AF815074

METATAXIS IN PRACTICE

Distributed Language Translation

The goal of these series is to publish texts which are related to computational linguistics and machine translation in general, and the DLT (Distributed Language Translation) research project in particular.

Series editor
Toon Witkam
B.S.O./Research
P.O. Box 8348, NL-3503 RH Utrecht
The Netherlands

Other books in this series:

1. B.C. Papegaaij, V. Sadler and A.P.M. Witkam (eds.)
   Word Expert Semantics
2. Klaus Schubert
   Metataxis
3. Bart Papegaaij and Klaus Schubert
   Text Coherence in Translation
4. Dan Maxwell, Klaus Schubert and Toon Witkam (eds.)
   New Directions in Machine Translation

Dan Maxwell
Klaus Schubert (eds.)

METATAXIS IN PRACTICE

Dependency syntax for multilingual machine translation

1989
FORIS PUBLICATIONS
Dordrecht - Holland/Providence RI - U.S.A.

Published by:
Foris Publications Holland
P.O. Box 509
3300 AM Dordrecht, The Netherlands

Distributor for the U.S.A. and Canada:
Foris Publications USA Inc.
P.O. Box 5904
Providence RI 02903
U.S.A.

Sole distributor for Japan:
Toppan Company, Ltd.
Sufunotomo Bldg.
1-6, Kanda Surugadai
Chiyoda-ku
Tokyo 101, Japan

CIP-DATA

Metataxis

Metataxis in Practice : Dependency Syntax for Multilingual Machine Translation / Dan Maxwell, Klaus Schubert (eds.). – Dordrecht [etc.] : Foris. – (Distributed language translation ; 6)
Publ. in co-operation with BSO, Utrecht. – With index, ref.
ISBN 90 6765 422 1 bound
ISBN 90 6765 421 3 paper
SISO 807 UDC 681.3: [801.56:800.3]
Subject heading: syntax ; machine translation.

In co-operation with BSO, Utrecht,
The Netherlands

ISBN 90 6765 421 3 (Paper)
ISBN 90 6765 422 1 (Bound)

© 1989 Foris Publications - Dordrecht

No part of this publication may be reproduced or transmitted in any form or by any means, electronic or mechanical, including photocopy, recording, or any information storage and retrieval system, without permission from the copyright owner.

Printed in The Netherlands by ICG Printing, Dordrecht.

Foreword

This volume contains a number of contributions that exemplify the model of dependency syntax described in the book *Metataxis* (no. 2 in this series). This model is used in the DLT machine translation system. When *Metataxis* was published in 1987, the first prototype of the DLT system then being completed heavily relied on the techniques accounted for in the book. The prototype contained only three languages, viz. English, French and Esperanto, the intermediate language of the system. The present volume includes studies that were written to prove the cross-linguistic feasibility of the suggested grammar model. The book falls into two parts. In the first part dependency syntaxes for eight diverse languages are given. They are arranged in a uniform way and provide abundant sample sentences, aimed especially at those readers who are not only interested in the theoretical model but primarily in its practical applicability to present-day written language. The second part contains metataxes, i.e., rule systems for the syntactic transfer in a given language pair. Each metataxis is based on dependency syntaxes of the source and the target language.

Of the authors of this volume, Dorine Tamis, Dan Maxwell, Job van Zuijlen and Klaus Schubert belong to the DLT team at BSO/Research in Utrecht. The other authors are scholars who have collaborated with the DLT project for periods of various length.

Utrecht, July 1989

Dan Maxwell
Klaus Schubert

Contents

Dependency syntax for parsing and generation

Klaus Schubert

Utrecht, Netherlands

In the first part of this book a number of languages are described in a model of **dependency syntax** that was developed for the DLT machine translation system. It is a special version of dependency syntax that has been tailored to meet the requirements of machine translation. It was derived from the primary source of modern dependency theory, Lucien Tesnière's *Éléments de syntaxe structurale* (1959/1982), and to a certain extent inspired by work from the Mannheim school (especially Engel 1982). The DLT model of dependency syntax was first suggested in the autumn of 1985 (Schubert 1986) with a short theoretical sketch and a fairly detailed description of Esperanto, which in the DLT system functions as an intermediate language. The model was then applied to the first source and target languages for which a prototype of the DLT system has been implemented, viz. English and French. But since the designers of DLT have always been aiming at a translation system for more than just a handful of closely related languages, it has been crucial to devise grammatical models that are in principle feasible for all human languages. DLT is meant to become a **multilingual** machine translation system, to which any language whatsoever can be added without requiring revisions of existing parts of the system. **Modular extensibility** is an essential precondition for all DLT design. As for the syntax model, it has therefore always been important to prove its feasibility for arbitrary languages. This is why the DLT project took an early interest in a broad variety of languages, even languages that are neither now nor in the nearby future likely to be included in the DLT system itself. The present volume has been compiled to show that it really can be done. It provides evidence for the general, cross-linguistic applicability of DLT's model of dependency syntax. Each of the contributions describes the central stock of syntactic regularities found in a particular language, renders them in a uniform way in accordance with the syntax model and furnishes the claims made with a substantial amount of samples from ordinary texts. The intention to prove the feasibility of the model for practical, machine translation-oriented work is also the reason why this volume does not include the syntaxes that have already proven their feasibility by being part of one of the operational DLT prototype modules, i.e., the English and the French dependency syntax. The same argument would of course apply also to DLT's intermediate language, but we have chosen to include the Esperanto syntax, since it is needed for all DLT metataxes to be written in the future.

The list of DLT dependency syntaxes completed so far comprises Esperanto, English, German, Danish, French, Italian, Czech, Polish, Bangla (Bengali), Finnish, Hungarian, Japanese, Chinese and Arabic. Others are being written. The editors wish to emphasize that the decision to omit some of the syntaxes from this volume does not imply any judgement whatsoever about their quality. Some of the reports were completed after the editorial deadline for this book.

In 1987, a second publication was concerned with DLT's model of dependency syntax with special attention to its use in that part of the overall translation process where the step from one language to another is actually taken, the metataxis or syntactic transfer step. This study could already be based on experience gained in applying the model to a variety of languages (Schubert 1987: 7). The contributions to follow below are some of the syntaxes worked out in the period 1987-1989. The present part of this book contains monolingual syntax descriptions that can be used for parsing and generating modules. The general characteristics of the specific syntax model used here implies that all these studies, although each written for a single language only, are oriented towards translation. They are not translation syntaxes, but they are syntaxes ready for translation. A metataxis, i.e., a transfer syntax that transforms pieces of text from the syntactic shape of one language into that of another, is a system of rules that account for the link between two dependency syntaxes of the type described here. How the translation step proper is carried out is described in the second part of this book.

As an introduction to the syntactic descriptions below, this article gives a concise outline of the theoretical model (section 1.), a short discussion of the relationship between this kind of syntactic description and parsing and synthesizing algorithms (2.) and between the trees handled in the syntaxes and the networks treated in the algorithms (3.). Finally, a few words are said about the choices left to the syntacticians within the framework of the given model (4.) and about the relationship of the present syntaxes to lower and higher levels of analysis (5.).

1. Dependency syntax: a theoretical sketch

The DLT model of dependency syntax has been described at length in an earlier work (Schubert 1987: 28-129). A short updated sketch should therefore suffice here.

Syntax is the theory about how the elements of the language system combine to form text. In the broad sense of the term adopted in this model (cf. Schubert 1987: 14-15), syntax is concerned with all levels of language structure, from morpheme to text. More so than other dependency models, this computational variant is strictly **form-oriented**. A clear distinction between form and content of the linguistic sign is maintained, so that syntax is concerned with form only.

The term "the elements of the language system", used above, is rather vague. The syntaxes in this volume focus mainly on the central part, sentence level syntax, since this is in many languages normally handled in parsers and generators, while word and text level analyses are carried out by other mechanisms. Because of this focus on the sentence, the basic element is in most cases the word. This is a deliberate choice, since by definition the smallest element is the morpheme and words normally include several morphemes. Words also normally occur in various (morphological or word-formational) forms, so that parsing with the word as basic unit, which is at present the most common way of parsing, has to be preceded by an analysis of word structure. This is often done by means of morphological redundancy rules over a syntactic dictionary. When the amount of work to be carried out by word analysis becomes too large, it is advisable to take the morpheme as the basic unit for parsing and generation. In this volume one language is described with such a morpheme-based approach: Hungarian, an agglutinative language with highly productive morphology and word formation. It may be noted as a characteristic feature that the dependency model is itself flexible as to the question what should be taken as the basic unit. While the Hungarian authors opted for a morpheme-based syntax, the other Finno-Ugric author – Kalevi Tarvainen of the university of Jyväskylä, who has done much dependency research in close cooperation with both the Mannheim and Leipzig schools – has chosen an essentially word-based approach for his Finnish dependency syntax, so to speak, of a Indo-European fashion. It is interesting to compare both solutions. The model as such allows for both choices.

The syntactic system of a given language can be described by a classification of the elements (words or morphemes) and a description of the possible relations between these elements (which I shall simply call "words" henceforth, even when they are in fact stems or morphemes). Classifying words in dependency syntax often comes down to a grouping which for the main groups of content words to a large extent conforms with traditional classifications. Function words, however, have to be re-considered more thoroughly according to the principles of dependency syntax, which normally results in a less orthodox classification. The relations between words are described in terms of syntactic dependencies. Some of the dependencies bear traditional names such as subject, object or attribute. But in spite of some familiar-looking names, all syntactic dependencies in these syntactic descriptions are defined according to the dependency model.

In this model, dependency is a directed relation between a governing and a dependent word. It is defined as directed co-occurrence (Schubert 1987: 29-37). Note that co-occurrence does not mean adjacency, but occurrence in the same piece of text (normally, in the same sentence). More precisely, two words are co-occurrent when the one word makes the occurrence of the other one syntactically possible. Co-occurrent words have a distinguishing feature that suggests an analysis in terms of **directed** relations: two words can be said to be linked by a dependency relation, if when taken together they behave according to the syntactic combination capacity of one of them. The word whose syntactic properties determine the behaviour of the whole set is taken as the **internal governor** (or "head") of the set, and the set is called a syntagma. The internal governor represents the syntagma towards the outside, i.e., towards governing words at higher levels. Here is a concrete example: In *Very many people attend the conference* the syntagma *very many people* combines with *attend* essentially in the way *people* alone could combine with it. Thus *people* is the internal governor of the syntagma. Its (external) governor is *attend.* (The next question to be answered is whether *very* and *many* depend each independently and directly on *people*, or one depends on the other. In the latter case, the syntagma headed by *people* contains another syntagma of an internal governor and a dependent.)

Dependency syntax not only describes what depends on what; it also classifies the dependency relations. Some dependents are paradigmatically interchangeable with other dependents (e.g., *very many people* with *they*). Interchangeable dependents are grouped in classes and the relations that are definitional for these classes are given names. In this way the list of possible dependent types is established.

Analyses based on dependency syntax are normally represented in the form of tree structures. The trees bear words on their nodes and dependent type labels on their branches. It is common to place the root of the tree at the top of the picture so that a dependent word is always shown below its governor. Dependency trees need not be projective.

This is one of the main features of dependency syntax that make it particularly well-suited for machine translation: The basic relation described in the model, the dependency relation, is a category of syntactic **function** rather than of syntactic **form**. In this way dependency syntax is **primarily** focussed on functional categories, which are directly relevant to translation. Form categories such as "genitive noun phrase" or the like normally cannot be translated without an intermediate transposition into functional categories ("genitive object", "genitive attribute" etc.). By taking functional categories as its basis, dependency syntax straightforwardly supports metataxis, which is dependency-based syntactic transfer (cf. Schubert 1987: 193-194).

2. Modularity

The reader may be surprised by the fact that a book from the realm of computational linguistics leaves computers, programs, algorithms etc. so much in the background. This is a result of DLT's general policy: All researchers who have seriously tried to automate translation (as well as many others) have understood how extremely complex the intellectual process of translating is. The designers of DLT approach this enormous but also challenging goal with the conviction that it can only be achieved if the complicated program system that is being built up is kept perspicuous. To this end, it has to be structured in a highly **modular** way.

One aspect of this modularity is a triple distinction of levels which is followed in the DLT system and in principle applies to all work on language processing done with computers. The three levels that constitute some of the main division lines of system modularity in DLT are **grammar**, **formalism** and **implementation**. The grammar level is concerned with the properties of language as such and has in principle no connection to computers. The implementation level includes those processes that control the computer and can be devised without knowledge about the languages to be processed. The formalism level is the interface between the two. To give a practical illustration: A parsing algorithm that reads words from the input of any given language, looks them up in a dictionary, stores them temporarily and retrieves them when needed, generates output structures, etc. belongs to the implementation level. A parser for a given language, written in a programming language or a special formalism provided by the implementation level, belongs to the formalism level. The syntactic description of the language in question, finally, is part of the grammar level. The grammar level is concerned with a static (declarative) description of the language and the formalism level with dynamic (procedural) algorithms for recognizing words as members of certain word classes, assigning dependent type labels etc. Roughly speaking, the grammar level is a general linguist's domain, the formalization level a computational linguist's and the implementation level a computer scientist's.

The contributions to this book belong to the grammar level. They are written according to a model of syntax that was devised for machine translation, but they are not concerned with parsing algorithms or their implementation in programming languages. Only Job van Zuijlen's contribution (in the second part of the volume) establishes the link to formalism and implementation.

3. Common features of the syntaxes in this volume

There are a number of features common to all syntactic descriptions in this volume that are not repeated in each of the contributions. Therefore a number of notes should be made here, in particular with respect to the arrangement of the descriptions, their scope, their interrelations with neighbouring modules of the DLT system and the structures they define.

The syntaxes are arranged in two parts, a classification of words on distributional grounds and a set of types of dependency relation. The former contains a short discussion, especially where the classification deviates from traditional ones. This has the consequence that it deals mainly with function words. The latter is given in the form of tables which for every possible governing word class show the dependent types it can govern and the syntactic form (word class, possibly syntactic features) these dependents can have. The tables are illustrated by sample sentences in which the governor and the dependent in the relation being illustrated are highlighted. The contributions are written with the purpose of applying a given model of syntax to a particular language. The solutions found by the authors illustrate how the model can explain the facts of the language in its special, machine translation-oriented manner. Note, however, that the articles are not written with the purpose of discussing or justifying the model itself. Those readers who are more interested in questioning the model than the facts it describes should therefore not direct their criticism to the articles in the first part of this book but preferably to my presentation here and to my more comprehensive account elsewhere (Schubert 1987).

The dependency syntaxes in this volume all have a deliberately chosen limitation in scope. They account for the syntax of the language in question at the levels of the syntagma and sentence. They cover present-day non-literary written texts, but not archaic, colloquial or substandard language. In addition, they are not meant to cover coordination or ellipsis at the sentence level. The latter are intricate problems which on the one hand would have expanded the scope of the contributions prohibitively and which on the other hand are likely to find cross-linguistic solutions. Suggestions for such general solutions have been made (Schubert 1987: 104-124) and more fully elaborated versions are being developed for the DLT system (especially by Dan Maxwell). Therefore the articles do not describe in any detail coordination at higher levels than the syntagma and although they sometimes refer to elliptic constructions they do not give a comprehensive account of the phenomena involved. It should, however, be pointed out that ellipses are not an objectively observable fact. Rather, the concept of ellipsis is determined by the grammar model on which the discussion is based. The model applied here has a tendency to describe the linguistic facts as they are rather than postulating an underlying structure from which elements "have been left out" (as the term "ellipsis" suggests). In this respect dependency syntax explains many constructions as normal syntagmata which are labelled elliptic in other models. Such syntagmata are covered in the descriptions of this book.

The articles in this part of the book give static syntactic descriptions. These belong to the grammar level (cf. 2.). They are neutral as to the question whether they (at the formalisation level) will be used for parsing or for generating sentences of the language in question. They are also neutral as to the implementation to be chosen for this purpose. I have earlier claimed with some discussion that a number of well-known parsing formalisms are suited for dependency parsing although not made for the purpose (Schubert 1987: 211-216), and I have discussed a few ideas concerning a more straightforwardly dedicated dependency parsing mechanism (Schubert 1987: 217-220).

The syntaxes in this volume describe the web of syntactic relations in a piece of text by means of tree structures which in the present model have been defined as true trees in the mathematical sense of the term. A dependency parser assigns a syntactically ambiguous sentence is assigned as many tree structures as there are parses. In view of the elegance of dependency trees, this is an appealingly simple picture of the complex problem of ambiguity. However, it is for practical reasons impossible to implement parsers in this way (cf. Schubert 1988: 136-137). A more complex structure has therefore been designed by Job van Zuijlen which represents all alternative representations of a given piece of text in a single complex network, called a **structured syntactic network**, which consists, as it were, of conflated trees. This representation accommodates the sentence during all transformations it undergoes during the various steps of the translation process, i.e., not only during the monolingual syntactic analysis, but also during metataxis, semantic and pragmatic treatment, syntactic synthesis etc. A dedicated parser for these complex structures has been designed and a metataxor is being constructed. These sophisticated mechanisms allow for a substantial increase in efficiency as compared with the 1988 prototype of the DLT system, and they at the same time avoid the danger of combinatorial explosion in syntactic analysis and in lexical transfer.

The networks designed by Job van Zuijlen belong to the formalism level. Thanks to the modularity of the general DLT design, it is possible to completely avoid any discussion of these compact representations at the grammar level, where the contributions of this part of the book are located. It is a perfectly true picture of the reality in DLT, when the grammar level descriptions discuss unambiguous tree structures which can, when needed, be split up into many slightly different but unambiguous trees. For the grammatical discussion the number of alternative trees is unimportant, whereas it is a serious problem in implementation. We have therefore chosen to stick to the picture of alternative dependency trees for the various readings of ambiguous sentences. The simplicity of the dependency trees is appealing enough to justify this step. Keep in mind that these alternative trees are represented in a single compact network at the formalism level, but this knowledge need in no way complicate the discussion of grammar.

In a similar way, the authors refer in seemingly vague terms to a "dictionary" that should accompany their syntaxes, without saying much about what these dictionaries look like or how they are actually implemented. The term dictionary is in this respect a ready abbreviation for a more complex system. At the formalism and the implementation level, there is not only a single source of syntactic knowledge, but normally a set of sources. One of them is a syntactic dictionary whose entries indicate the word class membership and possibly a number of syntactic features (such as gender, inflectional pattern class etc.) of the entry words. Another important source of syntactic knowledge is a set of redundancy rules dealing with information in the syntactic dictionary. These rules contain that part of the dictionary knowledge which applies to larger groups of entries and is therefore not repeated in full in all places where it is applicable. Given a suitable interface from, for instance, the parser to this set of sources, it is obviously totally unimportant for the outside modules, whether a particular piece of information is taken in its literal form from a dictionary entry or is derived by means of redundancy rules from other features, from the morphological form of the word or other phenomena. It is because of this effect of modularity that the authors in this volume are perfectly entitled not to pay any attention to the specific nature of the dictionary their syntaxes require. It should, however, be noted that the syntax both presupposes a dictionary and at the same time defines the content of the entries.

4. Dependency syntax in practice

The sample from current work with the DLT model of dependency syntax which is contained in this part of the book should not only illustrate the fact that the model is feasible for the function is has to fulfil in the construction of a modular, multilingual machine translation system. It shows at the same time flexibility of the model. All authors have worked according to the same guidelines (essentially what is said in Schubert 1987: 28-129), but the flexibility of the model has allowed them to approach the combinatorial properties of words in their languages with relatively diverse accentuations. I have already pointed out that the Finnish syntax is word-based, whereas the Hungarian one is morpheme-based. The German syntax, written by an author in close contact with Engel's Mannheim school of dependency syntax, has a strong accent on morphological form as a identifying feature of functional categories. The Danish syntax makes in an interesting way use of the fact that much of traditional and modern Danish grammatical writing is implicitly dependency-minded (cf. Bengt Sigurd's recent remarks about Jespersen; Sigurd 1988: 182).

The model used here is quite strictly word-oriented in the sense that in languages with orthographically marked word boundaries the basic unit may be smaller (e.g. Hungarian) but should not be larger than a word. It also means that there should be very good reasons for introducing empty nodes, i.e., nodes that do not carry a word. A ready way to evade these requirements of the model is using a notation for groups of words to be analysed elsewhere (as done in the Polish whole-page tree for using multi-word units on nodes) and using punctuation marks as words (cf. the Japanese whole-page tree). Really empty nodes (Ø) are used by the Hungarian authors in the case of defective paradigms.

This freedom in application is an inherent characteristic of this syntax model. The principles set up for the model are a useful guideline for those who apply the model to a specific language, but the principles need not be observed in every detail as long as the following superordinate principle is not violated: the strict orientation towards the **form** of the linguistic sign.

In view of this flexibility the editors of this book have not seen any need to unify the articles more than by providing guidelines.

5. Prospects

The basic view of grammar which underlies the model used in DLT suggests that syntax and semantics should each deal with their own side of the linguistic sign in its entirety. This means that syntax should cover all phenomena of linguistic form at all levels of analysis. A syntax which is complete in this sense therefore needs to cover not only the syntagma and sentence level in the way that most of the contributions in these volumes do, but it should also account for the levels below and above it. Although these levels, word syntax and text syntax, respectively, are not at issue in this volume, it ought to be kept in mind, that they are needed to yield a complete syntax of the degree of explanatory power needed for machine translation. As for word syntax, many of the relevant facts are relatively well known, but need a stringent treatment within a dependency-syntactic model before they can be applied in a computational system. The Hungarian contribution in this volume provides an interesting approach to these questions. In the realm of text syntax, however, research is needed not only on the most feasible way of accounting for these facts, but first of all into the mere facts themselves. A good deal of descriptive linguistic work has to be done in this field. None of the currently very popular fields of knowledge representation and acquisition, natural-language understanding, speech recognition of running text etc. can do without thorough investigations into both the semantics and the syntax of texts. Future work should show in what way the model discussed in this volume can be linked to grammatical mechanisms at its neighbouring levels.

References

Engel, Ulrich (1982): *Syntax der deutschen Gegenwartssprache.* Berlin: Schmidt, 2nd rev. ed.

Schubert, Klaus (1986): *Syntactic tree structures in DLT.* Utrecht: BSO/Research

Schubert, Klaus (1987): *Metataxis. Contrastive dependency syntax for machine translation.* Dordrecht/Providence: Foris

Schubert, Klaus (1988): The architecture of DLT – interlingual or double direct? In: *New directions in machine translation.* Ed. Dan Maxwell / Klaus Schubert / Toon Witkam. Dordrecht/Providence: Foris, pp. 131-144

Sigurd, Bengt (1988): [Review of Schubert (1987)] In: *Studia Linguistica* 42, pp. 181-184

Tesnière, Lucien (1959): *Éléments de syntaxe structurale.* Paris: Klincksieck, 2nd ed. 4th print. 1982

A dependency syntax of German

Henning Lobin

Bonn, Federal Republic of Germany

1. The German language: some general remarks

German is an inflected language with a rich morphology for derivation purposes. Nouns and adjectives derived from verbs with an extensive valency can function as the heads of very extensive phrases. In phrases of this kind, a lot of dependents precede the head. The derivation of the valency of such nouns or adjectives can be described in general by the use of valency transformations.

For German syntax, the word order is a typical issue, in particular, the position of the elements within the verbal complex (VC). If possible, the VC occurs in two parts or as one part of a two part frame:

- finite part in the second position, remainder of the VC in the last position (declarative clause word order)
- finite part in the first position, remainder of the VC in the last position (interrogative clause word order)
- imperative verb in the first postion (imperative clause word order)
- subjunction in the first position, VC in the last position (subordinate clause word order)

Every German clause contains such a "clause frame", but in some cases the frame is inherent in the clause (if the VC is a finite verb in the present or past tense). The clause frame appears, if the VC is transformed into another tense or into a modal verbal complex. The elements inside the clause frame are subject to several other constraints such as, for instance, that pronominal complements usually precede all lexical complements.

2. Word classes

Verb (V). Verbs are the words which can occur in a finite form or as participle II. Sample words in the infinitive form: *gehen, lachen, trinken, gewinnen, sein, werden, haben, scheinen, helfen, lassen, können, dürfen*; participle II, verbs like *gekommen* or *vergnügt*, are Vs just in case they function as a CVRB dependent.

Noun (N). Nouns are the words which always occur in the same gender. Sample words in the nominative singular: *Mann, Haus, Wohnung, Selbstverständlichkeit, Maschine, Gebirge, Laufen.*

Determiner (Det). Determiners are the words which commute with a proper noun in the genitive when placed in front of a noun (*Oskars Vater – mein Vater*). Sample words in the nominative singular: *der, die, das; dieser, diese, dieses; mein, dein, sein; all(e); viel; welcher, welche, welches; kein, keine; neunzig* (cardinal number); also the Dets, which introduce a relative clause: *dessen, deren.*

Adjective (A). Adjectives are the words, which can occur between a determiner and a noun. Sample words (all in the nominative singular masculine): *groß, schnell, hiesig, behördlich, Hamburger* (or *hamburger*), *eisern, laufend* (participle I), *vergnügt* (participle II, not in all cases an A), *zweite* (ordinal number).

Pronoun (Pro). Pronouns are the words, which commute with a noun phrase. Sample words (only in nominative singular): *ich, du, der, dieses, niemand, etwas, nichts, wer* (interrogative pronoun).

Preposition (P). Prepositions are the words, which are invariable and which can occur in front of a noun at any time. Sample words: *von, bei, an, auf, bis, mithilfe, vermöge, zeit.*

Subjunction (Sbj). Subjunctions are the words, which have the function to make clauses subordinate to other words. Sample words: *daß, ob, weil, nachdem, zu, obwohl, indem.*

Adverb (Adv). Adverbs are the words, which can occur in the first position within a clause and which can act as an answer to a wh-question. Sample words: *jetzt, hier, immer, aufwärts, rechtens, einmal; darin, darüber* (prepositional adverbs); *wann, worüber* (adverbial interrogatives); *gern, lieber, (am) liebsten* (comparative adverbs).

Conjunction (Con). Conjunctions are the invariable words which link homogeneous and equivalent constructions, whereby the linked word is not changed. Sample words: *aber, und, oder, denn* (links only VPs), *sowie* (links only NPs, ProPs, and DetPs), "," (comma syndesis).

Particle (Par). Particles are all other invariable words. Sample words: *möglicherweise, vielleicht, wohl, eigentlich, ja, erstens, wo, als, wie, sehr.*

In the following, "VP", "NP" and "DetP" mean verb phrase, noun phrase, determiner phrase and so on for all other word classes.

3. Short definition of the dependent types

In this grammar, the first step taken to distinguish complements from adjuncts is to ask whether or not a phrase is forced to occur with a certain word. All obligatory phrases are complements. Therefore, an optional phrase is a complement, if it only occurs with elements of a subclass from within a certain word class. All remaining phrases are adjuncts.

3.1. Complements

Subject (CSUB) in a narrow sense; cf. 3.3. All complements which are interchangeable with a personal pronoun in the nominative and which are always governed by a V.

Expletivum and suppletivum (CSUE). Different kinds of *es*, which are not interchangeable with any other phrase and which are always governed by a V.

Accusative complement (CACC). All complements, which are interchangeable with a personal pronoun in the accusative.

Dative complement (CDAT). All complements, which are interchangeable with a personal pronoun in the dative.

Genitive complement (CGEN). All complements, which are interchangeable with *dessen* oder *deren* (i.e. a demonstrative pronoun in the genitive).

Prepositional complement (CPRE). All complements, which are interchangeable with *da-* plus a specific P.

Situative complement (CSIT). All complements, which are interchangeable with place adverbs like *da* or *dort* and which always occur obligatorily.

Directive complement (CDIR). All complements which are interchangeable with directional adverbs like *dahin* or *daher* and which always occur obligatorily.

Expansive complement (CEXP). All complements, which are interchangeable with *(um) soviel, -lange, -weit* etc. (expansive adverbs or PPs with *um*).

Nominal complement (CNOU). All complements which, if governed by a V, are interchangeable with *es* and also occur obligatorily. CNOU can always be expressed by an NP. For other governors see the tables below.

Adjectival complement (CADJ). All complements which are interchangeable with *so* and which occur obligatorily. CADJ is always expressed by an AP or by a phrase which is interchangeable with an AP.

Verbal complement (CVRB). All complements which are interchangeable with *es geschehen, es tun, es sein* etc. CVRB is always expressed by a VP.

Subordinate complement (CSBJ). All complements which are always expressed by a SbjP.

Particle complement (CPAR). All complements which are always expressed by a ParP.

Comparative complement (CCOM). All complements which are always governed by the comparative morpheme of an Adj or Adv.

Reflexive complement (CREF). All obligatory ProPs which are always expressed by a reflexive pronoun (*mich, dich, sich*).

Prefix complement (CPRX). Only verbal prefixes, which are divided from the verb, if it occurs in the first or the second position of the clause.

3.2. Adjuncts

Verbal adjunct (AVRB). All VP adjuncts.

Nominal adjunct (ANOU). All NP and ProP adjuncts which are not AAPPs, and all DetPs which are not governed by an N.

Determinal adjunct (ADET). All DetP adjuncts which are governed by an N.

Adjectival adjunct (AADJ). All AP adjuncts which are not AAPPs.

Prepositional adjunct (APRE). All PP adjuncts, which are not AAPPs.

Subjunctional adjunct (ASBJ). All SbjP adjuncts.

Adverbial adjunct (AADV). All AdvP adjuncts.

Particle adjunct (APAR). All ParP adjuncts.

Apposition (AAPP). An adjunct to N or Pro which always follows its governor and which is always expressed by an NP, AP or PP.

3.3. Valency transformations

For a complete dependency syntax, a description of some fundamental valency transformations must be given. For instance, the subject can occur not only in the nominative case, but also in the accusative:

Peter läßt uns kommen.

Verbs like *lassen* force the CSUB of *kommen* to be transformed into a phrase in the accusative. The correct name for CSUB must be, strictly speaking, CNOM (Nominative complement), and the subject ought to be a category that can be expressed by CNOM or CACC, and CNOM and CACC ought in turn to be a category which can be expressed as VPs, NPs, DetPs etc. But up to now, these kinds of transformations are not very well developed.

4. Explicit definition of phrases and dependent types

Each of the following subsections illustrates the government capacity of a certain word class with an overview table and sample sentences. In the sentences, the governor of the illustrated relation is given in *italics* and the dependent in **bold face**.

4.1. Dependents of verbs

	V	N	Det	A	Pro	P	Sbj	Adv	Par	Con
CSUB	×	×	×		×		×			×
CSUE					×					
CACC	×	×	×		×		×			×
CDAT	×	×	×		×					×
CGEN	×	×	×		×		×			×
CPRE	×					×	×	×		×
CSIT	×					×		×		×
CDIR	×					×		×		×
CEXP	×	×	×			×	×			×
CNOU	×	×	×		×					×
CADJ	×			×			×	×	×	×
CVRB	×									×
CSBJ							×			×
CPAR									×	×
CCOM										
CREF					×					
CPRX						×				
AVRB	×									×
ANOU		×								×
ADET										
AADJ				×						×
APRE						×				×
ASBJ							×			×
AADV								×		×
APAR									×	×
AAPP										

CSUB/Verb

Wer jetzt nicht hier **ist**, *wird* auch nachher nicht hier sein.

CSUB/Noun

Meine **Schwester** *fährt* nach Lübeck.

CSUB/Determiner

(Deine Schwester wohnt in Berlin und) **meine** *wohnt* in Kiel.

CSUB/Pronoun

Das *gefällt* mir nicht.

CSUB/Subjunction

Daß es dir nicht gut geht, *tut* mir sehr leid.

CSUE/Pronoun ONLY *es*.

- (i) THERE IS NO OTHER WORD IN FRONT OF THE FINITE VERB IN A DECLARATIVE SENTENCE:

Es *sagt* niemand die Wahrheit.

- (ii) *es* IS AN OBLIGATORY COMPLEMENT:

Es *regnet*.

daß **es** *regnet*.

- (iii) *es* IS AN OPTIONAL COMPLEMENT:

Davor *ekelt* **es** mich.

- ONLY A FINITE VERB CAN GOVERN AN EXPLETIVUM (A KIND OF VALENCY TRANSFORMATION TAKES PLACE; CF. 3.3.):

Es *hat* niemand über diesen Witz gelacht.

- IN THE CASE OF A VERBAL COMPLEX IN SEVERAL PARTS, THE CAPABILITY TO GOVERN "CSUE" MOVES TO THE FINITE VERB:

Es *hat* geregnet.

CACC/Verb

Was ich nicht selbst gesehen **habe**, *glaube* ich nicht.

CACC/Noun

Er *gab* mir meinen **Schlüssel** wieder.

CACC/Determiner

Er *schenkte* mir **dieses** (und dir jenes Buch).

CACC/Pronoun

Das *braucht* Peter nicht mehr.

CACC/Subjunction

Daß sich die Erde um die Sonne dreht, *glaube* ich nicht.

CDAT/Verb

Wem nicht zu vertrauen **ist**, *leiht* Peter nichts.

CDAT/Noun

Man *hinterlegte* dem **Gast** eine Nachricht.

CDAT/Determiner

Mir *fehlten* **zwei** (und dir drei Punkte).

CDAT/Pronoun

Mir *kommen* die Tränen.

CGEN/Verb

Sie *entsann* sich, wessen sie sich nicht entsinnen **wollte**.

CGEN/Noun

Sie *entsann* sich ihrer ersten **Begegnung**.

CGEN/Determiner

Sie *entsann* sich **ihrer** ersten (und leider auch ihrer zweiten Begegnung).

CGEN/Pronoun

Man *bediente* sich **seiner**.

CGEN/Subjunction

Sie *entsann* sich, **daß** sie sich kein drittes Mal getroffen hatten.

CPRE/Verb

Worüber sich alle **ärgern**, *ärgere* auch ich mich.

CPRE/Preposition

Alle *setzen* **auf** diesen Mann.

CPRE/Subjunction

Sie *erinnerte* sich, **daß** sie ihn kannte.

CPRE/Adverb

Sie *erinnerte* sich **daran**.

CSIT/Verb

Wo Peter **wohnt**, *weiß* niemand.

CSIT/Preposition

Er *fand* einen Arbeitsplatz **in** einer Maschinenfabrik.

CSIT/Adverb

Das Gesuchte *befand* sich nicht **dort**.

CDIR/Verb

Er *ging*, wohin man ihn auch immer **schickte**.

CDIR/Preposition

Peter *fiel* **in** einen Graben.

CDIR/Adverb

Peter *fiel* **hinein**.

CEXP/Verb

Solange die Römer **herrschten**, *war* Ruhe in der Provinz.

CEXP/Noun

Er *lief* zehn **Kilometer**.

CEXP/Determiner

Peter *lief* **zehn** (und Katrin zwölf Kilometer).

CEXP/Preposition

Sie *verfehlten* sich **um** eine halbe Stunde.

CEXP/Subjunction

Sie *spielten*, **bis** der Morgen graute.

CNOU/Verb

Er *wurde*, was er immer werden **wollte**.

CNOU/Determiner

Dieser Mann *ist* **einer**, der immer schnell aufgibt.

CNOU/Noun

Er *wurde* **Politiker**.

CNOU/Pronoun

Er *blieb* **es** auch sein ganzes Leben lang.

CADJ/Verb

Er *benahm* sich, wie es nicht anders zu erwarten **war**.

CADJ/Adjective

Peter *ist* **krank**.

CADJ/Subjunction

Sie *tut*, **als** ob sie nichts verstanden hätte.

CADJ/Adverb ONLY *so*

Peter *ist* **so**.

CADJ/Particle

Peter *benimmt* sich **wie** ein Flegel.
Wir *sind* **quitt**.
Ich *bin* es **leid**.

CVRB/Verb

Peter *läßt* sich nicht **hintergehen**.
Ich *möchte* Klavier spielen **können**.
Ich möchte Klavier **spielen** *können*.

CSBJ/Subjunction

Peter *vergaß*, uns **zu** benachrichtigen.
Man *vermutet*, **daß** der Täter um zehn Uhr wieder fort war.
Peter *scheint* verhindert worden **zu** sein.

CPAR/Particle ONLY *als*

Das Buch *gilt* **als** Bestseller.
Das Buch *gilt* **als** lesbar.
Man *sah* ihn **als** einen offiziellen Teilnehmer an.

CREF/Pronoun ONLY REFLEXIVE PRONOUNS COREFERENTIAL WITH THE SUBJECT:

Er *verhielt* **sich** sehr sonderbar.

CPRX/Preposition VERBS WITH PREFIXOIDE (NON-FIXED PREFIX), WHICH OCCUR IN THE FIRST OR SECOND POSITION:

Das Fest *findet* auch bei Regen **statt**.

AVRB/Verb

Sie *verließ* uns plötzlich, was uns alle sehr **erstaunte**.
Sie *verpackten* die Geschenke, wie sie es immer **taten**.

ANOU/Noun

Maria *stand* eines **Tages** vor der Tür.
Das *ist* meines **Erachtens** falsch.
Nächsten **Dienstag** *heiraten* sie.

AADJ/Adjective

Man *verpackte* **vergnügt** die Geschenke.
Man *verpackte* **umständlich** die Geschenke.

APRE/Preposition

In drei Stunden *kommt* Peter.
Mit Ihnen *trinke* ich am liebsten.

ASBJ/Subjunction

Als Peter zehn Jahre alt war, *zog* seine Familie ins Ausland.
Georg *trainiert*, **um** Kondition zu bekommen.

AADV/Adverb

Dann *tranken* sie Kaffee.
Peter *fährt* **lieber** mit Katrin.

APAR/Particle

Dieses Argument *ist* **allerdings** recht überzeugend.
Er wird **wohl** *kommen*.

Correlates

All Vs, which govern a dependent of type X expressed as a VP (with the exception of CVRB), can optionally govern another dependent X´, which is always expressed by a Pro or an Adv. A dependent of this kind is called a correlate.

The possible correlates are:

CACC: *es, das*
CDAT: *dem, diesem* or *jenem*
CGEN: *dessen*
CPRE: prepositional adverb
CSIT: *das*
CDIR: *dahin, daher*
CEXP: *es*
CNOU: *das*
CADJ: *es*
CSBJ: *es, das* (only with *daß* or *ob* as the head of CSBJ)

CSUB´/Pronoun

Wer jetzt nicht hier ist, **der** *wird* auch nachher nicht hier sein.

CACC´/Pronoun

Was ich nicht selbst gesehen habe, **das** *glaube* ich auch nicht.

CDAT´/Pronoun
Wem nicht zu vertrauen ist, **dem** *leiht* Peter nichts.
CGEN´/Pronoun
Wessen sie sich nicht entsinnen wollte, **dessen** *entsann* sie sich doch.
CPRE´/Adverb
Worüber sich alle ärgern, **darüber** *ärgere* auch ich mich.
CSIT´/Pronoun
Das *weiß* niemand, wo Peter wohnt.
CDIR´/Adverb
Er *ging* **dahin**, wohin man ihn auch immer schickte.
CNOU´/Pronoun
Er *wurde* **das**, was er immer werden wollte.
CADJ´/Adverb
Er *benahm* sich **so**, wie es nicht anders zu erwarten war.
CSBJ´/Pronoun
Peter *vergaß* **es**, uns zu benachrichtigen.

4.2. Dependents of nouns

	V	N	Det	A	Pro	P	Sbj	Adv	Par	Con
CSUB										
CSUE										
CACC										
CDAT										
CGEN										
CPRE						×		×		×
CSIT										
CDIR						×		×		×
CEXP		×	×			×				×
CNOU		×								
CADJ										
CVRB										
CSBJ							×			×
CPAR										
CCOM							×	×	×	×
CREF						×				
CPRX										
AVRB	×									×
ANOU		×	×							×
ADET			×							×
AADJ				×						×
APRE						×				×
ASBJ										
AADV								×		×
APAR									×	×
AAPP		×	×	×		×				×

CPRP/Preposition
die *Hoffnung* **auf** Frieden
der *Gedanke* **an** Japan
CPRP/Adverb
die *Hoffnung* **darauf**
CDIR/Preposition
die *Fahrt* **in** die Berge
CDIR/Adverb
die *Fahrt* **dahin**
CEXP/Noun
das *Laufen* eines halben **Kilometers**
CEXP/Determiner
das *Laufen* **eines** halben (und das Gehen eines ganzen Kilometers)
CEXP/Preposition
eine *Theateraufführung* **von** einer Stunde
CNOU/Noun
Bundeskanzler *Kohl*
ein **Glas** warme *Milch*
CSBJ/Subjunction
der *Gedanke*, **daß** Hans bald kommt,
CCOM/Subjunction
eine *Qualität*, **wie** sie ihresgleichen sucht,
CCOM/Adverb ONLY *so*
so eine *Qualität*
CCOM/Particle
das *Größersein* **als** zwei Meter
CREF/Pronoun
das **sich** *Weigern*
AVRB/Verb
der *Mann*, der Birnen **verkauft**,
ANOU/Noun
das *Haus* meines **Vaters**
das *Laufen* der **Kinder**
ANOU/Determiner
das *Haus* **meines** (und der Garten deines Vaters)
das *Laufen* **der** vier (und das Schwimmen der fünf Schulkinder)
ADET/Determiner
der *Mann*
dieser *Mann*
alle *Männer*
zwanzig *Männer*
AADJ/Adjective
der **hohe** *Berg*
meine **wenigen** *Kenntnisse*
der **laufende** *Junge*
APRE/Preposition
der höchste *Berg* **in** dieser Gegend
AADV/Adverb
der *Mann* **dort**
APAR/Particle
mein *Vater* **als** Schüler
vielleicht mein *Vater*
AAPP/Noun
Herr *Meier*, **Vorsitzender** dieses Vereins,

AAPP/Adjective

Friederike, wie immer **vergnügt**,

AAPP/Preposition

ihre *Freundin*, **in** bester Laune,

4.3. Dependents of determiners

The dependents of Det are in general identical with the dependents of N. DetPs result from noun phrases in which an ellipsis of the head has taken place. For that reason, the dependents of Det are the same as those of N. The dependency representation itself makes no use of ellipsis.

	V	N	Det	A	Pro	P	Sbj	Adv	Par	Con
CSUB										
CSUE										
CACC										
CDAT										
CGEN										
CPRE						×		×		×
CSIT										
CDIR						×		×		×
CEXP		×	×			×				×
CNOU										
CADJ										
CVRB										
CSBJ							×			×
CPAR										
CCOM							×	×	×	×
CREF						×				
CPRX										
AVRB	×									×
ANOU		×	×							×
ADET			×							×
AADJ				×						×
APRE						×				×
ASBJ										
AADV								×		×
APAR									×	×
AAPP		×	×	×		×				×

CPRP/Preposition

(die Hoffnung auf Gerechtigkeit und) *die* **auf** Frieden

(der Gedanke an China und) *der* **an** Japan

CPRP/Adverb

(meine Hoffnung auf Frieden und) *deine* **darauf**

CDIR/Preposition

(unsere Fahrt an die See und) *eure* **in** die Berge

CDIR/Adverb

(unsere Fahrt in die Berge und) *eure* **dahin**

CEXP/Noun
(das Laufen eines ganzen und) *das* eines halben **Kilometers**
CEXP/Determiner
(das Laufen eines ganzen Kilometers und) *das* **eines** halben
CEXP/Preposition
(eine Aufführung von zwei und) *eine* **von** einer Stunde
CSBJ/Subjunction
(der Gedanke an Katrin und) *der*, **daß** Hans bald kommt,
etc. like N

4.4. Dependents of adjectives

	V	N	Det	A	Pro	P	Sbj	Adv	Par	Con
CSUB										
CSUE										
CACC		×			×					×
CDAT		×			×					×
CGEN		×			×					×
CPRE						×		×		×
CSIT						×		×		×
CDIR						×		×		×
CEXP		×				×		×		×
CNOU		×	×		×					×
CADJ				×			×	×	×	×
CVRB	×									×
CSBJ							×			×
CPAR									×	×
CCOM							×	×	×	×
CREF					×					
CPRX										
AVRB										
ANOU										
ADET										
AADJ										
APRE						×				×
ASBJ							×			×
AADV										
APAR									×	×
AAPP										

CACC/Noun MAINLY ADJECTIVAL PARTICIPLES:
der seine **Brille** *suchende* Peter
CACC/Pronoun
der **dieses** *suchende* Peter
CDAT/Noun
ein ihrer **Familie** *nahestehender* Bekannter
CDAT/Pronoun
der **ihm** etwas Geld *gebende* Mann
CGEN/Noun
ein sich seines **Erfolges** *sicherer* Mann

CGEN/Pronoun
ein sich **seiner** *sicherer* Mensch
CPRE/Preposition
der **an** Literatur *interessierte* Verwaltungsangestellte
CPRE/Adverb
der **davon** sehr *enttäuschte* Peter
CSIT/Preposition
meine **in** Kiel *wohnhafte* ältere Schwester
CSIT/Adverb
die **dort** *wohnende* Schwester
CDIR/Preposition
der **in** Richtung Norden *abgefahrene* Schnellzug
CDIR/Adverb
der **dahin** *fahrende* Zug
CEXP/Noun
der 15 **Jahre** *alte* Volvo
die zwei **Stunden** *dauernde* Vorstellung
CEXP/Preposition
die **um** eine Stunde *verlängerte* Vorstellung
CEXP/Adverb
die **solange** *dauernde* Vorstellung
CNOU/Noun
der **Peter** *heißende* Mann
CADJ/Adjective
der sich **schlecht** *benehmende* Peter
der rätselhaft **schnell** *laufende* Sprinter
CADJ/Adverb ONLY *so*
der **so** *aussehende* Mann
CADJ/Particle
der sich **wie** ein Flegel *benehmende* Peter
CVRB/Verb
der sich die Haare **schneiden** *lassende* Peter
CSBJ/Subjunction
Mein Bruder war nicht *gewillt*, zu uns **zu** kommen.
ein *solches* Unwetter, **daß** man nicht hinausgehen konnte,
CPAR/Particle
der **als** Betrüger *geltende* Bankier
zu *schön*, um wahr zu sein,
ein **sehr** *erfreuliches* Ereignis
CCOM/Subjunction
besser, **als** wir erwartet hatten,
CCOM/Adverb ONLY *so*
so *gut* wie im letzten Jahr
CCOM/Particle
besser **als** im letzten Jahr
CREF/Pronoun ONLY *sich*
der **sich** schlecht *benehmende* Peter
APRE/Preposition
ein meiner Meinung **nach** *unverdientes* Lob
die **in** ihrem blauen Kleid *weggehende* Katrin
ASBJ/Subjunction
alt, **wie** das Haus nun einmal war,
wohnhaft in Kiel, **wie** sie wahrheitsgetreu angegeben hat,

APAR/Particle

ein **wohl** recht *neues* Auto
eine **möglicherweise** *ungerechte* Entscheidung

4.5. Dependents of pronouns

	V	N	Det	A	Pro	P	Sbj	Adv	Par	Con
CSUB										
CSUE										
CACC										
CDAT										
CGEN										
CPRE						×		×		×
CSIT										
CDIR										
CEXP										
CNOU		×		×						×
CADJ				×			×		×	×
CVRB	×									×
CSBJ										
CPAR									×	×
CCOM										
CREF										
CPRX										
AVRB										
ANOU										
ADET										
AADJ										
APRE										
ASBJ										
AADV										
APAR										
AAPP										

CPRE/Preposition

du **mit** deinem Glück
etwas **von** der Mettwurst
er, **im** Vollbesitz seiner Kräfte,

CPRE/Adverb

du **dort**

CNOU/Noun

du **Idiot**
ich, ein aufrechter **Demokrat**,

CNOU/Adjective

er, schon nicht mehr ganz **nüchtern**,

CADJ/Adjective

nichts **Gutes**

CADJ/Subjunction

nichts, **wie** es sein soll,

CADJ/Particle

nichts **wie** bei uns

CVRB/Verb

du, der du mir geholfen **hast**,
nichts, was mir helfen **könnte**,

CPAR/Particle

er **als** Mathematiker

4.6. Dependents of prepositions

	V	N	Det	A	Pro	P	Sbj	Adv	Par	Con
CSUB										
CSUE										
CACC		×	×		×			×		×
CDAT		×	×		×					×
CGEN		×	×		×					×
CPRE										
CSIT										
CDIR										
CEXP										
CNOU										
CADJ										
CVRB										
CSBJ										
CPAR								×		×
CCOM										
CREF										
CPRX										
AVRB										
ANOU										
ADET										
AADJ										
APRE										
ASBJ										
AADV										
APAR										
AAPP										

CACC/Noun

für deinen **Freund**
in die **Grube**

CACC/Determiner

für **deinen** (, nicht für meinen Freund)
gegen **fünf**
um **sieben**

CACC/Pronoun

für **ihn**

CDAT/Noun
mit der **Straßenbahn**
aus diesem **Grund**
CDAT/Determiner
mit **dieser** (, nicht mit jener Straßenbahn)
CDAT/Pronoun
mit **niemandem**
CGEN/Noun
wegen des **Geldes**
CGEN/Determiner
wegen **deiner** (, nicht wegen meiner Erkrankung)
CGEN/Pronoun
wegen **ihr**
CPAR/Adverb
nach **unten**
bis **jetzt**

4.7. Dependents of subjunctions

	V	N	Det	A	Pro	P	Sbj	Adv	Par	Con
CSUB										
CSUE										
CACC										
CDAT										
CGEN										
CPRE										
CSIT										
CDIR										
CEXP										
CNOU										
CADJ				×						×
CVRB	×									×
CSBJ							×			×
CPAR										
CCOM										
CREF										
CPRX										
AVRB										
ANOU										
ADET										
AADJ										
APRE										
ASBJ										
AADV										
APAR										
AAPP										

CADJ/Adjective
falls vom Arzt nicht anders **verordnet**
obwohl noch sehr **jung**

CVRB/Verb

nachdem alle gekommen **waren**
daß sie nicht hier **ist**

CSBJ/Subjunction

Er ist schon zu weit entfernt, *als* **daß** wir ihn noch einholen können.
Es sieht aus, *als* **ob** es gebrannt hat.
Er verließ uns, *ohne* sich von uns verabschiedet **zu** haben.

4.8. Dependents of adverbs

	V	N	Det	A	Pro	P	Sbj	Adv	Par	Con
CSUB										
CSUE										
CACC										
CDAT										
CGEN										
CPRE										
CSIT										
CDIR										
CEXP										
CNOU										
CADJ										
CVRB										
CSBJ										
CPAR										
CCOM							×	×	×	×
CREF										
CPRX										
AVRB										
ANOU										
ADET										
AADJ										
APRE										
ASBJ							×			×
AADV								×		×
APAR									×	×
AAPP										

CCOM/Subjunction

eher, **als** wir erwartet hatten,

CCOM/Adverb ONLY *so*

so *gern* wie erwartet

CCOM/Particle

eher **als** Peter

ASBJ/Subjunction

gestern, **als** ich spazierenging,

AADV/Adverb

immer *hier*

APAR/Particle

möglicherweise *hier*
ganz *hinten*

4.9. Dependents of particles

	V	N	Det	A	Pro	P	Sbj	Adv	Par	Con
CSUB										
CSUE										
CACC										
CDAT										
CGEN										
CPRE						×		×		×
CSIT										
CDIR										
CEXP										
CNOU		×	×		×					×
CADJ				×						×
CVRB										
CSBJ							×			×
CPAR										
CCOM										
CREF										
CPRX										
AVRB										
ANOU										
ADET										
AADJ										
APRE										
ASBJ										
AADV										
APAR										
AAPP										

CPRE/Preposition

schöner *als* **in** dieser Gegend
so gern *wie* **im** letzten Jahr

CPRE/Adverb

schöner *als* **dort**
so schön *wie* **hier**
zu jung **dafür**

CNOU/Noun

so groß *wie* mein Freund **Peter**
lieber *als* diese **Leute**

CNOU/Determiner

kleiner *als* **mein** (, aber größer als dein Freund)

CNOU/Pronoun

so groß *wie* **du**

CADJ/Adjective

Das Buch gilt *als* **lesbar.**
Er sieht aus *wie* **betrunken.**

CSBJ/Subjunction

zu schön, **um** wahr zu sein,
Sie scheint eher zu lachen *als* **zu** weinen.

4.10. Coordination

Conjunctions always have the capability to double a dependency relation. For instance, if a word can govern a dependent of the CACC type, the conjunction *und* can govern two dependents of the same type, i.e. *und* <CACC, CACC>. The default valency of all conjunctions is <CVRB, CVRB>. Sample sentences with governors from various word classes:

CACC/Conjunction

Er *gab* mir den Schlüssel **und** das Buch wieder.

CADJ/Conjunction

Hans *benimmt* sich manchmal gut **und** manchmal schlecht.

CPRE/Conjunction

die *Hoffnung* auf Frieden **und** auf Gerechtigkeit

ADET/Conjunction

mein **und** dein *Buch*

AAPP/Conjunction

Friederike, wie immer vergnügt **und** in bester Laune,

CDIR/Conjunction

(eure Fahrt in die Berge und) *unsere* nach Italien **oder** nach Spanien.

CPAR/Conjunction

der als Betrüger **und** als der Kopf der Bande *geltende* Mann

CPRE/Conjunction

etwas von der Mettwurst **und** von der Salami

CGEN/Conjunction

wegen ihr **oder** ihres Geldes

CVRB/Conjunction

nachdem alle angekommen waren **und** sich gesetzt hatten

CSBJ/Conjunction

gestern, als ich spazierenging **und** darüber nachdachte,

CADJ/Conjunction

das Buch gilt *als* lehrreich **und** spannend.

A coordinate stucture behaves like a single word for elements which are not in one of the dependent phrases. That means that the capability of the heads of both coordinated phrases to govern certain dependents has moved to the conjunction. If there is, for instance, a structure involving coordination of two nouns, the conjunction can govern all the dependents which can also be governed by the nouns:

dein Freund und Helfer

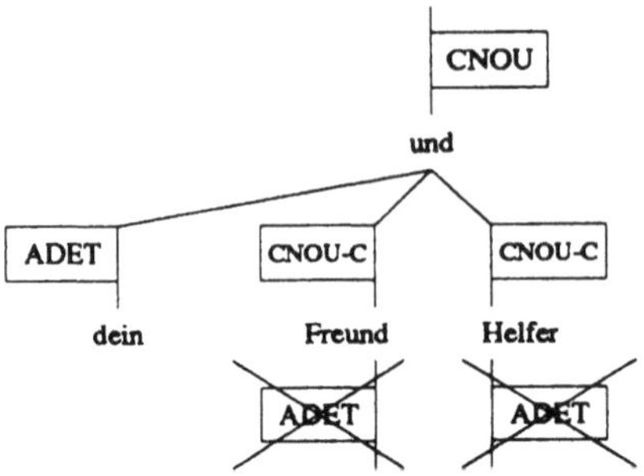

CSUB/Pronoun WHERE "CON" GOVERNS FINITE Vs
Sie lacht *und* weint gleichzeitig.
ADET/Determiner WHERE "CON" GOVERNS Ns
der Bundeskanzler *und* Parteivorsitzende
CPAR/Particle WHERE "CON" GOVERNS As
sehr groß *und* stark
etc.

5. Sample sentence

Nachdem Müller, gerade aus Berlin, wo er für seine Sache erfolgreich geworben hatte, zurückgekehrt, als erster geredet hatte und sich setzte, erhob sich frenetischer Beifall, anstatt daß die Leute schwiegen, und niemand wußte, was das zu bedeuten hatte.

'After Müller, having just come back from Berlin, where he had successfully fought for his case, had been the first to speak and sat down, there was frenzied applause instead of silence, and no-one knew what it might mean.'

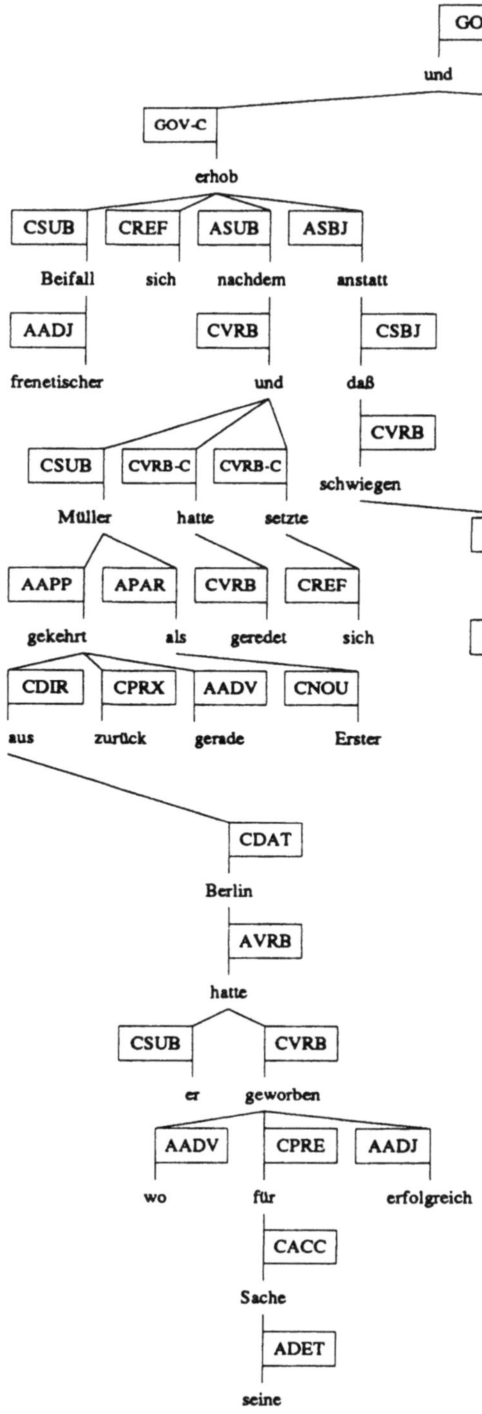
GOV
und
GOV-C
erhob
GOV-C
wußte
CSUB
Beifall
AADJ
frenetischer
CREF
sich
ASUB
nachdem
CVRB
und
CSUB
Müller
AAPP
gekehrt
CDIR
aus
CDAT
Berlin
AVRB
hatte
CSUB
er
CVRB
geworben
AADV
wo
CPRE
für
CACC
Sache
ADET
seine
AADJ
erfolgreich
CPRX
zurück
AADV
gerade
CNOU
Erster
APAR
als
CVRB-C
hatte
CVRB
geredet
CVRB-C
setzte
CREF
sich
ASBJ
anstatt
CSBJ
daß
CVRB
schwiegen
CSUB
Leute
ADET
die
CSUB
niemand
CACC
hatte
CSBJ
zu
CVRB
bedeuten
CSUB
das
CACC
was

Note

I am grateful to Prof. Ulrich Engel (Institut für Deutsche Sprache, Mannheim) for his valuable comments on a former version of this syntax. My work is by and large based on his studies of German grammar (especially Engel 1982, 1988).

References

Engel, Ulrich (1982): *Syntax der deutschen Gegenwartssprache.* Berlin: Schmidt, 2nd rev. ed.

Engel, Ulrich (1988): *Deutsche Grammatik.* Heidelberg: Groos

A dependency syntax of Danish

Ingrid Schubert
Utrecht, Netherlands

1. Introduction

This dependency syntax of Danish was written in the framework of the syntax model adopted for the DLT machine translation project. It accounts for the combinability of Danish words essentially in four steps, viz. (1) a definition of word classes, (2) a classification of the dependency relations among words (dependent types), (3) a specification of word class-specific dependencies and (4) a description of the syntactic shape in which the dependents can occur.

Theoretically, this would also be the order of working steps, although the steps in practice turn out to be so closely interrelated that one cannot be completed without the other. Word classes, for instance, cannot be marked off in a functional way, unless syntactic considerations are taken into account. Since word classes are ultimately defined in terms of syntactic co-occurrence patterns, this interrelatedness is obvious.

It should be mentioned that the descriptions suggested here are nothing but **possible** solutions. I hope they have logical relationships to each other, but the same linguistic facts can certainly be accounted for in alternative ways even within the given model.

This syntax is meant to cover contemporary written non-literary language, but in accordance with the other contributions in this volume I have refrained from dealing with certain intricate phenomena for which language-independent solutions may be applied, such as ellipsis (especially elliptic coordinations at the sentence level), interjections and syntactically free terms of address.

In addition, I have ignored constructions which are encountered in spoken Danish only. In this connection, however, I should like to point out a distinguishing characteristic of the language. Danish is a rapidly developing language. Evidence for this is found in the relative lowness of the thresholds between the sociolects of different social groups and as a consequence in a fairly immediate influence exercised by speech on written language. There is of course no sharp borderline between spoken and written styles. I have therefore included a number of typical spoken utterances, which in my view may be encountered in writing as well. This holds especially for their syntactic structure.

A number of idioms display irregular structures, which have to be accounted for at other levels such as valency entries in the dictionary or text-grammatical regularities.

Danish is a language with only a small number of noun cases and without verb inflection for person. As a consequence, it has a relatively bound word order. Accounts of Danish syntax therefore are typically much concerned with word order. To this end Paul Diderichsen (1946) developed the so-called sentence scheme (sætningsskema). After modifications by, among others, Nordentoft (1977b) and Erik Hansen (1977), Diderichsen's sentence scheme is today still the basis for most current syntactic work on Danish. It is a model which to a high degree accommodates the syntactic peculiarities of Danish.

Partial accounts based on dependency syntax of phenomena in Danish sentence structure are found in Vater (1973) and in Danish-German contrastive descriptions (Fabricius-Hansen 1979; Fabricius-Hansen/Falster Jacobsen/Olsen 1981). Work on Swedish can be used to some extent thanks to the syntactic similarity of the two languages. Monolingual studies on Swedish are for example those by Nikula (1976, 1986). A contrastive study of Swedish, German and English originates from Tarvainen (1983).

2. Danish word classes

The classification of Danish words suggested here coincides to a large extent with the traditional one. In order to fit in with a strictly form-oriented dependency syntax, however, the system should be freed of any semantic classification criteria. This brings about deviations from the traditional groupings, which are not as strictly based on distributional criteria as is required for the present purpose.

I describe the word classes on the basis of the traditional classification as given for example in Aage Hansen (1967) and Nordentoft (1977a). In addition, I distinguish content words and functions words in the way introduced by Tesnière (1959/1982: 53ff.: *mots pleins* vs. *mots vides*). Since my classification is purely syntactic, I take semantic criteria into consideration in only a few occasions, e.g. for subdividing certain word classes, where semantics has a direct reflex in syntactic distribution. In order to enhance parsing mechanisms that may be based on this syntax, I also mention the possible inflections of the words in question.

Since the goal of this study is an account of the system of dependency relationships of the language, word classes cannot be defined without taking into account the syntagmatic functions of the words. The syntactic approach to be developed in the body of this contribution has to play its role already in the first step. Its function in this respect is to view the borderlines between word classes, that often may seem vague and arbitrary, in the light of the fundamental question which makes up the entire system: "What depends on this word and what can it be governed by?" This view sharpens the required class delimitations.

2.1. Content words

As far as content words are concerned, the three basic classes defined by Tesnière (1959/1982: 63), verbs, nouns and adjectives, can in an uncontroversial way be taken over for Danish. This basic division can then be taken as a starting point for the distinctions to be made for other classes. When defining the function word classes, it is mainly important to maintain the contrast between them and the content words which are the basis of the word class system.

2.1.1. Verbs

Verbs occur in finite and infinite forms. Finite verbs are inflected for tense, voice and mood.

Tense. There are two morphologically marked tense forms:

Present tense:	jeg **tager** – 'I take'	hun **løfter** – 'she lifts up'
Past tense:	han **tog** – 'he took'	de **løftede** – 'they lifted up'

Other tense forms consist of a finite auxiliary verb (present or past tense) and an infinite form (past participle, supine, infinitive) of the content verb.

Voice. There are three passive-voice forms, one of which is marked morphologically. The other two are formed as syntagmata with a finite form of one of the auxiliary verbs *blive* 'become' or *være* 'be' and the past participle of the content verb.

tages – 'to be taken'
bliver taget – 'is (being) taken'
er taget – 'is (has been) taken'

There are deponents, i.e., verbs with passive form and active meaning (e.g. *det lykkedes ham at overbevise mig* 'he succeeded in convincing me'). Moreover, there are passive-marked verbs with a reciprocal meaning (*de skændes* 'they are quarrelling').

Mood. All verbs have imperative forms, whereas the optatives are rare.

Imperative:	**tag!** – 'take!'	**løft!** – 'lift up!'
Optative:	kongen **leve!** – 'long live the king!'	

Infinite verb forms are the infinitive and the supine.

Infinitive. The infinitive has no tense or mood markers, but can be inflected for voice:

> tage – 'to take'
> tages – 'to be taken'

The infinitive can be used with or without a preceding *at*, the use of which is determined by distributional regularities. I class this *at* as a subordinating conjunction (see 4.1.).

Supine. The supine is used in combination with the finite forms of auxiliary verbs. In contrast to the past participle, it is not inflected.

> jeg har **taget** – 'I have taken'
> jeg havde **taget** – 'I had taken'

The adjectival participle in predicative or attributive position is in this study considered to be an adjective, since it has the same distributional pattern as these. Similarly, the present participle is on syntactic grounds classed as either an adjective or an adverb (see 2.1.4.).

> Han er **rasende**. – 'He is outrageous.' (adjective)
> Han kom **gående**. – 'He came walking.' (adverb)

The central role in the sentence is played by the verb. Most other word classes can depend on it and in the model described here a verb, as the internal governor of a subordinate clause or an infinitive syntagma, can in turn depend on another verb.

> Jeg tror (at) han kommer. – 'I think (that) he will come.'

2.1.2. Nouns

The class of nouns consists of appellatives and proper names. Appellatives are inflected for number, case and definiteness. Proper names normally have only case inflection.

Number.

Singular:	dag – 'day'	bog – 'book'
Plural:	dage – 'days'	bøger – 'books'

Case. The are two cases, nominative and genitive.

Nominative:	by	byen – 'the town'
Genitive:	bys	**byens** historie – 'the history of the town'

Definiteness.

indefinite:	et hus – 'a house'	en bog – 'a book'	bøger – 'books'
definite:	huset – 'the house'	**bogen** – 'the book'	**bøgerne** – 'the books'

In traditional Danish grammar this definiteness marker is considered an inflectional form, due to its being morphologically integrated. Since this is so only in a certain type of construction, I adopt a different solution here (cf. 2.2.3.).

2.1.3. Adjective

The inflectional categories of adjectives are gender, number, definiteness and comparison.

Gender.

Common gender:	en *smuk* pige – 'a pretty girl'
Neuter:	et *smukt* hus – 'a pretty house'

Number.

Singular:	et *gammelt* hus – 'an old house'
	huset er *gammelt* – 'the house is old'
Plural:	*gamle* huse – 'old houses'
	husene er *gamle* – 'the houses are old'

Definiteness.

Indefinite:	et *gammelt* hus
definite:	det *gamle* hus

Comparison.

Positive:	smuk – 'pretty'	gammel – 'old'
Comparative:	smukkere – 'prettier'	ældre – 'older'
Superlative:	smukkest – 'prettiest'	ældst – 'oldest'

The comparative and superlative forms are subject to definiteness inflection as well.

Adjectives with three syllables or more, derived adjectives and participles lack morphologically marked comparative and superlative forms. The corresponding meanings are expressed by the combination of the adjective and a preceding *mere* or *mest*. *Mere* and *mest* are adverbs.

Positive:	intelligent – 'intelligent'
Comparative:	mere intelligent – 'more intelligent'
Superlative:	mest intelligent – 'most intelligent'

When used as an adjective, the present participle is not inflected:

Han er *rasende*. – 'He is outrageous.'

2.1.4. Adverb

Adverbs are a particularly incoherent group in traditional accounts, but its definition is fairly close to a strictly syntactic one in the sense needed here. As for their word-formational origin, I distinguish basic and in principle uninflected adverbs from derived, deadjectival adverbs. Due to the possibility of deriving adverbs from adjectives, this word class belongs to the open classes.

Basic adverbs are (with a few exceptions) uninflected and occur in constructions such as the following:

hun synger *gerne* – 'she likes to sing'
temmelig smuk – 'quite pretty'
huset *dérovre* – 'the house over there'

Deadjectival adverbs are normally formed by adding a *-t* to the adjective:

hun synger *højt* – 'she sings loudly'

Even a present participle can be used in an adverbial function. No *-t* can be added here, however:

hun synger *strålende* – 'she sings marvellously'

Only a few adverbs have comparative and superlative forms:

Positive:	ofte – 'often'
Comparative:	oftere – 'more often'
Superlative:	oftest – 'most often'

These forms are too rare for being included in the syntax rules. In a future implementation of this syntax, they should be dealt with in the dictionary.

A number of local adverbs distinguish a directional and a static form:

Directional:	Han kommer *op*. – 'He comes up/up here.'
Static:	Han er *oppe*. – 'He is up/up here.'

Adjective and adverb are very similar in their forms. Also their capacity of being governed by certain word classes display similarities:

Hun er *klog*. – 'She is clever.'
Hun synger *smukt*. – 'She sings nicely.'

The similarities notwithstanding, adjective and adverb cannot replace each other in these cases, since the dependency relations are of different types. The difference is due to the valency of the governing verbs.

2.2. The closed classes of function words

2.2.1. Pronoun

In traditional grammar, the class of pronouns is a large but closed word class which gives a somewhat incoherent impression as to the syntactic distribution of its various subclasses. Danish grammars (e.g. Nordentoft 1977a: 33ff.) normally distinguish two subclasses, viz. adjectival and nominal pronouns (pro-adjectives and pro-nouns). A similar subdivision suggests itself in a purely syntactic account. As a matter of fact, the question arises whether pronouns should be taken as a word class of their own at all, and if so, whether they form a single word class and how they are distinguished from nouns, adjectives and possibly from other word classes.

The group of nominal pronouns includes the following words (which I give here further subdivided in the traditional semantically motivated subgroups):

- Personal pronoun: (nominative) *jeg, du, han, hun, den, det, vi, I, de, De; man, folk*
  (oblique form) *mig, dig, ham, hende, os, jer, dem, Dem; eens.*

- Reflexive pronoun: *mig, dig, sig, os, jer, dem, Dem.*
- Reciprocal pronoun: *hinanden*
- Interrogative pronoun: *hvem, hvad*
- Relative pronoun: *som, der*
- Indefinite pronoun: *ingenting, nogenting;*
- Subject placeholder: *her, der, det* (see the subsection on placeholders, 2.2.7.)

(...)

The second subgroup of pronouns has syntactic functions that make it similar to another class of content words, i.e., the adjective. This group includes the following words:

- Possessive pronoun: *min, din, sin, hans, hendes, dens, dets, vores, jeres, deres, Deres*. Some of these pronouns are inflected for number and gender.
- Demonstrative pronoun: *den, denne, det, dette, disse, samme*
- Interrogative pronoun: *hvis, hvilken (hvilket, hvilke)*
- Relative pronoun: *hvis, hvilken (hvilket, hvilke)*
- Indefinite pronoun: *hver, enhver, ingen, nogen (noget, nogle), somme, alle (al, alt)*

(...)

If subdivided in this way, the class of pronouns has to be distinguished from adjectives and nouns on syntactic grounds.

The nominal pronouns have a similar governing capacity as nouns: They can govern a prepositional complement, an apposition, prepositional and adverbial adjuncts and post-attributes.

brevene **til** mig 'the letters for me'	*de* **til** dig 'those for you'
Jørgen, min gamle **ven** 'Jørgen, my old friend'	*han*, min gamle **ven**. 'he, my old friend'
manden **i** fjernsynet 'the man in the television'	*han* **i** fjernsynet 'he in the television'
kvinden **dérovre** 'the woman over there'	*hende* **dérovre** 'she over there'
manden som **kommer** idag 'the man who arrives today'	*han som* **kommer** idag 'he who arrives today'

However, nouns in addition to these common patterns can govern other dependents, which cannot be governed by nominal pronouns. Examples:

den **gode** *bog* – 'the good book'
denne *bog* – 'this book'
et *hus* – 'a house'
*hus***et** – 'the house'

One similarity between adjectives and adjectival pronouns is their capacity of being governed by the same governors, such as for instance nouns:

Adjective: den *gode* **ven** – 'the good friend'
Pronoun: **denne** *ven* – 'this friend'

The most important difference between the two classes is the fact that adjectival pronouns cannot govern any dependents themselves.

2.2.2. Numerals

Cardinal numerals are uninflected. Ordinal numerals are assigned to the class of adjectives. There is in principle no restriction on the number of numerals that can be combined to form a larger unit:

sekshundredefemoghalvfjerds – '675'
ottehundredetoogfirs – '882'

Unfortunately the orthography of Danish numerals is incoherent, especially with respect to writing compounds in one or in several words, which makes the syntactic definition more complicated. But since higher numerals are normally not spelled out, the problem need not be taken up here. Banks and similar institutions are in a habit of writing spelled-out numerals as one word.

Tusinde 'thousand', *million* 'million' etc. are inflected and should thus be classed as nouns.

2.2.3. Article

This class includes the indefinite article of the singular for common gender (*en*) and neuter (*et*), the definiteness morphemes attached to nouns, viz. *-(e)n*, *-(e)t* and *-(e)ne*, and *den*, *det* and *de*, which are governed by adjectives:

en bog – 'a book'
et hus – 'a house'

bog*en* – 'the book'
hus*et* – 'the house'
bøger*ne* – 'the books'

den store bog – 'the big book'
det smukke hus – 'the nice house'
de smukke huse – 'the nice houses'

The distributional syntactic analysis yields the article as a separate word class, distinguished from both pronouns and numerals, since the articles can only in part be paradigmatically exchanged for adjectives and pronouns. Definite and indefinite articles do to some extent share the demonstrative pronoun's syntactic patterns, but as opposed to pronouns they can never replace the noun in its typical functions:

en bog – 'a book'
denne bog – 'this book'

A nominally used article is incorrect:

*Jeg tager *en*. – 'I take a.'

whereas this construction is well-formed with a demonstrative pronoun:

Jeg tager *denne*. – 'I take this-one.'

The definite article *den* etc. can depend on (attributive) adjectives only. In this property the article clearly differs from pronouns.

2.2.4. Prepositions

Prepositions are uninflected particles whose main function is linking nouns or noun syntagmata to other elements of the sentence. Semantically this function may be seen as neither coordinating nor subordinating. Rather the entire syntagma can be conceived of as a whole.

Jeg danser *med* min ven. – 'I dance with my friend.'
Hun stoler *på* at vi kommer. – 'She is relying on us to come.'
taget *på* huset – 'the roof on the house'

2.2.5. Coordinating conjunctions

I distinguish coordinating conjunctions explicitly from subordinating ones. Coordinating conjunctions link sentences, syntagmata or words.

og 'and', *men* 'but', *samt* 'as well as', *eller* 'or'

Particles that are used with coordinating conjunctions, such as *hverken* in *hverken ... eller* 'neither ... nor' are classed as adverbs.

Since coordinating conjunctions can combine with almost any dependents, they have a nearly unlimited capacity of governing dependent syntagmata. The comma, used for linking dependents to the sentence, in this function parallels the coordinating conjunctions.

2.2.6. Subordinating conjunctions

Subordinating conjunctions introduce subordinate clauses or, in the case of *at*, infinitive syntagmata. These clause introducer may under certain circumstances be omitted in Danish. I have therefore decided not to let the subordinate clause depend on the subordinating conjunction or a clause-introducing relative pronoun (as is done in the analyses of a number of other languages), but to let it be governed directly by the verb (or some other word) of the superordinate sentence (cf. 4.1.).

The subordinating conjunctions include: *at, om, hvis, når, fordi, mens*; in comparison constructions alto *som* and *end* (cf. 4.4.).

2.2.7. Placeholders

Placeholders, also called dummies, are the unstressed forms of *her, der* and *det* in the special function they can assume in Danish sentences.

I distinguish the following cases in which *her, der* or *det* syntactically function as placeholders. I use the term *placeholder,* which originally derives from analyses of Danish word order in terms of Diderichsen's sentence scheme. This model postulates a certain position for the subject which always has to be filled; when this is for some reason not so, the placeholder fills the slot.

(1) *Her* and *der* used to avoid placing an indefinite subject at the beginning of a main or subordinate clause.

> Instead of: Er nogen kommet tilbage?
> it is more correct to say: Er *der* kommet nogen tilbage? – 'Has somebody returned?'

This use of *der* (or *her*) is valency-bound. Verbs with a direct object, for instance, cannot be included in such a pattern.

(2) In subordinate clauses, introduced by an interrogative pronoun (*hvem, hvad* ...), the clause introducer must be followed by *der* whenever it is the subject of the clause.

> *hvem der* er fornærmet – 'who is offended'
> *hvem* han har fornærmet – 'whom he has offended'

In other words, the position after the introducer of a subordinate clause must not be empty. It has to be filled with the subject of the clause, unless the introducer itself is the subject. (The combination *som der* with the relative pronoun *som* is encountered, but is not accepted as grammatical at all levels of style. *Som* can function either as subject and as object of the subordinate clause.)

(3) *Det* as a preliminary subject as in

> Det er godt at være hjemme. – 'Es ist gut, zu Hause zu sein'.

Her, der, and *det* may also occur as the only subject in a sentence, e.g.:

> Det regner. – 'It is raining.'
> Der danses. – 'People are dancing.', lit. 'it is being danced'
> Her tales dansk. – 'Danish is spoken here.'

In this function, however, I class them among the noun-like pronouns.

As a consequence, it is a common feature of the elements of this word class that they are used always in connection with another subject. They are thus a kind of additional subject. They cannot govern any other words.

2.2.8. Interjections

Interjections do not fit in the common sentence scheme, and no regularity in their positioning with respect to other word classes can be found, since they normally lack any syntactic link to the rest of the sentence (cf. Erik Hansen 1977: 36). I therefore do not take them up in the present account of dependency relationships in Danish sentences, also due to the fact that they are hardly ever encountered in the type of written non-literary texts to be covered by this syntax.

3. Word class-specific dependency patterns

The tables in this section follow the general model adopted for this book. For each possible governing word class a table is provided which accounts for the dependent types that belong to the specific government pattern of that word class. These are given in the left column of the tables. The upper line gives the word classes to which the dependents can belong. This table arrangement guarantees a high degree of coverage.

For each governor, the dependent type–word class combinations are illustrated with sample sentences. As elsewhere in this volume, the governor is shown in italics, the dependent in bold face. I refrain from illustrating the table for the coordinating conjunction, since almost every sample sentence use for the other tables might appear again here, augmented with a doubled syntagma. I do, however, inlcude the table for the coordinating conjunction, since it, as it were, sums up the preceding patterns.

I distinguish the following dependent types. Complements are valency-bound, whereas adjuncts are possible dependents of every element of the word class.

Complements:

SUBJ	subject
dOBJ	direct object
iOBJ	indirect object
PRED	predicative
ADVC	adverbial complement
PARG	argument of a preposition
PREC	prepositional complement
AUXC	auxiliary complement
VRBC	verb complement

Adjuncts:

PREATR	pre-attribute
POSTATR	post-attribute
APPO	apposition
PREA	prepositional adjunct
ADVA	adverbial adjunct
SBJA	subordinating conjunction as an adjunct

3.1. Dependent types governed by the verb

	Verb	Noun	Adj	Adv	Pron	Num	Prep	Sbj	Art	Plhld	Conj
SUBJ	×	×			×	×				×	×
dOBJ	×	×			×	×					×
iOBJ		×			×		×				×
PRED	×	×	×		×	×					×
ADVC	×			×							×
PARG											
PREC							×				×
AUXC	×										×
VRBC	×										×
PREATR											
POSTATR	×										×
APPO											
PREA							×				×
ADVA	×	×		×			×				×
SBJA								×			×

SUBJ/Verb

- VERB AS THE INTERNAL GOVERNOR OF A SUBORDINATE CLAUSE:

At han **havde** lyst *overraskede* mig. – 'that he would like [it] surprised me'

- INFINITIVE WITH *at*:

At **rejse** *er* dejligt. – 'travelling is nice'

- INFINITIVE WITH *at* AND PRECEDING SUBJECT PLACEHOLDER:

Det *er* dejligt at **rejse**. – 'it is nice to travel'

SUBJ/Noun

Huset *brænder*. – 'the house is-burning'

SUBJ/Pronoun

Han *gaber*. – 'he yawns'

SUBJ/Numeral

Enogtyve *er* tre gange syv. – 'twenty-one is three times seven'

SUBJ/Placeholder

Der *kommer* nogen. – 'there is somebody coming'

dOBJ/Verb

- FINITE VERB GOVERNING A SUBORDINATE CLAUSE INTRODUCED BY INTERROGATIVE PRONOUN:

Jeg *ved* ikke hvad du **ønsker** dig. – 'I do not know what you wish'

- FINITE VERB, GOVERNING SUBORDINATE CLAUSE, WITH OR WITHOUT SUBORDINATING CONJUNCTION:

Jeg *vidste* ikke at hun **er** syg. – 'I did not know that she is ill.'

- INFINITIVE (FOLLOWING MODAL VERB):

Han *skal* **komme** i morgen. – 'he will come tomorrow.'

- INFINITIVE, GOVERNING AN INFINITIVE SYNTAGMA:

Hun *lærer* at **tale** dansk. – 'she is-learning to speak Danish'

dOBJ/Noun

Hun *køber* en **bog**. – 'she is-buying a book'

oOBJ/Pronoun

Han *elsker* **hende**. – 'he loves her'

dOBJ/Numeral

Vi *har* **to**. – 'we have-got two-ones'

dOBJ/Coordinating conjunction

Vi *køber* bøger **og** plader. – 'we buy books and discs'

iOBJ/Noun

Jeg *giver* **barnet** et navn. – 'I give the child a name'

iOBJ/Pronoun

Jeg *giver* **ham** bogen. – 'I give him the book'

iOBJ/Preposition

Jeg *sendte* brevet **til** ham. – 'I sent the letter to him'

PRED/Verb

- FINITE VERB, GOVERNING A SUBORDINATE CLAUSE:

Spørgsmålet *er*, hvem der **kommer**. – 'the question is who will come'

PRED/Noun

Hun *er* **læge**. – 'she is a physician'

Det *er* **statsministerens**. – 'it is the prime-minister's'

PRED/Adjective

Værelserne *virker* **store**. – 'the rooms seem large'

PRED/Pronoun

Det må *være* **ham**. – 'it must be him'

PRED/Numeral

Vi *er* **fem**. – 'we are five'

PRED/Coordinating conjunction

Han *ærgrede* sig gul **og** grøn.

– idiom, lit. 'he upset himself yellow and green', i.e., 'he became very upset'

ADVC/Verb

- FINITE VERB, GOVERNING A SUBORDINATE CLAUSE:

Jeg *kom*, da klokken **var** tolv. – 'I arrived when it was twelve o'clock'

Hvis du **har** lyst, *kan* du jo gå med. – 'if you like, you might join [me]'

ADVC/Adverb

Det *varer* **længe**. – 'it takes a-long-time'

ADVC/Coordinating conjunction

Løb op **eller** ned. – 'run up or down'

PREC/Preposition

Jeg *taler* **om** det. – 'I speak about it'

AUXC/Verb

Han *er* **kommet**. – 'he has arrived'

Det skal *være* **gjort** i morgen tidligt. – 'it must be done by-tomorrow morning'

VRBC/Verb

- INFINITIVE, ALWAYS IN CONNECTION WITH AN ACCUSATIVE (PRO)NOUN (AcI):

Jeg *bad* ham **vente**. – 'I asked him to-wait'

Jeg *så* manden **komme**. – 'I saw the man arrive'

- INFINITIVE WITH at:

Jeg *har* noget at **sige**. – 'I have something to say'

Han *fik* det at **vide**. – 'he got to know this'

In this type of sentence, the verb complement does not depend on the pronoun (or the noun) as in constructions such as

fornemmelsen at **være** efterladt – 'the feeling of being abandoned'

Unlike the latter construction, in *Han fik det at vide* the infinitive *vide* is not governed by *det*. In such an analysis, the syntagma *det at vide* would as a whole function as a direct object of *fik*. Evidence against this analysis is found in the observation that *det at vide* as a unit, unlike the pronoun *det* alone, cannot fulfil other syntactic functions. It cannot, for instance, be a subject (***Det** at vide *er* vigtigt.) or a predicative (*Det *er* **det** at vide). Since *det at vide* thus does not function as a single unit in paradigmatic replacement, the occurrence of *at vide* is determined directly by the verb (*få*, past tense: *fik*), while *det* is to be explained as a normal object of *fik* without a direct dependency link to *at vide*.

POSTATR/Verb

- FINITE VERB GOVERNING A RELATIVE CLAUSE:

Han *sover*, hvilket jeg ikke **tør** gøre. – 'he is-sleeping, which I dare not do'

PREA/Preposition

Jeg *bor* **i** Danmark. – 'I live in Denmark'

ADVA/Verb

- FINITE VERB, GOVERNING A SUBORDINATE CLAUSE:

Hun *løb*, fordi det **regnede**. – 'she ran because it was-raining'

ADVA/Noun

De *kommer* næste **år**. – 'they will-come next year'

ADVA/Adverb

Jeg *kommer* **ikke**. – 'I do not come'

ADVA/Preposition

Hun *lukkede* døren **i**. – 'she closed the door'

SBJA/Subordinating conjunction

Han begynder **at** *tale*. – 'he begins to speak'

Jeg ved ikke **om** de *kommer*. – 'I do not know whether they will-come'

Han sover **fordi** han *er* træt. – 'he is-sleeping because he is tired'

3.2. Dependent types governed by the noun

	Verb	Noun	Adj	Adv	Pron	Num	Prep	Sbj	Art	Plhld	Conj
SUBJ											
dOBJ											
iOBJ											
PRED											
ADVC											
PARG											
PREC							×				×
AUXC											
VRBC	×										×
PREATR		×	×		×	×			×		×
POSTATR	×	×				×					×
APPO		×	×								×
PREA							×				×
ADVA				×							×
SBJA											

PREC/Preposition

brevet **til** chefen – 'the letter to the boss'

VRBC/Verb

- FINITE VERB, GOVERNING A SUBORDINATE CLAUSE:

kendsgerningen at han **har** løjet – 'the fact that he has lied'

Den *antagelse*, at jorden **var** flad, var almindelig.

– 'the assumption that the earth was flat was common'

- INFINITE VERB:
kunsten **at elske** – 'the art to love'
opgaven at **bekæmpe** arbejdsløsheden – 'the task of combatting unemployment'

PREATR/Noun
statsministerens *hat* – 'the prime-minister's hat'

PREATR/Adjective
den **gode** *ven* – 'the good friend'

PREATR/Pronoun
denne *bog* – 'this book'

PREATR/Numeral
to *biler* – 'two cars'

PREATR/Article
en *trøje* – 'a pullover'
*trøj***en** – 'the pullover'

POSTATR/Verb
en *kaffepunch*, **kogt** af cikorie – 'a coffee-punch, cooked from chicory'
Huset som **brændte** i går var min onkels.
– 'the house that burnt down yesterday was my uncle's'

POSTATR/Noun
Kong *Frederik* – 'King Frederik'
december **måned** – 'December', lit. 'December month'

POSTATR/Numeral
nummer **fem** – 'number five'

APPO/Noun
Hansen, min gamle **lærer**. – 'Hansen, my old teacher'

APPO/Adjective
en *gade*, **fuld** af mennesker – 'a street full of people'

PREA/Preposition
situationen **i** Danmark – 'the situation in Denmark'

ADVA/Adverb
manden **dérhenne** – 'the man over there'

3.3. Dependent types governed by the adjective

	Verb	Noun	Adj	Adv	Pron	Num	Prep	Sbj	Art	Plhld	Conj
SUBJ											
dOBJ											
iOBJ											
PRED											
ADVC											
PARG											
PREC							×				×
AUXC											
VRBC											
PREATR									×		×
POSTATR											
APPO											
PREA											
ADVA				×							×
SBJA											

PREC/Preposition

god **til** at lave mad – 'good at cooking'

PREATR/Article

den *blå* bog – 'the blue book'

ADVA/Adverb

meget *stor* – 'very big'

3.4. Dependent types governed by the adverb

	Verb	Noun	Adj	Adv	Pron	Num	Prep	Sbj	Art	Plhld	Conj
SUBJ											
dOBJ											
PRED											
ADVC											
PARG											
PREC							×				×
AUXC											
VRBC											
PREATR											
POSTATR	×					×					×
APPO											
PREA							×				×
ADVA				×							×
SBJA											

PREC/Preposition

op **til** over albuen – 'up until over the elbow'

POSTATR/Verb

Her, hvor vi nu **står** – 'here, where we are-standing now'
Dengang, du **var** lille. – 'that-time, you were small'

POSTATR/Numeral

begge **to** – 'both of them', lit. 'both two'

PREA/Preposition

her **i** Danmark – 'here in Denmark'

ADVA/Adverb

meget *lidt* – 'very little'

3.5. Dependent types governed by the pronoun

	Verb	Noun	Adj	Adv	Pron	Num	Prep	Sbj	Art	Plhld	Conj
SUBJ											
dOBJ											
iOBJ											
PRED											
ADVC											
PARG											
PREC							×				×
AUXC											
VRBC											
PREATR											
POSTATR	×	×									×
APPO		×									×
PREA							×				×
ADVA				×							×
SBJA											

PREC/Preposition

han **i** fjernsynet – 'he in the television'

POSTATR/Verb

Vi sender *dem*, der **kommer**, hjem igen. – 'we send those who come back home'

POSTATR/Noun

han **Jørgen** – lit. 'he, Jørgen'

APPO/Noun

Jeg mener *hende*, **kvinden** med det blå hår. – 'I mean her, the woman with the blue hair'
vi **danskere** – 'we Danes'

PREA/Preposition

vi **i** Danmark – 'we in Denmark'

ADVA/Adverb

han **dérovre** – 'he over there'

3.6. Dependent types governed by the numeral

	Verb	Noun	Adj	Adv	Pron	Num	Prep	Sbj	Art	Plhld	Conj
SUBJ											
dOBJ											
iOBJ											
PRED											
ADVC											
PREC											
AUXC											
VRBC											
PREATR											
POSTATR											
APPO											
PREA							×				×
ADVA											
SBJA											

PREATR/Article

de *to* mænd – 'the two men'

PREA/Preposition

to **af** os – 'two of us'

3.7. Dependent types governed by the preposition

	Verb	Noun	Adj	Adv	Pron	Num	Prep	Sbj	Art	Plhld	Conj
SUBJ											
dOBJ											
iOBJ											
PRED											
ADVC											
PARG	×	×	×	×	×	×	×				×
PREC											
AUXC											
VRBC											
PREATR											
POSTATR											
APPO											
PREA											
ADVA				×							×
SBJA											

PARG/Verb

- FINITE FORM:

fra han **kom** til han gik – 'from [the time] when he arrive until [the time] when he left'

- FINITE FORM, GOVERNING A SUBORDINATE CLAUSE:

Jeg tror *på* at han **kommer**. – 'I believe in that he will come'

- INFINITE FORM, GOVERNING AN INFINITIVE SYNTAGMA:
  Jeg er vant *til* at **vente**. – lit. 'I am used to waiting'

PARG/Noun
med **bilen** – 'by car'

PARG/Adjective
til **daglig** – 'daily'

PARG/Adverb
blandt **andet** – 'among other-things'

PARG/Pronoun
Jeg tænker *på* **ham**. – 'I am-thinking of him'

PARG/Numeral
Den er delt *i* **to**. – 'it is divided up in two'

PARG/Preposition
til **om søndagen** – 'until Sunday'

PARG/Coordinating conjunction
med toget **eller** bussen – 'by train or bus'

ADVA/Adverb
snart *efter* deres afrejse – 'soon after their departure'

3.8. Dependent types governed by the coordinating conjunction

(overview over all possible combinations)

	Verb	Noun	Adj	Adv	Pron	Num	Prep	Sbj	Art	Plhld	Conj
SUBJ	×	×			×	×				×	×
dOBJ	×	×			×	×					×
iOBJ		×			×		×				×
PRED	×	×	×		×	×					×
ADVC	×			×							×
PARG	×	×	×	×	×	×	×				×
PREC							×				×
AUXC	×										×
VRBC	×										×
PREATR		×	×		×	×			×		×
POSTATR	×	×				×					×
APPO		×	×	×							×
PREA							×				×
ADVA	×	×		×			×				×
SBJA								×			×

4. Problems and special cases

4.1. Subordinate clauses and infinitive syntagmata

In the realm of dependent syntagmata whose internal governor is a verb, three dependent types are distinguished:

(1) subordinate clauses, governed directly by the verb of the superordinate clause,

(2) subordinate clauses and infinitives governed by nouns,

(3) relative clauses.

These constructions, or rather, the verbs in these constructions, being their internal governors, can fulfil the following function in the superordinate syntagma:

	SUBJ	dOBJ	PRED	ADVC	PARG	VRBC	POSTATR
subord. cl.	×	×	×	×	×	×	
infinitive	×	×			×	×	
relative cl.							×

As far as subordinate clauses and infinitive syntagmata are concerned, I have decided not to let them be governed by a subordinating conjunction, but to consider the verb of the subordinate construction a direct dependent of the verb in the superordinate sentence.

Subordinate clause:

Jeg hader (at) han altid skal spise knækbrød til torsdagskoncerten.
'I hate (that) he always eats crispbread during the Thursday concert.'

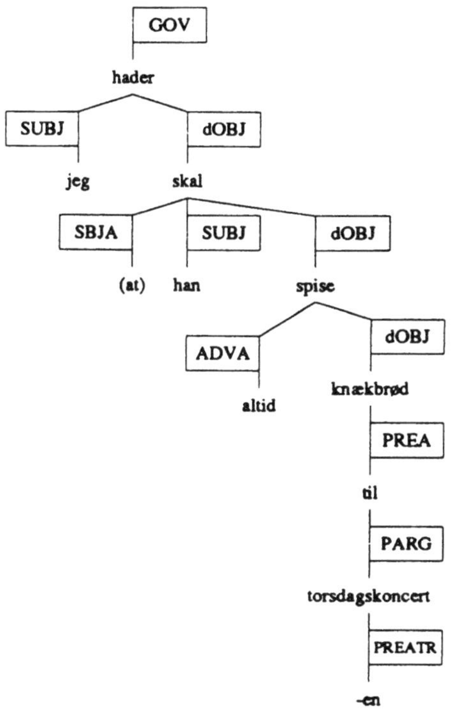

Infinitive:

Vi prøver at ringe i morgen. – 'we shall-try to call tomorrow'

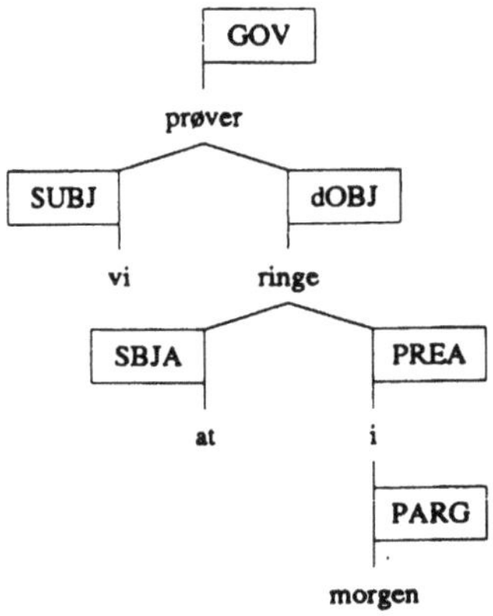

Relative clause:

Manden (som) du så i går var min onkel. – 'The man (whom) you saw was my uncle'

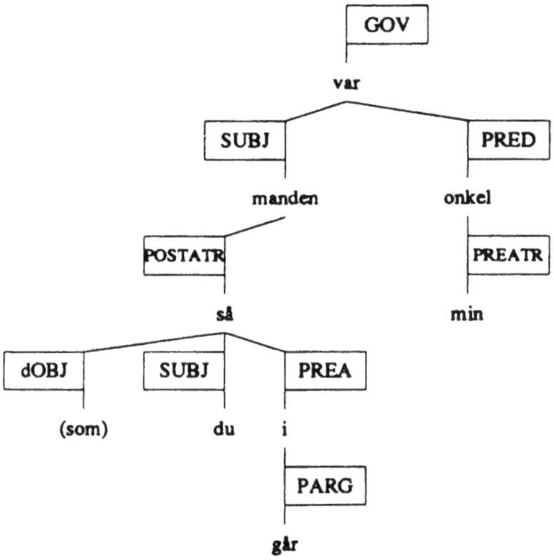

This solution seems expedient especially since *at* and *som* under certain circumstances are left out quite frequently.

4.1.1. Accusative with infinitive (AcI)

Diderichsen (1946/1968: 217) calls the accusative with infinitive infinitival nexus. In this construction the infinitive is never introduced by *at*. The construction can only occur with a number of specific verbs, the perceptions verbs, such as *se* 'see', *høre* 'hear', *føle* 'feel', *mærke* 'notice'. In a semantically different, but syntactically identical pattern, the construction also occurs with accusative verbs such as *bede* 'ask [to do something]', *byde* 'order [to do something]' and *lade* 'have [someone do something]'.

Jeg hører dig komme. – 'I hear you come'

This pattern is problematic, since *dig* is a direct object of the main clause, but at the same time semantically functions as the subject (agent) of the infinitive. Nordentoft (1977b: 90) calls this function "logisk subjekt" 'logical subject' or "neksussubjekt" 'nexus subject'.

If the double link is dissolved and the sentence is transformed into an ordinary sentence with a subordinate clause, the analysis looks like this:

Jeg hører at du kommer – 'I hear that you are-coming'

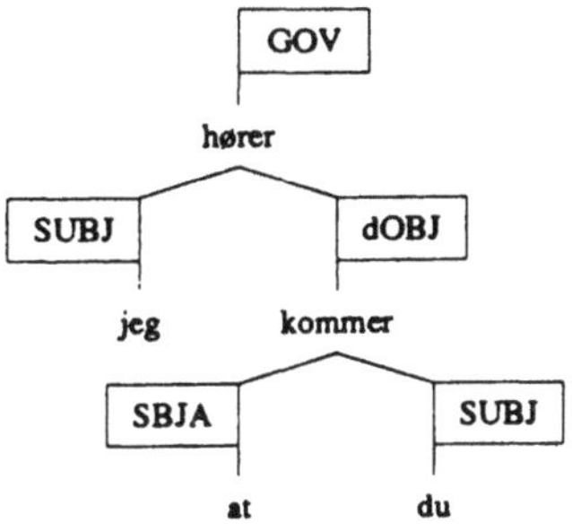

In contrast to this construction, the accusative with infinitive is analysed in this way:

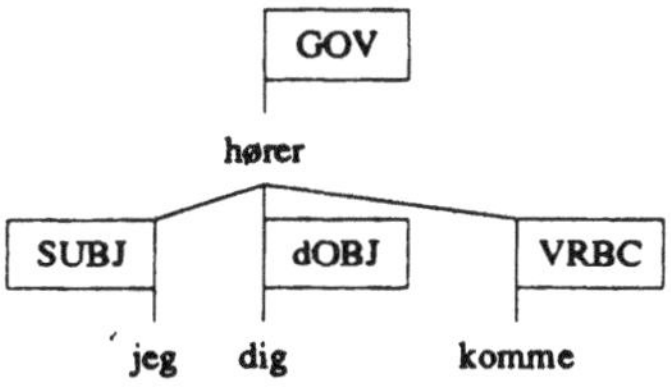

As a consequence, the accusative-with-infinitive construction parallels the following type of sentence which has the same pattern of dependency branches in its tree structure. In addition to the former sentence, this one has got a subordinating conjunction (*at*), but this has no influence on the rest of the tree.

Jeg har noget at sige. – 'I have something to say'

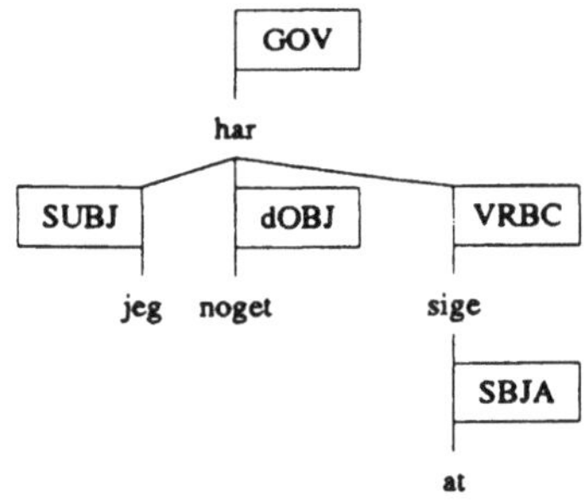

Unlike traditional grammar, the present, strictly syntactic, model is not aimed at identifying "logical" subjects in order to detect government relationships underlying the surface at a deeper level. I therefore find it appropriate to subsume these two patterns under a single heading. Accordingly, the analysis is not influenced by the fact that the accusative with infinitive can be transformed (as shown above), whereas the latter construction cannot.

Both sentence types are subsumed under the dependent type verb complement (VRBC). Since the subordinating conjunction *at* itself cannot govern other elements of the sentence, this is possible without complication. These sentence types are grouped together with infinitive syntagmata governed by nouns (e.g., *skikken at gå med slips* 'the custom to go with a tie'), which accounts especially well also for the semantic function of the accusative as the agent of the infinitive.

4.2. Sentence types with special word order regularities

Danish syntax comprises a number of special patterns, such as cleft and "knotted" sentences. If contrasted with other languages, the word order and in particular the text-grammatical function of these patterns are distinguishing peculiarities of Danish. They nevertheless do not present unexpected problems in the syntactic analysis according to the dependency model.

Cleft sentence:

Det er ham der har slået ruden. – 'it was him who broke the glass'

This sentence differs from its non-cleft counterpart (below) by by extraposing tthe subject to a superordinate clause and thus emphasizing it. It is introduced there by a placeholder (*det*) and in this way placed in a rhematic position.

Han har slået ruden. – 'he broke the glass'

Sentence knot:

Det har jeg aldrig sagt (at) du skal gøre. lit. 'this I never said that you should do'

Dissolving the "knot" the following construction is received:

Jeg har aldrig sagt (at) du skal gøre *det*. – 'I never said that you should do this'

In my view both sentences have the same dependency pattern:

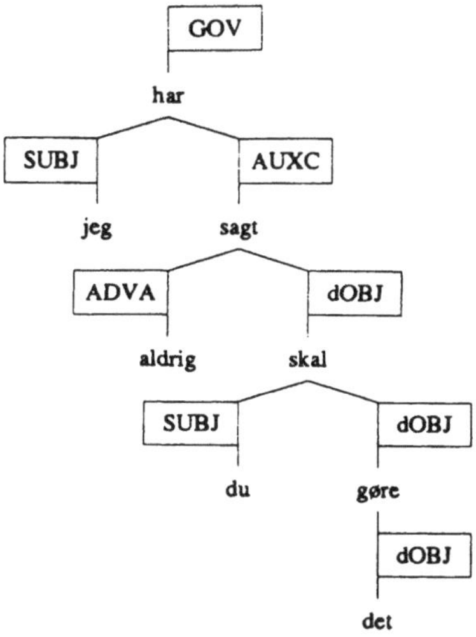

This structure should coincide with the structure of the sentence without a "knot", i.e., without a special emphasis on the extraposed object (*det*), since *det* in its semantic function is determined by the verb in the subordinate clause. The difference between the two varieties is text-grammatical and thus does not concern the level dealt with here.

4.3. Main clauses with subordinate-clause word order

Mon, gid, sikke, blot, bare and *måske* change the word order of the main clause into the word order pattern of subordinate clauses. Since these words cannot be glossed out of context, I illustrate them in sample sentences:

Mon han ikke kommer i morgen? – 'maybe he'll come tomorrow?'
Gid han kommer i dag. – 'o may he come today!'
Sikke du da kan larme! – 'what an awful noise you are making!'
Måske du lige kunne give et nap med! – 'maybe you could just give a hand'

These are exclamation-like utterances, but they may occur in written language as well. The etymology of these words cannot be taken up here, although it would in some cases provide a (historical) explanation for the word order encountered today. If these words are classed as normal adverbs, no special effect on the dependency structure of the sentences needs to be taken into account. It would be mistaken to see the word order as a reason to consider these sentences subordinate clauses.

Bare han dog havde sagt det i tide! – 'if only he had said it in time!'

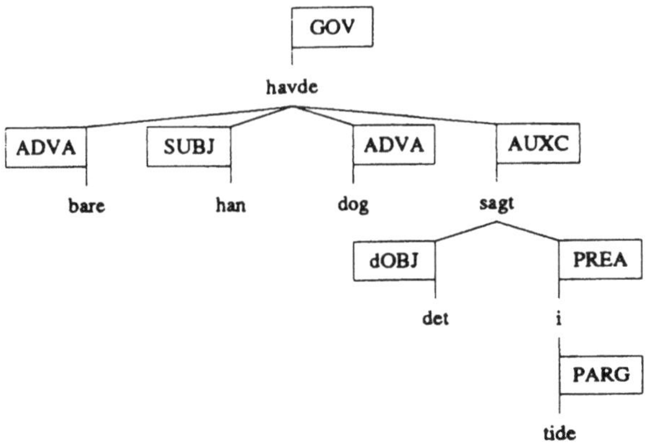

4.4. Comparison sentences

Another special case, which might as well be subsumed under the category of subordinate clauses, is the comparison sentence.

[1] Han er større end jeg. – 'he is taller than I'
[2] Han er mere smuk end klog. – 'he is more handsome than clever'
[3] Han er så stor som jeg. – 'he is as tall as I'
[4] Han har drukket sig fuld som sædvanlig. – 'he has got drunk as usual'

Som and *end* are subordinating conjunctions. This is especially evident when the sentences above are considered to be elliptic. When the "omitted" elements are restored, this yields:

[5] Han er større end jeg *er*. – 'he is taller than I am'
[6] Han er mere smuk end *han er* klog. – 'he is more handsome than he is clever'
[7] Han er så stor som jeg *er*. – 'he is as tall as I am'
[8] Han har drukket sig fuld som *han* sædvanlig *drikker sig fuld*.
'he has got drunk as he usually gets'

As was said above, ellipses are not treated in this study in any detail. Because of the frequency of the comparison constructions, a suitable solution is nevertheless required. It should be pointed out that the speakers of Danish are losing the awareness of the fact that these constructions are (or were) elliptic. As a consequence, the nominative pronouns as in [5] and [7] above are often replaced by the oblique form (*mig*). This means that *end* and *som* are already used as prepositions:

*Han er større end *mig*. – 'he is taller than me'

This form is not (yet) accepted as correct. I therefore do not see another solution than to consider the constructions in question to be elliptic and to refrain from adopting a non-elliptic solution for them here. I do so in particular since the individual valencies of the words involved cannot be included in this study. In any case the comparison sentences have to be analysed as special cases, since they cannot always be paradigmatically replaced by ordinary subordinate clauses.

5. Sample sentence

For at gøre det lettere at skabe bedre økonomiske betingelser, fremsætter Kommissionen 80 forslag med henblik på at nedbryde markedsskrankerne og sætte virksomhederne i stand til fuldt ud at drage fordel af den europæiske dimension.

'In order to make it easier to create better economic conditions, the Commission is putting forward 80 proposals which aim at removing the market barriers and at giving the companies an opportunity to fully take advantage of the European dimension.'

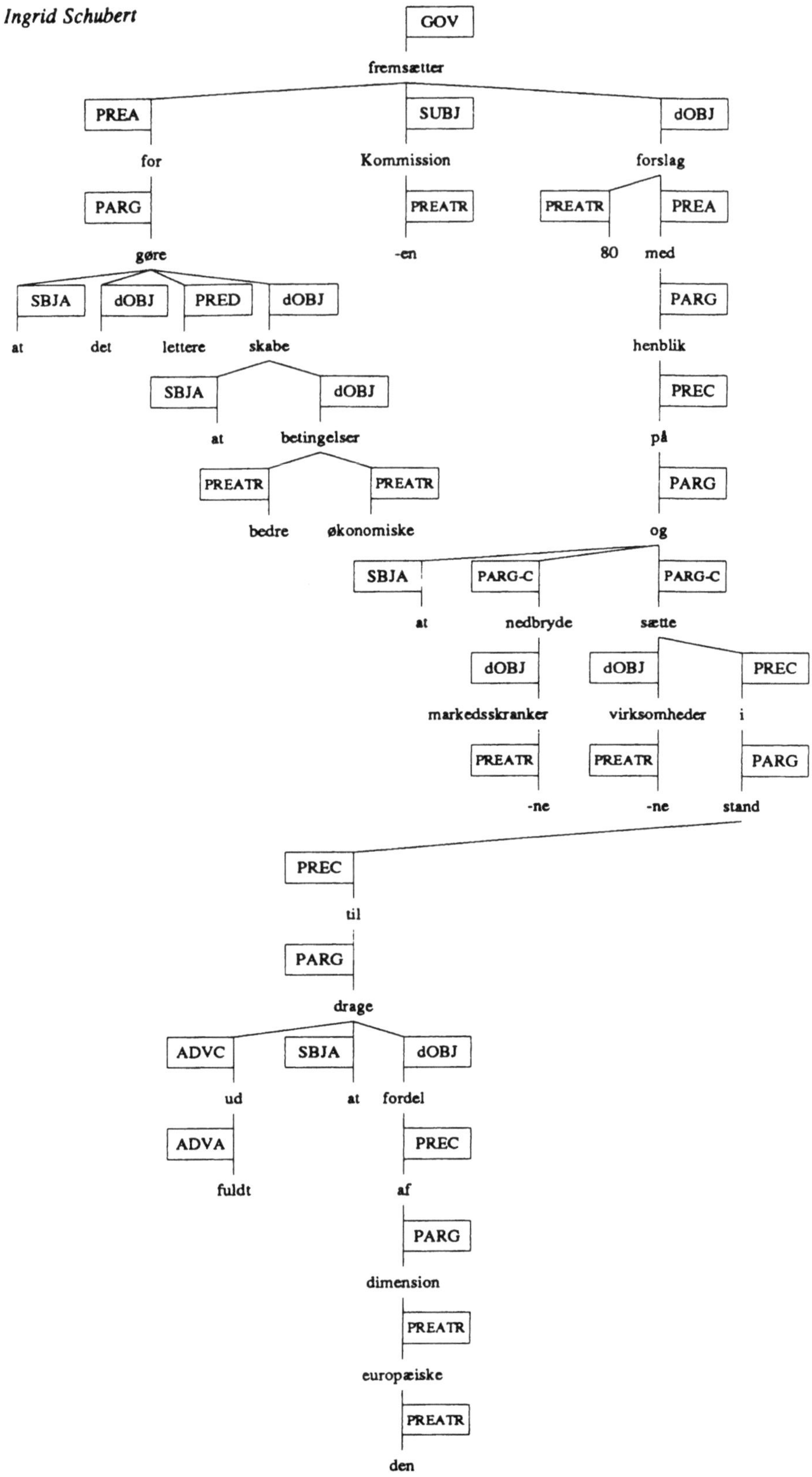
GOV
fremsætter
PREA
SUBJ
dOBJ
for
Kommission
forslag
PARG
PREATR
PREATR
PREA
gøre
-en
80
med
SBJA
dOBJ
PRED
dOBJ
PARG
at
det
lettere
skabe
henblik
SBJA
dOBJ
PREC
at
betingelser
på
PREATR
PREATR
PARG
bedre
økonomiske
og
SBJA
PARG-C
PARG-C
at
nedbryde
sætte
dOBJ
dOBJ
PREC
markedsskranker
virksomheder
i
PREATR
PREATR
PARG
-ne
-ne
stand
PREC
til
PARG
drage
ADVC
SBJA
dOBJ
ud
at
fordel
ADVA
PREC
fuldt
af
PARG
dimension
PREATR
europæiske
PREATR
den

References

Diderichsen, Paul (1946): *Elementær dansk Grammatik.*
København: Gyldendal, 3rd. ed. 1968

Fabricius-Hansen, Cathrine (1979): Valenztheorie und kontrastive Grammatik (Dänisch-Deutsch).
In: *Osloer Beiträge zur Germanistik* 3

Fabricius-Hansen, Cathrine / Lisbeth Falster Jacobsen / Jørgen Olsen (1981): *Die Satzbaupläne im Dänischen und Deutschen. 1. Vorüberlegungen.*
= KONTRA, Dänisch-deutsche kontrastive Grammatik, Arbeitsbericht 4. København: Københavns Universitet, Institut for Germansk Filologi

Hansen, Aage (1967): *Moderne dansk.*
Vol. I-III. København: Grafisk forlag

Hansen, Erik (1977): *Dæmonernes Port. Støttemateriale til undervisningen i nydansk grammatik.*
København: Reitzel

Nikula, Henrik (1976): *Verbvalenz. Untersuchungen am Beispiel des deutschen Verbs mit einer kontrastiven Analyse Deutsch-Schwedisch.*
= Acta Universitatis Upsaliensis, Studia Germanistica Upsaliensia 15. Uppsala

Nikula, Henrik (1986): *Dependensgrammatik.*
Malmö: Liber Förlag.

Nordentoft, Annelise Munck (1977a): *Hovedtræk af dansk grammatik. Ordklasser.*
København: Gyldendal, 2nd ed.

Nordentoft, Annelise Munck (1977b): *Hovedtræk af dansk grammatik. Syntaks.*
København: Gyldendal, 2nd ed.

Tarvainen, Kalevi (1983): The object as a syntactic category: a contrastive analysis of German, English and Swedish.
In: Tarvainen: *Two papers on dependency grammar.* = Umeå Papers in English 6 [Umeå], p. 29-52

Tesnière, Lucien (1959): *Éléments de syntaxe structurale.*
Paris: Klincksieck, 2nd ed. 4th print. 1982

Vater, Heinz (1973): *Dänische Subjekt- und Objektsätze.*
Tübingen: Niemeyer

A dependency syntax of Polish

Marek Świdziński

Warsaw, Poland

1. Some facts about Polish

Polish belongs to the group of West-Slavic languages, together with Czech, Slovak, Lower-, and Upper-Sorbian. Typologically, it is a representative of highly inflecting languages, like Latin or French, and unlike English or Chinese. Its syntax is, then, morphology-based; consequently, word order in Polish can be considered (relatively) free. An average lexical item (henceforth: LX) is exactly a set of wordforms (henceforth: *wf*), differing in shape, grammatical characteristics, and sometimes even in sets of dependents. LX's will be written down in capital letters (e.g., CHŁOPIEC 'boy'), *wf*'s in italic (e.g., *chłopiec* 'boy [nom, sg]').

Polish morphology is fairly developed. Not only does Polish have a great number of grammatical categories (which means that the paradigms of inflected lexemes are many-dimensional), but also there are a deal of declension and conjugation patterns. All this makes syntactic analysis of Polish sentences extremely complicated.

No simple procedure can be given to properly recognize a given *wf* as belonging to a respective LX, or to guess the headword of an (unknown) LX on the basis of that *wf*. The majority of Polish *wf*'s are synthetic (one-word); there are, too, several types of analytic *wf*'s, systemically rare but very frequent in texts, as well as analytic LX's. To account for all of such items, special dependency relations seem necessary, which, being of purely technical character, will not be dealt with here. A more detailed description is given in Świdziński (1988).

2. Part-of-speech classification

2.1. Classification

To avoid a vicious circle in definitions, LX-classes (and, possibly, LX-subclasses) in a dependency syntax have to be defined to some degree without reference to dependency properties. It seems natural that LX-classification be based primarily upon morphological criteria; only uninflected LX's will be defined in terms of distributional syntactic properties. The classification is taken from Saloni and Świdziński (1987).

Below, distributional definitions of the LX-classes are given. Some of the LX-classes are subclassified according to morphological-syntactic criteria (though not those of dependency-type). Also, *wf*'s representing LX's of particular LX-classes are subject to subclassification.

The classification can be illustrated by the following tree:

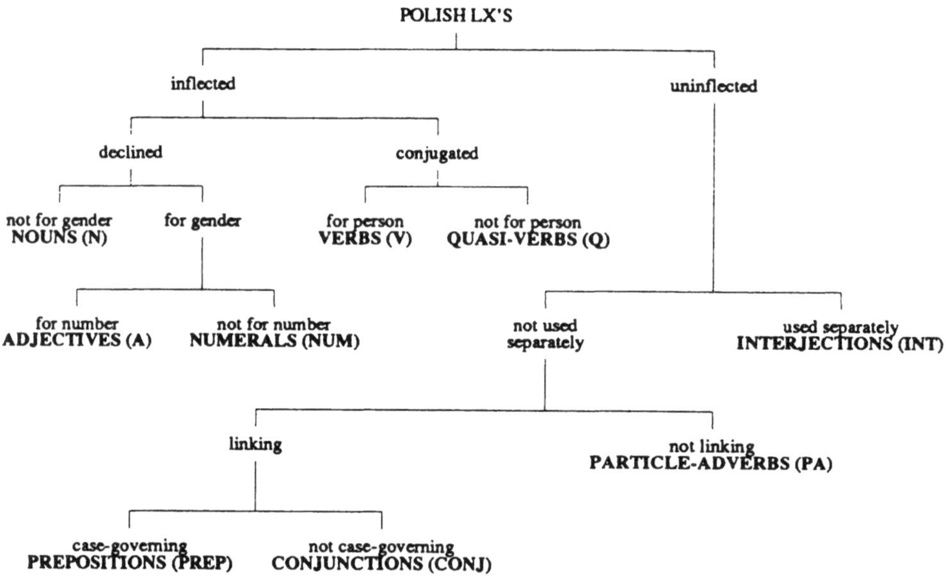

2.2. Verbs (V)

Verbs are conjugated for person, number, gender, tense, and mood. They also have the category of aspect: a given verb is either perfective (e.g. KUPIĆ 'buy'), or imperfective (e.g. KUPOWAĆ 'buy'). The structure of the 5-dimensional paradigm for Polish verbs depends on aspect: some *wf*'s are characteristic of perfectives, and not of imperfectives, or vice versa.

Wf-subclasses: personal *wf*'s (*kupię* 'I'll buy'), impersonal *wf*'s: the infinitive (*kupić* 'to buy'), the impersonal (*kupiono* '(one) bought'), adverbial participles (*kupując* 'buying') for KUPOWAĆ, *kupiwszy* 'having bought' for KUPIĆ). Personal *wf*'s, the impersonal and, in some cases, the infinitive form the superclass of **finite wordforms**, which always appear as head governors of a sentence.

Analytic *wf*'s: future tense *wf*'s of imperfectives (*będę* **kupować//kupował** '(I)'ll buy'), past tense *wf*'s (**kupiłem**//*-em* **kupił** '(I-[masc]) bought', **kupiły***śmy*//*-śmy* **kupiły** 'we-[fem] bought'), conditional *wf*'s (**kupiła***bym* '(I [fem])'d buy'), imperative third-person *wf*'s (*niech* **kupi** 'let him//her buy').

Analytic LX's: *reflexiva tantum* (BAĆ SIĘ 'be afraid').

2.3. Quasi-verbs (Q)

This class is typical of Slavic languages. Nothing like it is found in English, French, or German. Quasi-verbs are impersonal, subjectless verbal LX's.

Quasi-verbs do not have the category of person: they are conjugated solely for tense and mood. They also bear the category of aspect (e.g. LUNĄĆ 'start pouring' – perfective, TRZEBA 'be necessary' – imperfective). The above mentioned categories form a 2-dimensional paradigm for Polish quasi-verbs. Its structure depends on aspect as well.

Wf-subclasses: finite *wf*'s (*trzeba* 'it's necessary'), the infinitive (*lunąć* 'to start pouring').

Analytic *wf*'s: see 2.2. For some quasi-verbs: the infinitive (*być* **trzeba**).

Analytic LX's: see 2.2. (e.g. ZMIERZCHAĆ SIĘ 'darken').

2.4. Nouns (N)

Nouns are declined for case and number, which forms a 2-dimensional paradigm. They also have the category of gender, which is not an inflectional category.

LX-subclasses: regular nouns – standard (DZIEWCZYNA 'girl', STÓŁ 'table'), gerunds (KUPOWANIE 'purchasing', derived from KUPOWAĆ), deadjectivals (BIAŁOŚĆ 'whiteness', derived from BIAŁY 'white'); nominal pronouns – personal (JA 'I', ONO 'it-[neu]'), interrogative (CO 'what'), relative (KTÓRY 'who; which'), reflexive (SIĘ '-self'), indefinite (KTOŚ 'somebody'), negative (NIC 'nothing').

Analytic LX's: derivatives of *reflexiva tantum* verbs or quasi-verbs (BANIE SIĘ, ZMIERZCHANIE SIĘ).

2.5. Adjectives (A)

Adjectives are declined for case, number and gender. Most adjectives have also the category of degree. The inflectional categories form a 4-dimensional paradigm. To account for so-called deadjectival adverbs, it is convenient to enrich the paradigm with 3 adverbial *wf*'s which are solely degree-marked, being neutralized with respect to case, number, and gender.

Wf-subclasses: degree subclasses – positive *wf*'s (*wysoki* 'high-[nom, sg, masc]'), comparative *wf*'s (*wyższy* 'higher'), superlative *wf*'s (*najwyższy* '(the) highest'); "case-markedness" subclasses – adjectival *wf*'s (*wysoki*), adverbial *wf*'s (*wysoko* 'high(ly)').

Analytic *wf*'s: comparatives and superlatives of some adjectives (*bardziej chory* 'more ill', *najbardziej chory* 'most ill').

LX-subclasses: regular adjectives (WYSOKI 'high'), active participles (KUPUJĄCY 'buying', derived from the imperfective verb KUPOWAĆ), passive participles (KUPIONY 'bought', derived from KUPIĆ), ordinal numerals (DRUGI '(the) second'); pronouns - interrogative ($JAKI_1$ 'what... like?'), relative ($JAKI_2$ 'what'), possessive (NASZ 'our(s)'), indefinite (PEWIEN 'certain', 'some'), negative (ŻADEN 'no').

Analytic LX's: active participles derived from *reflexiva tantum* verbs (e.g., BOJĄCY SIĘ 'being afraid').

2.6. Numerals (NUM)

Of the LX's that are traditionally referred to as numerals, only cardinal numerals satisfy the morphology-based definition given in 2.1. Numerals are declined for case and gender, and not for number. Since complex numerals will not be dealt with in this paper, the NUM-class can be considered closed ($JEDEN_1$ 'one' will be treated here as an adjective containing only singular *wf*'s).

Examples: DWA 'two', SIEDEM 'seven', STO 'hundred'.

Syntactic properties of Polish numerals are so specific and systematically unprecedented that it requires much effort to deal with the class as a whole. Not only are there several LX-subclasses differing from each other both morphologically and syntactically; *wf*'s within an average NUM usually differ in their syntactic features.

Numerals always accompany a noun. I assume that for any numeral + noun construction and for any numeral *wf*, it is the numeral *wf*, and not the nominal one, that represents the whole construction, i.e., numerals are "centers" or heads of respective constructions. A number of serious arguments can be given for this solution (cf. Saloni/Świdziński 1987: 185-186).

Wf-subclasses: "government" *wf*'s (*wf*'s that govern the genitive case of the noun; e.g., *pięć* 'five-[nom, fem]' in *pięć kobiet* 'five women'), "agreement" *wf*'s (*wf*'s that are case-affected by the noun; e.g., *pięcioma kobietami* 'five women-[instr]').

2.7. Particle-adverbs (PA)

The class, though closed, is heterogeneous. Below, some examples are given: CZY$_1$ 'whether', NIE$_1$ 'not', NIESPEŁNA 'less than', NATYCHMIAST 'at once', NIE OPODAL 'nearby', OCZYWISTA 'obviously'.

2.8. Prepositions (PREP)

Prepositions are linking LX's that found case government patterns. There exist a number of analytic PREP's; sometimes it is hardly possible to tell if a given 2-word construction is a *wf* of an analytic PREP, or if it is a preposition + nominal construction.

Examples: DLA 'for', KOŁO 'close to', NA 'on', O 'about', PO 'after', PODCZAS 'during', W (*w, we*) 'in', Z POWODU 'because of'.

2.9. Conjunctions (CONJ)

Conjunctions are linking LX's which, unlike PREP's, do not found case government patterns. The two types of conjunctions are distinguished: **coordinate CONJ's** and **subordinate CONJ's**, both given by list. Some conjunctions are analytic, i.e., discontinuous.

Coordinate conjunctions (CONJ(c)): I 'and', ALE 'but', NIE TYLKO..., LECZ TAKŻE... 'not only... but also...', ZAŚ 'on the other hand', "," (= comma).

Subordinate conjunctions (CONJ(s)): BOWIEM 'because', CHOCIAŻ, CHOĆ 'although', GDY 'when', PÓKI..., PÓTY... '..., as long as...', JEŚLI 'if-[real]', ŻE 'that', ŻEBY 'in order to', 'to'.

2.10. Interjections (INT)

Interjections are LX's that are used separately (i.e., they can constitute a complete utterance). The class, if more thoroughly examined, turns out to be heterogeneous. Examples: AHA 'oh yes', CHOLERA 'shit', CZEŚĆ 'hi', DZIEŃ DOBRY 'good morning//afternoon', JEZU 'Jesus!', PA 'bye-bye'.

3. Dependent types

An inventory of the types of dependency relations applied in the present description is given below. It is based primarily on Schubert (1986).

Complements	**Abbreviation**
Subject	SUBJ
Object	OBJ
Prepositional complement	PREC
Predicative complement	PRED
Adverbial complement	ADVC
Infinitival complement	INFC
Propositional complement	PROC
Numeral argument	NARG
Prepositional argument	PARG
Subordinate conjunction argument	SARG
Coordination argument	X-C

Adjuncts	**Abbreviation**
Attribute	ATTR
Relative adjunct	RELA
Genitival adjunct	GENA
Apposition	APOS
Predicative adjunct	PREA
Adverbial adjunct	ADVA
Propositional adjunct	PROA
Free adjunct	FRA

The notion of **object** requires some comments. I do not here make a distinction between direct and indirect objects. I assume, too, that the only possible "sentence-like" (i.e., clausal) realization of OBJ is a relative clause (cf. *Kupił książkę//, co chciał*. 'He bought a book//what he wanted to.'). Subordinate clauses required by certain LX's (conjunctional clauses or indirect questions) are treated here as realizations of another type of a complement, namely the **propositional complement** (cf. *Wiem, kto przyszedł//, że Piotr przyszedł*. 'I know who came//that P. came.').

The **adverbial complement** has a number of realizations which seem distributionally equivalent: A (adverbial *wf*), PA, PREP, and even N or NUM (the latter two are textually rare). For some governors, the equivalence may be restricted. The same holds true for the **adverbial adjunct**. (Note, by the way, that the above inventory of adjuncts does not contain a prepositional adjunct.)

The **coordination argument** relation appears only in the description of Polish coordinate conjunctions. The symbol X-C stands for a variable; its fixed values, mentioned in 4.9. refer to the (intuitive) dependency characteristics of the conjuncts.

4. Dependency patterns for Polish LX-classes

4.1. Introduction

In this chapter, dependency properties of particular LX-classes are described, and the tables of possible realizations of all dependent types are presented.

Some dependent types are either *wf*-, or LX-specific, i.e., can be governed only by certain *wf*'s or by certain LX's. Such dependents are marked with an asterisk in the dependent tables and commented upon further. Those realizations that are textually or systemically rare are marked with R.

In the examples of Polish sentences, governors are written in italics, and dependents in boldface type(cf. **Jan** *śpi*. 'J. is sleeping.').

4.2. Dependents of verbs

	V	Q	N	A	NUM	PA	PREP	CONJ(c)	CONJ(s)	INT
SUBJ	×R	×R	×		×			×	×	
OBJ	×	×	×					×		
PREC							×	×		
PRED			×	×				×		
ADVC			×	×	×	×	×	×		
INFC	×							×		
PROC	×	×						×	×	
NARG										
PARG										
SARG										
ATTR										
RELA										
GENA										
APOS										
PREA	×			×						
ADVA			×	×	×	×	×	×		
PROA								×	×	
FRA			×					×		×

SUBJ (*wf*-SPECIFIC DEPENDENT TYPE: ONLY PERSONAL *wf*'S GOVERN IT. FOR NON-3RD-PERSON *wf*'S THE SUBJECT IS OPTIONAL.)

SUBJ/Verb (R)

Kto **przyjdzie**, *wygra*. – '(He) who'll come will win.'

SUBJ/Quasi-verb (R)

Nie *jest* jasne, czy już **świta**. – 'It isn't clear if it's dawning now.'

SUBJ/Noun

Studenci *przyszli*. – 'The students came';
Przyszedłem//**Ja** *przyszedłem*. – 'I came.'

SUBJ/Numeral

Przyszło **trzech** studentów. – 'The three students came.'

SUBJ/Coordinate conjunction

Jaś **i** Maria *przyszli.* – 'J. and M. came.'

SUBJ/Subordinate conjunction

Wydaje się, **że** pada. – 'It seems that it's raining.'

OBJ/Verb (R), Quasi-verb (R)

Zaprosimy, kogo **chcesz//**, kogo tam **nie było**.
– 'We'll invite (anybody) you want//(anybody) who wasn't there.'

OBJ/Noun, Numeral

Lubię **Marię//trzech** chłopców. – 'I like M.//(those) **three** boys.'

OBJ/Coordinate conjunction

Zaproś Jana **albo** Marię. – 'Do invite J. or M.'

PREC/Preposition

Myślę **o** was. – 'I think about you.'

PREC/Coordinate conjunction

Liczę na Ewę **i** na was. – 'I count on E. and on you.'

PRED/Noun, Adjective

Jaś *jest* **studentem//głupi.** – 'J. is a student//stupid.'

PRED/Coordinate conjunction

Jaś *jest* **bądź** studentem, **bądź** nauczycielem. – 'J. is either a student, or a teacher.'

ADVC/Noun, Adjective, Numeral, Particle-adverb, Preposition

To *kosztuje* **dolara//drogo//dwa** dolary//**trochę//nad** miarę.
– 'It costs a dollar//much//two dollars//a little//more than usual.'

ADVC/Coordinate conjunction

Mieszkamy w Warszawie **lub** tutaj. – 'We live either in Warsaw, or here.'

INFC/Verb

Każ mu **przyjść!** – 'Tell him to come!'

INFC/Coordinate conjunction

Każ mu przyjść , zaczekać! – 'Tell him to come, to wait!'

PROC/Verb, Quasi-verb

Wiem, kogo **zaprosić//**, kogo **mdli**. – 'I know whom to invite//who has nausea.'

PROC/Coordinate conjunction

Wiem, że pada, **a także** że nie przyjdziesz.
– 'I know that it's raining and also that you won't come.'

PROC/Subordinate conjunction

Wiem, **że** pada. – 'I know that it's raining.'

PREA/Verb

Przyszedł **płacząc**. – 'He came crying.'

PREA/Adjective

Przyszedł **zmęczony**. – 'He came tired.'

PREA/Coordinate conjunction

Przychodził **albo** płacząc, **albo** śmiejąc się.
– 'He used to come either laughing or crying.'

ADVA/Noun, Adjective, Numeral, Particle-adverb, Preposition

Spałem **godzinę//długo//pięć** godzin//**od** pó łnocy.
– 'I've been sleeping for an hour//for a long time//for five hours//since midnight.'

ADVA/Coordinate conjunction

Spałem godzinę **lub** dwie godziny.
– 'I've been sleeping for an hour or for two hours.'

PROA/Coordinate conjunction

Pójdę tam, choć nie mam czasu **i** chociaż się boję.
– 'I'll go there though I don't have much time and though I'm afraid of that.'

PROA/Subordinate conjunction

Ponieważ nie mam czasu, nie *pójdę* tam. – 'Since I have got no time, I won't go.'

FRA/Noun

On *umarł*, **chłopcze**! – 'He died, buddy!'

FRA/Coordinate conjunction

Kochani Janku i Marysiu, wszystko *jest* w porządku.
– 'Dear J. and M., everything is OK!'

FRA/Interjection

Jezu, *udało się*... – 'Jesus, got it...'

4.3. Dependents of quasi-verbs

	V	Q	N	A	NUM	PA	PREP	CONJ(c)	CONJ(s)	INT
SUBJ										
OBJ			×		×			×		
PREC							×	×		
PRED										
ADVC				×		×		×		
INFC	×	×						×		
PROC	×	×						×	×	
NARG										
PARG										
SARG										
ATTR										
RELA										
GENA										
APOS										
PREA										
ADVA			×	×	×	×	×	×		
PROA								×	×	
FRA			×					×		×

OBJ/Noun, Numeral

Brakuje **Marii//trzech** chłopców. – 'M.//(those) three boys are still missing.'

OBJ/Coordinate conjunction

Nie ma tutaj Jana **oraz** Marii. – 'Neither J. nor M. is here.'

OBJ/Preposition

Od Jana *czuć*. – 'J. stinks.'

OBJ/Coordinate conjunction

Ani od Jana, **ani** od Piotra nie *czuć*. – 'Neither J., nor P. stinks.'

ADVC/Adjective, Particle-adverb

Robi się **ciemno//akurat**. – 'It's getting dark//OK.'

ADVC/Coordinate conjunction

Było tam ciepło, **ale** nieprzyjemnie. – 'It was warm there, but not nice.'

INFC/Verb

Trzeba tam **pójść**! – 'It's necessary to go there!'

INFC/Quasi-verb

W samolocie *może* cię **mdlić**. – 'You can have nausea on the plane.'

INFC/Coordinate conjunction

Pora było **nie tylko** usiąść, **ale i** odpocząć!
– 'It was time not only to sit down, but also to rest.'

PROC/Verb, Quasi-verb

Było wiadomo, kogo **zaprosić**//, kogo **mdli**.

– 'It was obvious whom to invite//who has nausea.'

PROC/Coordinate conjunction

Słychać, że Piotr umarł, **a także** że wdowa nie ma pieniędzy.

– 'There are rumors that P. died, and also that the widow doesn't have any money.'

PROC/Subordinate conjunction

Chodzi o to, **że** Piotr umarł. – 'The problem is that P. died.'

ADVA/Noun, Adjective, Numeral, Preposition

Ściemniało się **godzinę**//**długo**//**dwadzieścia** minut//**od** piątej.

– 'It has been getting dark for an hour//for a long time//for twenty minutes//since 5 o'clock.'

ADVA/Particle-adverb

Ściemniało się **nagle**. – 'It used to darken suddenly.'

ADVA/Coordinate conjunction

Mdliło go godzinę **lub** dwie godziny.

– 'He has been suffering from nausea for an hour//for two hours.'

PROA/Coordinate conjunction

Jeśli Jan przyjdzie **albo** jeśli Maria przyjdzie, *będzie* dobrze.

– 'It'll be nice if J. comes or if M. comes.'

PROA/Subordinate conjunction

Jeśli Jan przyjdzie, *będzie* dobrze. – 'It'll be nice if J. comes.'

FRA/Noun

Czas na ciebie, **Mario**! – 'It's your turn, M.!'

FRA/Coordinate conjunction

Kochani Janku **i** Marysiu, już *świta*! – 'Dear J. and M., it's just dawning!'

FRA/Interjection

Psiakrew, *pada*! – 'Shit! It's raining!'

4.4. Dependents of nouns

	V	Q	N	A	NUM	PA	PREP	CONJ(c)	CONJ(s)	INT
SUBJ										
OBJ*	×R	×R	×		×			×		
PREC*							×	×		
PRED*			×	×				×		
ADVC*			×R	×	×R	×	×	×		
INFC*	×	×						×		
PROC*	×	×						×	×	
NARG										
PARG										
SARG										
ATTR*				×				×		
RELA*	×	×						×		
GENA*			×		×			×		
APOS			×		×			×		
PREA										
ADVA			×R	×R	×R	×R	×	×		
PROA										
FRA										

OBJ (FOR GERUNDIAL AND DEADJECTIVAL GOVERNORS ONLY)/Verb (R), Quasi-verb (R)

Zapraszanie, kogo **chcesz**//, kogo tam **nie było**, nie ma sensu.
– 'It's senseless to invite whoever you want//(those) who weren't there.'

OBJ/Noun, Numeral

Czytanie tej **książki** długo trwało. – 'It took (you) a lot to finish that book.'

OBJ/Coordinate conjunction

Zapraszanie Jana **albo** Marii nie ma sensu. – 'It's senseless to invite either J. or M.'

PREC (FOR GERUNDIAL AND DEADJECTIVAL GOVERNORS ONLY)/Preposition

Jego *wpływ* **na** Piotra jest niewątpliwy. – 'His influence on P. is beyond doubt.'

PREC/Coordinate conjunction

To jest *pytanie* do Jana, **ale i** do Marii.
– 'This question is (addressed) to J., but also to M.'

PRED (FOR SOME GERUNDIAL GOVERNORS)/Noun, Adjective

Bycie **księdzem**//**miłym** nie jest proste. – 'It is not easy to be a priest//to be nice.'

PRED/Coordinate conjunction

Bycie **i** księdzem, **i** marksistą wydaje się idiotyczne.
– 'It seems foolish to be both a priest and a marxist.'

ADVC (FOR SOME GERUNDIAL GOVERNORS)/Adjective, Particle-adverb, Preposition

Nie lubimy *mieszkania* tak **daleko**//**tam**//**w** Warszawie.
– 'We don't like to live so far (from here)//there//in Warsaw.'

ADVC/Noun (R), Numeral (R): *Czekanie* **rok**//**trzy** lata okazało się niepotrzebne.
– 'It has turned out to be futile to wait a year//three years.'

ADVC/Coordinate conjunction

Chodzenie tu **i** tam zabiera mu dużo czasu.
– '(His) walking to and fro is time-consuming.'

PROC (FOR SOME GERUNDIAL AND DEADJECTIVAL GOVERNORS; FOR INDIVIDUAL REGULAR NOUNS; FOR THE INDEFINITE PRONOUN *TO*)/Verb, Quasi-verb

Pytanie, kiedy **przyjdziemy**//, czy **pada**, zaskoczyło nas.
– 'We were caught by his question when we'd come//if it was raining.'

PROC/Coordinate conjunction

Odrzucono jego *radę*, **żeby** iść do chirurga.

– 'His advice to go to a surgeon was rejected.'

PROC/Subordinate conjunction

To, kiedy przyjdziemy **oraz** czy pada, ciekawiło Jana.

– 'J. was interested in when we would come and if it was raining.'

ATTR (NOT GOVERNED BY PERSONAL, REFLEXIVE, AND RELATIVE PRONOUNS)/Adjective

To jest **miłe** *miasto*. – 'This is a nice town.'

ATTR/Coordinate conjunction

To jest miłe , piękne *miasto*. – 'This is a nice, beautiful town.'

RELA (NOT GOVERNED BY PERSONAL, REFLEXIVE AND RELATIVE PRONOUNS)/Verb, Quasi-verb

Znam *chłopca*, który **widział** wypadek//, któremu **trzeba** pomóc.

– 'I know the boy who saw the crash//who should be helped.'

RELA/Coordinate conjunction

Znam *chłopca* który widział wypadek **i** któremu trzeba pomoć.

– 'I know the boy who saw the crash and who should be helped.'

GENA (NOT GOVERNED BY ANY PERSONAL, REFLEXIVE, OR RELATIVE PRONOUNS; RARE FOR OTHER PRONOUNS)/Noun, Numeral

Dom **Jana//trzech** małych świnek jest z cegieł. – 'J.'s//The three little pigs' house is made of bricks.'

GENA/Coordinate conjunction

Słyszałem *coś* Mozarta, **a nie** Haydna. – 'I've heard something by M., not by H.'

APOS/Noun

To jest *poeta* **Kowalski//***Kowalski***-poeta**. – 'This is K., a poet.'

APOS/Numeral

Zaprosiłam *je*, **pięć** skrzypaczek. – 'I invited them, the five violinists.'

APOS/Coordinate conjunction

Zaproś te *dziewczyny*, Marię **i** Annę. – 'Invite those girls, M. and A.'

ADVA/Preposition

Mieszkam w *domu* **bez** łazienki//**za** rogiem.

– 'I live in a house with no bathroom//around the corner.'

ADVA/Noun (R), Adjective (R), Numeral (R)

Mówienie **godzinę//głośno//sześć** godzin zmęczyło go.

– 'His one-hour//loud//six-hour speech made him exhausted.'

ADVA/Particle-adverb (R – THERE ARE ONLY A FEW ADNOMINAL PARTICLE-ADVERBS)

Nie przyszedł **prawie** *nikt*. – 'There came hardly anybody.'

ADVA/Coordinate conjunction

Mieszkam w *domu* bez łazienki, **natomiast** z ogrodem

– 'I live in a house with no bathroom, but with a garden.'

4.5. Dependents of adjectives

	V	Q	N	A	NUM	PA	PREP	CONJ(c)	CONJ(s)	INT
SUBJ										
OBJ*	×R	×R	×		×			×		
PREC*							×	×		
PRED*			×	×				×		
ADVC*			×R	×	×R	×	×	×		
INFC*	×							×		
PROC	×	×						×	×	
NARG										
PARG										
SARG										
ATTR										
RELA										
GENA										
APOS										
PREA										
ADVA			×R	×	×R	×	×R	×		
PROA										
FRA								×		

OBJ (GOVERNED BY SOME ACTIVE AND PASSIVE PARTICIPLES; BY INDIVIDUAL ADJECTIVES)/Verb (R), Quasi-verb (R)

Nie lubię *dających* ci, co **chcesz**//, czego ci **brakuje**.
– 'I hate those giving you whatever you want//whatever you lack.'

OBJ/Noun, Numeral

Szukam książki *danej* **Marii**//**trojgu** studentów.
– 'I'm looking for a book given to M.//to (those) three students.'

OBJ/Coordinate conjunction

One są *żądne* powodzenia, **ale i** pieniędzy.
– 'They-[fem] are eager for success, as well as for money.'

PREC (*wf*-SPECIFIC DEPENDENT TYPE: GOVERNED BY COMPARATIVE AND SUPERLATIVE *wf*'s; ALSO BY SOME ACTIVE AND PASSIVE PARTICIPLES; BY INDIVIDUAL ADJECTIVES)/Preposition

Oni są *lepsi* **od** Jana//**niż** Jan//*najlepsi* **wśród** fizyków.
– 'They are better than J.//the best among the physicists.'

PREC/Coordinate conjunction

Ta książka była *czytana* przez niego **bądź** przez Marię.
– 'This book was read by him, or perhaps by M.'

PREC (GOVERNED BY A FEW ACTIVE PARTICIPLES)/Noun, Adjective

Dziewczyna *będąca* **modelką**//**piękną** *sawsze zwycięża.*
– 'A girl who is a model//who is beautiful always wins.'

PREC/Coordinate conjunction

Znam człowieka *będącego* **nie tylko** dziennikarzem, **ale również** detektywem
– 'I know a guy who is not only a journalist, but also a detective.'

ADVC (GOVERNED BY INDIVIDUAL ACTIVE OR PASSIVE PARTICIPLES)/Noun (R), Adjective, Numeral(R), Particle-adverb, Preposition

Nie kupuję rzeczy *kosztujących* **dolara**//**drogo**//**dwa** dolary//**trochę**//**nad** miarę.
– 'I don't buy things costing a dollar//much//two dollars//a little//more than usual.'

ADVC/Coordinate conjunction

Będziemy *zakwaterowani* w Warszawie **lub** tutaj.
– 'We'll get accommodation either in Warsaw, or here.'

INFC (GOVERNED BY SOME ACTIVE PARTICIPLES)/Verb

Jan nie lubi facetów *każących* mu **pracować**.
– 'J. doesn't like people who use to tell him to work.'

INFC/Coordinate conjunction

Maria, *chcąca* tu przyjechać **albo** napisać do nas, nie ma pieniędzy.
– 'Mary, wanting to come or to write to us, has got no money.'

PROC (GOVERNED BY SOME ACTIVE PARTICIPLES; BY THE INDEFINITE ADJECTIVE PRONOUN *TAKI* 'SUCH (THAT)')/Verb, Quasi-verb

Nie jestem *pewien*, komu to **dać**//tego **potrzeba**.
– 'I am not sure whom to give that//who need that.'

PROC/Coordinate conjunction

Pytany, czy przyjdzie, **a także** kiedy przyjdzie, zaczął kląć.
– 'Asked if he'll come and also when he started to curse.'

PROC/Subordinate conjunction

On jest *taki*, **że** miło go zaprosić. – 'He's such that it's nice to invite him.'

ADVA/Adjective, Particle-adverb

On był **wyjątkowo**//**dosyć** *bogaty*. – 'He was very rich//rich enough.'

ADVA/Noun (R), Numeral (R), Preposition

Wyrzucił *czytających* **godzinami**//**dwie** godziny//**od** piątej.
– 'He kicked (those) who've been reading for hours (=permanently)//for two hours//since 5 o'clock.'

ADVA/Coordinate conjunction

Był bardzo , bardzo *bogaty*. – 'He was very, very rich.'

4.6. Dependents of numerals

	V	Q	N	A	NUM	PA	PREP	CONJ(c)	CONJ(s)	INT
SUBJ										
OBJ										
PREC										
PRED										
ADVC										
INFC										
PROC										
NARG			×					×R		
PARG										
SARG										
ATTR				×R						
RELA*	×R	×R						×R		
GENA*			×R					×R		
APOS										
PREA										
ADVA				×R		×R		×R		
PROA										
FRA										

NARG/Noun

Dwóch **chłopców** przyszło. //*Dwaj* **chłopcy** przyszli. – 'The two boys have come.'

NARG/Coordinate conjunction (R)

Spotkałem *pięć* studentek **albo** uczennic. – 'I met five (female) students or schoolgirls.'

ATTR/Adjective (R)

Dobre *dziesięć* kobiet zginęło. – 'Good ten (= no less than ten) women were killed.'

RELA (NUMERALS ALWAYS REFER TO PEOPLE)/Verb (R), Quasi-verb (R)

Znam *trzech*, którzy **widzieli** wypadek//, których tu **brakuje**.
– 'I know the three (men) who saw the crash//who are missing here.'

RELA/Coordinate conjunction (R)

Znam *trzech*, którzy widzieli wypadek **i** których można przesłuchać.
– 'I know the three (men) who saw the crash and whom you can interrogate.'

GENA (NUMERALS ALWAYS REFER TO PEOPLE)/Noun (R)

Jego *trzech* przyszło. – 'The three guys of his came.'

GENA/Coordinate conjunction (R)

Ci *trzej* Al Capone'a **i** ojca przyszli.
– 'The three guys of Al Capone and his father's came.'

ADVA/Adjective (R), Particle-adverb (R – THERE ARE ONLY A FEW ADNUMERAL MODIFIERS OF THIS TYPE)

Kupili **dokładnie//niemal** *dziesięć* puszek. – 'They bought exactly//almost ten cans.'

ADVA/Coordinate conjunction (R)

Kupili prawie, **ale nie** dokładnie *dziesięć* puszek.
– 'They bought almost, but not exactly, ten cans.'

4.7. Dependents of particle-adverbs

	V	Q	N	A	NUM	PA	PREP	CONJ(c)	CONJ(s)	INT
SUBJ										
OBJ										
PREC										
PRED										
ADVC										
INFC										
PROC										
NARG										
PARG										
SARG										
ATTR										
RELA										
GENA										
APOS										
PREA										
ADVA				×		×			×	
PROA										
FRA										

ADVA/Adjective, Particle-adverb

Przyjedziemy **dokładnie//na pewno** *jutro*. – 'We'll arrive just//certainly tomorrow.'

ADVA/Coordinate conjunction

Przyjedziemy prawdopodobnie, **a nawet** na pewno *jutro*.
– 'We'll come probably, and even surely, tomorrow.'

4.8. Dependents of prepositions

	V	Q	N	A	NUM	PA	PREP	CONJ(c)	CONJ(s)	INT
SUBJ										
OBJ										
PREC										
PRED										
ADVC										
INFC										
PROC										
NARG										
PARG			×		×					
SARG										
ATTR										
RELA										
GENA										
APOS										
PREA										
ADVA				×		×				
PROA										
FRA										

PARG/Noun, Numeral

Pytam *o* **Jana**//*o* tych **pięć** dziewczyn. – 'I'm asking about J.//about these five girls.'

PARG/Coordinate conjunction

Pracujemy *z* Janem **albo** Piotrem. – 'We work either with J., or with P.'

ADVA/Adjective, Particle-adverb

Krzyczeli **absolutnie**//**niemal** *bez* przerwy.
– 'They were shouting absolutely//almost uninterruptedly.'

ADVA/Coordinate conjunction

Pójdę tam **bądź** tylko, **bądź** również *z* nim.
– 'I'll go there either ONLY, or ALSO with him.'

4.9. Dependents of conjunctions

4.9.1. Dependents of coordinate conjunctions

Coordinate conjunctions appear in constructions that can be structured in the following way:

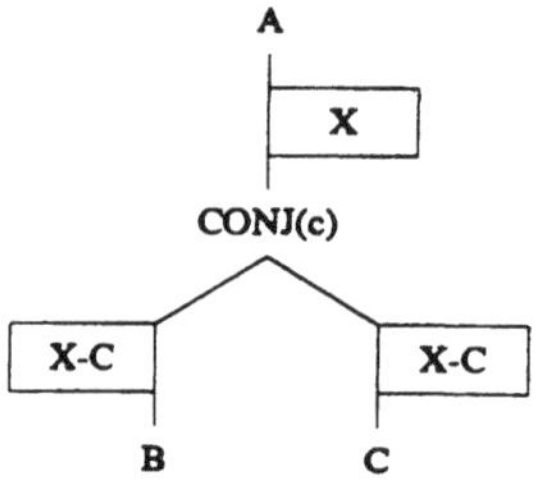

where the symbol X stands for a given dependent type, and the symbol X-C for conjuncts of the very type. E.g. in *Jan i Maria przyszli* 'J. and M. came' the conjunction *i*, being itself a subject of *przyszli*, governs the two subject-type conjuncts (SUBJ-C's) **Jan** and **Maria**, and in *Kup nowy albo stary samochód* 'Buy a new or used car' we have the two ATTR-C's **nowy** and **stary**.

Note that in sentences like *Zaproś Jana i Marię lub Annę* 'Invite J. and either M., or A.' there appear two OBJ-C-dependents **Maria** and **Anna**. They are governed by the conjunction *i* which is an OBJ-C of the verb *zaproś*, the other OBJ-C-conjunct of this conjunction being *Jana*. The reader can easily find appropriate examples in coordinate-conjunction lines of the paragraphs 4.2.-4.9.

Coordinate conjunctions can also govern (practically) all types of dependents. E.g., in *Jan czyta lub pisze listy* 'J. is reading or writing letters' the conjunction *lub*, as representing the predicate, is said to govern the subject (**Jan** czyta *lub* pisze) and, for the reading *(Jan) (czyta lub pisze) (listy)*, the object (czyta *lub* pisze **listy**). Again, it is easy for the reader to construct appropriate examples.

For another solution to the problem of coordinate constructions, see Mel'čuk (1988: 26-28, 40-41).

4.9.2. Dependents of subordinate conjunctions

	V	Q	N	A	NUM	PA	PREP	CONJ(c)	CONJ(s)	INT
SUBJ										
OBJ										
PREC										
PRED										
ADVC										
INFC										
PROC										
NARG										
PARG										
SARG	×	×								
ATTR										
RELA										
GENA										
APOS										
PREA										
ADVA										
PROA										
FRA										

CONJ/Verb, Quasi-verb

Ponieważ Jan nie **przyszedł//padało**, zostanę w domu.
– 'Since J. didn't come//it was raining I stayed at home.'

CONJ/Coordinate conjunction

Wiem, *że* Jan nie przyszedł, **a** Maria wyjechała.
– 'I know that J. didn't come, and M. was out.'

4.10. Interjections

No dependents.

5. Sample sentence

Uciec jeszcze można, kiedy więc inspektor spyta mnie, czy to wy kazaliście mi zabić Marię, będę utrzymywać, że nie tylko was, ale i ofiary nie znałem.

uciec jeszcze można, kiedy więc inspektor spyta mnie, czy to wy **kazaliście** [analytic *wf*] mi zabić Marię, Ø [empty word] **będę utrzymywać** że Ø **nie tylko** was, **ale i** ofiary nie **znałem**.

to-escape still is-possible, when so inspector asks me whether it you **told** me to-kill M. (I) **will assert** that (I) **not only** you **but also** victim not **knew**

'It's still possible to escape; so, when the inspector asks me whether it was you who told me to kill Mary, I'll assert that I didn't know you, as well as the victim.'

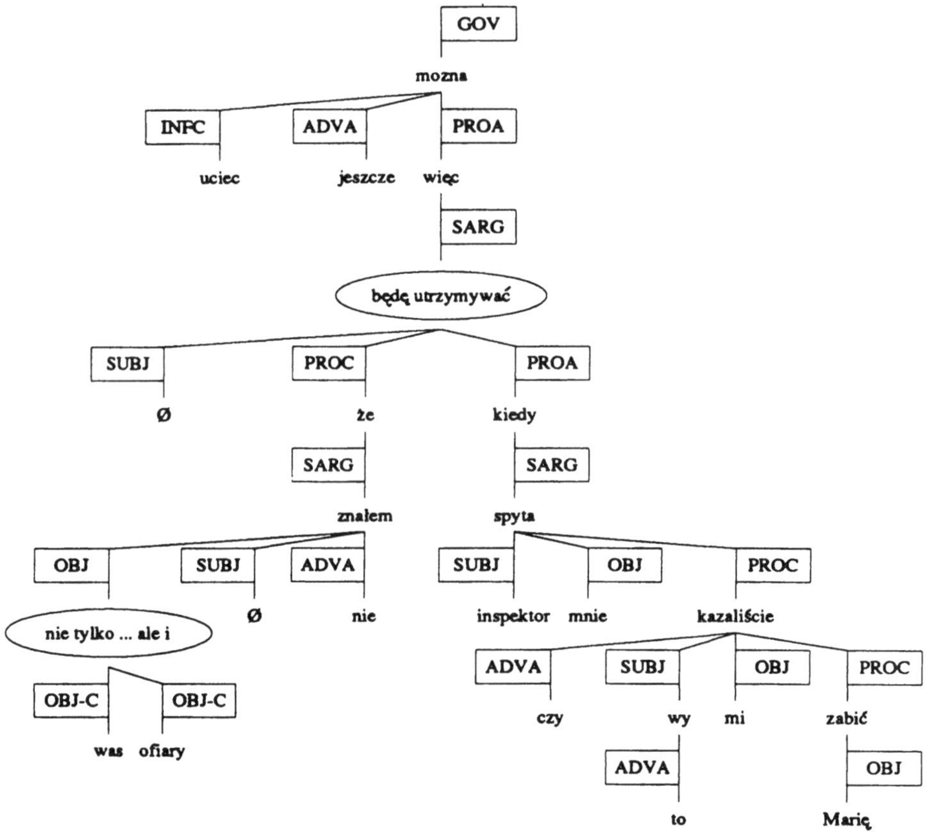

Editor's note

The author adopts word forms that consist of several, in some cases even discontinuous, orthographical words. Since these need to be analysed further in the DLT model of dependency syntax, we show these multi-word units in 5. in an ellipsis in a similar way as Tesnière does in his stemmas.

References

Mel'čuk, Igor A. (1988): *Dependency syntax.*
Albany: State University of New York Press

Saloni, Z. / Marek Świdziński (1987): *Składnia współczesnego języka polskiego.*
Warszawa, 3rd. ed.

Schubert, Klaus (1986): How to write a dependency syntax for DLT.
Unpublished report. Utrecht: BSO/Research

Świdziński, Marek (1987): Formalny opis składniowy polskich zdań o składniku zdaniowym.
Warszawa, mimeographed

Świdziński, Marek (1988): Dependency syntax of modern Polish.
Unpublished report. Utrecht: BSO/Research

A dependency syntax of Bangla

Probal Dasgupta
Hyderabad, India

1. Introduction

Bangla, also called Bengali, is a New Indo-Aryan language spoken in Bangladesh and the India state of West Bengal. Written Bangla uses one of the South Asian scripts (one that it shares with Assamese and Manipuri), underlyingly alphabetic and superficially syllabic. The transcription used here is phonemic and follows Ray, Ray and Hai (1966).

The vowel system is *i e E a O o u* (*E O* low) plus nasalized counterparts *iM eM* etc.; *y w* are high semivowels and *Y W* are mid; *h* is voiced in intervocalic position. The nasal *n* assimilates to the place of articulation of a following dental *t th d dh*, postalveolar (mildly retroflex) *T Th D Dh*, or palato-alveolar *c ch j jh*; *m* and the velar *N* are not stable. The fricatives *f v z* occur in partly naturalized loans, while *s* and palato-alveolar *S* occur also in native words. Pitch and stress are non-phonemic.

The basic fact about Bangla constituent order is that phrases are rigidly head-final, 1.(1)-(2) being the only permissible permutations for these expressions, while finite clauses, though basically of an SXOV type, as in (3)a, allow considerable freedom of reordering:

1.(1) ramer cee lOmba – 'taller than Ram'
Ram-GEN than tall

1.(2) bharote prokaSito boy kinte – 'to buy books published in India'
India-LOC published book buy-INF

1.(3) a. ram SEmke boyTa dilo – 'Ram gave Shyam the book'
Ram Shyam-DAT book-CLA gave
b. SEmke ram boyTa dilo
c. ram boyTa SEmke dilo
d. SEmke boyTa ram dilo
e. ram SEmke dilo boyTa
f. ram boyTa dilo SEmke
g. boyTa dilo SEmke ram

Such freedom is unavailable in the equative clause construction; as Dasgupta (1983) shows in detail, the equative verb is always medial:

1.(4) a. SEmol hocche dOler SOrdar – 'S. is the leader of the gang'
Shyamal is gang-GEN leader
b. dOler SOrdar hocche SEmol

Bangla permits verbless or "small" clauses as simple sentences:

1.(5) khOborTa khub bhalo – 'The (piece of) news is very good'
news-CLA very good

1.(6) ram jodur bhay – 'Ram is Yadu's brother'
Ram Yadu-GEN brother

1.(7) DakghOrTa baRir kache – 'The post office is near the house'
post-office-CLA house-GEN near

In such cases, it is unusual for the predicate to precede the subject as in 1.(8), and that order becomes normal only if emphasis or other marked devices come into play as in 1.(9), or if one can interpret the reversed sentence itself as a subject-predicate sequence as in 1.(10):

1.(8) ??baRir kache DakghOrTa – 'Is near the house the post office'

1.(9) baRir kachei DakghOrTa – 'Quite near the house is the post office'
house-GEN near-EMPH post-office-CLA

1.(10) jodur bhay ram – 'Yadu's brother is Ram'
Yadu-GEN brother Ram

Clearly, one can simply view 1.(6) and 1.(10) as having different subjects; neither is then a variant of the other.

Turning from syntax to morphology, the orthographic word in Bangla is not always a convenient unit for principled grammatical description. The true morphology of the noun of verb is inflectional; but the orthographic word often adds to it an agglutinative or enclitic layer which is best treated separately. The Emphasizer *i* introduced in 1.(9) is an example of material belonging to this layer. Consider 1.(11), an emphatic version of 1.(6):

1.(11) ram joduri bhay – 'Ram is *Yadu's* brother'

Here the orthographic word *joduri* (which the alphabeto-syllabic orthography of Bangla in any case shows as a complex word, indicating a syllable break between *r* and *i*) is best treated as the inflected Noun *jodur*, a true word, plus the clitic Emphasizer *i* which phonologically leans on it but is syntactically a distinct word.

Similarly the Classifier *Ta* of 1.(5) and 1.(7) counts as a clitic and may follow an inflectional affix as in *SEmerTa* in 1.(12):

1.(12) ramer pealaTa bORo, SEmerTa choTo – 'Ram's cup is big, Shyam's is small'
Ram-GEN cup-CLA big, Shyam-GEN-CLA small

Finally, many complexities of the Bangla verb become manageable if one segments forms like *dekheche* 'has seen' into *dekhe che*, the true Verb *dekhe* (the conjunctive form of 'see') and the cliticized Rhetic (as we shall call it) *che*, an element that marks the tense-aspect-mood in collaboration with the conjunctive inflection of the Verb. Such a segmentation, like that of *peala Ta* and *Semer Ta* in 1.(12) or *jodur i* in 1.(11), must be recognized for proper parsing, though normal orthography shows no word boundary before an Emphasizer, a Classifier, or a Rhetic. Furthermore, in a case like 1.(13), where normal orthography uses a hyphen to separate the Numeral-Classifier complex from the Noun, a proper segmentation would have to treat the sequences as three-word constructions, *peala du To*, *SEmer du To*:

1.(13) ramer peala-duTo bORo, SEmer-duTo choTo – 'The two cups of Ram are big, the two (cups) of Shyam are small'
Ram-GEN cup-two-CLA big, Shyam-GEN-two-CLA small

The reader should assume that, before a written Bangla text is submitted to analysis in terms of the present grammar, it must first be pre-segmented, i.e. rewritten in a canonical form which adds word boundaries of the above sorts to those recognized in conventional spelling. It is possible to carry out such pre-segmentation mechanically, although we present no algorithm here.

2. Word classes

2.1. Open classes

We postulate four open classes of words in Bangla:

- **Nouns**, like *deWal* 'wall', *baRi* 'house', *bataS* 'air, wind';
- **Adjectives**, like *halka* 'light (not heavy)', *patla* 'thin', *Sobuj* 'green';
- **Adverbs**, like *taRataRi* 'quickly', *SOrbotro* 'everywhere', *ekhane* 'here';
- **Verbs**, like *paTha-no* 'send-GRD' (we use the Gerund as the citation form), *dEkha-no* 'show-GRD', *dEkh-a* 'see-GRD', *Dak-a* 'call-GRD'.

The treatment of Noun declension and Verb conjugation is discussed in 2.3.; this will presuppose familiarity with the classes of Classifiers, Pronouns, Numerals, and Rhetics, introduced in 2.2. A word whose classification is dubious will be regarded as a Noun; the significance of this decision becomes clear in section 3., at example V(14) of 3.2. below.

2.2. Closed classes

The present analysis recognizes ten closed classes of words for Bangla:

- **Numerals**, like *Ek* 'one', *tin* 'three', *Onek* 'many';
- **Pronouns**, like *tuy* 'you INTIMATE SINGULAR', *ami* 'I', *o* 's/he DISTAL NEUTRAL';
- **Classifiers**, as in *paMc Ta beRal* 'five CLA cat', 'five cats', *aT jon amla* 'eight CLA bureaucrat', *beRal Ta* 'cat CLA', 'the cat', *amla ra* 'bureaucrat CLA', 'the bureaucrats';
- **Emphasizers**, viz. *i* 'rather than something else', *o* 'in addition to something else';
- **Rhetics**, like *lo* 'PAST', *cche* 'PRESENT PROGRESSIVE', *na* 'NEGATION';
- **Adpositions**, like *nie* 'about', *SONgė* 'with', *kore* 'by' – Bangla is postpositional;
- **Subjunctions**, like *je* and *bole* in *ami Sune chilam je tumi aS be na* 'I heard had that you come will not', and *tumi aS be na bole ami Sune chilam* 'you come will not that I heard had', both meaning 'I had heard that you were not coming', or like *karon* in *ami e lam na karon onno kaj chi lo* 'I come PAST not since other work be PAST', 'I didn't come since there was other work';
- **Anchors**, a class of enclitics like *to* in *jitu to ja be na* 'Jitu TOPICALIZATION go will not', '*Jitu* will not go' and *ki* in *jitu ki ja be* 'Jitu Q go will', 'will Jitu go?';
- **Conjunctions**, like *ar* 'and', *eboN* 'and', *ba* 'or', *kimba* 'or', zero (paratactic);
- **Interjections**, like *hEM* 'yes', *accha* 'okay', *na* 'not' (distinct from the Rhetic).

2.3. Declension and conjugation

2.3.1. Nouns

The case paradigm, in 2.3.1. below, includes an unmarked Nominative, a variably zero- and *ke*-marked Accusative, a consistently *ke*-marked Dative, and a Genitive whose ending is *-r* after a vowel, *-er* otherwise. Some Genitive Nouns end in the lexically restricted element *kar* (*ekhankar* 'here-GEN', *Se-din-kar* 'that day-GEN', *e-dik-kar* 'this-side-GEN', *Onek-din-kar* 'long-time-GEN', etc.) which is poorly understood.

	Nominative	Accusative	Dative	Genitive
a. 'paper'	*kagoj*	*kagoj / kagojke*	*kagojke*	*kagojer*
b. 'knee'	*haMTu*	*haMTu / haMTuke*	*haMTuke*	*haMTur*

2.3.2. Classifiers

Nouns, Pronouns, Classifiers, and marginally Numerals are declined in this manner. Classifiers mark the inflectional feature of Number lexically, thus marking it an inherent feature in Bangla, the way Gender is is many languages. Thus, the Classifiers *ra* (with an irregular paradigm, 2.3.2.(a), *gulo, brindo, bOrgo,* and others expressing what I once (Dasgupta 1985) called "collective aggregation" – in constructions like *beRal guloke* 'cat CLA-DAT', 'to the cats', of 2.3.2.(d) below – may be taken as manifesting Plural Number, in contrast to the Singular Number (or, in my 1985 terminology, the Individual Aggregation) expressed by Classifiers like *Ta, jon, khana* etc. The decision to treat the features differentiating these two sets of Classifiers as a language-particular instantiation of Singular and Plural Number – despite the semantically odd consequence that in *dOS Ta boy* 'ten CLA book', 'ten books' the Classifier *Ta* now counts as Singular – reverses my 1985 proposals and is a response to Mel'čuk's (1987, personal communication) criticism of those proposals. A Noun or Pronoun unaccompanied by any Classifier will be regarded as singular.

		Nominative	Accusative	Dative	Genitive
a.	plural human	*ra*	*der*	*der*	*der*
b.	literary plural human	*brindo*	*brindoke*	*brindoke*	*brinder*
c.	literary plural human	*bOrgo*	*bOrgoke*	*bOrgoke*	*bOrger*
d.	plural general	*gulo*	*gulo, guloke*	*guloke*	*gulor*
e.	literary plural general	*Somuho*	*Somuho, Somuhoke*	*Somuhoke*	*Somuher*
f.	singular human	*jon*	*jonke*	*jonke*	*joner*
g.	singular general	*Ta (/Te/To)*	*Ta, Take* (etc.)	*Take* (etc.)	*Tar* (etc.)
h.	singular segmental	*khana*	*khana, khanake*	*khanake*	*khanar*
i.	singular substantial	*khani*	*khani, khanike*	*khanike*	*khanir*
j.	singular diminutive	*Tuku (/Tu)*	*Tuku, Tukuke* (etc.)	*Tukuke* (etc.)	*Tukur* (etc.)
k.	singular individuative	*Ti*	*Ti, Tike*	*Tike*	*Tir*

2.3.3. Pronouns

The declension of Pronouns, on the present analysis, is as shown in 2.3.3. Plural pronominal expressions are treated as Pronoun-Classifier constructions, some of them easy to analyze, like *o ra* 'they', and some of them morphologically opaque, like *ama der* 'us', 'our' and *am ra* 'we', whose proper parsing involves recognizing *ama* and *am* as variants of *ami*:

	Nominative	Accusative	Dative	Genitive
'I'	*ami* (with some allomorphy)	*amake, amaY*	*amake, amaY*	*amar*
's/he'	*o*	*oke*	*oke*	*or*

2.3.4. Verbs

Identification of a reasonable range of morphological variants is also an essential condition for the proper parsing of verbal forms:

	'eat'	as in	'buy'	as in
Basic	*kha*	*ha Y* 'eats'	*khen*	*ken e* 'buys'
Infinitive	*khete*	*khete ka Y* 'wants to eat'	*kinte*	*kinte ca Y* 'wants to buy'
Conjunctive	*khee*	*khee che* 'has eaten'	*kine*	*kine che* 'has bought'
Protatic	*khele*	*khele bujh be* 'if you eat, you will understand'	*kinle*	*kinle bujh be* 'if you buy, you will understand'
Gerund (citation form)	*khaWa*	*khaWa ja Y* 'can be eaten'	*kena*	*kena ja Y* 'can be bought'
Gerundive	*khaWar* *khabar*	*khaWar lok* 'people to eat' *khaWar dOrkar* 'need to eat'	*kenar* *kinbar*	*kenar lok* 'people to buy' *kenar dOrkar* 'need to buy'

The morphological forms listed here must all be classified syntactically as Verbs in some contexts; but some of them must be cross-classified as non-Verbs elsewhere. Infinitive and Conjunctive forms may also be Adverbs; Gerunds may also be Nouns; Gerundives may also be Adjectives; and Adjectives of the Participle subclass are morphologically identical to Gerunds (cf. Dasgupta 1979, 1986).

3. Dependency examples

The tables in this section are followed by sample sentences in which the governor of the illustrated dependency relation is shown in *italics* and the dependent in **bold face**.

3.1. Dependents of nouns

	Noun	Adj	Adv	Vb	Num	Pron	Cla	Emp	Rhe	Adp	Sjc	Anc	Cj	Int
SUBJ	×	×	×	×		×	×			×	×		×	
DOBJ	×	×	×	×		×	×				×		×	
IOBJ	×					×	×			×			×	
CONV	×	×	×	×						×			×	
INFC				×									×	
ADVC			×										×	
PREC										×			×	
PARG														
PROC	×	×	×	×		×	×			×	×		×	
SUBC														
ATR1	×	×			×								×	
ATR2	×	×	×	×		×	×			×			×	
EPI	×												×	
APO	×					×	×						×	
ADVA			×					×	×			×	×	
PREA										×			×	
PROA											×			
NUMA														
CLAA							×						×	
LIA			×						×	×		×	×	

SUBJ/Noun

N(1) **dilip** *SObhapoti* – 'Dilip (is the) president'

N(2) Eto **bacca** *jOnmano* deSer pokkhe kharap – 'So many children being born is bad for the country'
so-many children being-born country-GEN for bad

SUBJ/Adjective

N(3) amar *dharona* dibbendu **dayi** – 'it is my belief (that) Divyendu (is) responsible'

SUBJ/Adverb, Verb, Pronoun, Classifier, Adposition: AS IN N(3), BUT WITH A NON-ADJECTIVE PREDICATE; SEE EXAMPLES M(7)-(12) IN 3.7.

SUBJ/Subjunction

N(4) amar*dharona* **je** dibbendu day – 'it is my belief that D. (is) responsible'

SUBJ/Conj

N(5) dilip**ar** prodip jugmo *SOmpadok* – 'Dilip and Pradip (are) joint editors'

DOBJ/Noun

N(6) **bimOlke** *paThano* bhul – 'it is wrong to send B.'
Bimal sending wrong

N(7) dilip aSol **lok** *bhaba* bhul – 'it is wrong to think Dilip is the real person'
Dilip real person thinking wrong

N(8) dilipke **malik** *bhaba* bhul – 'it is wrong to consider Dilip the owner'

N(9) **SObhapoti** *hOWa* bokami – 'it is folly to become president'
president becoming folly

DOBJ/Adjective, Adverb, Verb, Pronoun, Classifier, Adposition: AS IN N(7); CF. THE NOTE ABOVE AT N(3)

DOBJ/Subjunction

N(10) *bhaba* bhul hoe chilo **je** dilip aSol lok – 'it had been wrong to think that D. was the real person'
thinking wrong been had that Dilip real person

SUBJ/Conjunction

N(11) dilip(ke) **ar** prodipke jugmo *SOmpadok* bOla cOl e – 'D. and P. may be called joint editors'

Dilip(-DAT) and Pradip-DAT joint editors calling go PRES

IOBJ/Noun

N(12) **dilipke** Taka dhar *deWa* bOndho kOr o – 'Stop lending Dilip money'

Dilip- DAT money loan giving stop do IMP

N(13) **dilipke** malik *bhaba* bhul = N(8)

IOBJ/Pronoun, Classifier: AS ABOVE, WITH **oke** 'HIM/HER' OR lok **Take** 'THE MAN' SUBSTITUTED FOR **dilipke**

IOBJ/Adposition

N(14) sripotir **kache** Oto miSTi *paThano* bhul hoe chilo – 'it had been a mistake to send so many sweets to Sripati'

Sripati to so-many sweets sending wrong been had

CONV/Noun

N(15) dilipke Taka **dhar** *deWa* bOndho kOr o = N(12)

CONV/Adjective

N(16) pOtaka **uMcu** *kOra* SOhoj nOY – 'it is not easy to hoist a flag'

flag high making easy isn't

CONV/Adverb

N(17) choTobElar khOta **mone** *kOra* SOkto – 'it is hard to recall facts about one's childhood'

childhood about mind-LOC doing difficult

CONV/Verb

N(18) upenke e Ta **bujhie** *deWa* joruri – 'it is vital to explain this to Upen'

Upen-DAT this CLA explain-CONJV giving vital

CONV/Adposition

N(19) bhitu chele der **pichone** *laga* niSThurota – 'it is cruel to tease timid boys'

timid boy CLA behind sticking cruelty

CONV/Conjunction

N(20) Eto khObor dekhe **ba** bujhe *neWa* SomOYSapekkho kaj – 'it is a time-consuming task to take a good look at or attain a good understanding of so much news'

so-much news look-CONJV or understand-CONJV taking time-consuming job

INFC/Verb

N(21) baRi pherar icche Oneker i hO Y – 'many people feel an urge to get back home'

home return-GRDV wish many-GEN EMPH occur PRES

ADVC/Adverb

N(22) o der SON**geduSTumite** *para* koThin – 'it is difficult to be a match for them in naughtiness'

3 PL-ACC with naughtiness-LOC managing difficult

PREC/Adposition

N(23) ey Siddhanter karon Samir **SONge** *jhOgRa* – 'the reason for this decision was a quarrel with (her) husband'

this decision-GEN reason husband-GEN with quarrel

PROC/Noun

N(24) uni aSol **prarthi** e *kOtha* jan tam na 'he/she – 'I didn't know that s/he was the real candidate'

3-SG (HON) real candidate this fact know PAST not

PROC/Adjective, Adverb, Verb, Pronoun, Classifier, Adposition: AS IN N(24), CF. NOTE AT N(3)

PROC/Subjunction

N(25) e *kOtha* jan tam na **je** uni aSol prarthi = N(24), WITH **je** 'THAT'

ATR1/Noun

N(26) ini nil **rONer** *pOrda* ca n – 's/he wants a curtain of blue colour'

this-person (HON) blue colour-GEN curtain want PRES

ATR1/Adjective: **nil** *rONer* IN N(26)

ATR1/Numeral

N(27) o ra **baro** *bhuter* nritto dEkh e ni – 'they have not seen the dance of twelve ghosts (i.e. the chaos of uncoordinated effort)'

3-PL NOM twelve ghosts' dance see PERF not

ATR2/Noun

N(28) ini ey **dokaner** *pOrda* ca n – 's/he wants a curtain from this shop'

this-person (HON) this shop-GEN curtain want PRES

ATR2/Adjective

N(29) **Samprotik** kichu *skuTar* er protiddondi – 'some recent scooters are its competitors'

recent some scooters this-GEN competitor

ATR2/Adverb, Verb

N(30) tumi*kake* cen o je **srirampure**$_{ADV}$ (**thak**$_{V}$ e) – 'whom do you know who lives in S.?'

you whom know PRES who Srirampur-LOC (lives)

ATR2/Pronoun, Classifier

N(31) ami **or** (/o **der**) *gan* Sun bo – 'I will hear him/her (them) sing'

I his/her (/their) song hear will

ATR2/Adposition

N(32) am ra **Samner** du To *cheleke* cin i – 'we know the two boys in front'

1P PL in-front-GEN two CLA boy-ACC know PRES

EPI/Noun

N(33) **monipur** *rajjo* parbotto elakaY Obosthito – 'the state of M. is situated in a mountainous area'

Manipur state mountainous area-LOC situated

APO/Noun, Pronoun, Classifier

N(34) puroSkar pa be ekhankar Sera *khEloaR* toma **bhay/tumi/**oy **lok** Ta – 'the prize will go to the best player here, your brother/you/that man'

prize get will here-GEN best player, your brother/you/that man CLA

ADVA/Adverb, Emphasizer, Rhetic, Anchor

N(35) e Ta **adow**$_{ADV}$ *SOhor* **i**$_{EMP}$ **na**$_{RHE}$ **bujhi**$_{ANC}$ – 'is this not a city at all?'

this CLA at-all city EMP not Q

PREA/Adposition

N(36) ama der **moddhe** *kew* ja be na – 'none of us will go'

1-PL ACC out-of anybody go will not

PROA/Subjunction

N(37) tumi *ke* **je** am ra tomar kOtha Sun bo? – 'who are you that we should listen to you?'

you who that 1P PL your words hear will

CLAA/Classifier, Conjunction

N(38) ini Ek **Ta**$_{CLA}$ (**ba**$_{CONJ}$ du to) – 's/he wants one (or two) scooter(s)'

this-person (HON) one CLA (or two CLA) *skuTar* ca n scooter want 3P

LIA/Adverb

N(39) or prodhan gun **tay** *dhoyrjo* – 'his/her main quality, for that reason, is patience'

his/her main quality thus patience

LIA/Rhetic

N(40) o ra tor *bondhu* **re**! – 'they are your friends, you know!'

3-PL NOM your friends you-know

LIA/Adposition

or prodhan gun Se **jonne** *dhoyrjo* – 'For that reason, his/her main quality is patience'

his/her main quality that for (i.e. for that reason) patience: CF. N(39)

LIA/Anchor

N(41) uni karkhanar *malik* **to** – 's/he is a factory owner after all'

s/he-DISTAL-HONORIFIC factory-GEN owner PARTICLE

3.2. Dependents of verbs

	Noun	Adj	Adv	Vb	Num	Pron	Cla	Emp	Rhe	Adp	Sjc	Anc	Cj	Int
SUBJ	×	×	×	×		×	×			×	×		×	
DOBJ	×	×	×	×		×	×			×	×		×	
IOBJ	×					×	×			×			×	
CONV	×	×	×	×						×			×	
INFC				×									×	
ADVC			×										×	
PREC										×			×	
PARG														
PROC	×	×	×	×		×	×			×	×		×	
SUBC														
ATR1														
ATR2	×	×	×	×		×	×			×			×	
EPI														
APO														
ADVA			×					×	×			×	×	
PREA										×			×	
PROA											×			
NUMA														
CLAA														
LIA			×						×	×		×	×	

SUBJ/Noun, Pronoun, Classifier

V(1) **Omit**$_{NOUN}$/**o**$_{PRON}$/o **ra**$_{CLA}$ paTTho boy *likhe* che – '**Amit/ s/he /they** has/have *written* a text book'
text- book write have

SUBJ/Adjective

V(2) proman *ho* lo o ra **doSi** – 'it was proved (that) they were guilty'
proved be PAST 3-PL PL guilty

SUBJ/Adverb, Verb, Adposition: AS IN V(2); CF. NOTE AT N(3)

SUBJ/Subjunction

V(3) proman *ho* lo **je** o ra doSi: LIKE V(2), WITH **je** 'THAT'

DOBJ/Noun, Classifier

V(4) Sumit **boy**$_{NOUN}$ (**Ta**$_{CLA}$) *likhe* che – 'Sumit has written a (the) book'
Sumit book (CLA) written has

DOBJ/Adjective

V(5) promod **bORo** *hoe* che – 'Pramod has grown up'
Pramod big become has

DOBJ/Adverb

V(6) binod **ekhane** *e* lo – 'Binod came here'
Binod here come did

DOBJ/Verb

V(7) robi SaMtar **kaTte** *par* e – 'Robi can swim'
Robi swim cut can PRES

DOBJ/Pronoun

V(8) rajeS **tomake** *dekh* be na – 'Rajesh will not notice you'
Rajesh you-ACC notice will not

DOBJ/Adposition, Subjunction

V(9) probir *bhab* to (je) jaYga Ta DakghOrer **kache**$_{ADP}$ – 'Prabir used to think (that) the place was near the post office'

Prabir think PAST (that) place CLA post-office- GEN near

IOBJ/Noun, Pronoun, Classifier

V(10) kancon **bidiSake**$_{NOUN}$/**oke**$_{PRON}$/o **der**$_{CLA}$ boy *de* be – 'Kancham will give books to Bidisha him/her/them'

Kanchan Bidisha-DAT 3P-SG/PL book give will

V(11) **bidiSar/or/o der** boy *lag* be na – 'Bidisha / he or she / they do not need books'.

Bidisha-GEN 3P PL book be-needed will not

V(12) kancon **bidiSake** (etc.) nirdoS *bhab* e – 'Kanchan considers Bidisha (etc.) innocent'

Kanchan Bidisha-DAT (etc.) innocent consider PRES

IOBJ/Adposition

V(13) rajen hirenke debener **kache** *patha* lo – 'Rajen sent Hiren to Deben'

Rajen Hiren-ACC Deben-GEN to *send* PAST

CONV/Noun

V(14) Sudipto dilipke SOkto proSno **jigeS** *kor* lo – 'Sudipta asked Dilip hard questions'

Sudipta Dilip-DAT hard question ask do PAST

NOTE THAT *jigeS* IS AN ITEM THAT CANNOT BE CLASSIFIED ON ANY NON-ARBITRARY GROUNDS; AT THIS POINT, OUR DECISION TO TREAT SUCH ITEMS AS NOUNS PLAYS A ROLE.

CONV/Adjective

V(15) jiten pOtaka **uMcu** *kor* lo – 'Jiten hoisted the flag'

Jiten flag high make PAST

CONV/Adverb

V(16) o der tomake **mone** *poR* be – 'they will remember you, think of you'

3P GEN you-ACC mind-LOC fall will

CONV/Verb

V(17) rupen upenke kOtha Ta **bujhie** *di* lo – 'Rupen explained the matter to Upen'

Rupen Upen-DAT matter CLA explain-CONJV give PAST

CONV/Adposition

V(18) o ra bhitu chele der **pichone** *lag* e – 'they tease timid boys'

3P-NOM timid boy GEN behind stick PRES

CONV/Conjunction

V(19) oke khObor Ta bole **ba** likhe *di* o – 'please tell him/her this or write this down for him/her'

3P-DAT news CLA tell-CONJV or write-CONJV give IMP

INFC/Verb

V(20) uni baRi *jete* ceSTa **kor** chen – 'he is trying to go home'

he home go-INF effort make PRES-PROG

ADVC/Adverb

V(21) am ra kOm **TakaY** *cala* bo – 'we will manage with (very) little money'

1P PL little money-LOC manage will

PREC/Adposition

V(22) giriS Obosthar **SONge** *manie* ne be – 'Girish will adjust to the situation'

Girish situation-GEN with adjust-CONJV take will

PROC/Noun, Subjunction

V(23) aSol kOtha *ho* cche (je) horiS i aSol**prarthi**$_{NOUN}$ – 'the real point is that Harish is the real candidate'

real point be PRES-PROG (that) Harish EMP real candidate,

PROC/Adjective, Adverb, Verb, Pronoun, Classifier, Adposition: AS IN V(23); CF. NOTE AT N(3) ABOVE

ATR2/Noun

V(24) je jar **chatro** Se tar Samne *daMRie* che – 'for every x and every y such that x is a student of y, x is standing in front of y'

who whose student s/he of-him/her in-front standing is

ATR2/Adjective, Adverb, Verb, Pronoun, Classifier, Adposition: AS IN V(24); CF. NOTE AT N(3) ABOVE

ATR2/Verb: ALSO AS IN V(25)

V(25) cador gulo *poce* **poce** ja cche – 'the sheets are gradually becoming rotten'
sheet/shawl CLA rot-CONJV rot-CONJV go PRES-PROG

ADVA/Adverb, Emphasizer, Rhetic, Anchor

V(26) o **to bhalo** *gay* **be i** – 's/he will, of course, sing well, after all'
3P after-all well sing will of-course (**to**: Anchor, **bhalo**: Adverb, **be**: Rhetic, **i**: Emphasizer)

PREA/Adposition

V(27) am ra Sondher **pOr** *ja* bo – 'we will go after dusk'
1P NOM evening after go will

PROA/Subjunction

V(28) dipa SomeSke *mar* e o ni **je** o bEtha pa be, *bOk* e o ni **je** or kanna aS be – 'Dipa neither hit Somesh, which could have hurt him, nor scolded him, which could have made him cry'
Dipa Somesh-DAT hit PERF EMP not that he hurt feel FUT, scold Perf EMP not that his weeping come FUT

LIA/Adverb

V(29) o tay ca Y na – 'hence s/he doesn't want it'
s/he hence want PRES not

LIA/Rhetic, Adposition, Anchor: AS IN V(29); CF. N(40)-(42)

3.3. Dependents of adjectives

	Noun	Adj	Adv	Vb	Num	Pron	Cla	Emp	Rhe	Adp	Sjc	Anc	Cj	Int
SUBJ	×					×	×				×		×	
DOBJ	×	×	×	×		×	×			×	×		×	
IOBJ	×					×	×			×			×	
CONV	×	×	×	×						×			×	
INFC				×									×	
ADVC			×										×	
PREC										×			×	
PARG														
PROC	×	×	×	×		×	×			×	×		×	
SUBC														
ATR1		×											×	
ATR2	×	×	×	×		×	×			×			×	
EPI														
APO														
ADVA			×					×	×			×	×	
PREA										×			×	
PROA	×	×	×	×		×	×			×	×		×	
NUMA														
CLAA							×							
LIA			×						×	×		×	×	

SUBJ/Noun

Adj(1) ..**jOnmano**..*kharap*: SEE N(1) ABOVE IN 3.1.

SUBJ/Pronoun, Classifier

Adj(2) **o** / o **ra** *doSi* – 's/he is /they are guilty'
3-SG/3-PL PL guilty (**o**: Pronoun, **ra**: Classifier)

SUBJ/Subjunction

Adj(3) adaloter kache *spOSTo* **je** dibbendu doSi – 'it is clear to the court that Divyendu is guilty'
court-GEN to clear that Divyendu guilty

DOBJ/Noun, Verb

Adj(4) uni **gujraTi**$_{NOUN}$ (**likhte**$_{V}$) *jana* kerani ca n – 's/he wants a clerk who knows (how to write) Gujarati'
s/he Gujarati (to-write) knowing clerk want PRES

DOBJ/Adjective

Adj(5) amla der kache **Opodostho** *hOWa* lok Onek ach e – 'there are many who have been humiliated by the bureaucrats'
bureaucrat CLA by humiliated been people many be PRES

DOBJ/Adverb

Adj(6) ami *niScit* uni Ekhon **bOhorompure** – 'I am sure s/he is now in Baharampur'
I sure 3-SG now Baharampur-LOC

DOBJ/Pronoun

Adj(7) ami *niScit* e Ta **tumi** m – 'I (am) sure this CLA (is) you'

DOBJ/Classifier

Adj(8) ami *niScit* aSol kOtha e **Ta** i – 'I (am) sure (the) main point (is) this CLA EMP'

DOBJ/Adposition

Adj(9) ami *niScit* o ra Ekhon SOhorer **bayre** – 'I am sure they are now outside the city'
I sure 3P PL now city-GEN outside

DOBJ/Subjunction, Verb

Adj(10) ami *niScit* (**je**$_{SJC}$) ama der dOl **jit**$_{V}$ – 'I am sure that our team will win'
I (am) sure (that) 1-PL GEN team win FUT'

IOBJ/Noun, Pronoun, Classifier, Adposition

Adj(11) o ra **modhur** / **or** /lok**Tar** *bhOkto* – 'they are fond of Madhu / him/her / the man'
3-PL NOM Madhu-GEN / 3-PL-GEN / man CLA-GEN fond

Adj(12) **modhuke** / **oke** / lok **Take** / or **kache** *paThano* pEkeT harie che – 'a parcel sent to **Madhu**/ to **him or her** / to the man / **to** him or her has got lost'
Madhu-DAT / 3-PL-DAT / man CLA-DAT 3P to sent parcel got-lost has

CONV/Noun

Adj(13) o der **dOkhol** *kOra* jomite caS hO Y na – 'the land occupied by them is not cultivated'
3-PL GEN occupation done land-LOC cultivation happen PRES not

CONV/Adjective

Adj(14) ekhane **gocchit** *rakha* Taka nirapOd thak be – 'money deposited here will be safe'
here deposited kept money safe be will

CONV/Adverb

Adj(15) Eto Ta **gae** *pORa* lok dekhle OSSosti hO Y – 'one feels uneasy when one sees such an obtrusive man'
so much body-on falling man see-PROTATIC unease occur PRES

CONV/Verb

Adj(16) **bheNe** *jaWa* durgo o ra abar goR be – 'they will rebuild the ruined fort'
break-CONJV gone fort 3-PL NOM again build will

CONV/Adposition

Adj(17) beRaler **Samne** *pORa* iMdur ki kor be? – 'what can a mouse do when it suddenly faces a cat?'
cat-GEN in-front fallen mouse what do will

INFC/Verb

Adj(18) am ra **jete** *raji* – 'we are willing to go'
1-PL NOM to-go willing

ADVC/Adverb

Adj(19) uni **iSSOre** *biSSaSi* – 's/he believes in God'
3-SG-DISTAL-HONORIFIC God-LOC believing

PREC/Adposition

Adj(20) uni iSSOrer **proti** *asthaSil* – 's/he trusts in God'
3-SG God-GEN in trustful

PROC/Noun

Adj(21) uni aSol **prarthi** *Emon* Sun i ni – 'I have not heard that s/he is the real candidate'
s/he real candidate such heard have not

PROC/Adjective, Adverb, Verb, Pronoun, Classifier, Adposition: AS IN Adj(21); CF. NOTE AT N(3)

PROC/Subjunction

Adj(22) *Emon* Sun i ni **je** uni aSol prarthi = Adj(21) WITH **je** 'THAT'

ATR1/Adjective

Adj(23) uni **halka** *nil* jama pOr en – 'She is wearing a light blue shirt'
3-SG light blue shirt wear PRES

ATR2/Verb

Adj(24) ami *Emon* lokkc cin i je ete mOja **pa** be – 'I know a man who will be amused at this'
I such man know PRES who at-this amusement get will

ATR2/Noun, Adjective, Adverb, Pronoun, Classifier, Adposition: AS IN Adj(24); CF. NOTE AT N(3)

ADVA/Adverb

Adj(25) bojha Ta **beS** *halka* – 'the burden is quite light'
burden CLA quite light

ADVA/Emphasizer, Rhetic, Anchor

Adj(26) mal Ta *SOsta* **o na bujhi**? – 'you mean the stuff is not even cheap?'
stuff CLA cheap even not Q

PREA/Adposition

Adj(27) jama Ta rOkter **mOto** *lal* – 'The shirt is as red as blood'
shirt CLA blood-GEN like red

PROA/Verb

Adj(28) o khun **kore** che *erOkom* proman koy? – 'Where is the proof that s/he has committed ad r murder?'
s/he murder done has such proof where?

PROA/Noun, Adjective, Adverb, Pronoun, Classifier, Adposition: AS IN Adj(28); CF. NOTE AT N(3)

CLAA/Classifier

Adj(29) tOrkari Ta ek **Tu** *ThanDa* – 'The vegetables are a bit cold'
vegetable Classifier **bit** *cold*

LIA/Adverb

Adj(30) o **tay** *OSohiSnu* – 'hence s/he is intolerant'
3P hence intolerant

LIA/Rhetic, Adposition, Anchor: AS IN Adj(30); CF. N(40)-(42)

3.4. Dependents of adverbs

	Noun	Adj	Adv	Vb	Num	Pron	Cla	Emp	Rhe	Adp	Sjc	Anc	Cj	Int
SUBJ	×	×	×	×		×	×			×			×	
DOBJ	×	×	×	×		×	×			×	×		×	
IOBJ	×					×	×			×			×	
CONV	×	×	×	×						×			×	
INFC				×									×	
ADVC			×										×	
PREC										×			×	
PARG														
PROC	×	×	×	×		×	×			×	×		×	
SUBC	×	×	×	×		×	×			×			×	
ATR1	×	×			×								×	
ATR2	×	×	×	×		×	×			×			×	
EPI	×	×	×		×	×	×			×			×	
APO			×										×	
ADVA			×					×	×			×	×	
PREA										×			×	
PROA	×	×	×	×		×	×			×	×		×	
NUMA														
CLAA							×						×	
LIA			×						×	×		×	×	

SUBJ/Noun, Pronoun, Classifier

Adv(1) **raY o / o ra** *ekhane* – 'Ray/he/she/they is/are here'
Ray / 3 PL here

SUBJ/Adjective

Adv(2) o **doSi** proman *hoe* karo kono labh ho lo na – 'nobody benefited from his/her being proved guilty'
s/he guilty proved being anybody-GEN any use be PAST not

SUBJ/Adverb, Verb, Adposition: AS IN Adv(2); CF. NOTE AT N(3)

DOBJ/Noun, Adjective, Adverb, Verb, Pronoun, Classifier, Adposition, Subjunction: SUBSTITUTE AN ADVERBIAL CONJUNCTIVE FOR THE VERB AT V(4)-V(9) TO GET EXAMPLES

IOBJ/Noun, Pronoun, Classifier, Adposition: LIKEWISE AT V(10)-(13)

CONV/Noun, Adjective, Adverb, Verb, Adposition: LIKEWISE AT V(14)-(18)

INFC/Verb: LIKEWISE AT V(20)

ADVC/Adverb: LIKEWISE AT V(21)

PREC/Adposition

Adv(3) ama der **pokkhe** *beSi* aste col che bas – 'The bus is running too slowly for us'
1-PL ACC **for** *too* slowly running is bus

PROC/Noun

Adv(4) uni aSol **prarthi** *erOkom* Odbhut dabi Sun i ni – 'I have not heard such a strange claim that s/he is a real candidate'
s/he real **candidate** *such* strange claim heard have not

SUBC/Noun

Adv(5) SureS karkhanar **malik** *tate* tor ki? – 'what is it to you that S. is the owner of the factory?'
suresh factory-GEN **owner** *that-LOC* your what

SUBJ/Adjective, Adverb, Verb, Pronoun, Classifier, Adposition: AS IN Adv(5); CF. NOTE AT N(3)

ATR1/Noun

Adv(6) nil **rONer** *pOrdaY* hO be na – 'a curtain of blue colour won't do'
blue colour-GEN curtain-LOC be will not

ATR/Adjective

Adv(7) **nil** *rONe* oMr mon uTh be na – 'the blue colour will not satisfy him/her'
blue colour-LOC his/her mind rise will not

ATR/Numeral

Adv(8) **baro** *bhute* nac be – 'there will be chaos'
twelve ghosts-LOC dance will

ATR2/Noun, Adjective, Adverb, Verb, Pronoun, Classifier, Adposition: SUBSTITUTE AN ADVERBIAL LOCATIVE FOR THE NOUN AT N(28)-N(32) TO OBTAIN EXAMPLES

EPI/Noun

Adv(9) o **monipur** *rajje* thak e – 's/he lives in the state of Manipur'
s/he Manipur state- LOC live PRES

EPI/Adjective

Adv(10) kaj Ta **bhalo** *kore* kOr o – 'do the job well'
job CLA good ly do IMP

EPI/Adverb

Adv(11) aste kore gaRi cala W – 'drive the car slowly'
slowly ly car drive IMP

EPI/Numeral

Adv(12) **tiner** *Tate* jOl ney – 'there's no water in the third one'
three-GEN CLA-LOC water is not

EPI/Pronoun, Classifier

Adv(13) **tor** / to **der** *Tate* jOl ney – '...no water in yours'
your/you CLA/GEN *CLA-LOC*...,

EPI/Adposition

Adv(14) **pOrer** *Tate* jOl ney – '..no water in the next one'
after-GEN *CLA-LOC*..,

APO/Adverb

Adv(15) o ra paSer *deSe*, **bOrmaY**, ja cche – 'they're going to the country next door, Burma'
PL NOM neighbouring *country-LOC*, **Burma-LOC**, go PRES-PROG

ADVA/Adverb

Adv(16) e pahaR Ta **Onek** *beSi* uMcu – 'This mountain is much taller'
this mountain CLA **much** *more* tall

ADVA/Emphasizer

Adv(17) aj *khub* **i** gOrom – 'It is indeed very hot today'
today (it is) *very* **indeed** hot

ADVA/Rhetic, Anchor

Adv(18) o Ta **to**$_{ANC}$ amar *hate* **na**$_{RHE}$ – 'That is not in my contral after all'
that CLA, after-all, my control-LOC not

PREA/Adposition

Adv(19) ami or **cee** *aste* gaRi cala y – 'I drive the car more slowly than him/her'
I him/her **than** *slow*(er) car drive PRES

PROA/Verb

Adv(20) o rag **kor** be *Emon* biroktikOr kichu ami bol i ni – 'I have said nothing so irritating as to anger him/her'
s/he anger **do** will *so* irritating anything I said have not

PROA/Noun, Adjective, Adverb, Pronoun, Classifier, Adposition: AS IN Adv(20); CF. NOTE AT N(3)

PROA/Subjunction

Adv(21) ami *Emon* biroktikOr kichu bol i ni **je** o rag kor be = Adv(20) WITH **je** 'THAT'

CLAA/Classifier

Adv(22) du **To** *gelaSe* jOl ney – 'Water isn't in the two glasses'
two CLA *glass- LOC* water isn't

Adv(23) o ra Onek **Ta** *aste* gaRi cala cche – ‘they are driving a lot more slowly’
3 PL much CLA slowly car drive PRES-PROG

LIA/Adverb

Adv(24) o tay ekhane – ‘Hence s/he is here’
s/he hence here (CF. Adj(30))

LIA/Rhetic, Adposition, Anchor: AS IN Adv(24); CF. N(40)-(42)

3.5. Dependents of classifiers

	Noun	Adj	Adv	Vb	Num	Pron	Cla	Emp	Rhe	Adp	Sjc	Anc	Cj	Int
SUBJ	×					×	×						×	
DOBJ														
IOBJ														
CONV														
INFC														
ADVC														
PREC														
PROC														
ATR1														
ATR2							×							
EPI	×	×			×	×	×			×			×	
APO	×					×	×						×	
ADVA			×					×	×			×	×	
PREA														
PROA											×			
NUMA					×								×	
CLAA														
LIA			×						×	×		×	×	

SUBJ/Noun

Cla(1) aSol **malik** tom *ra* – ‘the real owners are you’
real owner you CLA

SUBJ/Pronoun

Cla(2) **tumi** ki ama *der*? – ‘are you one of us?’
you Q 1-PL GEN

SUBJ/Classifier

Cla(3) e **Ta** ki tomar *Ta*? – ‘is this one yours?’
this CLA Q your CLA

EPI/Noun, Adjective

Cla(4) **ramer**$_{\text{NOUN}}$ *Ta* ar **ey**$_{\text{ADJ}}$ *Ta* bhalo – ‘Ram’s and this one are good’
Ram’s CLA this good CLA

EPI/Numeral

Cla(5) **tiner** *Ta* khali – ‘the third one is empty’
third CLA empty (CF. Adv(12))

EPI/Pronoun: **tomar** *Ta* IN Cla(3)

EPI/Classifier: SUBSTITUTE toma **der** *Ta* IN Cla(3); ALSO,

Cla(6) tom *ra* baNali **ra** juddhe poTu nO W – ‘you Bengalis are not good at fighting’
you CLA Bengali CLA war-LOC good not-be PRES

EPI/Adposition

Cla(7) **bayrer** *Ta* beSi Sundor – 'the one outside is more beautiful'
outside-GEN CLA more beautiful

APO/Noun

Cla(8) to *ra*, SOhorer **chele**, okhane thakte ca S? – 'you, city boys, want to stay there?'
you PL city-GEN boys, there stay-INF want PRES

EPI/Pronoun

Cla(9) ditio *jon*, **ami**, jete par lam na – 'the second one, I, could not go'
second CLA, I, go able PAST not

EPI/Classifier

Cla(10) o *ra* – oy choMRa **gulo** – khelte par e?
3 PL – those brats – play can PRES?

ADVA/Adverb, Emphasizer, Rhetic, Anchor

Cla(11) e Ta **adow** o *der* **i na bujhi**? – 'Is this theirs at all?'
this CLA at-all 3 PL EMP not Q?

PROA/Subjunction

Cla(12) **kaj** Ta to ama *der* na **je** am ra matha ghama bo – 'the job is not ours that we should rack our brains over it'
job CLA ANC 1P GEN not that 1 PL head sweat FUT

NUMA/Numeral

Cla(13) ami **du** *To* boy ne bo – 'I will take two books'
I two CLA book take will

LIA/Adverb

Cla(14) kichu i **tay** ama *der* **na** – 'hence, there is nothing that is ours'
anything EMP hence 1P GEN not (CF. N(39)-(42))

LIA/Rhetic, Adposition, Anchor: AS IN Cla(14) (CF. N(39)-(42))

3.6. Dependents of pronouns

	Noun	Adj	Adv	Vb	Num	Pron	Cla	Emp	Rhe	Adp	Sjc	Anc	Cj	Int
SUBJ	×					×	×						×	
DOBJ														
IOBJ														
CONV														
INFC														
ADVC														
PREC														
PARG														
PROC	×	×	×	×		×	×			×			×	
SUBC														
ATR1														
ATR2	×	×	×	×		×	×			×			×	
EPI	×												×	
APO	×						×						×	
ADVA			×					×	×			×	×	
PREA														
PROA											×			
NUMA														
CLAA														
LIA			×						×	×		×	×	

SUBJ/Noun

Pron(1) aSol **malik** *tumi* – 'the real owner is you'
real owner you

SUBJ/Pronoun

Pron(2) **ami** ki *tumi*? – 'am I you?'
I Q you

SUBJ/Classifier, Conjunction

Pron(3) e **Ta**$_{CLA}$ (**ba**$_{CONJ}$ o Ta) niScoy *tomar* – 'This one (or that one) is definitely yours'
this CLA (or that CLA) definitely yours

PROC/Noun

Pron(4) tumi **aSami** *ta* jan tam na – 'I did not know that you are the accused'
you accused that know PAST not

PROC/Adjective, Adverb, Verb, Pronoun, Classifier, Adposition: AS IN Pron(4); CF. NOTE AT N(3)

ATR2/Noun

Pron(5) je Ta SObcee bORo **SOmoSSa** *ta* ho lo tomar sthanabhab – 'what is the greatest problem is your lack of space'
which CLA most great problem that be RHE your lack-of-space

ATR2/Adjective

Pron(6) ja SObcee **joruri** *ta* ho lo tomar kaj – 'what is most vital is your work'
what most vital that be RHE your work

ATR2/Adverb, Verb, Pronoun, Classifier, Adposition: AS IN Pron(6); CF. NOTE AT N(3)

EPI/Noun

Pron(7) *tuy* **bETa** er moddhe kOtha bolte aS iS kEno? – 'why do you-bastard poke your nose into this?'
you bastard of-this in-the-middle talk to-talk come PRES why

APO/N

Pron(8) *apni*, Ek jon **buddhijibi**, e kaj kEno kor ben? – 'Why do you, one intellectual, do this?'
you, one CLA intellectual, this action why do will?

APO/Classifier

Pron(9) *o*, baRir SObcee phaltu cakor **Ta**, ki kore par be? – 'How will he, the most useless servant of the house, be able to do this?'
he, house-GEN most useless servant CLA, Q how be-able FUT?

ADVA/Adverb, Emphasizer, Rhetic, Anchor

Pron(10) e Ta **tahole** *tomar* **o na bujhi**? – 'is this not even yours, then?'
this CLA then yours even not Q

PROA/Subjunction

Pron(11) kaj Ta ki *amar* **je** ami bEsto hO bo? – 'is the task mine that I should be anxious?'
task CLA Q mine that I anxious be FUT

LIA/Adverb

Pron(12) e Ta **tay** *tomar* – 'hence this is yours'
this CLA hence yours

LIA/Rhetic, Adposition, Anchor: AS IN Pron(12); CF. N(40)-(42)

3.7. Dependents of minors

Minors are Subjunctions, Numerals, Emphasizers, Interjections, Adpositions, Anchors and Rhetics.

Note: The following abbreviations are used to indicate governing category in the table for these seven minor categories: **N** for Numeral, **I** for Interjection, **A** for Adposition, and **S** for Subjunction. Other abbreviations are as in previous tables and the text.

	Noun	Adj	Adv	Vb	Num	Pron	Cla	Emp	Rhe	Adp	Sjc	Anc	Cj	Int
SUBJ	A					A	A						A	
DOBJ														
IOBJ														
CONV														
INFC														
ADVC														
PREC														
PARG	A		A			A	A			A			A	
PROC														
SUBC	S	S	S	S		S	S			S			S	
ATR1														
ATR2					N									
EPI														
APO														
ADVA			NIA					NA	NA			NA	NA	
PREA										N			N	
PROA														
NUMA														
CLAA														
LIA														

SUBJ/**Noun** or **Pronoun** or **Classifier**/*Adposition*

M(1) **ram / o / o ra** dOrjar *kache* – 'They are near the door'
Ram / s/he / 3P PL door *near*

PARG/**Noun**/*Adposition*

M(2) **Sormilar** *SONge* ja W – 'go with Sharmila'
Sharmila-GEN with go IMP

PARG/**Adv**/*Adposition*

M(3) **base** *kore* ja W – 'go *by* **bus**'
bus-LOC by go IMP

PARG/**Pronoun**/*Adposition*

M(4) **or** *SONge* ja W – 'go *with* **him/her**'

PARG/**Classifier**/*Adposition*

M(5) o **der** *SONge* ja W – 'go with 3P PL'

PARG/**Adposition**/*Adposition*

M(6) o ra ghOrer **bhitor** *theke* bero lo
they room inside from emerged PAST – 'they emerged *from* **inside** the room'

SUBC/**Noun**/*Subjunction*

M(7) Sune chi *je* tumi Ek jon **prarthi** – 'I have heard that you are a candidate'
heard have *that* you a CLA **candidate**

SUBC/**Adjective**/*Subjunction*

M(8) Sune chi *je* tumi **agrohi** – '...*that* you (are) **interested**'

SUBC/**Adverb**/*Subjunction*

M(9) Sune chi *je* tumi **ekhane** – '...*that* you **here**'

SUBC/**Verb**/*Subjunction*

M(10) Sune chi *je* tumi **aS** be – '... that you will come'
...*that* you **come** will

SUBC/**Pronoun**/*Subjunction*

M(11) Sune chi *je* karkhana Ta **tomar** – '...that the factory is yours'
...*that* factory CLA **yours**

SUBC/**Classifier**/*Subjunction*

M(12) Sune chi *je* karkhana Ta toma **der** – '...*that* the factory is yours(PL)

SUBC/**Adposition**/*Subjunction*

M(13) Sune chi *je* jaYga Ta **kache** – '...*that* the place is **near**'

ATR2/**Numeral**/*Numeral*

M(14) ami *tin* **tin** Te ciThi likhe chi – 'I have written three letters, no less'
I three three CLA letter written have

ADVA/**Adverb** or **Emphasizer** or **Rhetic** or **Anchor**/*Adposition*

M(15) baRi Ta **to**$_{ANC}$ **bodhOY**$_{ADV}$ *kache* **o**$_{EMP}$ **na**$_{RHE}$ – 'the house is after all probably not even near by'
house CLA after-all probably near even not

ADVA/**Adverb** or **Emphasizer**/*Numeral*

M(16) duye duye **niScoy**$_{ADV}$ *car* **i**$_{EMP}$ hO be – 'two and two must definitely be four'
two-LOC definitely four indeed be FUT

ADVA/**Rhetic** or **Anchor**/*Numeral*

M(17) duye duye *car* **na**$_{RHE}$ **bujhi**$_{ANC}$? – 'isn't two and two four?'
... *four* **not** Q

PREA/**Adposition**/*Numeral*

M(18) ama der **moddhe** *du* jon aS be – '*two* **of** us will come'
1P GEN of two come FUT

PROA/**Subjunction**/*Adposition*

M(19) baRi ki *kache* **je** heMTe ja bo? – 'is the house near by that I can go there on foot?'
house Q near that walking go will

NUMA/**Num**/*Num*

M(20) o ra **du** *hajar* Taka ca Y – 'they want **two** *thousand* rupees'

LIA/**Adverb**/*Adposition*

M(21) bOndor Ta **tay** jelar Simar *bayre* – 'the port is, hence, outside the district limits'
port CLA hence district-GEN limit-GEN outside

LIA/**Rhetic, Adposition, Anchor**/*Adposition*: AS IN M(21); CF. N(40)-(42)

3.8. Dependents of conjunctions

	Noun	Adj	Adv	Vb	Num	Pron	Cla	Emp	Rhe	Adp	Sjc	Anc	Cj	Int
SUBJ	×	×	×	×		×	×			×	×		×	
DOBJ	×	×	×	×		×	×			×	×		×	
IOBJ	×					×	×			×			×	
CONV	×	×	×	×						×			×	
INFC				×									×	
ADVC			×										×	
PREC										×			×	
PROC	×	×	×	×		×	×			×	×		×	
SUBC														
ATR1	×	×			×	×	×			×			×	
ATR2	×	×	×	×		×	×			×			×	
EPI	×	×			×	×	×			×			×	
APO	×		×			×	×						×	
ADVA			×					×	×			×	×	
PREA										×			×	
PROA	×	×	×	×		×	×			×	×		×	
NUMA														
CLAA							×						×	
LIA			×						×	×		×	×	

No separate listing is necessary; general conventions make it obvious what kinds of examples are involved, as conjunctions take on the character of the elements they conjoin.

4. Analytical decisions: summary

(1) The CONV **Converbial** dependent plus Verb governor, the bilexemic verb construction, has two special cases in Bangla: the compound verb with a Verb as Converbial, and the composite verb (M. Dasgupta 1986) with a non-Verb as Converbial. We allow a Converbial element to govern other elements only if the Converbial is a Verb; in composite verb clauses, all actants depend on the governing Verb, not on the non-Verb Converbial. Thus in V(16) above, *tomake* is the DOBJ of poR, while in V(17) *Ta* is the DOBJ of *bujhie*.

(2) ATR2, the **Secondary Attribute** dependency, is employed for two special purposes in this grammar. In cases of full-word reduplication, like *poce poce* in V(25) above, the second item is treated as an ATR2 of the first. And when a relative clause exhibits multiple dependency as in V(24) above, the head of the relative clause (the verb, usually) is treated as an ATR2 of the head of the main clause; to indicate that this is a special use of the ATR2 dependency, a special mark, ATR2-*k*, will be used in the system.

(3) DOBJ, the **Direct Object** dependency, is extended so that it also covers predicative complements as in V(5) above, following up on an idea due to

Shiroratna (1860). The case marking pattern in Bangla makes it rational to do this, and to extend IOBJ or Indirect Object also in an unorthodox way, so that it covers *bidiSake* in V(12). These decisions are related to the decision not to postulate zero copula elements in Bangla (Benveniste 1966 argues against zero copula theories in general), which leaves the headship of, say, a sentence like Adj(2) *o doSi* 's/he guilty, i.e. s/he is guilty' in the hands of the predicated element, here the Adjective *doSi* 'guilty'. While many types of words may thus head a Bangla clause, a Rhetic (the element often bearing finiteness morphology) cannot, but must depend on the clausal head. One consequence is that, when finiteness and predication are fused, as in *ney* 'is not (present, available)', the word must be treated as a Verb, not a Rhetic, despite its finite character.

(4) **Locatives** are uniformly treated as Adverbs; this leaves open the status of the locative element as an inflection or otherwise.

(5) INFC, the **Infinitival Complement** dependency, is invoked only for slots that are not in complementary distribution with standard Direct Objects.

5. Sample sentence

Sentence:

indrojiter baRite phire amar mone ho lo je ram je dolil du To kawke dEkhate ca Y ni ey SOhoj kOtha Ta hOYto du jon dOrSoker kache kuaSar mOto jhapSa

Indrojit's house-LOC come-back-Conjunctive I-GEN mind-LOC be PAST that Ram that document two CLA anyone-DAT to-show want PRES Neg-PAST this simple fact CLA perhaps two CLA onlooker-GEN to mist-GEN like obscure

'When I returned to Indrojit's house, it struck me that the simple fact that Ram had not wanted to show the two documents to anybody was perhaps as unclear as mist to two observers'

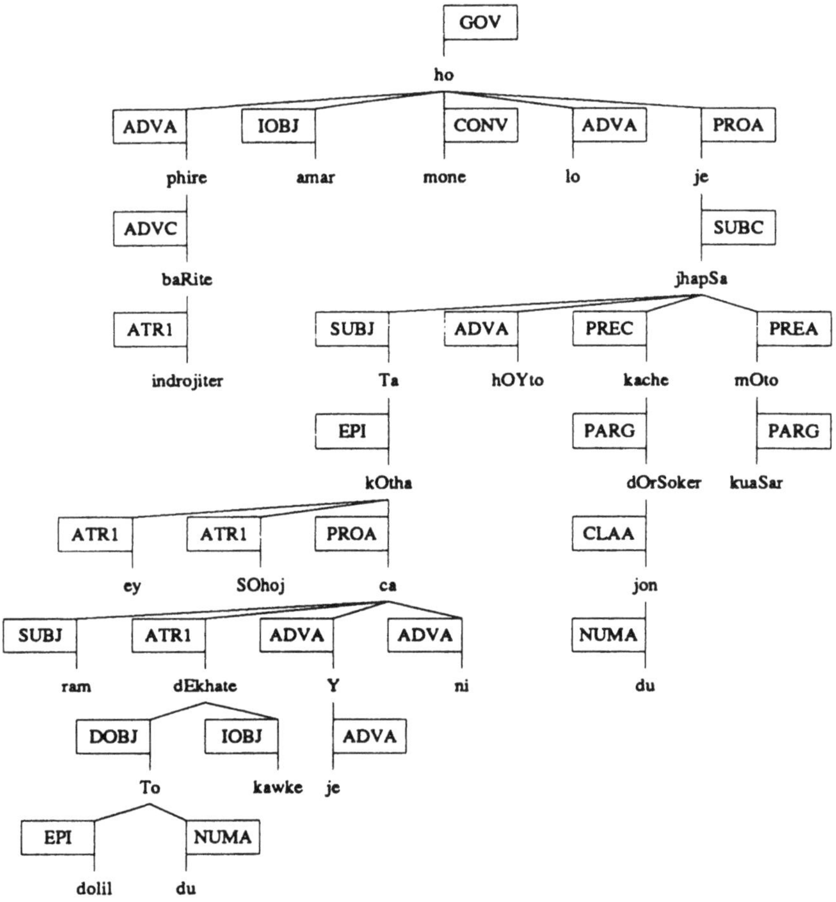

References

Benveniste, Émile (1966): *Problèmes de linguistique générale.* Paris: Gallimard

Dasgupta, Malasree (1986): Composite verbs in Bangla. M.A. dissertation, Pune: Deccan College

Dasgupta, Probal (1979): The Bangla *Wa-no* form as participle and gerund. In: *Indian Linguistics* 40[3], pp. 185-197

Dasgupta, Probal (1983): Bangla equatives, complementizers, final foci, and roots. In: *Linguistic analysis* 11[2], pp. 103-137

Dasgupta, Probal (1984): Bangla emphasizers and anchors. In: *Indian Linguistics* 45, pp. 102-117

Dasgupta, Probal (1985): On Bangla nouns. In: *Indian Linguistics* 46[1-2], pp. 37-65

Dasgupta, Probal (1986): Gerunds, participles, and the theory of categories. In: *Bulletin of Deccan College Research Institute* 45, pp. 7-18

Dasgupta, Probal (1987): Sentence particles in Bangla. In: *Select papers from SALA-7.* Ed. Elena Bashir / Madhav Deshpande / Peter Edwin Hook. Bloomington: Indiana University Linguistics Club, pp. 49-75

Ray, Punya Sloka / Lila Ray / Muhammad Abdul Hai (1966): *Bengali language handbook.* Washington, D.C.: Center for Applied Linguistics

Shiroratna, Loharam (1860): *Bangla byakaran* [in Bangla: 'Bangla grammar']. Calcutta: New Sanskrit Press

A dependency syntax of Finnish

Kalevi Tarvainen

Jyväskylä, Finland

1. Introduction

Finnish is one of the few non-Indo-European languages spoken in contemporary Europe. It belongs to the Finno-Ugric language family, having e.g., Hungarian as a distant, and Estonian as a close linguistic relative. Finnish is the native language of about 95% of Finland's population of circa 5 million. It is also one of the official languages, the other for historical reasons being Swedish, which is still spoken natively by circa 300,000 Finns (often called Finland Swedes).

Finnish differs both in its basic vocabulary and in its grammar from familiar Indo-European languages like English, German, etc. As for the sound structure, there are 21 phonemes in Finnish: 8 vowels and 13 consonants. The writing system is phonemic – a given phoneme is always written with the same letter (grapheme) and on the other hand a given letter always corresponds to the same phoneme. Morphologically and syntactically, Finnish is mainly an agglutinative language with a rich system of various endings for syntactic functions and with a relatively free word order, although it is not as agglutinative as Hungarian. The most important characteristics and peculiarities of Finnish grammar are as follows:

(1) Finnish has no articles and no grammatical gender: *auto* 'a/the car'; *hän* 'he/she'.

(2) When adjectival words (e.g., adjectives, determiners, numerals) occur as pre-attributes they agree in number and case with their headword, i.e., they take the same endings:

iso auto 'the big car'
iso/*ssa* auto/*ssa* 'in the big car'
iso/*t* auto/*t* 'the big cars'
iso/*issa* auto/*issa* 'in the big cars'

(3) The sentential negation in Finnish is indicated by a verb form with the same personal endings as the "normal" finite verb, e.g.,

minä e/*n* tule 'I don't come' – minä tule/*n* 'I'll come'
sinä e/*t* tule 'you don't come' – sinä tule/*t* 'you'll come'

(4) Adding endings (suffixes) to a word stem is a morphological feature of many European languages, but Finnish nevertheless differs from most of them. Firstly, it has more inflectional endings (e.g., 15 nominal case endings) and secondly, Finnish often uses suffixes where Indo-European languages have independent words (e.g., the possessive suffix *-ni* corresponds to the English possessive pronoun *my*: talo/*ni* '*my* house'; the enclitic particle *-kin* can be translated into English by the word *too* or *also*: minä/*kin* 'I, too'; 'also I'). Thirdly, one word can have many suffixes of different kinds, thus becoming a real morpheme "conglomerate". A noun, for example, can have five different suffixes attached to the nominal stem in the following fixed order: (1) number suffix, (2) case ending, (3) possessive suffix, (4) enclitic particle, (5) interrogative particle, e.g., talo/*i*/*ssa*/*ni*/*kin*/*ko?* 'in my houses, too?' (lit. 'house-s-in-my-too-whether?'). It might be asked whether some or all of these suffixes could be regarded as analytical entities of their own, that is, as "non-independent" enclitic words, in a metataxis-oriented dependency syntax. In order to facilitate discussion of this problem, the main groups of Finnish suffixes are given below:

(a) Inflectional endings, e.g., the case endings of the noun and the conjugational endings of the verbs, e.g.,

talo/*n* (genitive) 'of the house', talo/*ssa* (inessive) 'in the house'
tule/*n* 'I'll come', tule/*t* 'you'll come' etc.
(conjugational personal endings)

(b) The interrogative particle *-ko* attached to the finite verb as a syntactic sign of the interrogative sentence or to another word as a question particle, e.g.,

Tulee/*ko* hän 'Does he come' (lit. 'Comes-whether he?')
Sinä/*kö* tulit 'Was it you that came?'

(c) Possessive suffixes: talo/*ni* 'my house', talo/*mme* 'our house' etc.

(d) Enclitic particles often translated with particle words into English, e.g., *-kin* 'also', 'too'; *-kaan* 'not either'; *-pa* [emphasis], *-han* [emphasis]:

Sinä/*kin* tulit 'You came, too'
Kekkonen/*kaan* ei tullut 'Kekkonen didn't come, either'

It would surely be possible to analyse many of the above suffixes as words of their own, as has been done to a great extent in the Hungarian dependency syntax by Prószéky, Koutny and Wacha (1987; see also their contribution to this volume). For example in the sentence *Tulin tänään kaupunkiin* 'I came to town today' the personal ending *-n* could be considered as a "suffixal word" in the function of the subject, so also the illative ending *-in* in *kaupunki/in* as a "suffixal" adverbial complement corresponding to the English preposition *to*. From the point of view of metataxis, this solution may be practical in the dependency analysis of the sentence above, as shown by the tree diagram below:

It would, however, hardly be practical to regard all Finnish inflectional endings or other suffixes as words of their own, for "it would imply that the limit between the word and the sentence is given up entirely" (Schubert 1987: 86). My analysis is based on the one-word principle of Schubert allowing only one "real" word to occur in each dependency node. But the principle is restricted here by two exceptions: the possessive suffixes and most of the so-called enclitic particles (e.g., *-kin* 'also') are regarded as words of their own. These exceptions are metataxis-oriented in that these suffix words have either syntactic functions – the possessive suffix can for example function as the subject in the so-called clause equivalents – or lexical ones, expressed in most languages by normal words. Purely morphological, inflectional endings (e.g., the case endings) are regarded as parts of their "headwords". This is also true for the interrogative particle *-ko*, even if it is syntactic, because it is a characteristic of an interrogative sentence. Its syntactic properties have nothing to do with dependency relationships, but are rather of a pragmatic nature on the sentence level, expressing a sentence type, not a dependency structure in a sentence.

2. Word classes

The traditional Finnish word classification is based on inflectional criteria and has only three main word classes, further subdivided on the basis of semantic criteria: (1) Nominals with a case inflection (declination): nouns, adjectives, numerals, pronouns, (2) Verbs with a person inflection (conjugation), (3) Particles without any inflection: adverbs, pre- and postpositions, conjunctions, interjections.

The word classification used in this paper is based mainly on the syntactic distribution of the words, but also partly on their morphology (inflection). The word class list consists of the following 15 classes: (1) verbs, (2) nouns, (3) adjectives (adj),

(4) pronouns (pron), (5) determiners (det), (6) numerals (num), (7) adverbs (adv), (8) modal particles (mod), (9) pre- and postpositions (prep), (10) gradation particles (grad), (11) specification particles (spec), (12) comparison particles (comp), (13) subjunctions (sub), (14) conjunctions (conj), (15) interjections. In some cases, a word in a given class is not a "real" word but a lexical suffix, e.g., the possessive suffix in the class of the pronouns (kirja/*ni* '*my* book') or the enclitic particle *-kin* 'too' (hän/*kin* 'he, *too*'). The word classes "modal particle", "determiner", "gradation particle", "specification particle", "comparison particle" and "subjunction" are definitely non-traditional. The capacity of functioning as a certain dependent type is in Finnish normally a property not of a word as a member of a particular word class, but rather of a specific subset of its morphological forms (e.g., predicative complement: noun in nominative/partitive/essive etc.). That is why in dealing below with the word classes, the main morpho-syntactic features of a word class must be given, too.

2.1. Verbs

Morphologically, the word class verb in Finnish consists of a finite verb with markings for normal verbal categories (tense, mood, person, voice) and various non-finite forms – e.g., infinitives and participles – with mainly nominal endings. In terms of dependency relationships, one can make a distinction between lexical (or main) verbs with normal dependent types (subject, direct object etc.) and a heterogeneous group of auxiliaries (*olla* 'be'; modal verbs, etc.) with a non-finite verbal form as their only complement. This is here called "verbative complement" (as e.g., in the traditional analytic past tenses: *on* **tullut** 'has come').

Finite Verb. The Finnish finite verb has two voices (active and passive), four moods (indicative, conditional, potential and imperative) and two tenses (present and past) as the table below shows.

ACTIVE				PASSIVE
Indicative				
Present:	sg.	1.	saavu/*n* 'I come'	saavu/*ta*/*an* 'people come'
		2.	saavu/*t* 'you come' etc.	
Past:	sg.	1.	saavu/*i*/*n* 'I came'	saavu/*tti*/*in* 'people came'
		2.	saavu/*i*/*t* 'you came'	
Conditional				
Present:	sg.	1.	saapu/*isi*/*n* 'I would come'	saavu/*tta*/*isi*/*in* 'people would come'
Potential				
Present:	sg.	1.	saapu/*ne*/*n* 'I may come'	saavu/*tta*/*ne*/*en* 'people may come'
Imperative				
Present: e.g.,	sg.	2.	saavu 'come'	saavu/*tta*/*koon* 'people shall come'

The Finnish finite verb has in the active (indicative, conditional, potential) six grammatical persons. They correspond to the personal pronouns, which in the 1. and 2.

p. sg./pl. are, however, optional and are often omitted, for the personal endings have each a unique meaning and can express the subject person alone, without a subject pronoun:

singular	plural
1. (*minä*) saavu*n* 'I come'	(*me*) saavu*mme* 'we come'
2. (*sinä*) saavu*t* 'you come'	(*te*) saavu*tte* 'you come'
3. *hän* saapu*u* 'he comes'	*he* saapu*vat* 'they come'

In the passive voice, there is no subject word at all and only one personal ending expressing indefinite persons as performers of the action ("impersonal passive" or "indefinite"). These personal endings, though they could be regarded as suffixal (enclitic) subjects, are here considered to be at the structural center of the sentence as parts of the finite verb, which is then considered to be without a subject:

Minä näin hänet tänään – Näin hänet tänään

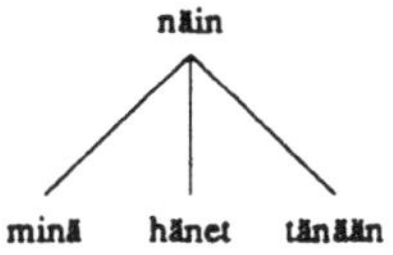

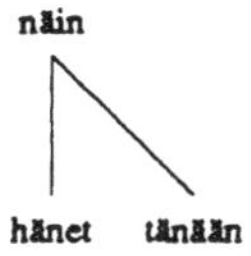

A characteristic of Finnish is that also the sentence negator is a verbal form (called "negation verb") with the same personal endings as the "normal" verb:

(minä) e/*n* saavu (cf. minä saavu/*n*)
'I don't come'

(sinä) e/*t* saavu (cf. sinä saavu/*t*)
'you don't come'

hän e/*i* saavu (exceptional ending -*i*; cf. hän saapu/*u*)
'he doesn't come', etc.

In terms of dependency relationships, this means that in the case of negative verb forms, the negation verb is the structural governor of the sentence and the main verb (mostly as a verbal stem without an ending) is its complement (verbative complement):

Minä *en* **tunne** häntä 'I don't know him'
Minä *en* ole nähnyt häntä 'I haven't seen him'

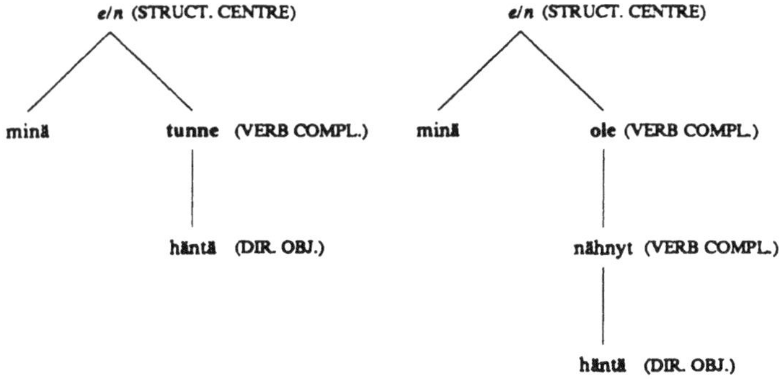

Non-finite verb forms. The infinitives have a nominal case inflection, although it may be defective, and occur in a sentence in functions similar to those of nouns (e.g., subject, direct object, adverbial complement or adjunct), whereas the participles act mainly as attributive adjectives.

(1) Finnish has four infinitives, three of which are in common use. The main one is the first infinitive, whose so-called short form (e.g., *syödä* 'to eat') is the dictionary form of the verb; the others are the 2nd (inessive and instructive) and the 3rd (inessive, elative, illative, adessive, ablative). The infinitive form as a word consists of a verbal stem, a so-called function suffix, the case ending and an eventual possessive suffix, e.g.,

syö/de/ssä/mme 'while we eat'
1 2 3 4

(1) verbal stem,
(2) function suffix of the 2nd inf.,
(3) case ending of the inessive,
(4) the poss. suffix of the 1st p. pl.

The following table shows the main features of the Finnish infinitive system (stem, function suffix, case ending, meaning):

1st		
(a) short form	*-a*:	sano/*a* 'to say' (no case ending)
(b) longer form	*-a/kse*:	sano/*a/kse*/ni (translative) 'in order to say'
2nd	*-e*:	sano/*e/ssa*/ni (inessive) 'while I am saying'
		sano/*e/n* (instructive) 'saying'
3rd	*-ma*:	sano/*ma/ssa* (inessive) '(he is) saying (that) ...'
		sano/*ma/sta* (elative) lit. 'from saying'
		sano/*ma/an* (illative) '(in order) to say'
		sano/*ma/lla* (adessive) 'by saying'
		sano/*ma/tta* (abessive) 'without saying'

The short form of the 1st infinitive is used above all as a subject and a direct object, the other infinitives are used as other objects ("case complements") and as adverbials replacing as "clause equivalents" subordinate clauses. The verbal character of the infinitives is shown by the fact that they govern the same dependents as the finite verb, e.g.,

> *Lukiessani* **lehteä** (partit. obj.) hän tuli huoneeseen
> 'While I was reading a paper he entered the room'
> (Kun *luin* **lehteä** (partit. obj.) 'When I read the paper')

(2) Finnish has two participles, the present and the past, which both have active and passive forms. They occur, above all the past, as verbative complements in the traditional compound forms of verbs (e.g., Hän *on* **tullut** 'He has come'), but mainly they function as attributive adjectives, their verbal word class character appearing in that they still take the same dependents as the verb, e.g.,

> Näetkö tuon **kirjaa** *lukevan* pojan? 'Do you see that book-reading boy'
> (*lukevan* is a present participle as an adjective attribute of the noun *pojan*, but it is preceded by the partitive direct object **kirjaa**; cf. Hän *lukee* **kirjaa** 'He is reading a book')

Participles are also used as "clause equivalents" in the functions of a direct object and an adverbial adjunct:

> Minä näin *hänen* **tulevan** 'I saw him coming'
> Minä näin **että** *hän* **tuli** 'I saw that he came'
> (the present participle *tulevan* as the internal governor of a clause equivalent as a direct object)

The forms of the participles are given below.

ACTIVE	PASSIVE
Present: *-va*: luke/*va* 'reading	lue/*tta/va* 'to be read'
Past: *-nut*: luke/*nut* 'read'	lue/*ttu* 'read'

2.2. Nouns

(1) Finnish nouns have some 15 cases (singular and plural) expressed by declinational suffixes called case endings. The table below shows the grammatical names of the cases as well as examples of their main endings and meanings.

NOMINATIVE	auto 'the car'
GENITIVE	auto/*n* 'of the car'
PARTITIVE	auto/*a* 'the car': En osta autoa (OBJ) 'I don't buy a car'
"Accusative" (OBJ)	auton (GEN. SG.): Ostin auton 'I bought a car' auto (NOM. SG.): Osta auto! 'Buy a car!' autot (NOM. PL.): Ostin autot 'I bought the cars'
ESSIVE	auto/*na* 'as a car': Pidän sitä hyvänä autona 'I regard it as a good car'
TRANSLATIVE	auto/*ksi* '(into) a car': Fiat kehittyi hyväksi autoksi 'Fiat became a good car'
INESSIVE	auto/*ssa* 'in the car'
ELATIVE	auto/*sta* '(out) of the car'
ILLATIVE	auto/*on* 'into the car'
ADESSIVE	pöydä/*llä* 'on the table'
ABLATIVE	pöydä/*ltä* 'off the table'
ALLATIVE	pöydä/*lle* 'onto the table'
COMITATIVE	auto/i/*ne*/en (pl.): mies autoineen 'the man with his car(s)'
ABESSIVE	auto/*tta* 'without a car'
INSTRUCTIVE	käs/i/*n* (pl.) 'with hands'

The cases above can be divided into different functional groups. The **grammatical cases** (nominative, partitive and genitive) are above all cases for the subject, the direct object, and the predicative complement (genitive also for an attribute; the "accusative" is a collective functional name for some nominative and genitive forms as an object ["total object"] as opposite to the partitive object ["partial object"]). The **half-grammatical cases** (essive and translative) are grammatically mainly predicative cases, but they have also some adverbial functions (e.g., temporal). The basic function of the six **local cases** is the expression of place and direction in the two dimensions of "inside" (inessive, elative, illative) and "outside" (adessive, ablative, allative), but they are also used in many other adverbial functions (e.g., temporal, modal, causal) and even in purely grammatical meanings: the allative and ablative as case complements (objects) are e.g., equal to the indirect object in English (annoin *miehelle* rahat 'I gave the man the money'). The **marginal cases** (comitative, abessive, instructive) are seldom used.

(2) A characteristic subclass of Finnish nouns is the so-called "verbal noun", which has a complete nominal case inflection and nominal syntactic functions (e.g., subject) but a verbal meaning. It is formed by various derivational suffixes, above all by the suffix *-minen*, which in principle can change any verb into a noun, e.g.:

luke/a 'to read' – luke/*minen* (nom.) 'the reading' (cf. German *das Lesen*), luke/*misen* (gen.) 'of the reading'
tul/la 'to come' – tule/*minen*, also tul/*o* 'the coming'

Semantically, most nominal phrases formed by verbal nouns are equal to sentences with a finite verb and must often be translated into other languages as a clause:

isän ***meneminen*** **kaupunkiin – isä** ***menee*** **kaupunkiin**
'father's going to town' – 'father goes to town'
isän meneminen kaupunkiin oli yllätys 'that father went to town was a surprise'

The dependents (traditionally attributes) of *meneminen* correspond to the dependents of the finite verb *menee*: the subjective genitive *isän* corresponds to the nominative subject *isä* and the illative attribute *kaupunkiin* to the adverbial complement in the same form. From the point of view of metataxis, the dependents of verbal nouns are not called attributes in this paper, but are regarded as subjects (e.g., *isän*), adverbials (*kaupunkiin*) etc., as in the case of a real verbal governor.

(3) Many adjectives can function like a noun. In this paper they are considered as nouns, e.g.,

kaikki *kaunis* (subj.) kiinnostaa minua 'everything beautiful interests me'

2.3. Adjectives

Adjectives can in general have the same case endings as the nouns, but unlike these most of them form comparative and superlative by adding the suffixes *-mpi* (*-mpa*, *-mma*) and *-in* (*-impa*, *-imma*), respectively, to the stem, e.g.,

Nom. sg. iso 'big' (positive) – iso/*mpi* (comparative) 'bigger' - iso/*in* 'the biggest'; iso/*mman* (comparative in genitive) - iso/*imman* (superlative in genitive).

Adjectives are used as pre-attributes and predicatives. Three different groups can be distinguished.

(1) Most adjectives can be used both attributively and predicatively. When used as an attribute, the adjective agrees with its head noun in case and number, having the same 14 cases as the noun, e.g.,

iso talo (nom. sg.) 'a big house'
iso/*t* talo/*t* (nom. pl.) 'the big houses'
iso/*n* talo/*n* (gen. sg.) 'of the big house'
iso/*ssa* talo/*ssa* (iness. sg.) 'in the big house'
iso/*mma*/*ssa* talo/*ssa* (iness. sg. comp.) 'in the bigger house'
iso/*imma*/*ssa* talo/*ssa* (iness. sg. sup.) 'in the biggest house', etc.

In a predicative use, the case of the predicative complement is traditionally nominative or partitive, that of the predicative adjunct mostly essive, e.g.,

mies on *vanha* (nom. sg.) 'the man is old'
miehet ovat *vanho*/*ja* (part. pl.) 'the men are old'
hän palasi kotiin sairaa/*na* (ess. sg.) 'he came home sick'

(2) There are some short adjectives (e.g., *pikku* 'small', *eri* 'different') which are only used as attributes, but are undeclined agreeing not in case or number with the noun, e.g., *pikku* poika (nom. sg.) 'the small boy', *pikku* pojat (nom. pl.) 'the small boys', *pikku* poja/lle (allat. sg.) 'to the small boy'. These adjectives have no comparison, either.

(3) Traditional Finnish grammars don't mention any adjectives used as predicatives only. In this paper some traditional "adverbs" are regarded as predicative adjectives, because they form a paradigm with normal adjectives and can often be replaced by a real adjective of the same stem, e.g.,

auto on *rikki* (= rikkinäinen) 'the car is broken'
uusi new'
mies on *juovuksissa* (= juopunut) 'the man is drunk'
(in many cases such an adjective is a fossilized case form, here an inessive)

The ordinal numbers as well as present and past participles used as pre-attributes are counted in adjectives, e.g.,

kolmas (ord. num.) mies oli isäni 'the third man was my father'
lisääntyvä (present participle) työttömyys on ongelma
'the increasing unemployment is a problem'

2.4. Pronouns

Pronouns are here only substitutes for noun phrases: the so-called adjectival pronouns of the traditional grammar are regarded as determiners. The Finnish pronouns have the same 14 cases as the nouns, some even 15. The discrepancy is caused by the fact that the accusative is a distinct form for some pronouns (e.g., the personal pronouns) but not nouns, e.g., *minä* 'I' – *minut* 'me'. There are some clear classes of pronouns; in some cases, determiners can also act as pronouns (e.g., *tämä* 'this').

(1) Personal pronouns

Nominative:	*minä* 'I', *sinä* 'you', *hän* 'he/she'
	me 'we', *te* 'you', *he* 'they'
Accusative:	*minut* 'me', *sinut* 'you', *hänet* 'him/her'
	meidät 'us', *teidät* 'you', *heidät* 'them'
Genitive:	*minun* 'my/mine', *sinun* 'your(s)', etc.

(2) Possessive suffixes

(minun)	kirja/*ni* 'my book'
(sinun)	kirja/*si* 'your book'
(hänen)	kirja/*nsa* 'his/her book'
(meidän)	kirja/*mme* 'our book'
(teidän)	kirja/*nne* 'your book'
(heidän)	kirja/*nsa* 'their book'

Possessive suffixes are "enclitic words" corresponding to the possessive pronouns or determiners of many other languages and often having a genitive of the personal pronoun as a mostly optional pre-attribute of the noun. The possessive suffixes can also act as subjects in the so-called clause equivalents, e.g., *Tullessa/ni* kotiin hän itki 'When I came home, he was crying'.

(3) Interrogative pronouns

e.g., *kuka* (nom. sg.) – *ketkä* (nom. pl.) 'who'
kenen (gen. sg.) – *keiden* (gen. pl.) 'whose', etc.

(4) Relative pronouns

joka (nom. sg.) – *jotka* (nom. pl.) 'who, which, that'
mikä (nom. sg.) – *mitkä* (nom. pl) 'which'

(5) Indefinite pronouns

The numerous indefinite pronouns (e.g., *joku* 'someone', *jokin* 'something', *kukaan* 'anyone', *mikään* 'anything', *jompi kumpi* 'one (of the two)'), most of which are also used as determiners, constitute as a whole a very complicated and irregular system, differing from that of Indo-European languages in many respects.

(a) Finnish has no negative indefinite pronouns (cf. Engl. *nobody, nothing*). Also for pronouns, the negative is always a verb form, even if it is placed before a (positive) indefinite pronoun, e.g.,

Ei **kukaan** nähnyt minua 'Nobody ("not anybody") saw me'
Kukaan *ei* nähnyt minua 'Nobody ("anybody not") saw me'

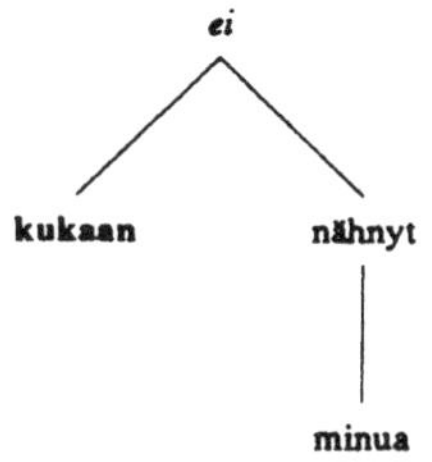

(b) Finnish has no reflexive pronouns. Their functions are expressed by the appropriate case forms of the indefinite pronoun *itse* 'myself, yourself' etc. followed by a possessive suffix, e.g.,

Me rakastamme *itse/ä/mme* (partit. of *itse* + poss. suff. *-mme*)
'We love ourselves'

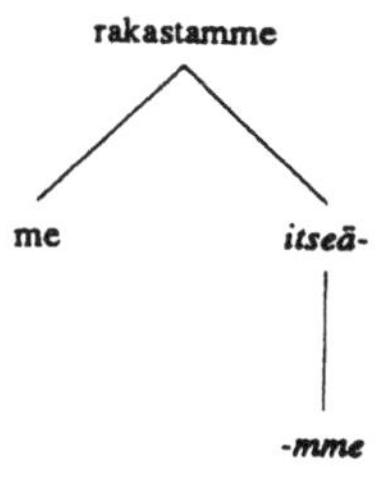

(c) The indefinite pronoun *toinen* 'other' has also a reciprocal function. This pronoun is either used in a plural case form followed by a poss. suff. of the 1st/2nd/3rd p. pl. (e.g., *toisia/mme*: *toisia* [part. pl.] + *-mme* [poss. suffix 1st p. pl.]) or in a double construction with the nom. sg. + an oblique case of sg. of *toinen* followed by a poss. suff. 1st/2nd/3rd p. pl. (e.g., *toinen toistamme*: *toinen* [nom. sg.] + *toista-* [part. sg.] + *-mme* [poss. suff. 1st p. pl.]), e.g.,

Me rakastamme *toisiamme* 'We love each other'
Me rakastamme *toinen toistamme* 'We love each other'

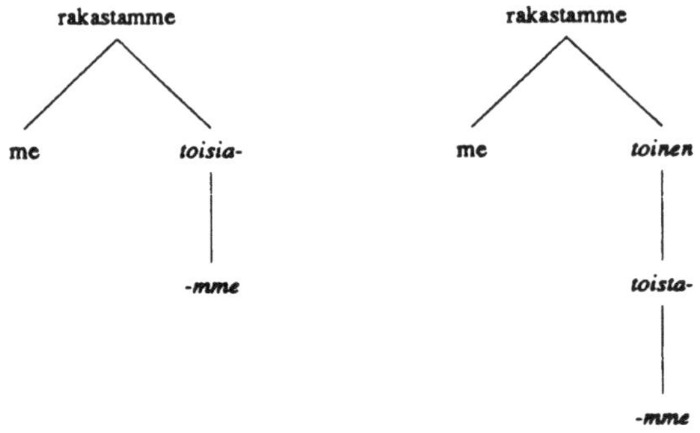

2.5. Determiners

Determiners, which correspond to the adjectival pronouns of traditional grammar, appear as the first element of a noun phrase, but are to be regarded, unlike for example in English, as facultative pre-attributes, since the Finnish noun needs no article word as a distinctive grammatical sign, e.g.,

poika 'the/a boy'
tämä *poika* 'this boy'
tämä pieni *poika* 'this little boy'
tämä hyvin pieni *poika* 'this very little boy'

Most determiners can be used as pronouns, too:

tämä *poika* (determiner) 'this boy'
tämä *on* suomalainen poika (pronoun) 'this is a Finnish boy'

The determiners can be divided into the following groups:

(1) Demonstratives, e.g., *tämä* 'this', *tuo* 'that', *se* 'it'

(2) Interrogatives, e.g., *mikä* 'what', 'which', *kumpi* 'which' (of two)

(3) Relatives: *mikä* 'which' (e.g., Hän uskoo yhteisomistukseen, **mitä** *ajatusta* minä vastustan 'He believes in public ownership, which idea I'm opposed to')

(4) Indefinites, e.g., *jokin* 'some', *mikään* 'any', *kumpikin* 'each (of two)', *kaikki* 'all', *jokainen* 'every'

2.6. Numerals

Traditionally, the numerals are divided into cardinal and ordinal numerals (numbers). The ordinal numbers of Finnish agree with the headword in case and number like adjective attributes, wherefore they are classified as adjectives in this paper, e.g.,

> **kolma/s** *mies* (nom. sg.) 'the third man'
> **kolma/nne/lle** *miehelle* (allat. sg.) 'to the third man'

The numerals dealt with here are cardinal numbers, e.g., 1 = *yksi*, 2 = *kaksi*, 10 = *kymmenen*, 13 = *kolmetoista*, 20 = *kaksikymmentä*, 24 = *kaksikymmentäneljä*, 1000 = *tuhat*, 2354 = *kaksituhatta kolmesataaviisikymmentäneljä*, 1,000,000 = *miljoona*, 4,000,000 = *neljä miljoonaa*.

Like other nominals, cardinal numbers are declined in case. The noun phrases with a cardinal are, however, syntactically rather complicated. The number of the noun following the numeral is always singular, but the problem is the dependency relation: according to the traditional Finnish grammar the headword (governor) of the phrase is in some cases the noun, in other cases the number. There can be distinguished three different constructions.

(1) The cardinal *yksi* 'one' (= 1), always agrees in case and number with the noun, which is the governor in the syntagm:

> Kadulla seisoo (vain) **yksi** *mies* (nom. sg. as subj.)
> 'There is (only) one man standing in the street' (lit. 'In the street stands (only) one man')
> Näin **yhden** *miehen* (gen. sg. as dir. obj.) 'I saw one man'
> Olin (vain) **yhdessä** *talossa* (iness. sg. as an adv. compl.) 'I was in one house (only)'

(2) When the noun in a cardinal noun phrase – except in the phrase with *yksi* 'one' – is in a case other than the partitive, the cardinal agrees in case with the noun, which is the governor, the numeral being the dependent (attribute), as in construction 1), e.g.,

> Minä olin matkallani **kolme/ssa** *kaupungi/ssa* 'I was in three towns on my journey' (inessive as an adverbial complement)

The similar dependency structure of these first types of phrase (1-2) can be shown by the following tree diagrams or dependency trees:

> [1] Kadulla seisoo **yksi** *mies* 'In the street stands one man'
> [2] Minä olin **kolmessa** *kaupungissa* 'I was in three towns'

[1]

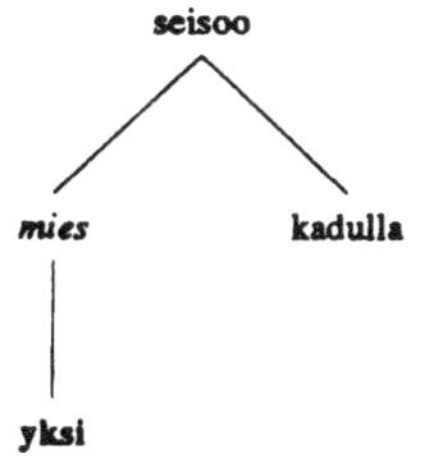

[2]

(3) When the noun phrase with a cardinal number is the subject, direct object or

predicative complement, the noun is always in the partitive singular and the numeral in nominative or partitive singular, e.g.,

> Kadulla seisoo *kolme miestä* (subject phrase)
> 'There are three men standing in the street'
> Eilen kirjoitin *seitsemän sivua* (direct object phrase in the "accusative")
> 'Yesterday I wrote seven pages'
> En omista *kahta autoa* (direct object phrase in the partitive)
> 'I don't own two cars'

Purely formally and according to the traditional Finnish grammar, the cardinal is here the governor (the subject or object proper) and the noun in the partitive its dependent. The dependency tree of the first sample sentence would then be the following:

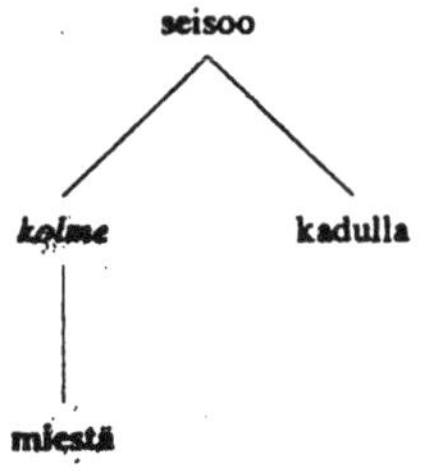

This is theoretically right, for the sentence without the numeral, but not the one without the partitive, would be ungrammatical:

> Kadulla seisoo kolme miestä
> Kadulla seisoo kolme
> *Kadulla seisoo miestä

It is, however, from the point of view of metataxis, problematic to separate this case structurally from the cases [1] and [2], where the noun is the governor and the numeral the dependent (attribute). That is why I have decided to regard the noun also here (in part. sg.) as the governor (subject or object) and the numeral as its dependent. The dependency tree of sentence [3] would then conform with the tree graphs of types 1 and 2 and with those of most other languages:

[3]

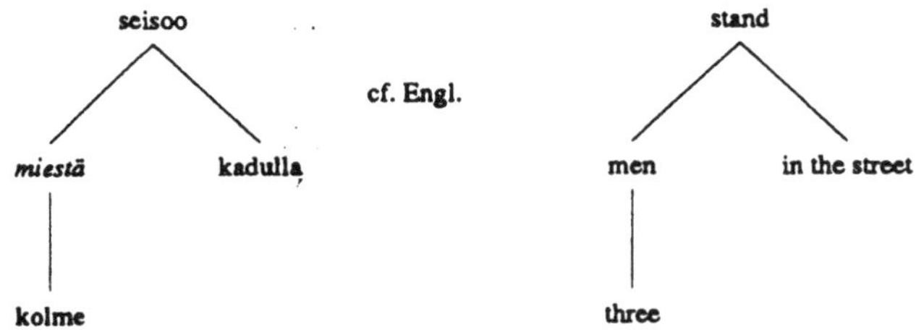

2.7. Adverbs

Adverbs, as they are understood in this paper, are only dependents of a verb as adverbials in a paradigm (traditional adverbs as dependents of adjectives or adverbs – e.g., **sangen** *suuri* 'very big' – for example are classified as "gradation particles").

Finnish adverbs can be members either of an open or a closed word class. The most common type of the open adverbs is formed by adding the suffix *-sti* (Engl. *-ly*) to the inflectional stem of the adjective and can have a comparison with the endings *-mmin* (comp.) *-immin* (superl.):

> (voimakas 'strong') – voimakkaa/*sti* – voimakkaa/*mmin* 'more strongly' – voimakka/*immin* 'most strongly'

Many of Finnish adverbs are old or still living nominal case forms (*mai/tse* 'by land', *meri/tse* 'by sea'; *-tse* is a survival of the obsolete case "prolative"), forming even short case paradigms, e.g., *sisä/llä* (adessive) 'inside', *sisä/ltä* (ablative) 'from within', *sisä/lle* (allative) 'into', 'in'.

2.8. Modal particles

Modal particles are invariable words as *ehkä*, *kai* 'perhaps', 'maybe', 'probably', *tietysti* 'of course', resembling the so-called modal adverbials (e.g., *huonosti* 'badly'), but differing from them in having no pro forms (Germ. *Anapher*) as a part of a paradigm.

> **Tietysti/ehkä** hän *tulee* 'Of course/maybe he comes'
> ***Niin** hän *tulee* *'So he comes'
> (Modal particle)

Hän *käyttäytyi* **huonosti**		'He behaved badly'
	tällä tavalla	'in this way'
	niin	'so'
(Adverb)		

A modal particle can also occur together with an adverb in a sentence. This shows that it presents a word class different from the adverb.

> *Ehkä* hän käyttäytyi *huonosti* 'Perhaps he behaved badly'

2.9. Pre- and postpositions

The functions of the analytic prepositional phrases of Indo-European languages are fulfilled in Finnish mostly by synthetic case forms, especially for cases indicating location, e.g., *in* the house = talo/*ssa*. The inflectional case system is, however, completed by analytic constructions formed by "word morphemes" corresponding to e.g., English prepositions. But these functional words are in Finnish mainly postpositions and are accordingly placed after their headword, even though prepositions also occur, e.g.,

pihan *yli* (postposition)
yli pihan (preposition) 'over the courtyard'

Prepositions govern the partitive and the genitive, postpositions mostly the genitive, but the partitive and some local cases (especially the illative) are possible, too; e.g.,

ennen **sotaa** (prep. with a partitive) 'before the war'
sodan *aikana* (postp. with a genitive) 'during the war'
aamuun *asti* (postp. with an illative) 'until the morning'
koululle *saakka* (postp. with an allative) 'as far as the school'
maanantaista *lähtien* (postp. with an elative) 'since Monday'

Many of the Finnish pre-/postpositions are old "fossilized" case forms, some even today inflecting in three local cases:

takana (essive) 'behind'
alla (adessive): Koira on **pöydän** *alla* 'The dog is under the table'
alle (allative): Koira ryömi **pöydän** *alle* 'The dog crawled under the table'
alta (ablative): Tule esiin **pöydän** *alta* 'Come out from under the table'

In connection with the genitive of a personal pronoun, a possessive suffix must be obligatorily attached to the headword, the genitive itself being optional, e.g.,

Hän tuli (**minun**) *kanssa*/**ni** 'He came with me'

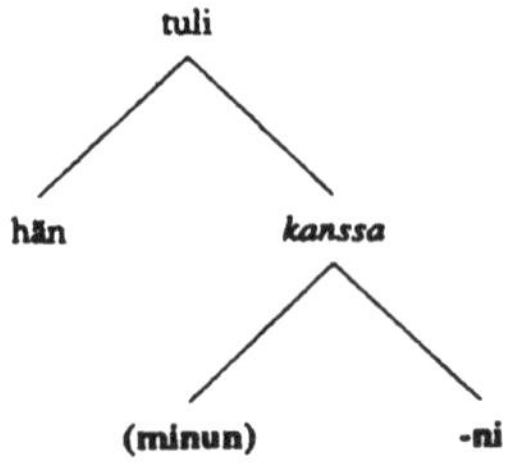

2.10. Gradation particles

Gradation particles, which in traditional grammar normally are treated as a class of adverbs, are invariable (non-declinable) words standing as intensifiers before adjectives or adverbs (in the positive, comparative, or superlative degree):

Hän on **kovin** *älykäs* 'He is very clever' (adj. pos.)
Hän tuli **kovin** *nopeasti* 'He came very fast' (adv. pos.)
Hän on **paljon** *vanhempi* kuin minä (adj. comp.) 'He is much older than me'
Hän on **kaikkein** *paras* (adj. superl.) 'He is the very best'

2.11. Specification particles

Specification particles – also adverbs in traditional grammar – are a small group of invariable (non-declinable) words which are able to stand as closer specifiers of any word class, e.g., *jopa* 'even', *myös* 'too', *-kin*, *-kaan* 'too', 'even' (enclitic particles), *juuri* 'just', *vain* 'only':

> **jopa** *Jussi/hän* voisi tehdä sen tänään 'Even Jussi/he could do it today'
> *Jussi* voisi **jopa** tehdä sen tänään 'Jussi could even do it today'
> *Jussi* voisi tehdä sen **jopa** tänään/täällä 'Jussi could do it even today/here'

2.12. Comparison particles

Finnish has only one comparison particle *kuin*, which occurs after both the positive (engl. 'as', 'like') and the comparative (Engl. 'than') degree of an adjectival or adverbial headword (governor), e.g.,

> Hän on kaunis *kuin* jumalatar 'She is beautiful like a goddess'
> Hän on kauniimpi *kuin* äitinsä 'She is more beautiful than her mother'

If the adjective (adverb) is preceded by a gradation particle as an intensifier (*yhtä* 'as', *niin* 'so'), the comparison particle must be regarded as a dependent of the intensifier:

> Hän on *yhtä* kaunis **kuin** äitinsä 'She is as beautiful as her mother'

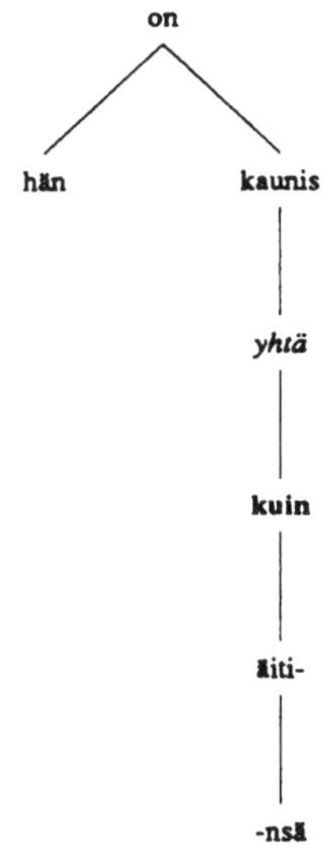

2.13. Subjunctions

Subjunctions, which correspond to the subordinating conjunctions of traditional grammar, act as internal governors of subordinate finite clauses, e.g., *että* 'that', *jotta* 'that', *jos* 'if', *kun* 'when', *koska* 'because', *vaikka* '(al)though':

Minä tiedän, *että* hän tulee 'I know that he comes'

2.14. Conjunctions

Conjunctions here are equal to the coordinating conjunctions of traditional grammar. They link two phrases or propositions with each other, e.g., *ja* 'and', *sekä* 'as well as', *tai*, *vai* 'or', *mutta* 'but', *sekä* ... *että* 'both ... and'.

2.15. Interjections

Interjections are words which do not have a syntactic function in a sentence. They could be regarded as independent (elliptical) sentences of their own. They are mostly one-word expressions, but they can also be connected with some case forms or clauses. They are not treated any further in this paper.

Voi! Voi voi! 'Alas!'
Voi sinua! 'Poor you!'
Voi, kuinka pieni sinä olet! 'Oh, how small you are!'

3. Basic dependent types

This chapter begins with a list of the basic dependent types of Finnish, with one sample sentence for each. The list is followed by a discussion of the main principles and problems in establishing the types. Their forms are exemplified with numbered sample sentences after the tables of the dependent types and their word classes in the third part of this chapter.

3.1. A list of the dependent types

Complements

SUBJ	**Subject**	**Mies** lukee kirjaa 'The man is reading a book'
DOBJ	**Direct object**	Mies lukee **kirjaa** 'The man is reading a book'
CASC	**Case compl. (object)**	Minä puhuin **siitä** 'I spoke about it'
PREPC	**Prepositional compl. (object)**	Minä puhuin miehen **kanssa** 'I spoke with a man'
ADVC	**Adverbial complement**	Hän asuu **Lontoossa/siellä** 'He lives in London/there'
PREDC	**Predicative complement**	Minä olen **opettaja/vanha** 'I am a teacher/old'

VERBC	**Verbative complement**	Olen **ollut** **siellä** 'I have been there'
PROPC	**Propositional complement**	Luulen, **että** hän on oikeassa 'I think that he is right'
COMC	**Comparison complement**	Hän on **kauniimpi kuin** minä 'She's more beautiful than I'
COMARG	**Comparison argument**	Hän on kauniimpi kuin **minä** 'She's more beautiful than I'
PARG	**Prepositional argument**	ennen **sotaa** 'before the war'
SUBARG	**Subjunctional argument**	Minä luulen, että hän **tulee** 'I think that he'll come'

Adjuncts

ADVA	**Adverbial adjunct**	Näin hänet **yöllä/tänään** 'I saw him at night/today'
MODA	**Modal adjunct**	**Ehkä** hän tulee 'Maybe he'll come'
PREDA	**Predicative adjunct**	Enoni kuoli rikkaana **miehenä** 'My uncle died as a rich man'
PREATR	**Pre-attribute**	**iso** poika 'a big boy'
POSTATR	**Post-attribute**	Lintu **katolla** oli varis 'The bird on the roof was a crow'
APP	**Apposition**	Kalle, paras **ystäväni** ... 'Kalle, my best friend ...'
INT	**Intensifier**	Hän on **sangen** älykäs 'He is very clever'
SPEC	**Specifier**	Osaan **vain** saksaa 'I only know German'
COMA	**Comparison adjunct**	Hän on komea **kuin** prinssi 'He is handsome like a prince'

3.2. Principles used in establishing the dependent types

(1) The verb as a governor of a dependent type (e.g., the direct object) can be either a finite verb (or a negation verb) as the structural center of the sentence or one of the numerous non-finite verb forms, which themselves are already dependents, e.g.,

> Tyttö *joi* **maitoa** (partit. as dir. obj. of finite verb) 'The girl was drinking milk'
> Hän hymyili *juodessaan* **maitoa** 'She smiled while drinking milk'
> (partit. as dir. obj. of 2nd inf. iness. as adverbial clause equiv.)
> Näin **maitoa** *juovan* tytön 'I saw the milk-drinking girl'
> (partit. as dir. obj. of pres. participle as adj. attr.)

(2) The traditionally attributive dependents of a verbal noun are considered as dependents of a verb (cf. 2.2., 2)), e.g.,

> **isän** *meneminen* **kaupunkiin** 'father's going to town'
> subject adverbial complement

(3) The main formal characteristic of the complements **subject, direct object** and the **predicative complement** is a semantically based case alternation: between the nominative (subject and predicative complement) or genitive/nominative as "accusative" (direct object) on the one hand and the partitive on the other hand.

The basic meaning of the former cases is to express a concrete or abstract whole or a definite quantity while "the partitive often expresses an indefinite, non-limited quantity of something, allowing the possibility that more of it may exist" (Karlsson 1978: 72), e.g.,

> *Maito* on pullossa (nominative as a definite subject) 'The milk is in the bottle'
> Pullossa on *maitoa* (partit. as an indef. subj.) 'There is milk in the bottle'.

In some cases, e.g., in infinitival and participial sentence equivalents, the subject is in genitive (cf. samples 5-6). As predicative complements, which as dependents of the verb normally also agree in number with the subject or object, I consider, besides the traditional nominative and partitive, also some other cases (e.g., translative, essive, ablative; cf. samples 53-55). The legitimacy of the **predicative adjunct** as a dependent type of its own is based on the fact that its cases, essive and translative, also agree in number with the subject or object, e.g.,

> *Hän* palasi takaisin rikkaana *miehenä* (subj. and essive both in sg.) 'He came back as a rich man'
> *He* tulivat takaisin rikkaina *miehinä* (subj. and essive both in pl.) 'They came back as rich men'

(4) The **case complements** (or **case objects**), normally corresponding to prepositional objects of English, German etc., are complements whose noun form (mostly a local case) is determined by its governor and whose pro-form (Germ. *Anapher*) is a pronoun, e.g.,

> Isä *uskoo* **Jumalaan** (ill.) – Isän *usko* **Jumalaan**
> **Häneen** **Häneen**
> 'Father believes in God' – 'Father's belief in God'
> in Him in Him
> (Both the finite verb *uskoo* and the verbal noun *usko* have the illative of the noun *Jumala* as their case complement (object) and the pronominal illative *Häneen* as its pro-form.)
> Olen *tietoinen* **asiasta** 'I'm aware of the matter'
> **siitä** of it
> (the complement of the adjective *tietoinen* is in the elative case)

The **prepositional complement (object)**, formed in Finnish with a postposition, corresponds to the prepositional object of German etc., but is very rare (cf. sample 36).

(5) **Adverbial complements** and **adjuncts** do not consist only of adverbs as in many DLT-grammars, but also of noun phrases, clauses, clause equivalents etc., in a paradigm with an adverb as its member:

Viime tiistaina tapasin hänet	'Last Tuesday I met her'
Kun tulin kotiin tapasin hänet	'When I came home I met her'
Tullessani kotiin tapasin hänet	'When coming home I met her'
Eilen tapasin hänet	'Yesterday I met her'
Silloin tapasin hänet	'Then I met her'

(6) **Verbative complements** are various non-finite verb forms (infinitives, participles,

verbal stems) as dependents which are not members of a paradigm (as e.g., in traditional compound verb forms and modal constructions; cf. samples 67-77). If a non-finite form is e.g., a member of an object paradigm, it is not a verbative complement but an object, e.g.,

> Minä näin **pojan** 'I saw the boy'
> Minä näin pojan **tulevan** 'I saw the boy coming'
> (the present participle *tulevan* is the internal governor of the direct object *pojan tulevan*; cf. also the inessive of the 2nd inf. *tullessani* above)

(7) The **propositional complement** differs from other verbal complements by being a finite clause or a participle clause equivalent, but not having other members in its paradigm, e.g.,

> Minä luulen, **että hän puhui asiasta** (clause)
> Minä luulen **hänen puhuneen asiasta** (clause equiv.) 'I think he spoke about the matter'

In sentences like *Minä tiedän,* **että hän on puhunut/hänen puhuneen** the finite clause and the participial clause equivalent are members of the paradigm of a direct object (cf. *Minä tiedän* **hänen nimensä/sen** 'I know his name/it').

(8) **Arguments** are complements of the following purely grammatical function words: comparison particle (**comparison argument**; cf. 2.12.), pre- and postpositions (**prepositional argument**; cf. 2.9.) and subjunctions (**subjunctional argument**; cf. 2.13.). Dependents like the **comparison complement** and **comparison adjunct**, on the other hand, are normally complements and adjuncts with a comparison particle as their internal governor followed by a comparison argument (cf. samples 155, 158).

(9) As for the **pre-attributes**, a characteristic construction in Finnish consists of an appellative noun undeclined in the nominative before a proper noun (cf. samples 126-127). **Post-attributes** (cf. samples 135, 137-138) are rare in written Finnish. An **apposition** is normally an appellative noun (or an adjective) following a proper noun (with a comma) or a proper noun following an appellative (without comma), both in case concord with their headword (cf. samples 139-140).

(10) **Intensifiers** and **specifiers** are adjuncts based on gradation particles and specification particles as word classes of their own, different from adverbs.

3.3. Tables of the dependent types with sample sentences

The tables below with sample sentences have been given for the following word classes as governors: verb, noun, adjective, pronoun, numeral and adverb. The tables are accompanied by sample sentences each of which illustrates a single dependency relation. The governing word of this relation is shown in *italics*, the dependent in **bold face**.

The other word classes are dealt with briefly here.

(1) **Conjunctions** as internal governors can occur in most dependent types, e.g.,

> Ostimme **kirjan** *ja* **äänilevyn** (dir. obj.) 'We bought a book and a record'
> Kieltäydyimme **syömästä** *ja* **juomasta** 'We refused to eat or drink'
> (3rd inf. elat. as case compl.)

The dependent types with a conjunction are given in the last table, where all combinations of word classes and dependent types are given (combination table).

(2) The **comparison particle** and the **preposition** govern only one dependent type each, but this consists of various word classes (given in the combination table).

(a) The **comparison argument**, which can also be regarded as an elliptic clause, can consist of most word classes (cf. the combination table), e.g.,

> Tänään hän oli iloisempi *kuin* **eilen** (adverb) / **minä** (pron. in nom.)
> 'Today he was more cheerful than yesterday / I'
> (Cf.: Tänään hän oli iloisempi *kuin* hän oli eilen
> 'Today he was more cheerful than he was yesterday')

(b) The **prepositional argument** consists of nouns in various cases (cf. 2.9.), pronouns, numerals, adverbs and subjunctions (cf. the combination table), e.g.,

> Kello oli neljännestä *vaille* **seitsemän** (numeral in nom.) 'It was a quarter to seven'
> **Sinne** *asti* (adverb) 'as far as there'

(3) The **subjunction** governs various types of clauses (sentences) with a finite verb as the internal governor, e.g.,

> Tiedän, *että* hän **tulee** tänään 'I know he'll come today'

(4) The **determiner** can govern a specification particle only, e.g.,

> Minä tunnen **vain** *tämän* pojan 'I know only this boy'

(5) The word class **gradation particle**, which is identical to the dependent type **intensifier**, can't normally govern anything (cf. however *yhtä* in 2.12.). If it is in comparative or superlative, it can, however, have another intensifier (gradation particle) as its dependent, e.g.,

> Hän ei ole **kovin** *paljon* isompi kuin minä 'He is not very much taller than I'

(6) The **specifiation particle**, which can depend on any word class or dependent type (cf. 2.11.), can't have any dependents of its own. That is true of the **modal particles** (e.g., *ehkä* 'perhaps', cf. 2.8.), too.

3.3.1. The dependent types governed by the verb

	Verb	Noun	Adj	Pron	Det	Num	Adv	Mod	Prep	Grad	Spec	Comp	Sub	Conj
SUBJ	×	×		×		×							×	×
DOBJ	×	×		×		×							×	×
CASC	×	×		×		×								×
PREPC									×					
ADVC	×	×		×		×	×		×			×		×
PREDC	×	×	×	×		×	×					×		×
VERBC	×													×
PROPC	×												×	×
COMC														
COMARG														
PARG														
SUBARG														
ADVA	×	×		×		×	×		×			×	×	×
MODA								×						
PREDA	×	×	×											×
PREATR														
POSTATR														
APP														
INT														
SPEC											×			×
COMA														

SUBJ/Verb

- FINITE VERB AS THE INTERNAL GOVERNOR OF A CLAUSE

[1] *On* epävarmaa, mitä hän **tekee** – 'It is uncertain what he'll do'

- 1ST INFINITIVE (SHORT FORM)

[2] *On* aika vaikea **oppia** suomea – 'It is quite difficult to learn Finnish'

SUBJ/Noun

- NOMINATIVE VS. PARTITIVE

[3] **Maito** *on* pullossa (nom.) – 'The milk is in the bottle'

[4] Pullossa *on* **maitoa** (partit.) – 'There is (some) milk in the bottle'

- GENITIVE

[5] **Isän** *täytyy* lähteä – 'Father must leave'

[6] **Talven** *tullessa* ... – 'When winter comes ...'

SUBJ/Pronoun (the case forms as in the noun; also poss. suff.), e.g.,

[7] **He** (nom.) *leikkivät* ulkona – 'They are playing outdoors'

[8] *Tullessa*/**ni** (poss. suff. 'my') kotiin näin hänet – 'When I came home I saw him'

SUBJ/Numeral (the case forms as in the noun)

[9] **Kolme** (nom.) *on* enemmän kuin kaksi – 'Three is more than two'

SUBJ/Subjunction (as the internal governor of a clause)

[10] Minua *ilahdutti*, **että** sinä tulit – 'I was glad that you came'

DOBJ/Verb

- FINITE VERB AS THE INTERNAL GOVERNOR OF A CLAUSE

[11] *Tiedätkö*, **tuleeko** hän? – 'Do you know if he comes?'

- PRESENT AND PAST PARTICIPLE AS THE INTERNAL GOVERNOR OF A CLAUSE EQUIVALENT

[12] Minä *näin* hänen **tulevan** (present) – 'I saw him come'

[13] *Tiedän* hänen **tulleen** (past) – 'I know that he has come'

- 1ST INFINITIVE (SHORT FORM)

[14] Lapsi *pelkää* **mennä** kotiin – 'The child is afraid of going home'

DOBJ/Noun

- GENITIVE OR NOMINATIVE (AS "ACCUSATIVE") VS. PARTITIVE

[15] *Söin* **leivän** (gen. as. "acc.") – 'I ate the bread'

[16] *Syö* **leipä**! (nom. as. "acc.") – 'Eat the bread!'

[17] *Söin* **leipää** (partit.) – 'I was eating bread'

- PARTITIVE

[18] *Ajattelen* **tyttöä** – 'I think of the girl'

DOBJ/Pronoun

- GENITIVE OR NOMINATIVE (AS "ACCUSATIVE") VS. PARTITIVE (AS IN THE NOUN), E.G.,

[19] *Söin* **sen** (gen. as "acc.") – 'I ate it'

[20] *Söin* **sitä** (partit.) – 'I was eating it'

- PARTITIVE (AS IN THE NOUN)

[21] *Rakastan* **häntä** – 'I love her'

- ACCUSATIVE

[22] *Tunnen* **hänet** – 'I know her'

DOBJ/Numeral

- NOMINATIVE (AS "ACCUSATIVE") VS. PARTITIVE

[23] *Tunnen* **kaksi** (nom.) heistä – 'I know two of them'

- PARTITIVE

[24] *Rakastan* **kahta** heistä – 'I love two of them'

DOBJ/Subjunction (as the internal governor of a clause)

[25] *Tiedän*, **että** hän tuli – 'I know that he came'

CASC/Verb

- 3RD INF. ELATIVE

[26] *Kieltäydyin* **tulemasta** – 'I refused to come'

- 3RD INF. ILLATIVE

[27] *Pystytkö* **ajamaan** Helsinkiin? – 'Can you drive to Helsinki?'

CASC/Noun

- ELATIVE

[28] Pentti *kertoi* **matkastaan** – 'Pentti told about his trip'

- ILLATIVE

[29] *Uskon* **tulevaisuuteen** – 'I believe in the future'

- ABLATIVE

[30] *Kysy* **häneltä** missä posti on – 'Ask him where the post office is'

- ALLATIVE

[31] *Puhun* **sinulle** – 'I talk to you'

[32] *Näytän* **sinulle** tien – 'I'll show you the way'

- ADESSIVE

[33] **Paavolla** *on* uusi pyörä – 'Paavo has a new bicycle' ("at Paavo is ...")

CASC/Pronoun (the case form as in the noun), e.g.,

[34] Mitä *luulet* **tästä**? (elative) – 'What do you think of this?'

CASC/Numeral (the case form as in the noun), e.g.,

[35] *Rakastuin* **yhteen** näistä tytöistä (illative) – 'I fell in love with one of these girls'

PREPC/Postposition

[36] Minä *puhuin* miehen **kanssa** – 'I spoke with the man'

ADVC/Verb

- 3RD INFINITIVE IN INESSIVE, ELATIVE, ILLATIVE

[37] Kalle *on* **kalastamassa** (inessive) – 'Kalle is fishing'

[38] Kalle *tuli* **kalastamasta** (elative) – 'Kalle came from fishing'
[39] Kalle *meni* **kalastamaan** – 'Kalle went fishing'
- PAST PARTICIPLE PASSIVE IN ESSIVE AND TRANSLATIVE
[40] Auto *on* **korjattavana** – 'The car is being repaired'
[41] Auto *vietiin* **korjattavaksi** – 'The car was taken to be repaired'

ADVC/Noun
- LOCAL CASE, E.G.,
[42] Hän *asuu* **Lontoossa** (inessive) / **rannikolla** (adessive) – 'He lives in London / on the coast'
- GENITIVE OR NOMINATIVE (AS "ACC.") VS. PARTITIVE
[43] Kokous *kesti* **tunnin** (Gen.) / useita **tunteja** (partitive) – 'The meeting lasted for an hour / for several hours'

ADVC/Pronoun in local case
[44] **Muutamissa** näistä taloista *asutaan* – 'In some of these houses people still live'

ADVC/Numeral
[45] Kokous *kesti* **kymmeneen** (illative) – 'The meeting lasted till ten o'clock'

ADVC/Adverb
[46] Hän *asuu* **siellä** – 'He lives there'

ADVC/Pre- or postposition
[47] Hän *asuu* vanhempiensa **luona** – 'He lives with his parents'

ADVC/Comparison particle
[48] Hän *käyttäytyy* **kuin** hupsu – 'He behaves like a fool'

PREDC/Verb
- FINITE VERB AS THE INTERNAL GOVERNOR OF A CLAUSE
[49] Hän *on* millainen hänen **tuleekin** olla – 'He is as he should be'
- PRESENT PARTICIPLE PASSIVE IN INESSIVE PLURAL
[50] Hän *ei ole* **tavoitettavissa** – 'He cannot be reached'

PREDC/Noun
- NOMINATIVE VS. PARTITIVE
[51] Pekka *on* **mies** (nom.) – 'Pekka is a man'
[52] Aika *on* **rahaa** (partit.) – 'Time is money'
- ESSIVE
[53] Heikki *on* Jämsässä **lääkärinä** – 'Heikki is (working) as a doctor in Jämsä'
- TRANSLATIVE
[54] Tyttö *aikoo* **insinööriksi** – 'The girl intends to become an engineer'
- ABLATIVE
[55] Mies *näyttää* **opettajalta** – 'The man looks like a teacher'
- GENITIVE
[56] Kirja on **isän** – lit. 'The book is father's'

PREDC/Adjective
- CASE FORMS AS IN THE NOUN (EXCEPT GENITIVE), E.G.,
[57] Kuppi *on* **kuuma** (nom.) – 'The cup is hot'
[58] Kahvi *on* **kuumaa** (partit.) – '(The) coffee is hot'
[59] Hän *on* **kaikkeen tottunut** (past. participle nom.) – 'He is used to everything'
[60] Isä on *tullut* **vanhaksi** (translat.) – 'Father has become old'
[61] Isä *näyttää* **sairaalta** (ablat.) – 'Father looks ill'
- NON-DECLINABLE
[62] Auto *on* **rikki** – 'The car is broken'

PREDC/Pronoun (rare; forms as in the noun), e.g.,
[63] Hän *on* **se** (nom.) – 'He is it'

PREDC/Numeral in nominative
[64] Meitä *on* **kolme** – 'We are three'

PREDC/Adverb
[65] Se *on* **ohi** – 'It is over'

PREDC/Comparison particle

[66] Hän *on* **kuin** sinä – 'He is like you'

VERBC/Verb

- 1ST INFINITIVE (SHORT FORM)

[67] Hän *taitaa* **olla** kotona – 'He may be at home'

- 1ST INFINITIVE (LONGER FORM)

[68] *Tulin* sen todella **sanoneeksi** – 'I really happened to say it'

- 3RD INFINITIVE IN INESSIVE, ILLATIVE, ADESSIVE, ABESSIVE, E.G.,

[69] *Olin* **lukemassa** (iness.) lehteä, kun ... – 'I was reading a paper, when ...'

[70] *Tulen* **lähtemään** (illat.) pois – 'I will go away'

[71] *Olin* **lähtemäisilläni** (adess.), kun ... – 'I was about to leave when ...'

- PRESENT PARTICIPLE ACTIVE IN NOMINATIVE

[72] Hän *on* sen **tekevä** – 'He will do it'

- PRESENT OR PAST PARTICIPLE ACTIVE IN GENITIVE

[73] Hän *näyttää* **tietävän** (present) / **tienneen** (past) sen – 'He seems to know / to have known it'

- PRESENT PARTICIPLE PASSIVE IN NOMINATIVE

[74] Minun *on* **lähdettävä** – 'I have to leave'

- PAST PARTICIPLE ACTIVE OR PASSIVE IN NOMINATIVE

[75] *Olen* / *olisin* **lukenut** (active) kirjan – 'I have / would have read the book'

[76] Kirja *on* / *olisi* **luettu** (passive) – 'The book has been / would have been read'

- VERBAL STEM

[77] *En* **lue** kirjaa – 'I don't read the book'

PROPC/Verb

- PRESENT OR PAST PARTICIPLE ACTIVE OR PASSIVE IN GENITIVE AS THE INTERNAL GOVERNOR OF A CLAUSE EQUIVALENT, E.G.,

[78] *Luulen* hänen **puhuneen** (past active) asiasta – 'I think he has spoken about the matter'

[79] *Luulen* asiasta **puhuttavan** (present pass.) – 'I think the matter will be spoken about'

PROPC/Subjunction (as the internal governor of a clause)

[80] *Luulen*, **että** hän puhui asiasta – 'I think that he spoke about the matter'

ADVA/Verb

- FINITE VERB AS THE INTERNAL GOVERNOR OF A CLAUSE

[81] Missä hän **onkin**, minä *rakastan* häntä – 'Wherever she is, I love her'

- 1ST INFINITIVE (LONGER FORM) AS THE INTERNAL GOVERNOR OF A CLAUSE EQUIVALENT

[82] Ihminen *syö* **elääkseen** – 'Man eats in order to live'

- 2ND INFINITIVE INESSIVE OR INSTRUCTIVE AS THE INTERNAL GOVERNOR OF A CLAUSE EQUIVALENT

[83] Pekan **herätessä** (inessive) Liisa *lähtee* töihin – 'When Pekka wakes, Liisa goes to work'

[84] Lapsi *tuli* **itkien** (instructive) kotiin – 'The child came home crying'

- 3RD INF. INESSIVE, ELATIVE, ILLATIVE, ADESSIVE, ABLATIVE, ABESSIVE AS THE INTERNAL GOVERNOR OF A CLAUSE EQUIVALENT

[85] Ville *on* kirjastossa **lukemassa** (inessive) lehtiä – 'Ville is in the library reading papers'

[86] Tuula *tuli* rannalta **uimasta** (elative) – 'Tuula came from the beach, where she had been swimming'

[87] *Menen* ulos **syömään** (illative) – 'I'll go out to eat'

[88] Hän *elää* **kirjoittamalla** (adessive) kirjoja – 'He lives by writing books'

[89] Kalle *teki* sen meidän **tietämättämme** (abessive) – 'Kalle did it without our knowing'

- PRESENT PARTICIPLE PASSIVE IN ESSIVE OR TRANSLATIVE AS THE INTERNAL GOVERNOR OF A CLAUSE EQUIVALENT

[90] Matti *on* sairaalassa **tutkittavana** (essive) – 'Matti is in the hospital for examination'

[91] Matti *vietiin* sairaalaan **tutkittavaksi** (translative) – 'Matti was taken into a hospital for examination'

- PAST PARTICIPLE PASSIVE IN PARTITIVE AS THE INTERNAL GOVERNOR OF A CLAUSE EQUIVALENT

[92] Kallen **tultua** Pekka *lähti* – 'When Kalle had come Pekka left'

ADVA/Noun

- LOCAL CASE

[93] Näin hänet **kaupungissa** (inessive) / **kadulla** (adessive) – 'I saw her in the town / in ("on") the street'

- GENITIVE OR NOMINATIVE (AS "ACCUSATIVE") VS. PARTITIVE

[94] Hän *työskenteli* **tunnin** (gen.) / useita **tunteja** (partit.) – 'He worked for one hour / several hours'

- NOMINATIVE

[95] Hän *työskenteli* joka **päivä** – 'He worked every day'

- ESSIVE

[96] Isä *tulee* **maanantaina** – 'Father will come on Monday'

- TRANSLATIVE

[97] *Tulen* kotiin **jouluksi** – 'I'll come home for Christmas'

ADVA/Pronoun in the local case

[98] *Tapasin* hänet **jossakin** noista taloista – 'I met him in one of those houses'

ADVA/Numeral

- ABLATIVE

[99] Hän *tulee* **kymmeneltä** – 'He'll come at ten o'clock'

- ILLATIVE

[100] Minä *viivyn* siellä **kymmeneen** – 'I'll be there till ten o'clock'

- TRANSLATIVE

[101] **Kolmeksi** minun täytyy *ehtiä* kotiin – 'I must be home by three o'clock'

ADVA/Adverb

[102] *Näin* hänet **siellä** / **eilen** – 'I saw him there / yesterday'

ADVA/Pre-/Postposition

[103] Hän *asui* täällä **ennen** sotaa / sodan **jälkeen** – 'He lived here before the war / after the war'

ADVA/Comparison particle

[104] Hän *työskentelee* **kuin** sinä – 'He works like you'

ADVA/Subjunction (as the internal governor of a clause)

[105] *Näin* sinut, **kun** tulit kotiin – 'I saw you, when you came home'

MODA/Modal particle

[106] **Ehkä** hän *tulee* tänään – 'Maybe he'll come today'

PREDA/Verb

- 3RD INFINITIVE IN ELATIVE OR INESSIVE

[107] *Löysin* ystäväni **nukkumasta** (elat.) – 'I found my friend sleeping'

PREDA/Noun

- ESSIVE

[108] Hän *palasi* takaisin rikkaana **miehenä** – 'He came back (as) a rich man'

- TRANSLATIVE

[109] Vaimoni *antoi* minulle kirjan **lahjaksi** – 'My wife gave me book as a present'

PREDA/Adjective

- ESSIVE

[110] Hän *palasi* takaisin **rikkaana** – 'He came back rich'

- UNDECLINED

[111] Mies *tuli* takaisin **juovuksissa** – 'The man came back drunk'

SPEC/Specification particle

[112] Hän **vain** *syö* – 'He only eats'

3.3.2. The dependent types governed by the noun

	Verb	Noun	Adj	Pron	Det	Num	Adv	Mod	Prep	Grad	Spec	Comp	Sub	Conj
SUBJ		×		×		×								×
DOBJ		×		×		×								×
CASC	×	×		×		×								×
PREPC									×					
ADVC	×	×		×		×	×		×					×
PREDC		×	×	×										×
VERBC	×													×
PROPC													×	×
COMC														
COMARG														
PARG														
SUBARG														
ADVA	×	×		×		×	×		×				×	×
MODA														
PREDA		×	×											×
PREATR		×	×	×	×	×								×
POSTATR	×	×		×			×		×					×
APP		×	×											×
INT														
SPEC											×			×
COMA														

SUBJ/Noun in genitive

[113] Olen iloinen **isän** *tulosta* – 'I am glad of father's arrival

SUBJ/Pronoun in genitive / possessive suffix

[114] Olen iloinen (**sinun**) *tulosta*/**si** – 'I am glad of your arrival'

SUBJ/Numeral in genitive

[115] Iloitsen niiden **kolmen** *tulosta* – 'I am glad of the arrival of the three'

DOBJ/Noun/Pronoun/Numeral in the same forms as in the subject, e.g.,

[116] **Ystävän** (noun in gen.) *rakastaminen* on helppoa – 'Loving a friend is easy'

[117] Kiitän sinua *auttamisesta*/**ni** (poss. suff.) – 'I thank you for helping me'

CASC/Verb/Noun/Pronoun/Numeral in the same forms as with a verb, e.g.,

[118] *Uskoni* **tulevaisuuteen** ... (noun in illative) – 'My belief in the future'

PREPC/Postposition (as with the verb), e.g.,

[119] *Keskusteluni* naapurin **kanssa** – 'My discussion with the neighbor'

ADVC/Verb/Noun/Pronoun/Numeral/Adverb/Preposition (mainly in the same form as with a verb), e.g.,

[120] *Asuminen* **kaupungissa** (noun in iness.) / **siellä** (adv.) on kallista – 'Living in town / there is expensive'

PREDC/Noun/Adjective/Pronoun in translative or essive (as with the verb), e.g.,

[121] Jussin *nimittäminen* **puheenjohtajaksi** ... (noun. in transl.) – 'Appointing Jussi as the chairman ...'

VERBC/Verb (1st infinitive, short form)

[122] Hänen *aikomuksensa* **auttaa** minua ... – 'His intention to help me ...'

PROPC/Subjunction as the internal governor of a clause

[123] Miehen *väite*, **että** hän oli ratkaissut ongelman – 'The man's claim that he had solved the problem'

ADVA/Verb/Noun/Pronoun/Numeral/Adverb/Preposition/Subjunction (in nearly the same forms as with a verb), e.g.,

[124] Hänen *saapumisensa* **maanantaina** (noun. in ess.) / **eilen** (adverb) / **kymmeneltä** (num. in ablat.) – 'His arrival on Monday/yesterday/at ten o'clock'

PREDA/Noun/Adjective in the same form as with a verb, e.g.,

[125] Hänen *paluunsa* **humalaisena** / **humalassa** oli yllätys – 'His coming back drunk was a surprise'

PREATR/Noun

- NOMINATIVE

[126] **Maalari** *Syvänen* 'The painter Syvänen'

[127] Annoin kirjan **maalari** *Syväselle* – 'I gave a book to the painter Syvänen'

- GENITIVE

[128] **Opettajan** *auto* – 'The teacher's car'

PREATR/Adjective (in case concord with the noun), e.g.,

[129] Hänellä on **iso** *talo* – 'He has a big house'

PREATR/Pronoun in genitive

[130] **Jokaisen** *ystävä* ei ole **kenenkään** *ystävä* – 'Everybody's friend is nobody's friend'

PREATR/Determiner

[131] Annoin kirjan **tuolle** *pojalle* – 'I gave the book to that boy'

PREATR/Numeral

[132] Minulla on **kaksi** *autoa* 'I have two cars'

[133] Hän kertoi **kolmesta** *miehestä* – 'He told about three men'

POSTATR/Verb (as the internal governor of a clause)

[134] *Mies*, joka **seisoo** tuolla, on isäni – 'The man who is standing there is my father'

POSTATR/Noun in local case

[135] Tuo *lintu* **katolla** (adess.) on varis – 'That bird on the roof is a crow'

POSTATR/Pronoun (as possessive suffix)

[136] Olen *ystävä*/**si** – 'I am your friend'

POSTATR/Adverb

[137] *Tilanne* **siellä** on vaikea – 'The situation there is difficult'

POSTATR/Preposition

[138] *Talo* meidän taloamme **vastapäätä** ... – 'The house opposite to ours ...'

APP/Noun (in case concord with the noun)

[139] Annoin kirjan *Matille*, parhaalle **ystävälleni** (allat.) – 'I gave the book to Matti, my best friend'

[140] Minä annoin sen *sedälleni* **Otolle** – 'I gave it to my uncle Otto'

APP/Adjective (in case concord with the noun)

[141] *Veljeni*, neljä vuotta **nuorempi** kuin minä, ... – 'My brother, four years younger than I, ...'

SPEC/Specification particle

[142] **Vain** *parlamentti* voi säätää lakeja – 'Only the parliament can give laws'

3.3.3. The dependent types governed by the adjective

	Verb	Noun	Adj	Pron	Det	Num	Adv	Mod	Prep	Grad	Spec	Comp	Sub	Conj
SUBJ														
DOBJ														
CASC	×	×		×		×							×	×
PREPC									×					
ADVC		×					×							×
PREDC														
VERBC														
PROPC														
COMC		×		×								×		
COMARG														
PARG														
SUBARG														
ADVA														
MODA														
PREDA														
PREATR														
POSTATR														
APP														
INT										×				
SPEC											×			
COMA												×		

CASC/Verb (3rd infinitive in illative)

[143] Hän on aina *valmis* **auttamaan** – 'He's always ready to help'

CASC/Noun

- GENITIVE

[144] Hän on **isän** *kaltainen* – 'He is like father'

- LOCAL CASE (ELATIVE, ILLATIVE, INESSIVE, ALLATIVE), E.G.,

[145] Hän pysyi *uskollisena* **ystävälleen** (allative) – 'He remained faithful to his friend'

CASC/Pronoun (in the same forms as the noun), e.g.,

[146] Olen *tietoinen* **siitä** (elat.) – 'I am aware if it'

CASC/Numeral (in the same forms as the noun), e.g.,

[147] Olen *tyytyväinen* **kolmeen** heistä – 'I am satisfied of three of them'

CASC/Subjunction (as the internal governor of a clause)

[148] Olen *iloinen*, **että** tulit – 'I am glad that you came'

PREPC/Preposition

[149] Olen tuttu *miehen* **kanssa** – 'I am acquainted with the man'

ADVC/Noun in elative or ablative

[150] Hän on *kotoisin* **Kuopiosta** (elat.) / **Tampereelta** (abl.) – 'He is from Kuopio/Tampere'

ADVC/Adverb

[151] Hän on *kotoisin* **sieltä** – 'He is from there'

COMC/Noun in partitive or elative

[152] Poika on *isompi* **isää** (partit. after adj. in comp.) – 'The son is taller than father'

[153] Hän on *paras* **pojista** (elat. after adj. in superl.) – 'He is the best of the boys'

COMC/Pronoun in partitive and elative (like the noun), e.g.,
[154] Hän on *isompi* **minua** (partit.) – 'He is taller than I'
COMC/Comparison particle
[155] Poika on *isompi* **kuin** isä – 'The son is taller than father'
INT/Gradation particle
[156] Hän on *sangen* **älykäs** – 'He is very clever'
SPEC/Specification particle
[157] Hän on **myös** *älykäs* / *älykäs*/**kin** – 'He is also clever / clever, too'
COMA/Comparison particle
[158] Hän on *komea* **kuin** prinssi – 'He is handsome like a prince'

3.3.4. The dependent types governed by the pronoun

	Verb	Noun	Adj	Pron	Det	Num	Adv	Mod	Prep	Grad	Spec	Comp	Sub	Conj
SUBJ														
DOBJ														
CASC		×		×										×
PREPC														
ADVC														
PREDC														
VERBC														
PROPC														
COMC														
COMARG														
PARG														
SUBARG														
ADVA														
MODA														
PREDA														
PREATR														
POSTATR	×	×		×			×						×	×
APP		×	×	×										×
INT														
SPEC											×			×
COMA														

CASC/Noun/Pronoun in elative
[159] Tunnen *muutamia* **ystävistäsi** / **heistä** – 'I know some of your friends / of them'
POSTATR/Verb (finite verb as the internal governor of a clause)
[160] Minä autan *niitä*, jotka **auttavat** minua – 'I help those who help me'
POSTATR/Noun in local case, e.g.,
[161] Tunnetko *ketään* **Hankasalmelta**? (abl.) – 'Do you know anybody in Hankasalmi?'
POSTATR/Adverb
[162] Tunnetko *nuo* **tuolla**? – 'Do you know those over there?'
POSTATR/Subjunction (as the internal governor of a clause)
[163] Hän kieltää *sen*, **että** hän tuntisi miehen – 'He denies that he knows the man'

APP/Noun/Adjective/Pronoun (in case concord with the headword), e.g.,

[164] Minä tarkoitan *häntä*, parasta **ystävääni** *häntä* **itseään** – 'I mean him, my best friend (lit.:) him himself'

[165] *Te* **tanskalaiset** olette ystävällisiä *meille* **suomalaisille** – 'You Danes are friendly to us Finns'

SPEC/Specification particle

[166] Minä tunnen **myös** *hänet* / *hänet*/**kin** – 'I know also him / him, too'

3.3.5. The dependent types governed by the numeral

	Verb	Noun	Adj	Pron	Det	Num	Adv	Mod	Prep	Grad	Spec	Comp	Sub	Conj
SUBJ														
DOBJ														
CASC		×		×		×								
PREPC														
ADVC														
PREDC														
VERBC														
PROPC														
COMC														
COMARG														
PARG														
SUBARG														
ADVA														
MODA														
PREDA														
PREATR					×									
POSTATR														
APP														
INT														
SPEC											×			
COMA														

CASC/Noun/Pronoun/Numeral in elative

[167] Tunnen *kaksi* **miehistä** / **heistä** / **kolmesta** – 'I know two of the men / of them / of the three'

PREATR/Determiner

[168] **Nämä** *kaksi* miestä – 'These two men'

SPEC/Specification particle

[169] **Vain** *kaksi* (miestä) tiesi sen – 'Only two (men) knew it'

3.3.6. The dependent types governed by the adverb

	Verb	Noun	Adj	Pron	Det	Num	Adv	Mod	Prep	Grad	Spec	Comp	Sub	Conj
SUBJ														
DOBJ														
CASC														
PREPC														
ADVC														
PREDC														
VERBC														
PROPC														
COMC		×		×		×						×		×
COMARG														
PARG														
SUBARG														
ADVA														
MODA														
PREDA														
PREATR														
POSTATR	×	×					×		×				×	×
APP														
INT										×				
SPEC											×			
COMA												×		

COMC/Noun/Pronoun/Numeral in partitive
[170] Hän laulaa **äitiään/minua/**noita **kahta** *paremmin* – 'She sings better than her mother / than I / than those two'
COMC/Comparison particle
[171] Hän laulaa *paremmin* **kuin** äitinsä/minä ... – 'She sings better than her mother / I ...'
POSTATR/Verb (as the internal governor of a clause)
[172] *Tässä*, missä me nyt **seisomme**, ... – 'Here where we are now standing ...'
POSTATR/Noun in a locative case, e.g.,
[173] *Täällä* **Suomessa** (iness.) – 'Here in Finland'
POSTATR/Adverb
[174] Hän on *tuolla* **keskellä** – 'He is there in the middle'
POSTATR/Preposition
[175] *Tuolla* talon **takana** – 'There behind the house'
POSTATR/Subjunction (as the internal governor of a clause)
[176] Näin hänet *silloin*, **kun** hän kävi täällä – 'I saw him ("then") when he was here'
INT/Gradation particle
[177] Hän puhuu englantia **oikein** *hyvin* – 'He speaks English very well'
SPEC/Specification particle
[178] **Vain** *silloin* minä näin hänet – 'Only then I saw him'
COMA/Comparison particle
[179] Hän puhui *kauniisti* **kuin** piispa – 'He spoke beautifully like a bishop'

3.3.7. The dependent types governed by the conjunction

(at the same time a **combination table**)

	Verb	Noun	Adj	Pron	Det	Num	Adv	Mod	Prep	Grad	Spec	Comp	Sub	Conj
SUBJ	×	×		×		×								×
DOBJ	×	×		×		×								×
CASC	×	×		×		×								×
PREPC									×					
ADVC	×	×		×		×	×		×			×		×
PREDC	×	×	×	×		×	×					×		×
VERBC	×													×
PROPC	×												×	×
COMC		×										×		×
COMARG	×	×	×	×		×	×		×				×	×
PARG		×		×		×	×						×	×
SUBARG	×													×
ADVA	×	×		×		×	×		×			×	×	×
MODA								×						
PREDA	×	×	×											×
PREATR		×	×	×	×	×								×
POSTATR	×	×		×			×		×				×	×
APP		×	×											×
INT										×				
SPEC											×			×
COMA												×		

4. Sample sentence

The following is a sample sentence with a labelled dependency tree.

Lahden kirjailijakokouksen teemat valitaan yleensä varsin väljästi, koska kirjalijat kuitenkin puhuvat siitä mistä he itse haluavat puhua.

'The-Lahti writer-convention's themes are-chosen usually rather loosely, because the-writers however speak about that about which they themselves want to-speak'

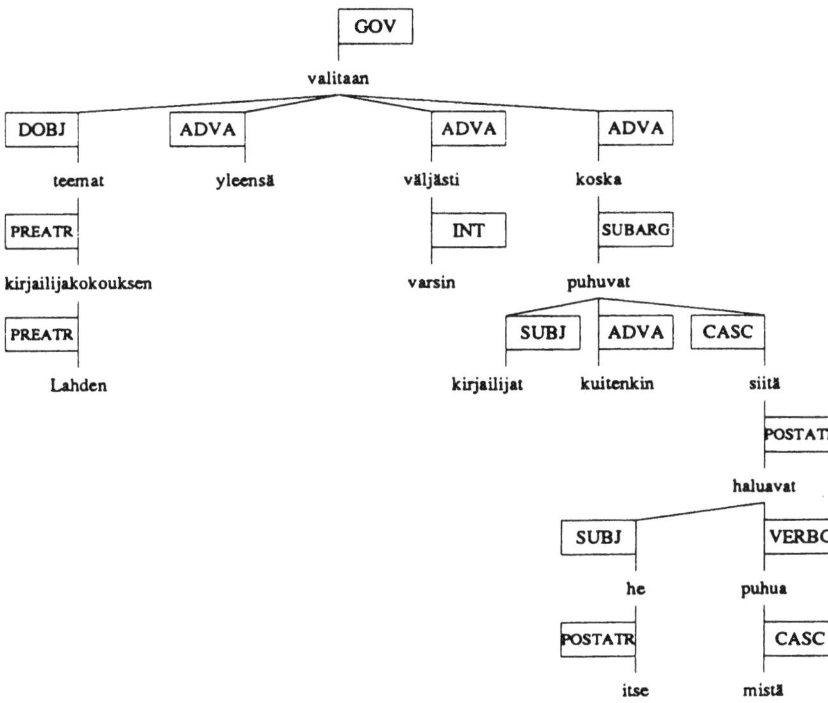

References

Engel, Ulrich (1988): *Deutsche Grammatik.*
Heidelberg: Groos

Fromm, Hans (1982): *Finnische Grammatik.*
Heidelberg: Winter

Hakulinen, Auli / Fred Karlsson (1979): *Nykysuomen lauseoppia.*
Jyväskylä: Gummerus

Holman, Eugene (1984): *Handbook of Finnish verbs.*
Vaasa: SKS

Ikola, Niilo (1968): Suomen kielioppi ja oikeakielisyysopas.
In: *Suomen kielen käsikirja.* Ed. Niilo Ikola. Helsinki: WSOY, pp. 103-315

Isaac, Luc (1986): Syntaxe dependantielle du français.
Unpublished report. Utrecht: BSO/Research

Karlsson, Fred (1983): *Finnish grammar.*
Juva: WSOY

Korst, Bieke van der (1986): A dependency syntax for English.
Unpublished report. Utrecht: BSO/Research

Penttilä, Aarni (1963): *Suomen kielioppi.*
Porvoo/Helsinki: WSOY

Prószéky, Gábor / Ilona Koutny / Balázs Wacha (1987): A dependency syntax of Hungarian (for use in DLT).
Unpublished report. Utrecht: BSO/Research

Schubert, Ingrid (1987): Dänische Dependenzsyntax für DLT.
Unpublished report. Utrecht: BSO/Research

Schubert, Klaus (1986): *Syntactic tree structures in DLT.*
Utrecht: BSO/Research

Schubert, Klaus (1987): *Metataxis. Contrastive dependency syntax for machine translation.*
Dordrecht/Providence: Foris

Tarvainen, Kalevi (1985): *Kielioppia kontrastiivisesti. Suomesta saksaksi.*
= Jyväskylän yliopisto, Saksan kielen laitoksen toimituksia // Universität Jyväskylä, Veröffentlichungen des Germanistischen Instituts 4
Jyväskylä

Tarvainen, Kalevi (1985): *Kontrastive Syntax Deutsch-Finnisch.*
= Deutsch im Kontrast 4.
Heidelberg: Groos

Tarvainen, Kalevi (1987): Formale Dependenzgrammatik des Finnischen.
Unpublished report. Utrecht: BSO/Research

Tarvainen, Kalevi (1988): Braucht die Valenzgrammatik Objekte und Adverbiale?
In: *Valenzen im Kontrast. Ulrich Engel zum 60. Geburtstag.* Ed. Pavica Mrazović / Wolfgang Teubert. Heidelberg: Groos, pp. 380-397

A dependency syntax of Hungarian

Gábor Prószéky
Ilona Koutny
Balázs Wacha

Budapest, Hungary

1. Introduction

1.1. Main characteristics of the Hungarian language

Hungarian belongs to the **Finno-Ugric language family**, whose other well-known representative is Finnish. The relation is obvious at the grammatical level, but very distant for vocabulary. Typologically it is generally considered to be an **agglutinative** language (like Finnish or Japanese). This means that grammatical roles like object or locative are often expressed by suffixes in Hungarian sentences. Consequently, word forms are morpheme-sequences consisting of a stem and several grammatical morphemes with additional syntactic information such as person, possession, and so on. The **vowel harmony** (as in Turkish) determines the necessary form of the suffix (e.g. *ház***ban** '**in** the house', but *kert***ben** '**in** the garden').

The rich morphological structure of the language enables a relatively **free word order**, but it is influenced significantly by the topic-comment structure in question. The neutral form is SOV, e.g.

A fiú levelet ír. – 'The boy is writing a letter.'
the boy letter-ACC writes

or SVO, e.g.

> A fiú írja a levelet. – 'The boy is writing **the** letter.'
> the boy writes the letter-ACC

but other orders are also possible (the focus falls on whichever unit directly precedes the verb):

> **Levelet** ír a fiú.
> **A fiú** ír levelet.
> **Ír** levelet a fiú.
> Levelet **a fiú** ír.
> **Ír** a fiú levelet.

Languages such as English, German or French have already several grammatical descriptions on the basis first of all of constituency, but also of dependency. Attempts have already been made to apply some form of constituency theory to describe different structures in Hungarian, but there is no fully elaborated dependency description up to now.

1.2. A morpheme based grammar

It is necessary to point out that Hungarian cannot always be analysed in the same way as the Indo-European Languages. Both constituency and dependency grammars handle words as basic units. To construct a grammar for agglutinative languages such as Hungarian, it would be better to define the basic unit as **an element of the output of a morphological analyser**. This will form the minimal syntactic unit in our study. Concerning its internal structure it can be a word in the usual sense or a morpheme block, but must consist of at least one morpheme.

Each Hungarian noun, for example, can occur in nearly 1000 word forms as a stem, because the majority of the Indo-European prepositions and possessive determiners are expressed by suffixes (it would be too much to store them in the dictionary!), thus we request morphological segmentation as the first phase of parsing. Let us present some examples. The Hungarian sentence

> Írhatok a barátomnak. – 'I can write to my friend.'
> write-can-I the friend-my-to

would without morphological analysis give a very implicit structure where the relevant elements (e.g., *barátomnak*) could not be found in the dictionary:

In order to construct a structure which is as explicit as those used for other languages in DLT, we have to pass the sentence through the morphological analyser and build the dependency tree from its output:

ír--hat--ok a barát--om--nak

Note: The morphemes with "-" express their need for a link on the left, the right or on both sides; these are the output of the morphological analyser.

Now the dependency tree will be similar to that of English:

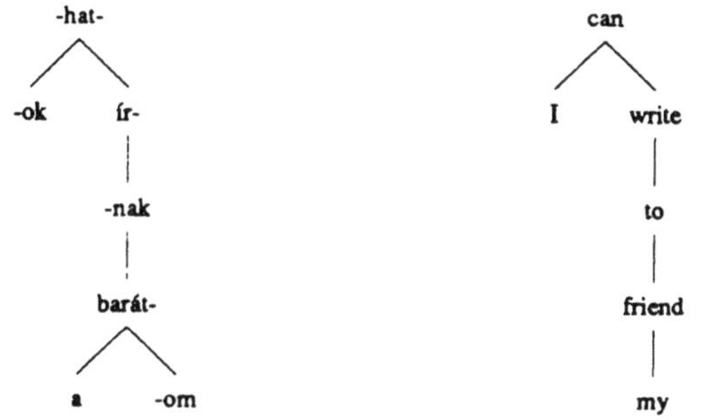

Another example is the sentence:

Dolgoztatlak. – 'I make you work.'
work-make-you-I

which consists of only one word. After word analysis the following dependency tree can be built:

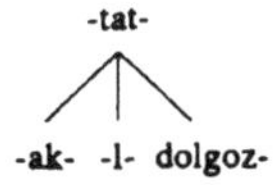

Another phenomenon which requires the splitting of words is the necessity of shifting verbal endings in certain cases:

Meg akarlak érteni. – 'I want to understand you.'
PREF want-you-I understand

The ending *-lak* expresses both the subject and the object of the main verb *megért* 'understand' at the same time. In this system, both the subject and the object will be assigned formally to the modal verb. The above sentence presents us with a further problem, the verbal prefix (which, as you may notice, has a near analogue in German). The morphological analyser provides us with the possibility of identifying the two parts of the verb *megért*, namely *meg* ___ *ért* and *ért* ___ *meg*. This approach enables the **homogeneous treatment** of cases (accusative, locative, etc.), e.g.

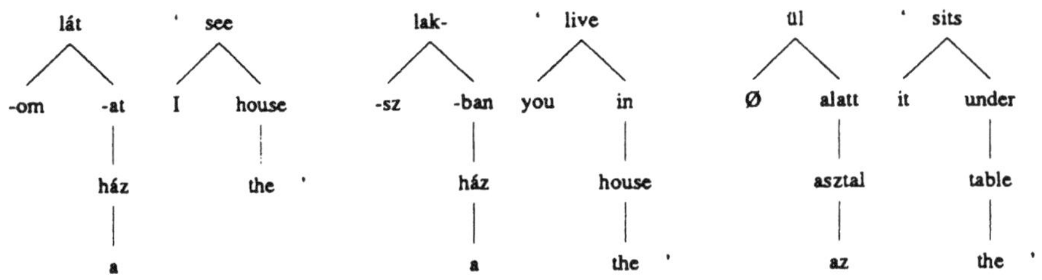

This means that syntactic roles are consequently separated from the content part of the word and directly linked to the verb which causes this role.

In order to build a homogeneous system that covers similar structures in a similar way we have to introduce the zero morpheme (Ø) in several cases. For example, the subject in the third person singular is expressed by a Ø suffix at the end of the verb (*lát--Ø*) or the verb *van* 'be' as a copula is omitted in the singular 3rd person of the present tense:

A lány szép volt. – 'The girl was beautiful.'
but: A lány szép Ø. – 'The girl is beautiful.'

In Hungarian there are several allomorphs for a given ending because of morphonological reasons (vowel harmony). In the analysis of a word we use the one applicable in that case (e.g. *-ban* or *-ben*), in the systematic treatment of endings below we show only one representative, but the variable part is indicated by a capital letter (eg: *-bAn* stands for *-ban* and *-ben*).

Our description is not complete. Rare structures and ellipses have been omitted. We do not deal with word order either.

2. Classification of Hungarian morphemes (basic syntactic units)

The first part of a dependency description of Hungarian must be the classification of morphemes and not only words, because word forms in Hungarian sentences consist of a stem and several other morphemes which carry independent grammatical and semantic information like, for example, pronouns or prepositions in other languages. Members of the same class are characterized by **similar morpho-syntactic patterns.** As for the stems, we classify them by the usual category names, but what is unusual, bound morphemes will also be cross-classified as pronouns, adjectives, adverbs and so on. The reason for this is to conserve the advantages of the agglutinative nature of the language and at the same time to conform to the use of word classes in Indo-European languages concerning their content.

2.1. Verbs (V)

The verb (traditionally the verbal stem) can have finite (see 2.3), participial (2.4), gerund (see 2.6), infinitive (see 2.7) and verbal noun (see 2.2) endings. The finite verb is the main element of a sentence, while verbs with other endings are the heads of verbal phrases. The morphological segmentation separates the verb stem from its endings, thus the verb is responsible only for the complements belonging to it and the finite ending (see: Pronouns) is the subject of the sentence (like pronouns in other languages). The other above mentioned endings link the word containing the verb to other word classes such as Adj, Adv, etc. and so they are treated there (e.g. the participial endings under the adjectives). So the double nature of the participles, gerunds, infinitives and deverbal nouns can be easily treated. The ending – here an emancipated member of the system – enables a word form to fulfil a syntactic role linked to its word class and the verbal stem governs its complements as usual, e.g.:

A feladatot elvégezve távozott. – 'After having performed the task he left.'
the task-ACC performing left-he

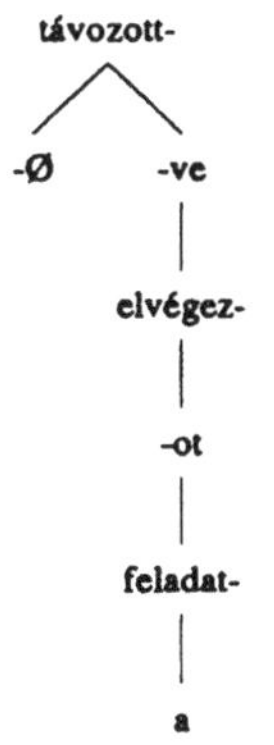

So we do not need to introduce an OBJ complement for the gerund, because the object belongs to the case frame of the verb. The verb carries markings for tense (past and present) and mood (conditional and imperative). These elements can be found in the finite endings' lexical entries and they are added as features to the verb during the segmentation:

láttam 'I saw it' → lát-PAST--am

Main Verbs (mV). The verbs not belonging to any other specific subclasses constitute this biggest subclass and in contrast to the other ones only this class of main verbs is open.

Hungarian verbs can have 0, 1, 2, 3 or 4 valencies. This means that there are 0 to 4 case-endings belonging to their lexical form. (The verbal prefixes are discussed under adverbs.) The basic form of the Hungarian verbs we use is a pure stem. This means that all the suffixes (e.g. infinitival or finite suffixes) follow this stem.

0-valency verbs: *havazik* 'it is snowing', *fagy* 'it is freezing'
1-valency verbs: *él (valaki)* 'live (somebody)', *megy (valaki)* 'go (somebody)'
2-valency verbs: *olvas (valamit)* 'read (something)', *lakik (valahol)* 'live (somewhere)'
3-valency verbs: *ad (valakinek valamit)* 'give (somebody something)',
tekint (valakit valaminek) 'consider (somebody something)'
4-valency verbs: *mond (valakinek valamit valamiről/valakiről)*
'tell (somebody something about somebody/something)'

Remark: We could consider verbs of the first group above as 1-valency verbs while the morphological analyser identifies the zero and the -ik endings of verbs as the finite ending of the 3rd person singular.

Linking Verbs (Cop). The linking verbs (otherwise copula) have a lexical subject and a predicative complement (e.g. *van* 'be', *marad* 'remain').

The main linking verb in Hungarian *van* has an obligatory Ø-allomorph in the singular

3rd person present tense. In past and future tenses or in 1st and 2nd persons of the present tense there are lexical forms, so we hope the reader will be convinced of the usefulness of a Ø verbal stem. Otherwise we should have to introduce a verbal role for nouns and adjectives. This would unnecessarily complicate the system. Thus

A lány szép. – 'The girl is beautiful.'

is analysed in a way which parallels the analysis of *A lány szép volt* – 'the girl was beautiful':

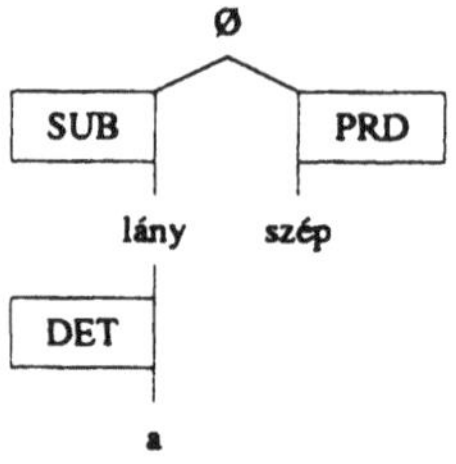

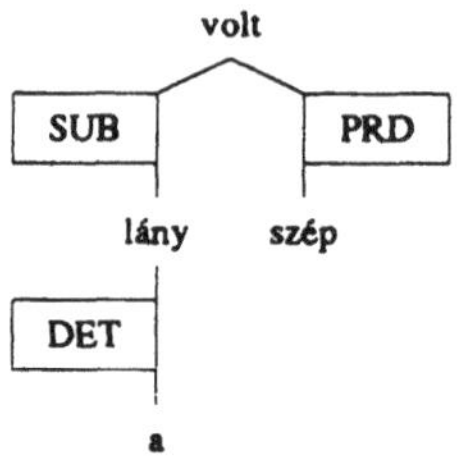

Auxiliaries (Aux). Auxiliaries are accompanied by other verbs with infinitive endings. Some of the Hungarian equivalents of the so-called auxiliary verbs show a similar structure to those of Indo-European languages: they mark tense mood, number and person. For example, *fog* used to form the future tense:

A férfi olvasni **fog**. – 'The man **will** read.'
or: Nem **tudok** úszni. – 'I **cannot** swim.'

The others (*kell* 'must, have to', *szabad* 'be allowed, can' and so on) – in general the so-called modal verbs – have an ending which shows only the tense and the mood, but the number and person are shifted to the other verb, e.g.

El **kell**--ett men--n--ünk. – 'We **had to** leave.',
PREF must-PAST leave-INF-we

where *kell* 'must' is an auxiliary, *men-* 'go' is a verbal stem with the infinitive ending (*-n-*); *-ett* bears the marking of the past tense, but *-ünk* means 1st person plural. If there is an explicit agent, it is in the dative instead of the expected nominative:

A tanár--**nak** el kell--ett men--ni--e. – 'The teacher had to leave.'
the teacher-DAT PREF must-PAST leave-INF-he.

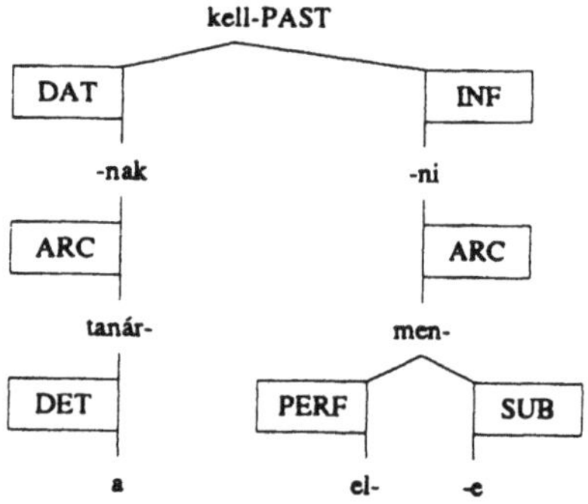

Auxiliaries^0 (Aux^0). We have to introduce this category because two of the Hungarian auxiliaries are represented by bound morphemes (further on we use the sign ^{0} for bound morphemes of a word class): *-hAt-* 'to be able, can' and *-(t)At-* 'make', e.g.

A gyerekek játsz**hat**nak. – 'The children **can** play.'

2.2. Nouns (N)

Nouns are the words directly followed by nominal suffixes and case endings or postpositions (see 2.7.). Nouns are the heads of noun phrases. Determiners and attributes join the noun from the left:

a nagy ház – 'the big house'

The order of the suffixes and endings is fixed; the case ending is the last one, e.g.:

a barát--om--é--**ban** – '**in** that of my friend'
the friend my that in

or: a barát--aim--éi--**val** – '**with** those of my friends'
the friend--s my those with

The plural will be marked as a feature: *barát--ok* → *barát*-PL.

Common Nouns (cN). In spite of the identifiability of Hungarian nouns before case endings, we give some of the most frequent possible derived endings of common nouns, because of the existence of the -Ø case ending (nominative, sometimes genitive): *-Ász, -mÁny, -vÁny, -AlOm, -sÁg, ...*

Proper Nouns (pN). Proper nouns are considered here as a subclass of nouns, although sometimes they can consist of more than one word (e.g. *San Francisco* or *Amerikai Egyesült Államok* 'United States of America'). In this case one of them is considered arbitrarily as the head of the expression, the relation between them is lexical (LEX) and so given in the dictionary. They begin with capital letters.

Verbal Noun Endings (vN^0). Nouns can also be formed from all of the verbs with the help of a particular morpheme *-Ás*. They are considered in the proposed grammar as nouns, but they need an obligatory left argument, a verbal stem (e.g. *lát--ás* 'sight, seeing', *ül--és* 'sitting'). So it is enough to put information about the verbal stem into the dictionary once, and there is no need to distinguish between normal nouns and nouns with a verbal character. (Nouns with *-Ás* can have verbal complements.)

Adjectival Nouns (aN). Some nouns can serve as an adjective or qualifier of another noun; they are adjacent words without any marking. These adjectival nouns denote nationality, profession, colour, age or material of the entity specified by the head of the phrase, e.g.

műanyag táska – 'plastic bag'
tanár barátom – 'my friend who is a teacher'

Measurement Nouns (mN). Measurement nouns are either official units of measure (e.g. *méter, gramm, liter*) or unofficial but common ones (e.g. *pohár* 'glass') that can form a particular adverbial with the case ending *-nyi*. The only attributes of measurement nouns which precede them are numerals.

3 **liter** tej – '3 **litres** of milk',
egy **ujjnyi** kakaó – 'one finger **of** cocoa'

2.3. Pronouns (Pr)

Pronouns are morphemes directly followed by nominal suffixes, case endings and postpositions. They have neither left attributes, nor determiners. Pronouns which are bound morphemes have an obligatory left argument. They constitute a closed class. Pronouns refer to other grammatical elements. We use the term **pronoun** in a strict sense: pronouns are only noun-like elements; in addition there are **pro-adjectives proadverbs** and **pronumerals** discussed under the main categories as their subclasses.

Personal Pronouns (prsPr). Personal pronouns are: *én, te, ő, mi, ti, ők, ön, ...*

Remarks: (i) No difference in the 3rd person between genders; there are no genders in Hungarian. (ii) The accusative forms and all the other inflected forms consisting of a case ending and a personal suffix (*engem, téged, minket* etc.) are transformed by the morphological analyser into a "prsPr--Cas" form. This procedure is very important for handling suffixed nominals elegantly. Without it, case-endings beginning a word form would have to be supposed with all of their unwanted consequences, e.g.

engem → én--t
neked → te--nek
róla → ő--ról

Another reason to support this method is the similar behaviour of the postpositions:

utánam → én után
like: Péter után

Reflexive pronoun: *maga-*.
Reciprocal pronoun: *egymás-*.

Demonstrative Pronouns (demPr). E.g., *ez* 'this' and *az* 'that' standing outside of a nominal phrase:

ez (egy) lány – '**this** is a girl'
abban lakom – 'I am living in **that one**'

Finite Endings (Fin). Finite endings follow the verbs directly: *-Em, -Ed, -(j)A, -ik, ...* (Attention! Intersection of finite endings and personal endings is not empty.) There are parallel endings series for both the definite and indefinite verbal conjugations in Hungarian. The ending for the 3rd person singular indefinite conjugation is the Ø (e.g. *lát-* is the verbal stem).

Some definite and indefinite forms:

lát--**om**	'I see'	lát--t--**am**	'I saw'	lát--ná--**m**	'I would see'
lát--**ok**		lát--t--**am**		lát--né--**k**	

The definite forms contain potentially the object; its place should accordingly be generated with the help of a Ø-morpheme (*lát--om--Ø* 'I see **it**') or only by the metataxis if there is no explicit object. It is more explicit in the 2nd person singular:

lát--l--ak – 'I see **you**'

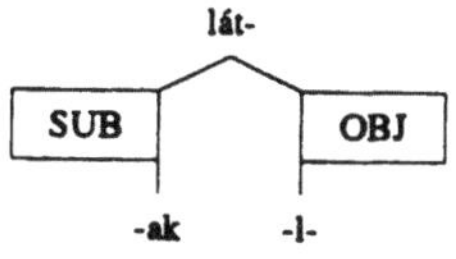

Personal Endings (Prs). Personal endings mark the possessive relation between two nominal elements: *ház*--**am** '**my** house', *ház*--**aitok** '**your** houses' ... In the 3rd person they can have a facultative argument, viz. a noun *Péter ház--a* or *Péter*--**nek** *a ház--a* 'Peter's house' or a pronoun. For the first and the second person only the personal pronoun can figure in a correlative position with the personal ending: *az* **én** *ház***am**. The personal ending is often accompanied by an article or demonstrative determiner: *a házad, ez a könyved.*

Possessive Endings (Poss⁰). Possessive endings (*-é, -éi*) stand for a noun phrase whose referent is possessed by the referent of the nominal element directly before them (e.g. *Péter*--**é** '**that of** Peter'). If the nominal element is a personal pronoun, see possessive pronouns.

Possessive Pronouns (posPr). E.g., *enyém* 'mine', *tied* 'yours', ... They are in general used with the definite article:

A könyv **az enyém**. – 'The book is **mine**.'

Question Pronouns (qPr). Question or *wh*-pronouns are e.g. *mi* 'what', *ki* 'who', ... They are only rarely used as relative pronouns.

Relative Pronouns (relPr). Relative pronouns consist of an *a-* morpheme and a question pronoun: *aki* 'who', *ami* 'what', *amely* 'which', ...

Negative Pronouns (negPr). Negative pronouns consist of a *sem-* morpheme and a question pronoun: *senki* 'nobody', *semmi* 'nothing', ...

General Pronouns (genPr). General pronouns usually consist of a *minden-* morpheme and a question pronoun: *mindenki* 'everybody', *minden* 'everything', ...

Indefinite Pronouns (indPr). Indefinite pronouns usually consist of a *vala-, akár-* or *bár-* morpheme and a question pronoun: *valami* 'something', *akármi, bármi* 'anything', ...

2.4. Adjectives (Adj)

Adjectives can have in general the same endings as the nouns, and the majority of them can form comparative and superlative and, by the suffix *-An*, an adverb. Adjectives can be left attributes of nouns or predicative complements of linking verbs. In the former case the adjective is invariable:

a **nagy** ház – 'the **big** house'
a **nagy** házakban – 'in the **big** houses'
but: A virágok **frissek** maradtak. – 'The flowers remained fresh.'
a **nagyokban** – 'in the big **ones**'

The comparative ending in Hungarian is *-(E)bb*, the superlative can be be formed by the only nominal prefix *leg-* and the suffix *-bb*: *legnagyobb*.

Main Adjectives (mAdj). This is an open class of the Hungarian adjectives (e.g. *szép* 'beautiful', *zöld* 'green'). Some of them can govern case complements, e.g.

hal**ban** gazdag – 'rich **in** fish'
indulás**ra** kész – 'ready **to** go'

Participle Endings (Part⁰). The participle endings follow a verbal stem to form an adjective-like element. Complements and adjuncts of the verbal part of a participle can only be its left attributes if the participle has an attributive role, e.g.:

a szobában könyvet olvasó fiú – 'the boy **reading** a book in the room'
the room-in book-ACC reading boy

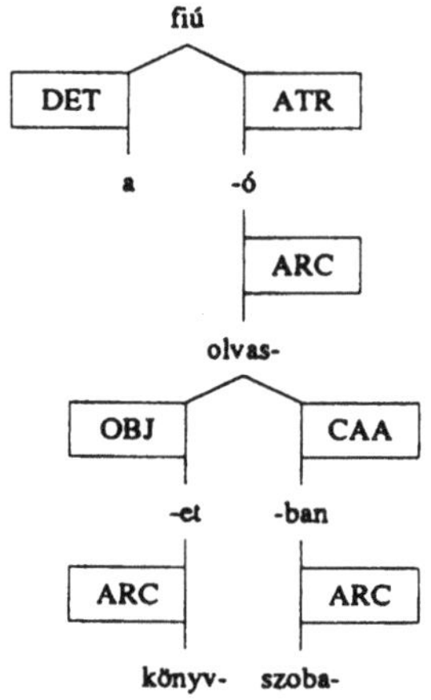

Morpheme-by-morpheme glossing is often much more precise in Esperanto. Here are the participle endings with their Esperanto equivalents:

-(Et)t
Esp. -inta (itr V) elszáradt virág 'dried flower'
Esp. -ita (perf tr V) megírt levél 'written letter'
Esp. -ata (imp tr V) tisztelt uram Esp. 'mia estimata sinjoro'
-O
Esp. -anta dolgozó emberek 'working people'

-AndO

Esp. -ota	(tr V)	elolvasandó könyv 'book to be read'
Esp. -enda	(tr V)	(as above, with a nuance of necessity)
Esp. -onta	(itr V)	születendő gyermek 'child to be born'

The ending *-hatólhető* '-able' is also classified here because splitting this word into *-hat--ó* would suggest a misleading translation, e.g.:

a moziban látható film – 'the film which can be seen in the movies'
the movies-in see-able film

Determinative Adjective (dAdj). These adjectives (e.g. *alsó* 'lower', *felső* 'upper') determine one element of a set. They require a determiner and precede the other attributes of a noun:

a felső piros sor – 'the upper red row'.

The *-bbik* suffix (Sufik^0). The suffix *-(E)bbik* transforms an adjective to a dAdj:

a nagy--obbik – 'the bigger one'

Ordinal number ending (Ord^0). E.g. *-Edik*, in *öt--ödik* 'fifth'. It requires a numeral as a left argument and in general a determiner.

Comparative Suffix (cAdj^0). The comparative suffix -Abb forms the comparative of an adjective. It governs generally a case. For example, the sentence

She is more beautiful than Mary

can be expressed as follows:

szebb, mint Mária
or: szebb Máriánál

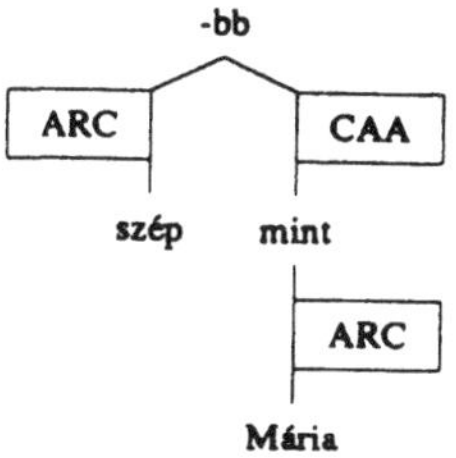

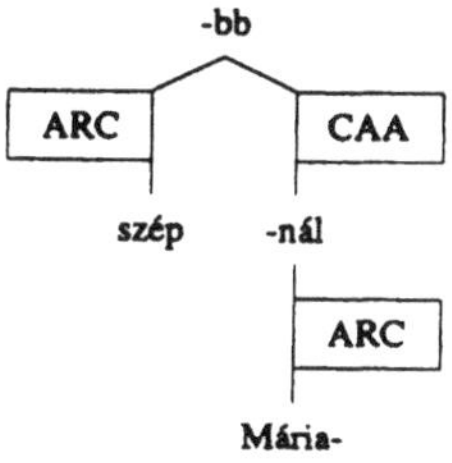

At the same time it can govern two cases, e.g.

5 cm-rel magasabb Máriánál – 'He is 5 cm taller than Mary'.

Adjective Ending (Adj^0). The *-i* and the *-s* ending make an adjective from a noun, e.g.:

Budapest → budapesti
víz 'water' → vizes 'wet'

The adjectival forms of geographic nouns are formed in general by the suffix *-i*.

The *ú*-ending (Sufu^0). This suffix makes an adjective from a nominal expression (attribute + noun), it is joined to the noun:

barna haj 'brown hair' → barna hajú 'brown-haired'

Some lexicalised forms are written in one word as compounds (e.g. *féllábú* – 'having one leg').

Proadjectives (prAdj). The words excluded from the pronouns and having an adjectival character belong to this category. They can be classified in the same way as the pronouns (e.g., indefinite prAdj: *valamilyen* Esp. 'ia', negative prAdj: *semmilyen* Esp. 'nenia'). The question prAdj *milyen* 'which' and the relative prAdj *amilyen* play an important role.

Empty Adjectives (eAdj). There are some adjectives (*való, levő* 'being', *történő* 'occurring') which are semantically empty. They serve only to link a case complement to a head noun (otherwise nouns can in general have only attributes in Hungarian):

az asztalon **levő** könyv – 'the book on the table'

2.5. Numerals (Num)

All numerals can be formed from a finite set of numbers (0, 1, 2, ...). The numerals can have the same endings as a noun and in addition the numeral suffixes *-Ed, -Edik, -En*. They can also have the same syntactic role as a noun or an adjective. If it stands alone, it cannot have any left attribute or article (**öt** *megmaradt* '**five** remained'), if it is the left attribute of a noun, in general it is the first. Hungarian nouns do not take a plural after numerals.

Cardinal Numbers (cNum). Cardinal numbers can occur alone:

kettő meg **kettő** az **négy** – '**2** + **2** = **4**'
öten jöttek – '**five** people arrived'
5-ből talált **3**-at – 'he scored **3** out of **5**'

and as left attributes:

két szép lány – '**two** beautiful girls'

Fraction Number Ending (frNum^0). This is the *-Ed* suffix: *öt*-**öd** 'one fi**fth**'. It needs a numeral as a left argument and can have a cardinal number as a numeral complement.

Quantifiers (Qua). These elements (e.g. *sok* 'many', *néhány* 'several') precede the other attributes of a noun, but they do not need a determiner.

Pronumerals (prNum). The words excluded from the pronouns and having a numeral character belong to this category, they can be classified in the same way as the pronouns (e.g., indefinite prNum: *valahány* Esp. 'iom', negative prNum: *sehány* Esp. 'neniom'). The question prNum *hány* 'how many/much' and the relative prNum *ahány* have an important role.

2.6. Adverbs (Adv)

Adverbs are invariable and do not take any ending generally. They constitute a closed class. They depend on verbs – sometimes on adjectives (gAdj) – as a complement or free adjunct. They can govern only an apposition. The bound morphemes need a left argument.

Main Adverbs (mAdv). E.g.: *ma* 'today', *itt* 'here', ...

Gerund Endings (Ger^0). These suffixes (*-vA, -vÁn*) make gerund forms from verbs: *ír-*-**va** '**writing**'.

Adverbial Endings (Adv^0). These suffixes (*-An, -lAg, -Ul*) make an adverb-like element from an adjective, so they need an adjective as a left argument: *gyors--an* 'quickly'. The *-lAg* often depends on adjectives:

> **szemantikailag hibás mondat 'semantically wrong phrase'.**

Adverbs of Degree (gAdv). They can depend both on verbs and adjectives: **nagyon** *tetszik* 'I like it **very much**' and **nagyon** *szép* '**very** beautiful'.

Verbal Prefixes ($Pref^0$). The verbal prefix (e.g. *ki-* 'out', *be-* 'in') is part of the verb, but in several cases (negative, imperative) it occurs separately: **ki***megy* 'it goes **out**', *menj* **ki**! 'go **out**!'. It must be linked to the verb, because in many cases they together have a meaning and sometimes the verb alone cannot subsist: e.g. *kifejez* 'express', *fejezd ki!*, but there is no *fejez*. The dictionary must indicate the possible prefixes of a verb.

Proadverbs (prAdv). The words excluded from the pronouns and having an adverbial character belong to this category, they can be classified as was done for the pronouns (e.g., indefinite prAdv: *valahogy* Esp. 'iel', negative prAdv: *sehogy* Esp. 'neniel'). The question prAdv *hogy* 'how' and the relative prAdv *ahogy* play an important role.

2.7. Case morphemes (Cas)

We treat a closed subset of the suffixes and some autonomous words as case morphemes. All the heads of nominal phrases except the nominative are followed directly by case endings. Case morphemes play the same role in Hungarian as prepositions in Indo-European languages. They have an obligatory argument on their left side.

Case Endings (Cas^0). There are approximately 20 case-suffixes in Hungarian. The number of case endings depends on where the boundary lies between real case suffixes, which can govern any substantive, and derivational suffixes, which govern only special classes or are not productive. Considering the surface word forms, there are in all more than 60 different morphemes which form the 20 subclasses mentioned above. Because of the vowel harmony, a case ending can have up to 5 allomorphs, as in the example of the accusative *-(A)t*:

> ház-**-at**, kez-**-et**, pötty-**-öt**, lom-**-ot**, fá-**-t**

The *-An* ending after numerals indicates nominative and refers to persons, e.g.:

> **Hatan** jöttek. – 'Six **people** arrived.'

Postpositions (Post). Postpositions are independent words that occur only directly after the head of a noun phrase (e.g. *a ház* **alatt** 'under the house', *Péter* **szerint** 'according to Peter'). Some postpositions give a case-suffix to the noun they follow (e.g. *az erdő*--**n keresztül** 'across the forest'). A postposition can belong to several nouns and more than one postpositions can belong to a single noun:

> Péter és Pál **előtt** – '**in front of** Peter and Paul'
> Péter **előtt** és **mögött** – '**in front of** and **behind** Peter'

Infinitive Suffix (Inf^0). All the verbal stems can be followed by an infinitive suffix (e.g. *-ni, -ani*). The infinitive is used in Hungarian sentences in three cases: beside auxiliaries (*mennem kell* 'I have to go') and as complements or adjuncts of verbs (*szeret játszani* 'he likes to play') and of some adjectives such as *kész elmenni* 'he is ready to go'. In the former case, the "head" is semantically the verb followed directly by the infinitive suffix. There are some auxiliaries that allow the infinitive suffix to be followed by an ending containing some information about the number and person of the subject (see Auxiliaries, 2.1.).

Comparative Particle (Comp). The comparative particle *mint* can occur after adjectives and has a compulsory argument on its right side.

> **olyan nagy, mint** egy ház – 'it is **as big as** a house'
> **nagyobb, mint** egy ház – 'it is **bigger than** a house'

The argument can also be a proposition:

> Nem olyan szép, mint **ahogy elképzeltem.** – 'It is not as beautiful as **I imagined.**'

Notice that there is a comma before it. It can depend on verbs too:

> fut, **mint** a nyúl – 'it runs **like** a rabbit'

This particle has another special use after nouns, distinguished by the absence of the comma:

> Kovács **mint** tanár – 'Kovács **as** a teacher'

2.8. Determiners (Det)

The determiner is the leftmost element of a noun phrase and takes the whole phrase in its scope, e.g.:

> **egy** három éve épült ház – '**a** house that was built three years ago'
> a three years-ago built house

Articles (Art). Definite: *a*, before words beginning with a consonant and *az*, before words beginning with a vowel.
Indefinite: *egy*.

Demonstrative Determiners (dDet). Demonstrative determiners *ez, az* (do not confuse these with the demPr!) require a definite article before the noun:

ez a ház – 'this house'

Their suffixed forms e.g. *ebben, abban, ehhez*, present a strange structure in Hungarian: the case ending has to be the same as that of the head noun:

abban a **házban** – '**in** that house'

The dDet *e, ezen, ...* can be substituted for the structures *ez/ebben/ehhez/... a*:

ebben a házban = **e** házban

2.9. Coordinating conjunctions (Con)

Coordinating conjunctions are linkers of two phrases or two propositions. The two subclasses of the conjunctive elements are not disjunct. Besides the simple ones, there are some double conjunctions:

vagy a fiúk, **vagy** a lányok indulnak – '**either** the boys **or** the girls start'

Coordinating conjunctions between phrases (phCon). Conjunctions between phrases include *és, meg* 'and', *vagy* 'or', *de* 'but', ...

Coordinating conjunctions between propositions (prpCon). Conjunctions between propositions include not only the elements of this class, but also those of the other subclass: *azonban* 'however', *ellenben* 'but', *és* 'and', ...

2.10. Subordinating conjunctions (Sbj)

There are some lexical subordinators, e.g. *hogy* 'that', *ha* 'if', *mert* 'because' with an obligatory comma before them. E.g.

Olvasnék, **ha** megtalálnám a könyvemet. – 'I would read if I could find my book.'

All the relative pronouns can play the role of a subordinating conjunction.

2.11. Modifiers (Mod)

Modifiers (*is* 'also', *nem* 'not', *csak* 'only', ...) can modify almost every element of a sentence. *Nem* and *talán* 'maybe' precede the related word, *is* follows it:

Péter **nem** megy moziba. – 'Peter does **not** go to the movies.'
Nem Péter megy moziba. – 'It is **not** Peter who is going to the movies.'
Péter **nem** moziba megy. – 'Peter is **not** going to the movies (but maybe somewhere else).'

There is also a verbal modifier (used only in interrogative sentences): *-e*, e.g.:

Megy-**e** moziba? – 'Does he go to the movies?'

Modifiers cannot govern anything.

2.12. Interjections (Int)

Interjections are independent (elliptical) sentences belonging to the main verb only formally. Here we classify interjections in the traditional sense (*oh, jaj,* ...) and other particles which do not depend on a concrete element of the sentence, but are related to the whole (*igen* 'yes', *bizony* 'certainly', ...). They cannot govern anything.

2.13. Overview

An overview over the morpheme classes and their subdivisions is given in the table on the next page.

Abr.	Subclasses	Abr.	Examples
V	main verb	mV	*ül, lógat ...*
	linking verb	Cop	*van, vol-, marad, ...*
	auxiliary	Aux	*kell, akar, fog, ...*
	auxiliary^0	Aux^0	*-tat-, -het-, ...*
N	common noun	cN	*liba, kacsa, ...*
	proper noun	pN	*MTA, Magyarország, ...*
	verbal n. end.	vN^0	*-ás, -és*
	measur. noun	mN	*kg, méter, ...*
	adjectival n.	aN	*orvos, ifjú, ...*
PR	personal pr.	prsPr	*én, te, maga, ...*
	demonstr. pr.	demPr	*ez, az*
	finite ending	Fin^0	*-om, -unk, ...*
	poss. ending	Poss^0	*-é, -éi*
	pers. ending	Prs^0	*-m, -d, -ja, -eink, ...*
	question pr.	qPr	*ki, mi, ...*
	relative pr.	relPr	*aki, ami, ...*
	possess. pr.	posPr	*enyém, tied, ...*
	negative pr.	negPr	*senki, semmi, ...*
	general pr.	genPr	*mindenki, minden, ...*
	indefinite pr.	indPr	*valaki, akárki, ...*
ADJ	main adjective	mAdj	*zöld, nagy, ...*
	participle end.	Part^0	*-ó, -hető, -ett, ...*
	determ. adj.	dAdj	*alsó, középső, ...*
	-bbik suffix	Sufik^0	*-bbik*
	proadjective	prAdj	*milyen, amekkora, ...*
	adj. ending	Adj^0	*-s, -os, -es, -ös, -i*
	comparative suf	cAdj	*-abb, -ebb, -obb*
	ú-ending^0	Sufu^0	*-ú, -ű, -jú, -jű*
	empty adj.	eAdj	*való, történő, ...*
	ord. number end	Ord^0	*-odik, -ödik, ...*
NUM	cardinal number	cNum	*három, ezer, ...*
	fraction number	frNum	*-ad, -ed, -od, -öd*
	pronumeral	prNum	*annyi, hány, ...*
	quantifier	Qua	*sok, kevés, ...*
ADV	main adverb	mAdv	*tegnap, otthon, ...*
	gerund ending	Ger^0	*-va, -ve, -ván, -vén*
	adverbial end.	Adv^0	*-an, -lag, -ül, ...*
	adv. of degree	gAdv	*nagyon, alig, ...*
	verbal prefix^0	Pref^0	*ki-, alá -, haza-, ...*
	proadverb	prAdv	*hol, hová, amikor, ...*
CAS	case ending	Cas^0	*-nak, -ból, -ra, -t, ...*
	postposition	Post	*után, alatt, mögé, ...*
	infinitive end.	Inf^0	*-ni, -ani, -eni, ...*
	comp. particle	Comp	*mint*
DET	article	Art	*a, az, egy*
	demonstr. det	dDet	*ez, e, az, eme, ama*
CON	con b. phrases	phCon	*és, vagy, ...*
	con b. prop.	prpCon	*azonban, csakhogy ...*
SBJ	subjunction		*hogy, mert, ha*
MOD	modifier		*nem, csak, talán, is, ...*
INT	interjection		*igen, bizony, óh, jaj, ...*

3. Basic dependent types

The following two tables show the entire set of dependent types.
(3) The object is marked generally by the case ending *-t*. The other object-like elements are treated in a different way (PRC, CAC).

3.1. Complements

Abr	Complement Name	Relations: Governor → Dependent
ADC	adverbial complement	V → {ADV, CAS}
ARC	argument	CAS → {V, N, PR, ADJ, NUM, CON}, PR → {ADJ, N}, ADV → {V, ADJ}, NUM → NUM, SBJ → V
-C	conjunctive arguments	CON → {V, N, PR, ADJ, NUM, ADV, CAS, DET, CON, SBJ}
CAC	case complement	{V, ADJ, CAS, N, ADV} → CAS
DAT	dative subject	V → CAS
INF	infinitive complement	V → CAS
LEX	lexical relation	...
NUC	numeral complement	{N, ADV, PR, ADJ} → NUM
OBJ	object	V → CAS
PRD	predicative	V → {N, PR, ADJ, NUM}
PRC	proposition	{V, CON} → SBJ, V → V
PRV	preverbal modifier	V → ADV
SUB	subject	V → PR

3.2. Adjuncts

Abr	Adjunct Name	Relations: Governor → Dependent
ADA	adverbial adjunct	V → {ADV, CAS}, N → CAS
APP	apposition	N → {N, ADJ}, ADJ → {N, ADJ}, ADV → {ADV, CON, CAS}, CAS → ADV
ARA	argument	PR → {N, PR, ADJ, CAS, CON}
ATR	(only left) attribute	{V, N, ADJ, ADV} → ADV, NUM → NUM, {N, ADJ, NUM} → ADJ
CAA	case adjunct	{V, N, ADJ, NUM} → CAS
DET	determining adjunct	{N, ADJ, NUM, DET} → DET
EQU	equivalence	CAS → CAS
LIA	linking adjunct	V → {INT, N, PR}
MOD	modifier	{V, N, PR, ADJ, NUM, ADV, CAS, DET} → MOD
NUA	numeral adjunct	{N, ADJ} → NUM
PRD	predicative	V → {N, PR, ADJ, NUM}
PRA	proposition	{V, N, PR, ADJ, ADV, DET} → SBJ
PSS	possessive adjunct	{N, ADJ} → PR
REL	relative clause	{N, PR, ADJ, ADV} → V

Remarks to the tables in 3.1. and 3.2.:

(1) The arrow (→) marks the direction of the relation between governor (G) and dependent (D).

(2) In this system the verbal ending – classified as a pronoun – is always the subject of the sentence. If there is an explicit subject, it depends on the finite ending as an argument. The metataxis will eliminate the redundancy.

4. Morpheme class specific dependency patterns

Remarks to the following examples for the dependency patterns

(1) Each of the sample sentences in the subsections below illustrates a single governor-dependent relation as given in the relevant table. The governing morpheme is shown in *italics*, the dependent in **bold face**. Notes to the right of the glosses refer to the governor (G) or the dependent (D) of the illustrated relation.

(2) To save space, we mostly use 'he' in glossing the 3rd person singular, but out of context the translation could be 'she' or 'it' as well.

(3) We split the words at the morpheme boundaries if this is necessary to present its components better.

(4) Sometimes we give some subclass specific restrictions.

(5) Modifiers and interjections are not in the separate dependency tables (except 4.11.), because the former can depend on almost any other word class (the dependency relation is always labelled MOD) and the latter does not depend really on any one class, but is arbitrarily put with the main verb as a case of LIA. A number of sample sentences are, however, given for this relation.

(6) The lexical relation (LEX) is not class specific, so it is not treated here (it can be found in the dictionary).

(7) The relation EQU does not figure in the table, because it is used only to identify the case ending of the demonstrative determiner with that of the related noun.

4.1. Dependents of the verb

	V	N	PR	ADJ	NUM	ADV	CAS	DET	CON	SBJ
ADC						×	×		×	
ARC	×									
CAC							×		×	
DAT							×		×	
INF							×		×	
NUC										
OBJ							×		×	
PRD		×	×	×	×				×	
PRC	×								×	×
PRV						×			×	
SUB			×							
ADA						×	×		×	
APP										
ARA										
ATR										
CAA							×		×	
DET										
NUA										
PRA									×	×
PSS										
REL										

ADC/adverb

Fest-**-ve** *volt*--ak. – 'They were painted.' (quasi passive, G = Aux)
Itt *lak*--ik. – 'He lives here.' (D ≠ gAdv, Pref^{0})

ADC/case morpheme

Budapest-**-en** *lak*--ik. – 'He is living in Budapest.'

ARC/verb

dolgoz--*tat* – 'he makes somebody work' (G = Aux^{0})

CAC/case morpheme

Elnök-**-nek** *választott*--ák. – 'He was elected as president.'
Péter-**-nek** *ad*--om a könyvet. – 'I give Peter the book.'
Szeret--ek olvas-**-ni**. – 'I like to read.'

DAT/case morpheme

Péter-**-nek** el *kell* mennie. – 'Peter has to leave.' (D = *-nAk*, G = Cop or Aux)

INF/case morpheme

Olvas-**-ni** *fog*--ok. – 'I shall read.' (G = Aux, D = Inf^{0})

OBJ/case morpheme

Könyv-**-et** *olvas*--*Ø*. – 'He is reading a book.' (D = *-(A)t*)

PRD/noun

Péter **gyerek** *maradt*. – 'Peter has remained a child.' (G = Cop)

PRD/pronoun

ő **az** *volt*. – 'He was that.' (G = Cop)

PRD/adjective

Okos *vagy*. – 'You are intelligent.' (G = Cop

PRD/numeral

Kétszer kettő **négy** *Ø*. – '2 × 2 = 4' (G = Cop)

PRC/verb

Tudom, mit **csinál**--sz. – 'I know what you are doing'

PRC/subordinating conjunction

Lát--om, **hogy** jó. – 'I see that it is good.'

PRV/adverb

El--*ment*. – 'He has left.' (D = $Pref^0$)

SUB/pronoun

Fut--**ok**. – 'I run.' (D = Fin^0)

ADA/adverb

Gyors--**an** *fut*--Ø. – 'He runs quickly.'
Siet--**ve** *jön*--Ø. – 'He comes hurrying.'

ADA/case morpheme

A kert--**ben** *dolgoz*--ik. – 'He is working in the garden.'

CAA/case morpheme

Pál 5 óra--**kor** *jött*--Ø meg. – 'Paul arrived at 5 o'clock.'
Megy--ek sétál--**ni**. – 'I go for a walk.'

CAA/coordinating conjunction

A nővéremmel **vagy** a barátnőmmel *megy*--ek moziba.
– 'I go to the movies with my sister or my friend.'

PRA/coordinating conjunction

Megigérte, **de** nem tette meg. – 'He promised it, but he has not done it.'

PRA/subordinating conjunction

Elmegy--ek, **hogy** megnézzem őt. – 'I shall go to see him.'

NOT SHOWN IN THE TABLE:

MOD/modifier

A gyerekek *játsz*--anak **is** és *tanul*--nak **is**.
– 'The children are also playing and learning.'

LIA/interjection

Nem, holnap nem *megy*--ek. – 'No, tomorrow I shan't go.'

4.2. Dependents of the noun

	V	N	PR	ADJ	NUM	ADV	CAS	DET	CON	SBJ
ADC										
ARC										
CAC							×		×	
DAT										
INF										
NUC					×				×	
OBJ										
PRD										
PRC										
PRV										
SUB										
ADA							×		×	
APP		×		×					×	
ARA										
ATR				×		×			×	
CAA							×		×	
DET								×	×	
NUA					×				×	
PRA									×	×
PSS			×							
REL	×								×	

CAC/case morpheme

igény a szép--**re** – 'pretention of beauty' (rare)

NUC/numeral

3 *méter* – '3 meters' (G = mN)

ADA/case morpheme

hidak a Duná--**n** – 'bridges on the Danube'
csirke krumpli--**val** – 'chicken with potatoes'

APP/noun

Kovács, a **tanár** – 'Kovács, the teacher'

APP/adjective

Pista, az **okos** – 'Pista, the intelligent'

ATR/adjective

szép *ház* – 'nice house'

ATR/adverb (rare constructions)

a **hazafelé** *út* – 'the way home'
A *helyzet* **ott** rossz. – 'The situation there is bad.'

DET/determiner

a *fiú* – 'the boy'
ez *a* fiú – 'this boy'

NUA/numeral

5 *lány* – '5 girls'

PRA/subordinating conjunction

A *döntés*, **hogy** elmegyünk, megszületett.
– 'The decision that we shall start, has been made.'

PSS/pronoun

ház--**unk** – 'our house' (D = Prs⁰)

REL/verb

az *ember*, aki el--**ment** – 'the man who left'

NOT SHOWN IN THE TABLE:

MOD/modifier

Judit **is** – 'Judy too'

4.3. Dependents of the pronoun

	V	N	PR	ADJ	NUM	ADV	CAS	DET	CON	SBJ
ADC										
ARC		×		×	×					
CAC										
DAT										
INF										
NUC										
OBJ										
PRD										
PRC										
PRV										
SUB										
ADA										
APP										
ARA		×	×	×			×		×	
ATR										
CAA							×			
DET										
NUA										
PRA									×	×
PSS										
REL	×								×	

ARC/noun

a **gyerek**--*é* – 'that of the child' (G = Poss⁰)

ARC/adjective

a **szorgalmas**--*é* – 'that of the diligent one'

ARC/numeral

három--*é* – 'that of three'

ARA/noun

A **gyerekek** játsz--*anak*. – 'The children are playing.' (G = Fin)

az **erdő** fá--*i* – 'the trees of the forest'

ARA/pronoun

én mondt--*am* – 'I have said it' (G = Fin)

az **én** könyv--*em* – 'my book'

ARA/adjective

a **kiváncsiak** meg--jött--*ek* – 'the curious ones arrived'

ARA/case morpheme

 hárm--**an** énekel--*nek* – 'three people are singing'

CAA/case morpheme

 ő **teveled** nagyon csinos pár – 'she and you make a nice couple.'

PRA/subordinating conjunction

 Az, **hogy** rossz, senkit sem érdekel. – 'It does not bother anybody that it is bad.' (G = demPr)

REL/verb

 ő, **aki** el--men--t 'he who left' (G ≠ Prs⁰)

 Aki nem **akar--Ø**, nem megy--*Ø*. – 'Those that don't want to, don't go.'

NOT SHOWN IN THE TABLE:

MOD/modifier

 én **is** – 'me too'

4.4. Dependents of the adjective

	V	N	PR	ADJ	NUM	ADV	CAS	DET	CON	SBJ
ADC										
ARC										
CAC							×		×	
DAT										
INF										
NUC					×					
OBJ										
PRD										
PRC										
PRV										
SUB										
ADA										
APP		×		×					×	
ARA										
ATR				×		×			×	
CAA							×		×	
DET								×	×	
NUA					×				×	
PRA									×	×
PSS			×							
REL	×								×	

CAC/case morpheme

 tett--**re** *kész* – 'ready for action'

NUC/numeral

 öt--*ödik* – 'fifth' (G = Ord⁰)

APP/noun

 a *jobboldali*, a **barát**--om – '(the man on) the right, my friend'

APP/adjective

 a *baloldali*, a magas--**abb** – '(the man on) the left, the taller (one)'

ATR/adjective

a **nagy** *barna* – 'the big brown one'

ATR/adverb

erős--**en** *piros* – 'strongly red'

CAA/case morpheme

matematiká--**ból** *kiváló* – 'outstanding in mathematics'

DET/determiner

a *szép* – 'the beautiful one'

NUA/numeral

három *szegény* – 'three poor (ones)'

PRA/subordinating conjunction

olyan szép, **hogy** csodájára járnak
– 'she is so beautiful that people come to admire her'

PSS/pronoun

szép--**ei** – 'his beautiful ones'

REL/verb

Olyan magas, amilyen te **vagy**. – 'He is as tall as you are.'

NOT SHOWN IN THE TABLE:

MOD/modifier

majdnem *zöld* – 'almost green'

4.5. Dependents of the numeral

	V	N	PR	ADJ	NUM	ADV	CAS	DET	CON	SBJ
ADC										
ARC										
CAC										
DAT										
INF										
NUC					×					
OBJ										
PRD										
PRC										
PRV										
SUB										
ADA										
APP										
ARA										
ATR				×	×				×	
CAA							×		×	
DET								×	×	
NUA										
PRA										
PSS										
REL										

NUC/numeral

hat--*od* – 'sixth'

ATR/adjective

a **kisebbik** *három* – 'the smaller three'

ATR/numeral

négy öt--*öd* – 'four fifths'

CAA/case morpheme

hat--**szor** *hat* – 'six times six'

DET/determiner

az a *három* – 'those three'

NOT SHOWN IN THE TABLE:

MOD/modifier

csak *négy* – 'only four'

4.6. Dependents of the adverb

	V	N	PR	ADJ	NUM	ADV	CAS	DET	CON	SBJ
ADC										
ARC	×			×						
CAC							×			
DAT										
INF										
NUC					×					
OBJ										
PRD										
PRC										
PRV										
SUB										
ADA										
APP						×	×		×	
ARA										
ATR						×				
CAA										
DET										
NUA										
PRA	×								×	×
PSS										
REL	×								×	

ARC/verb

lát--*va* – 'seeing' (G = Ger^0)

ARC/adjective

gyors--*an* – 'quickly' (G = Adv^0)

CAC/case morpheme

ott ült a mozi--**ban** – 'he was sitting in the cinema'

NUC/numeral

három *napja* – 'for three days'

APP/adverb

ott, **alatta** – 'there, under it'

APP/case morpheme

ott, a mozi--**ban** – 'there, in the cinema'

ATR/adverb

nagyon *hátul* – 'a long way over there'

PRA/verb

úgy, ahogy **mond**--od – 'as you say'

PRA/subordinating conjunction

úgy, **hogy** zöld le--gy--en – 'in order to be green'

REL/verb

itt, áhol **áll**--unk – 'here where we are standing'

NOT SHOWN IN THE TABLE:

MOD/modifier

nem *nagyon* magas – 'not very tall'

4.7. Dependents of the case morpheme

	V	N	PR	ADJ	NUM	ADV	CAS	DET	CON	SBJ
ADC										
ARC	×	×	×	×	×	×			×	
CAC							×		×	
DAT										
INF										
NUC										
OBJ										
PRD										
PRC										
PRV										
SUB										
ADA										
APP						×			×	
ARA										
ATR										
CAA							×			
DET										
NUA										
PRA										
PSS										
REL										

ARC/verb

lát--*ni* – 'to see'

ARC/noun

a **ház**--*ból* – 'from the house'

ARC/pronoun

ki--*vel* – 'with whom'

ARC/adjective

kicsi--*hez* – 'to the small one'

ARC/numeral

öt--*ből* – 'from five'

ARC/adverb

holnap--*ra* – 'for tomorrow'

CAC/case morpheme

a város--**on** *keresztül* – 'across the city' (G = Postp)

APP/adverb

a konyhá--*ban*, **lenn** – 'in the kitchen, downstairs'

CAA/case morpheme

gyerek--**kel** a karjá--*n* – '"with a child in her hand"'

NOT SHOWN IN THE TABLE:

EQU/case morpheme

eb--**ben** a ház--*ban* – 'in this house'

A FEW EXAMPLES OF COORDINATION:

ARC/coordinating conjunction

mint Judit **és** Márta – 'like Judy and Martha' (G = Postp, Comp)

a ház **vagy** a kert *mögött* – 'behind the house or the garden'

CAC/coordinating conjunction

a városon **és** a folyón *keresztül* – 'across the town and the river'

MOD/modifier

az asztal *alatt* **is** és *fölött* **is** – 'both under and above the table'

4.8. Dependents of the determiner

	V	N	PR	ADJ	NUM	ADV	CAS	DET	CON	SBJ
ADC										
ARC										
CAC										
DAT										
INF										
NUC										
OBJ										
PRD										
PRC										
PRV										
SUB										
ADA										
APP										
ARA										
ATR										
CAA										
DET								×		
NUA										
PRA										
PSS										
REL										

DET/determiner

ez *a* könyv – 'this book'

NOT SHOWN IN THE TABLE:

MOD/modifier

csak *ez* a könyv – 'only this book'

4.9. Dependents of the conjunction

Dependents of the conjunction bear the label of the conjunction, augmented with the extension -C.

4.10. Dependents of the subjunctive

	V	N	PR	ADJ	NUM	ADV	CAS	DET	CON	SBJ
ADC										
ARC	×									
CAC										
DAT										
INF										
NUC										
OBJ										
PRD										
PRC										
PRV										
SUB										
ADA										
APP										
ARA										
ATR										
CAA										
DET										
NUA										
PRA										
PSS										
REL										

ARC/verb mond--ta, *hogy* jö--ssz – 'he said that you will come'

4.11. Table of Hungarian dependency patterns

Possible governor → Possible head word of dependent ↓	**V**	**N**	**PR**	**ADJ**	**NUM**	**ADV**	**CAS**	**DET**	**CON**	**SBJ**
V	ARC PRC	REL	REL	REL		REL ARC PRA	ARC		-C	ARC
N	PRD LIA	APP	ARC ARA	APP			ARC		-C	
PR	SUB PRD LIA	PSS	ARA	PSS			ARC		-C	
ADJ	PRD	ATR APP	ARA ARC	APP ATR	ATR	ARC	ARC		-C	
NUM	PRD	NUA NUC	ARC	NUC NUA	NUC ATR	NUC	ARC		-C	
ADV	ADC ADA PRV	ATR		ATR		APP ATR	ARC APP		-C	
CAS	OBJ DAT ADC ADA CAC CAA INF	CAC ADA CAA	ARA CAA	CAC CAA	CAA	CAC APP	CAC EQU CAA		-C	
DET		DET		DET	DET			DET	-C	
CON	*	*	*	*	ATR CAA	REL PRA APP	ARC CAC APP		-C	
SBJ	PRC PRA	PRA	PRA	PRA		PRA			-C	
MOD	MOD	MOD	MOD	MOD	MOD	MOD	MOD	MOD		
INT	LIA									

*: Almost all of the dependent types could be mentioned here (except SUB) because of the compound sentences

5. Sample sentence

A barátom sokat szokott sétálni a kicsi fiával ebben az erdőben azért, hogy friss levegőt szívjanak, és megismerkedjenek az erdő állataival és madaraival.

(a barát--om sokat szok--ott--Ø sétál--ni a kicsi fi--á--val eb--ben az erdő--ben azért, hogy friss levegő--t szív--janak, és meg--ismerked--jenek az erdő állat--ai--val és madar--ai--val.)

the friend-my much-ACC used-to-he walk-to the small son-his-with this-in the forest-in in-order-to, that fresh air-ACC breathe-they, and get-know-they the forest's animals-its-with and birds-its-with

'My friend often used to walk with his small son in this forest to enjoy the fresh air and th become familiar with the animals and birds of the forest.'

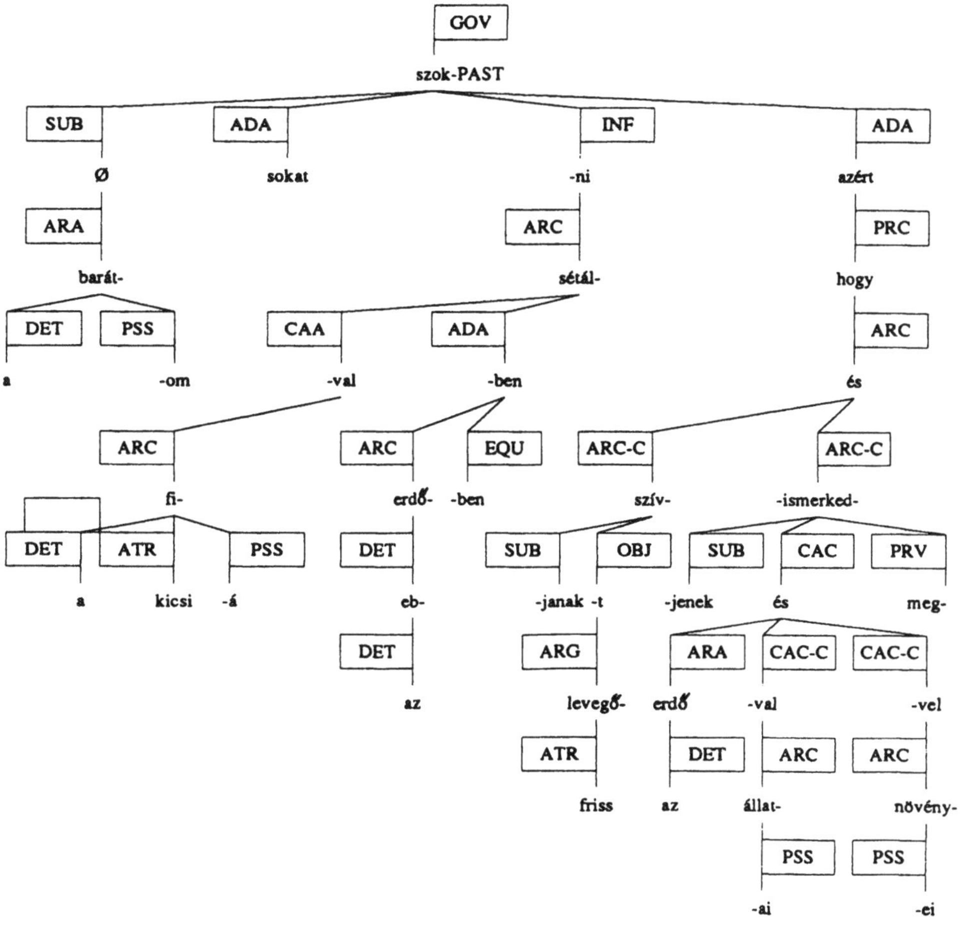

A dependency syntax of Japanese

Shigeru Sato

Sendai, Japan

1. Introduction

Japanese is not an Indo-European language, nor has it been linguistically demonstrated that it has a genetic kinship with other languages. It is easy to see, however, that there are a large number of morphosyntactic similarities it shares with Altaic languages such as Korean, Mongolian, Uzbek, and Turkish: (1) instead of nominal declensions, lexically independent case suffixes are attached to nouns; (2) instead of verbal inflections, agglutination of auxiliary elements is used to form a predicate phrase; (3) instead of prepositions, there are postpositions; (4) noun modifiers occur before the noun; (5) there are no relative pronouns; (6) there are subordinate conjunctions at the end of the subordinate clause; (7) the verb complex is sentence-final; (8) there is no plural form for nouns after a numeral representing plurality, (9) there is no grammatical gender. Furthermore, Japanese has no orthography of the sort that is established in English and other European languages; that is, there is no authorized representation of Japanese sentences using a Latin alphabet. On the other hand, for Japanese as much as for Altaic languages, a word defined by the orthography of English as an element delimited by spaces, for instance, may not be particularly useful as a unit for use in grammatical description. In these circumstances, we employ for convenience of representation a tentative orthography based on the morphological analysis to be shown in detail in due course. Roughly, a word is an adverb, a demonstrative adjective, a coordinate conjunction, or a noun/verb/adjective phrase. The first of these categories includes etymologically analogous subordinate conjunctions and postpositions. With a word thus defined, its internal structure will show a clearcut morpheme concatenation, as exemplified in (1-2):

[1] Kodomo-ga pan-wo tabe-sase-rare-ta. – 'The child was made to eat bread'
child-NOMINATIVE bread-ACCUSATIVE eat-CAUSATIVE-PASSIVE-PAST

[2] Haha-ga sono kodomo-ni pan-wo tabe-sase-te-i-ta. – 'The mother was making her child eat bread.'
mother-NOMINATIVE DEMONSTRATIVE/POSSESSIVE child-DATIVE bread-ACCUSATIVE eat-CAUSATIVE-GERUNDIVE-DURATIVE-PAST

where the hyphens indicate morpheme boundaries.

1. Morpheme classification

The word, as referred to in the previous section, may rather be regarded as a conciliatory unit devised for the ease of introduction of agglutinative morphology to readers familiar with the Indo-European concept of a word. But in what follows we let this word play a role in the recursive formation of stem-suffix compounds, which we call words, by-products in the classification of Japanese morphemes, autonomous and suffixal. Compared to its European counterparts, the second of these types manifests fewer instances of allomorphic variation as a result of contextual influences. This makes clear morphological segmentation possible. Thus, a word is a single autonomous word or such a unit with one or more suffixes. Word formation is accordingly regarded as a process of recursive affixation of a suffix to a stem that is an autonomous word. Autonomous words and suffixes correspond roughly to content words and function words, respectively.

[3] Boku-ni-wa kane-ga ar-u. – 'As for me, I have money.'
I-DATIVE-TOPIC money-NOMINATIVE exist-PRESENT

The following classification will mainly be based on traditional lexical class names, but careful attention will be paid to the autonomy of the morpheme, whether it is a stem or a suffix, according to which a number of subclasses are created under the given class name. Classes or subclasses are provided with information on whether a given member of the class acts as a stem (H: Head) or as a suffix (T: Tail). Each class is labelled either with (H) or (T) to show its role in word formation. We also give detailed explanations of those classes that involve a clear-cut departure from the traditional usage of grammatical categories.

1.1. Verbs

Lexical verbs (H). Japanese verbs have inflections in the sense that agglutination of morphemes is regarded as an affixation of a suffix to a stem and that the stem-suffix construct is considered to be a word that inflects. They can be classified into two major inflectional types: the vowel verbs and the consonant verbs. The names have their origin in the different stem-final phonemes and in the inflectional patterns caused thereby. Examples are given in [4].

[4] Verb inflections

Inflectional Form	Vowel Verb	Consonant Verb
Stem	*tabe* 'eat'	*kat* 'win'
Indicative Present	*tabe-ru*	*kat-u*
Indicative Past	*tabe-ta*	*kat-ta*
Imperative	*tabe-ro*	*kat-e*
Infinitive	*tabe*	*kat-i*
Gerund	*tabe-te*	*kat-te*
Provisional	*tabe-reba*	*kat-eba*
Conditional	*tabe-tara*	*kat-tara*
Alternative	*tabe-tari*	*kat-tari*

The verbs can have 1 to 3 valencies, on the basis of which they can be divided into three subclasses:

(1) 1-valent:	*tob* 'fly'	*Hikouki-ga tob-u* 'An airplane flies.'
(2) 2-valent:	*tobas* 'fly'	*Hikouki-wo tobas-u* 'fly an airplane'
	sum 'live'	*Tokyo-ni sum-u* 'live in Tokyo'
(3) 3-valent:	*ager* 'give'	*inu-ni pan-wo ager-u* 'give bread to a dog'

The existential verb (T). Not only verbs but also adjectives are inflectional and can be predicates in Japanese. In addition, we have a special morpheme *da* that accepts predication. We call it the existential verb.

The existential verb is suffixed to an adjectival noun to derive an adjective. A table of inflections and some example sentences now follow.

[5] The existential verb inflections

Inflectional Form	Vowel Verb
Stem	*da*
Indicative Present	*da*
Indicative Past	*datta*
Gerund	*de*
Infinitive	*ni*
Noun-modifying	*na*
Conditional	*nara*

[6] Umi-wa sizuka-da. – 'The sea is calm.'
sea-DETERMINER calmness-EXISTENTIAL PRESENT

cf. Umi-wa hiro-i. – 'The sea is wide.'
sea-DETERMINER wide-PRESENT

Unlike true adjectives, this adjectivalizer needs a different inflectional suffix *-na* to modify a noun:

[7] Sizuka-na umi – 'calm sea'
calmness-EXISTENTIAL NOUN MODIFIER sea

cf. hiro-i umi – 'wide sea'
wide-PRESENT sea

A common noun can also be made a predicate by affixing the existential verb. In this case, the existential verb carries the role of a linking verb, otherwise known as a "copula".

[8] Kinou-wa yasumi-datta. – 'yesterday was a holiday.'
yesterday-DETERMINER holiday-EXISTENTIAL PAST

[9] Kare-wa gakusei-da. – 'He is a student.'
he student-EXISTENTIAL PRESENT

1.2. Auxiliaries (T)

An auxiliary can be classified according to the inflectional form it requires (stem/infinitive/gerund) of the lexical verb that comes to the left of it, and to its own inflectional pattern (verbal/adjectival/noninflectional).

(1) Causative *sase* (stem-dominant verbal)

[10] kodomo-ni pan-wo tabe-sase-ru. – 'make the child eat bread'
child-DATIVE bread-ACCUSATIVE eat-CAUSATIVE-PRESENT

(2) Passive *rare* (stem-dominant verbal)

[11] Kuruma-ni butuka-rare-ta. – 'hit by a car'
car-DATIVE hit-PASSIVE-PAST

(3) Potential *re* (stem-dominant verbal)

[12] Furansugo-wo hanas-e-ru. – 'can speak French'
French-ACCUSATIVE speak-POTENTIAL-PRESENT

(4) Volitional *you* (stem-dominant noninflectional)

[13] Tokyo-e mukaw-you. – 'head for Tokyo'
Tokyo-DIRECTIONAL head-VOLITIONAL

(5) Durative *i* (gerund-dominant verbal)

[14] Pan-wo tabe-te-i-ru. – 'eating bread'
bread-ACCUSATIVE eat-GERUND-DURATIVE-PRESENT

(6) Desirative *ta* (infinitive-dominant adjectival)

[15] Hon-wo yom-i-ta-i. – 'want to read a book'
book-ACCUSATIVE read-INFINITIVE-DESIRATIVE-PRESENT

(7) Negative *na* (stem-dominant adjectival)

[16] Pan-wo tabe-na-i. – 'do not eat bread'
bread-ACCUSATIVE eat-NEGATIVE-PRESENT

1.3. Adjectives (H)

Japanese has two major subclasses of adjectives: inflectional (ordinary) adjectives and noninflectional demonstrative adjectives. In attributive usage, both are located before the nouns they modify, whereas the latter is never used in predicative situations. The morphological difference between an adjectival stem and an adjectival noun (cf. 1.4.) is that only the former can accept inflectional suffixes.

Ordinary adjectives (H).

[17] Adjective inflections

Inflectional Form	Adjective
Stem	*aka* 'red'
Indicative Present	*aka-i*
Indicative Past	*aka-katta*
Infinitive	*aka-ku*
Gerund	*aka-kute*
Provisional	*aka-kereba*
Conditional	*aka-kattara*
Alternative	*aka-kattari*

[18] Hana-wa aka-i. – 'The flower is red.'
flower-DETERMINER red-PRESENT

[19] Yama-wa siro-katta. – 'The mountain was white.'
mountain-DETERMINER white-PAST

[20] Syoujo-wa utukusi-ku-nar-u – 'The girl becomes beautiful.'
girl-DETERMINER beautiful-INFINITIVE-PERFECTIVE-PRESENT

Demonstrative adjectives (H). Noninflectional demonstrative adjectives are: *kono* 'this', *sono* 'that', *ano* 'that' and *dono* 'which'. Their position is always in front of a noun, since this is the noun-modifying position.

1.4. Nouns

Japanese nouns have no inflections, nor is the gender grammatically relevant.

Common nouns (H). Common nouns include:

(1) common nouns: *yama* 'mountain', *pan* 'bread', etc
(2) pronouns (personal): *boku* 'I', *kare* 'he', *dare* 'who', etc.
(demonstrative): *koko* 'here', *doko* 'where', etc.

But there is no distinction between them in morphological usage.

Formal nouns (H). A formal noun is either a noun that implies the content of what the preceding clause or demonstrative adjective signifies, or it is a nominalizer that nominalizes the clause that precedes it, without which this noun cannot appear independently. Formal nouns include: *koto*, *mono*, and *no*. Examples:

[21] Sensei-ga it-ta koto-wa tadasi-i. – 'What the teacher said is right.'
teacher-NOMINATIVE say-PAST what-DETERMINER right-PRESENT

[22] Asa hayaku oki-ru koto-wa kenkou-ni yo-i. – 'Getting up early in the morning is good for one's health.'
morning early getup-PRESENT to-DETERMINER health-DATIVE good-PRESENT

[23] kare-ga sou it-ta no-wa matigai-datta. – 'That he said so was a mistake.'
he-NOMINATIVE so say-PAST that-DETERMINER mistake-EXISTENTIAL PAST

Adjectival nouns (H). An adjectival noun plus an existential verb together indicate adjectival predication. Adjectival nouns include *sizuka* 'quietness', *yukai* 'delight', *kandai* 'generosity', etc. They are used as in:

[24] Kinou kyousitu-wa sizuka-datta. – 'Yesterday it was quiet in the classroom.'
yesterday classroom-DETERMINER quiet-PAST

[25] Ano hito-wa yukai-na hito-da. – 'That man is a delightful man.'
that man-DETERMINER delightful EXISTENTIAL NOUN MODIFIER man-PRESENT

[26] Kono soti-wa kandai-da. – 'This measure is generous.'
this measure-DETERMINER generous-PRESENT

Enumerative nouns (T). Enumeration of countable nouns in Japanese is done with the help of enumerative nouns like *ken*, *mai*, *hiki*, *kai*, etc. It must take a numeral as its argument, that is, it is a numeral-dominant suffix.

[27] Mukasi kono toori-ni ie-ga san-ken at-ta. – 'Once there were three houses on this street.'
once this street-LOCATIVE house-DETERMINER three-ENUMERATIVE exist-PAST

[28] Gakusei-wa kami-wo ni-mai morat-ta. – 'The student received two sheets of paper.'
student-DETERMINER paper-ACCUSATIVE two-sheet(ENUMERATIVE) receive-PAST

[29] Koko-ni go-hiki-no inu-no koya-ga ar-u. – 'Here is a hut of the five dogs.'
here-LOCATIVE five-ENUMERATIVE-GENITIVE dog-GENITIVE hut-NOMINATIVE exist-PRESENT

Numerals (H). Numerals are nouns expressing numbers, usually followed by enumerative nouns. See examples in [27-30].

[30] Nan-byak-kai iw-ase-ru-no-da. – 'How many hundred times do you make me say it?'
how many-hundred-times(ENUMERATIVE) say-CAUSATIVE-PRESENT-FORMAL NOUN-EXISTENTIAL PRESENT

1.5. Adverbs (H)

True Japanese adverbs are lexically stable, rarely affected by suffixal agglutination, and constitute a closed class. On the other hand, adjectives and adjectival nouns may act as adverbials with the help of adverbializing suffixes.

Lexical adverbs. Those words like *kyou* 'today', *yuube* 'last night', *koko* 'here', etc.

that are naturally included in the temporal and spatial adverbs in European languages are treated as common nouns because of their behavior as nouns in suffixal agglutination. They of course function as adverbs either in the stem form (*kyou*) or with adverbializing suffixes (*koko-ni*).

[31] *yukkuri* 'slowly', *dandan* 'gradually', *tatimati* 'quickly', *kitto* 'surely', *mada* 'yet', *hotondo* 'hardly'

Derived adverbs. Infinitive suffixes *-ku* and *-ni* are used as adverbializers for the adverb stem and the adverbial noun, respectively.

[32] Yuube hagesi-ku kaze-ga hui-ta. – 'Last night the wind blew fiercely.'
lastnight fierce-ly wind-NOMINATIVE blow-PAST

[33] Ima-wa sizuka-ni yuki-ga fut-te-i-ru. – 'Now it is quietly snowing.'
now-TOPIC quiet-ly snow-NOMINATIVE fall-GERUND-be-PRESENT

1.6. Postpositions (T)

Postpositions are considered to be functional extensions of case suffixes. Morphologically they are derived from two sources: the noun and the verb. Also, there are two forms for each postposition according to the role the postpositional phrase plays in the given sentence. A postposition needs a noun argument with a case suffix specified for it. Otherwise, it can also have a proposition as its argument.

For example, *issyo* 'together with', *tame* 'for the sake of' *kawari* 'instead of', etc. are morphologically nouns though they never act as independent nouns.

[34] Tomodati-to issyo-ni Amerika-e ik-u. – 'I go to America with a friend.'
friend-with together-DATIVE(EXISTENTIAL INFINITIVE) America-to go-PRESENT

Tomodati-to issyo-no Amerika ryokou – 'trip to America with a friend'
friend-with together-GENITIVE(EXISTENTIAL NOUN-MODIFYING) America trip

[35] Kane-no tame-ni hatarak-u. – 'I work for money.'
money-GENITIVE sake-DATIVE(EXISTENTIAL INFINITIVE) work-PRESENT

Kane-no tame-no sigoto – 'labor for the sake of money.'
money-GENITIVE sake-GENITIVE(EXISTENTIAL NOUN-MODIFYING) labor

[36] Kazoku-wo siawase-ni su-ru tame-ni hatarak-u. – 'I work in order to make the family happy.'
family-ACCUSATIVE happiness-DATIVE make-PRESENT sake-DATIVE work-PRESENT

[37] Gakkou-e ik-u kawari-ni ie-de benkyousi-ta. – 'I studied at home instead of going to school.'
school-to go-PRESENT instead-of house-in study-PAST

On the other hand, *kansite* 'about, concerning', *yotte* 'by, through the action of', and *oite* 'in, in point of' are a few of the verb-originated postpositons used in adverbial contexts, thus having the following counterparts in noun-modifying positions, respectively: *kansuru*, *yoru*, and *okeru*. This group of postpositions may not take propositions as arguments.

[38] kare-wa zibun-no kenkyuu-ni kansite houkokusi-ta. – 'He reported on his own study.'
he-DETERMINER himself-GENITIVE study-DATIVE concerning report-PAST

[39] kare-wa zibun-no kenkyuu-ni kanssuru houkoku-wo si-ta. – 'He gave a report on his own study.'
he-DETERMINER himself-GENITIVE study-DATIVE concerning report-ACCUSATIVE make-PAST

1.7. Conjunctions (T)

Subordinate conjunctions. A subordinate conjunction is placed at the end of a subordinate clause. Subordinate conjunctions include: *toki(ni)* 'when', *nara(ba)* 'if', *mae(ni)* 'before', *ato(de)* 'after', *keredo(mo)* 'although', *node* 'as, since', *to* 'that'.

[40] Kare-ga eki-ni tui-ta toki, daremo i-na-katta. – 'When he arrived at the station, nobody was there.'
he-NOMINATIVE station-LOCATIVE arrive-PAST when nobody exist-not-PAST

Coordinate conjunctions. *sikasi* 'but', *dakara* 'therefore', *sosite* 'and', etc.

Internominal conjunction. *to* 'and'.

[41] otoko to onna – 'man and woman'

1.8. Suffixes (T)

Tense. Tense suffixes are *ru* (Present) and *ta* (Past) for verbs, *da* (Present) and *datta* (Past) for existential verbs, and *i* (Present) and *katta* (Past) for adjectives. A tense suffix is attached to the stem, as in:

[41] *tabe-ta* 'ate', *tabe-ru* 'eat', *kirei-da* 'is pretty', *kirei-datta* 'was pretty', *maru-i* 'is round', *maru-katta* 'was round'

Imperative. Imperative suffix *ro/e*

[42] Takusan tabe-ro. – 'Eat a lot.'
Motto nom-e. – 'Drink more.'

Verb/adjective-inflectional.

(1) Infinitive suffix *i*, *ni* and *ku* for the verb, existential and adjective, respectively.

(2) Gerundive suffix *te/de*, *de*, and *kute* for the verb, existential and adjective, respectively.

Case. Case suffixes are attached to the nouns to meet the valency requirements the verbal imposes on the arguments. Except for those playing adverbial roles, the Japanese nouns never appear in their stem forms in propositions. The following is an exhaustive list of case suffixes:

[43] Case suffixes

Suffix class	**Suffix**	**Example**
Nominative	*ga*	*Kane-ga nar-u* 'A bell rings.'
Accusative	*wo*	*Kane-wo naras-u* 'ring a bell'
Dative	*ni*	*Kimi-ni hon-wo age-ru* 'give you a book'
Locative	*ni*	*London-ni sum-u* 'live in London'
	de	*kouen-de asob-u* 'play in the park'
Source	*kara*	*Tokyo-kara ku-ru* 'come from Tokyo'
	yori	*boku-yori kimi-e* 'from me to you'
Destinational	*made*	*Utrecht-made ik-u* 'go to Utrecht'
Directional	*e*	*gakko-e muka-u* 'head for school'
Concern	*ni*	*haha-ni ni-ru* 'resemble mother'
Transitive	*ni*	*isya-ni nar-u* 'become a doctor'
Coopreative	*to*	*kodomo-to asob-u* 'play with children'
Comparative	*yori*	*kimi-yori waka-i* 'younger than you'
Circumstantial	*de*	*hitori-de ik-u* 'go alone'
Instrumental	*de*	*pen-de kak-u* 'write with a pen'
Emphatic	*mo*	*10-kg-mo ar-u* 'weigh even 10 kg'
Topic/Determinant	*wa*	*mizu-wa tumeta-i* 'the water is cold.'
Co-occurrent	*mo*	*boku-mo it-ta.* 'I, too, went.'
Genitive	*no*	*Tom-no hon* 'Tom's book'

Noun plural. Noun suffixes include plural suffixes *tati* and *ra*.

[44] *boku* 'I', *boku-ra* 'we', *musume* 'girl', *musume-tati* 'girls'

Interrogative. To interrogativize a declarative sentence, the interrogative suffix *ka* is affixed at the end of the sentence.

[45] Ano yarou-ni kane-ga ar-u-ka. – 'Does that fellow have money?'
that fellow-DATIVE money-NOMINATIVE exist-PRESENT-INTERROGATIVE

1.9. Comma and period

The comma and period are included in the word classes to govern clauses and sentences.

2. Dependent types

2.1. Complements and adjuncts

[46-47] are the tables of complements and adjuncts used for Japanese. Before going into the detailed description of the dependent types and their morpheme classes, we will give a brief discussion of the main decisions made in establishing these dependent classes.

[46]

Abbr.	Complements
PRED	predicative
CASC	case complement
ADVC	adverbial complement
INFC	infinitival complement
GERC	gerundive complement
STMC	stem complement
PROC	propositional compelement
CLSC	clausal complement
POSC	postpositional complement
CARG	casal argument
NARG	numeral argument
PARG	plural argument
JARG	conjunction argument

[47]

Abbr.	Adjuncts
ATTR	attribute
CASA	case adjunct
ADVA	adverbial adjunct
PROA	propositional adjunct
MODA	modal adjunct
POSA	postpositional adjunct
CJCA	conjunctional-clausal adjunct

Although these dependents were basically designed according to those for DLT's IL, observation of Japanese data and native speakers' intuition led us to deviate from the original guideline to the extent of abolishing labels like "subject" and "object", and, instead, introducing "case complement". By doing this, we claim that, in the case of a verb governing noun phrases, for instance, the subject and the object do not, as in European languages, enjoy syntactically or morphologically privileged positions; these and other dependent nouns are connected in the same way to the governing verb with the help of case suffixes.

We have devised "gerundive and stem complements" in addition to "infinitival complement". Note that, as mentioned in 1.2., verbal morphemes and inflectional suffixes require their dependents to take one of these three inflectional forms.

Here we present the morpheme classes with the abbreviations to be used in the description of the dependent types in the following section.

[48]

Abbr.	Morpheme Class
VB	Lexical Verb
EX	Existential Verb
AX	Auxiliary
AJ	Adjective
NO	Noun
EN	Enumerative Noun
AD	Adverb
PS	Postposition
SC	Subordinate Conjunction
CC	Coordinate Conjunction
IC	Internominal Conjunction
TN	Tense Suffix
IM	Imperative Suffix
VS	Verbal-Inflectional Suffix
CS	Case Suffix
PL	Plural Suffix
IR	Interrogative Suffix
PR	Period
CM	Comma

2.2. Dependent type tables

[49] **Verb-dependents**

	VB	EX	AX	AJ	NO	EN	AD	PS	SC	CC	IC	TN	IM	VS	CS	PL	IR	PR	CM
PRED																			
CASC															×				
ADVC						×	×							×					
INFC														×					
GERC														×					
STMC																			
PROC									×										
CLSC																			
POSC																			
CARG																			
NARG																			
PARG																			
JARG																			
ATTR																			
CASA															×				
ADVA						×	×							×					
PROA																			
MODA																			
POSA																			
CJSA																			

The most normal dependency pattern for complements of the verb is the combination of noun and case suffix required by the verb valency. This is given the functionally descriptive name "case complement". In the case of a verb governing another verb, on the other hand, an inflectional suffix between the two elements is necessary, thus avoiding immediate government of the verb by a nominal or verbal. A proposition also depends on the verb with the help of a subordinate conjunction, *to* 'that'. Unlike the English *that*-clause, where *that* is optional, Japanese *to* should never be omitted. Only syntactic-adverbial/enumerative nouns are directly adjoined to verbs.

[50] CASC/Case Suffix
pan-**wo** *tabe*-ru – 'eat bread'
bread-ACCUSATIVE eat-PRESENT
inu-**ga** *ku*-ru – 'a dog comes.'
kodomo-**ni** hon-**wo** *age*-ru – 'give a book to a child'
child-DATIVE book-ACCUSATIVE give-PRESENT

[51] INFC/Inflectional Suffix
hon-wo yom-**i**-*hazime*-ru – 'begin to read a book'
book-ACCUSATIVE read-INFINITIVE-begin-PRESENT

[52] GERC/Inflectional Suffix
hon-wo yon-**de**-*sima*-u – 'finish reading a book'
book-ACCUSATIVE read-GERUND-finish-PRESENT

[53] PROC/Subordinate Conjunction
sono yama-wa kirei-da-**to** *omo*-u – 'I think that the montain is beautiful.'
that mountain-DETERMINER beautiful-EXISTENTIAL PRESENT-SUBORDINATE CONJUNCTION think-PRESENT

[54] ADVC/Inflectional Suffix
Kyousitu-wa sizuka-**ni** *nat*-ta. – 'The class became quiet.'
the class quiet-EXISTENTIAL INFINITIVE become-PAST

[55] ADVC/Enumerative Noun
Kaigi-wa iti-**zikan** *tuzui*-ta. – 'The meeting lasted for one hour.'
the meeting one-hour continue-PAST

[56] PRED/Enumerative Noun
kono hon-(ni)-wa 300-**peezi** *ar*-u. – 'This book has 300 pages.'
this book-(DATIVE)-DETERMINER 300-pages exist-PRESENT
Ie-kara Eki-made 15-**hun** *kakar*-u. – 'It takes 15 minutes from the house to the station.'
house-SOURCE station-DESTINATION 15-minutes take-PRESENT

[57] ADVA/Noun
Yuube boku-wa biiru-wo *non*-da. – 'Last night I drank beer.'
last night I-DETERMINER beer-ACCUSATIVE drink-PAST

[58] **Existential-dependents**

	VB	EX	AX	AJ	NO	EN	AD	PS	SC	CC	IC	TN	IM	VS	CS	PL	IR	PR	CM
PRED					×	×	×	×	×						×	×			
CASC																			
ADVC																			
INFC																			
GERC																			
STMC																			
PROC												×					×		
CLSC									×										
POSC																			
CARG																			
NARG																			
PARG																			
JARG																			
ATTR																			
CASA																			
ADVA																			
PROA																			
MODA							×												
POSA																			
CJSA																			

The relatively large group of categories dependent on the existential verb has the label PRED (predicative), since the governor da functions as a predicativizer over the morpheme classes in table [58].

[59] PRED/Noun

Hanako-wa **gakusei**-*da*. – 'Hanako is a student.'

PRED/Enumerative

Kono hon-wa 300-**peezi**-*da*. – 'This book is 300 pages long.'

kare-wa 175-**cm**-*da*. – 'He is 175 cm tall.'

PRED/Adverb

Kare-no hanasi-kata-wa **yukkuri**-*da*. – 'The way he speaks is slow.'

PRED/Postposition

Kougi-wa Amerika keizai-ni **kansite**-*datta*. – 'The lecture was about American economy.'

PRED/Case Suffix

Sono okurimono-wa kimi-**ni**-*da*. – 'That present is for you.'

PRED/Plural Suffix

Kati-wa boku-**tati**-*da*. – 'Winners are we.'

[60] PROC/Interrogative Suffix

Mondai-wa ano ko-ni sore-ga deki-ru-**ka**-*da*. – 'The question is whether the girl can do it.'

PROC/Tense Suffix

Kare-no kotae-wa hitori-de ik-**u**-*datta* – 'His answer was that he would go alone.'

[61] CLSC/Subordinate Conjunction

Paatii-wa kougi-ga owat-ta **atode**-*da*. – 'The party is after the lecture is over.'

[62] MODA/Adverb

Tabun are-wa uso-*da*. – 'Maybe that is a lie.'

maybe that-DETERMINER lie-EXISTENTIAL PRESENT

[63] **Auxiliary-dependents**

	VB	EX	AX	AJ	NO	EN	AD	PS	SC	CC	IC	TN	IM	VS	CS	PL	IR	PR	CM
PRED																			
CASC															×				
ADVC																			
INFC														×					
GERC														×					
STMC																			
PROC																			
CLSC																			
POSC																			
CARG																			
NARG																			
PARG																			
JARG																			
ATTR																			
CASA														×					
ADVA							×	×	×										
PROA																			
MODA																			
POSA																			
CJSA																			

[64] CASC/Case Suffix

Haha-**ga** kodomo-**ni** pan-wo tabe-*sase*-ta. – 'Mother made the child eat bread.'
mother-NOMINATIVE child-DATIVE bread-ACCUSATIVE eat-CAUSATIVE-PAST

[65] GERC/Verbal Suffix

Tabe-**te**-*i*-ru – 'be eating (it)'
eat-GERUND-Progressive-PRESENT

[66] INFC/Verbal Suffix

Yom-**i**-*ta*-i – 'want to read (books)'
read-INFINITIVE-want-PRESENT

INFC/Adjectival Suffix

Aka-**ku**-*nar*-u – 'turn red'
red-INFINITIVE-become-PRESENT

[67] STMC/Verb

tegami-wo **yoma**-*na*-i – 'do not read the letter'
letter-ACCUSATIVE read-not-PRESENT

[68] ADVA/Adverb

Zettai isya-ni nar-i-*ta*-i – 'I absolutely want to be a doctor.'
absolutely doctor-TRANSITIVE become-INFINITIVE-want-PRESENT

ADVA/Postposition

Kare-zisin-no **tameni** hatarak-*ase*-ta. – 'I made him work for the benefit of himself.'
he-self-GENITIVE for the benefit of work-CAUSATIVE-PAST

ADVA/Subordinate Conjunction

Boku-wa zibun-ga ne-ru **maeni** kodomo-wo ne-*sase*-ta. – 'I made my child sleep before I went to bed.'
I-DETERMINER self-NOMINATIVE sleep-PRESENT before child-ACCUSATIVE sleep-CAUSATIVE-PAST

[69] Adjective-dependents

	VB	EX	AX	AJ	NO	EN	AD	PS	SC	CC	IC	TN	IM	VS	CS	PL	IR	PR	CM
PRED															×				
CASC																			
ADVC																			
INFC																			
GERC																			
STMC																			
PROC																			
CLSC																			
POSC																			
CARG																			
NARG																			
PARG																			
JARG																			
ATTR																			
CASA																			
ADVA					×	×	×												
PROA																			
MODA																			
POSA																			
CJSA																			

[70] CASC/Case Suffix

Sono hana-**wa** *aka*-i. – 'The flower is red.'
that flower-DETERMINER red-PRESENT

[71] ADVA/Enumerative

Kare-wa boku-yori 5-**kg** *omo*-i. – 'He is 5 kg heavier than I am.'
he-NOMINATIVE I-COMPARATIVE 5 kg heavy-PRESENT

ADVA/Adverb

Motto *omosiro*-i eiga-ga mi-ta-i. – 'I want to watch a more interesting movie.'
more interesting-PRESENT movie-NOMINATIVE watch-(INFINITIVE)-want-PRESENT

ADVA/Noun

Konogoro maiban *suzusi*-i. – 'Its cool every night recently.'
recently every night cool-PRESENT

[72] Noun-dependents

	VB	EX	AX	AJ	NO	EN	AD	PS	SC	CC	IC	TN	IM	VS	CS	PL	IR	PR	CM
PRED																			
CASC																			
ADVC																			
INFC																			
GERC																			
STMC																			
PROC												×							
CLSC																			
POSC																			
CARG																			
NARG																			
PARG																			
JARG																			
ATTR					×							×		×					
CASA															×				
ADVA																			
PROA									×			×							
MODA																			
POSA								×											
CJSA																			

[73] PROC/Tense Suffix

Kare-ga it-**ta** *koto*-wo omoidas-e. – 'Remember what he said.'

he-NOMINATIVE say-PAST what-ACCUSATIVE remember-IMPERATIVE

[74] ATTR/Tense Suffix

Aka-**i** *hana*. – 'red flower'

ATTR/Existential-Inflectional Suffix

Kirei-**na** *musume* – 'pretty girl'

ATTR/Noun

Amerika *keizai* – 'American economy'

[75] CASA/Case Suffix

Ken-**no** *tukue* – 'Ken's desk'

[76] PROA/Tense Suffix

kouen-de hasir-**u** *hito* – 'man who runs in the park'

park-LOCATIVE run-PRESENT man

PROA/Subordinate Conjunction

kare-ga ki-ta **toiu** *zizitu* – 'the fact that he came'

he-NOMINATIVE come-PAST that fact

[77] POSA/Postposition

seizi-ni **kansuru** *kizi* – 'articles about politics'

politics-DATIVE about article

syougaisya-no **tameno** *gakkou* – 'school for the handicapped'

[78] **Enumerative-dependents**

	VB	EX	AX	AJ	NO	EN	AD	PS	SC	CC	IC	TN	IM	VS	CS	PL	IR	PR	CM
PRED																			
CASC																			
ADVC																			
INFC																			
GERC																			
STMC																			
PROC																			
CLSC																			
POSC																			
CARG																			
NARG					×														
PARG																			
JARG																			
ATTR																			
CASA																			
ADVA																			
PROA																			
MODA																			
POSA																			
CJSA																			

Enumerative nouns require only numeral noun complements as dependents.

[79] NARG/Noun (Numeral)

Kono hon-wa **300**-*peezi*-da. – 'This book is 300 pages long.'

100-wa 25-no **4**-*bai*-da. – '100 is 4 times as much as 25.'

[80] **Adverb-dependents**

	VB	EX	AX	AJ	NO	EN	AD	PS	SC	CC	IC	TN	IM	VS	CS	PL	IR	PR	CM
PRED																			
CASC																			
ADVC																			
INFC																			
GERC																			
STMC																			
PROC																			
CLSC																			
POSC																			
CARG																			
NARG																			
PARG																			
JARG																			
ATTR																			
CASA																			
ADVA							×												
PROA																			
MODA																			
POSA																			
CJSA																			

An adverb as a governor has only adjuncts as dependents.

[81] ADVA/Adverb

Motto *takusan* rensyu-wo su-ru beki-da. – 'You should practice a lot more.'
a lot more

[82] **Postposition-dependents**

	VB	EX	AX	AJ	NO	EN	AD	PS	SC	CC	IC	TN	IM	VS	CS	PL	IR	PR	CM
PRED																			
CASC																			
ADVC																			
INFC																			
GERC																			
STMC																			
PROC																			
CLSC																			
POSC												×			×				
CARG																			
NARG																			
PARG																			
JARG																			
ATTR																			
CASA																			
ADVA																			
PROA																			
MODA																			
POSA																			
CJSA																			

Postpositional complements are the only dependents of postpositions. The dependent can either be a noun plus a case suffix, or a proposition.

[83] POSC/Case Suffix

Kane-**no** *tameni* hatarak-u. – 'I work for money.'
money-GENITIVE for-the-benefit-of work-PRESENT

POSC/Tense Suffix

Kazoku-wo siawase-ni su-**ru** *tameni* hatarak-u. – 'I work in order to make the family happy.'
family-ACCUSATIVE happiness-DATIVE make-PRESENT for-the-benefit-of work-PRESENT

[84] Conjunction-dependents

	VB	EX	AX	AJ	NO	EN	AD	PS	SC	CC	IC	TN	IM	VS	CS	PL	IR	PR	CM
PRED																			
CASC																			
ADVC																			
INFC																			
GERC																			
STMC																			
PROC												×							
CLSC																			
POSC																			
CARG																			
NARG																			
PARG																			
JARG					×														
ATTR																			
CASA																			
ADVA																			
PROA																			
MODA																			
POSA																			
CJSA																			

In 1.7., we created three subclasses of conjunctions: subordinate, coordinate and internominal conjunctions. The first two of these always govern propositions, whereas the last links nouns.

[85] PROC/Tense Suffix

Kare-ga eki-ni tui-ta *toki*, daremo i-na-katta. – 'When he arrived at the station, nobody was there.'
he-NOMINATIVE station-at arrive-PAST when nobody exist-not-PAST

Natu-wa atu-i *ga*, huyu-wa samu-i. – 'Summer is hot, but winter is cold.'
summer-DETERMINER hot-PRESENT but winter-DETERMINER cold-PRESENT

[86] JARG/Noun

otoko *to* **onna** – 'man and woman'

[87] **Suffix-dependents**

	VB	EX	AX	AJ	NO	EN	AD	PS	SC	CC	IC	TN	IM	VS	CS	PL	IR	PR	CM
PRED					×														
CASC															×				
ADVC							×												
INFC																			
GERC																			
STMC			×	×															
PROC					×							×				×			
CLSC									×										
POSC																			
CARG					×														
NARG																			
PARG					×														
JARG																			
ATTR																			
CASA																			
ADVA																			
PROA																			
MODA																			
POSA																			
CJSA																			

Since the suffixes cannot exist as independent words, the suffix- dependents are all complements.

- (1) TENSE SUFFIX-DEPENDENTS

[88] STMC/Verb

Hanako-wa **oyoi-*da*.** – 'Hanako swam.'
swim-PAST

STMC/Auxiliary

Hanako-wa ringo-wo tabe-**ta-*katta*.** – 'Hanako wanted to eat an apple.'
eat-DESIRATIVE-PAST

STMC/Adjective

Waka-katta koro, Hanako-wa **utukusi-*katta*.** – 'When young, Hanako was pretty.'
pretty-PAST

- (2) IMPERATIVE SUFFIX-DEPENDENTS

[89] STMC/Verb

Yukkuri **tabe-*ro*.** Takusan **nom-*e*.** – 'Eat slowly. Drink a lot.'

- (3) VERBAL/ADJECTIVAL-INFLECTIONAL SUFFIX-DEPENDENTS

[90] STMC/Verb

Kare-wa hon-wo **yon-*de***-i-ru. – 'He is reading a book.'

STMC/Auxiliary

kodomo-ni pan-wo tabe-**sase-*te***-mi-ta. – 'I tried having the child eat bread.'

STMC/Adjective

Sora-ga **aka-*ku***-nat-ta. – 'The sky turned red.'

- (4) CASE SUFFIX-DEPENDENTS

[91] CARG/Noun

Hanako-*ga* Taro-*ni* ame-*wo* age-ta. – 'Hanako gave Taro a candy.'
Hanako-NOMINATIVE Taro-DATIVE candy-ACCUSATIVE give-PAST

[92] CASC/Case Suffix

Kono mondai-wa kare-**ni-*wa*** muzukasi-i. – 'This problem is too difficult for him.'

- (5) PLURAL SUFFIX-DEPENDENTS

[93] PARG/Noun

kodomo-*tati* – 'children'

boku-*ra* – 'we'

- (6) INTERROGATIVE SUFFIX-DEPENDENTS

[94] PRED/Noun

Hontou-*ka*. truth-INTERROGATIVE – 'really?'

[95] CASC/Case Suffix

Kore-wa kare-**no**-*ka*. – 'Is this his?'
this-DETERMINER he-GENITIVE

[96] ADVC/Adverb

Sigoto-wa **yukkuri**-*ka*. – 'Is the work done slowly?'

[97] PROC/Noun

kare-wa **sensei**-*ka*. – 'Is he a teacher?'

PROC/Tense Suffix

Inu-wa kusa-wo tabe-**ru**-*ka*. – 'Does the dog eat grass?'

PROC/Plural Suffix

Sore-wa kodomo-**tati**-*ka*. – 'Are they children?'

[98] CLSC/Subordinate Conjunction

Sore-wa kare-ga uso-wo tui-ta **kara**-*ka*. – 'Is it because he told a lie?'

[99] Period/comma-dependents

	VB	EX	AX	AJ	NO	EN	AD	PS	SC	CC	IC	TN	IM	VS	CS	PL	IR	PR	CM
PRED					×														
CASC															×				
ADVC																			
INFC																			
GERC																			
STMC																			
PROC		×										×					×		
CLSC									×	×									
POSC																			
CARG																			
NARG																			
PARG																			
JARG																			
ATTR																			
CASA																			
ADVA																			
PROA																			
MODA																			
POSA																			
CJSA																			×

- (1) COMMA-DEPENDENTS

[100] CLSC/Subordinate Conjunction

yama-wa taka-i **node**, kuuki-ga usu-i. – 'Since the mountain is high, the air is thin.'

CLSC/Coordinate Conjunction

Boku-wa sensei-da **ga**, kimi-tati-wa gakusei-da. – 'I am a teacher, and you are students.'

- (2) PERIOD-DEPENDENTS

[101] PRED/Noun

Boku-wa **gakusei** . – 'I am a student.'

[102] CASC/Case Suffix

Boku-**wa** gakusei .

[103] PROC/Existential

Umi-wa sizuka-**da** . – 'The sea is calm.'

PROC/Tense Suffix

Sora-wa ao-**i** . – 'The sky is blue.'

PROC/Interrogative Suffix

Sora-wa ao-i-**ka** . – 'Is the sky blue?'

[104] CLCA/Comma

yama-wa taka-i node **,** kuuki-ga usu-i . – 'Since the mountain is high, the air is thin.'

3. Sample sentence

omo-i hosi-wa tatimati moetuki-te sima-u-ga, karu-i hosi-wa yukkuri moe-ru node, 100-oku-nen izyou nagaikisu-ru mono-mo ar-u.

heavy-PRES star-DETERMINER quickly burn-out-(GERUND) finish-PRES-but light-PRES star-DETERMINER slowly burn-PRES since-(SUBORDINATE CONJUNCTION) 10-billion-years more-than live-long-PRES FORMAL NOUN-COOCCURRENT CASE exist-PRES

'heavy stars burn out quickly, but light stars burn so slowly that some even live for more than 10 billion years'

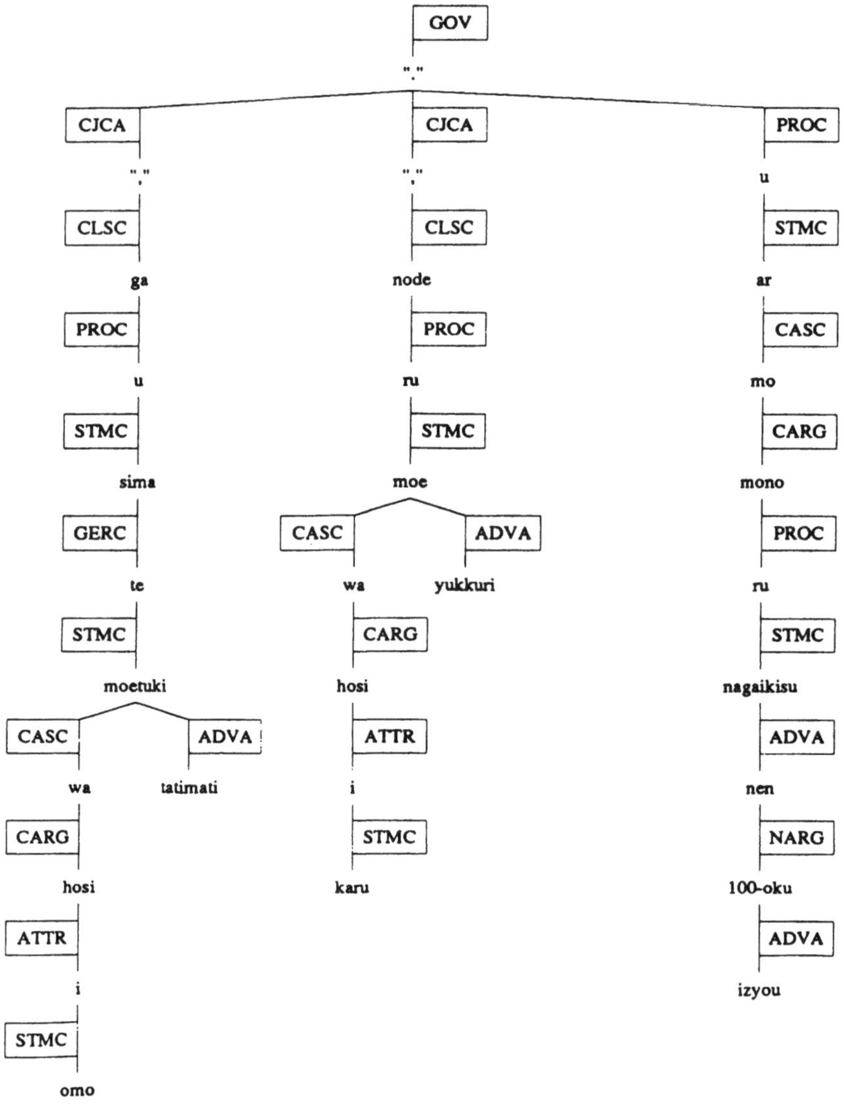

A dependency syntax of Esperanto

Klaus Schubert

Utrecht, Netherlands

1. Esperanto for people and Esperanto for computers

This article offers a dependency syntax of Esperanto. Like all the syntax descriptions in this volume, it is written within the framework of the model of dependency syntax developed for the DLT machine translation system.

Among the languages dealt with in the DLT project and in this volume, Esperanto occupies a special position in that it is not one of DLT's source or target languages, but rather its intermediate language (IL). None of the languages translated in DLT is in direct contact with any other source or target language, but each of them interfaces with Esperanto only. Translation in DLT is always from a source language into Esperanto and from Esperanto on into one or more target languages.

Since Esperanto still seems to be a new departure for many in theoretical and computational linguistics, I give a very concise characterisation of the language in section 1.1. In 1.2. I sketch the special function of Esperanto as an intermediate language in machine translation.

1.1. Esperanto at a glance

Esperanto is a planned language. From about a thousand projects of planned languages suggested so far (Duličenko 1988) Esperanto is the only one which has completed the transition from an artificial symbol system to a full-fledged human language (Blanke 1985: 105ff. and *Tabelle* 2). That is, since it was first published a century ago (Zamenhof 1887), Esperanto has grown into communicative use. Today it has a (second-)language community which develops the language in both reflected and unconscious ways in much the same way as with ethnic languages. Concerning the size of Esperanto's language community I do not know of any verifiable figures. Estimates range from half a million to more than 20 million speakers worldwide, the more serious figures being closer to the lower end of the scale. In the context relevant here, it is not so much the quantity as the quality that counts: whatever the precise number is, it can confidently be said that the Esperanto community is today big enough to maintain the language in a natural way. There is plenty of evidence for this claim.

All formal features of Esperanto grammar are extremely regular. Esperanto is 99% agglutinative (Wells 1978: 33). The content words (verbs, nouns, adjectives and adverbs) bear a word class-identifying morpheme. Nouns and most nominal pronouns are declined for number (singular, plural) and case (nominative, accusative). Both features are also found in adjectives and adjectival pronouns that agree with a noun. Personal pronouns have the case distinction, but not number as a syntactic feature, since it is semantically inherent in the root. Esperanto is a rather extreme representative of the so-called free word order languages, thanks to case marking of subjects, objects etc. The case distinction is also used to distinguish the static from the directional meaning of prepositions (*en la domo* 'in the house' vs. *en la domon* 'into the house') and of adverbs (*hejme* 'at home' vs. *hejmen* 'home'). Verbs are inflected for tense-mood and voice. The tense system has three tenses (past, present, future) and three forms expressing relative time (anterior, simultaneous, posterior) for each of the tenses. For an esperantologist, Hans Reichenbach's (1947) often-quoted system of three times three time relations reads as a true depiction of Esperanto tense grammar.

Esperanto is an a-posteriori planned language, which means among other things that its vocabulary consists of loans from ethnic languages. Due to its agglutinative structure, Esperanto takes loan words into its grammatical system as morphemes, not directly as words. The meaning of words and morphemes in Esperanto today does not depend on any reference languages, but is autonomously maintained by convention in the language community. Esperanto is a schematic planned language, which means that unlike naturalist planned-language projects it is not meant to be immediately intelligible for those acquainted with a certain set of reference languages. As a schematic language Esperanto has to be learned, but once learnt, it enhances active use rather than passive understanding only (cf. Schubert 1989b: 252).

Readers unacquainted with the terms I use here to characterise Esperanto are referred to a more extensive introduction to interlinguistics, the science of planned languages (Schubert 1989a).

1.2. Esperanto in DLT

The DLT machine translation system uses Esperanto as its intermediate language. The specific requirements of machine translation have made it necessary to apply a few modifications in Esperanto for making it suit the role of an intermediate language. But let it be said right away: The modifications applied to Esperanto in DLT are in no way due to any insufficiency whatsoever of Esperanto as a human language, but rather to the unsuitability of human languages for the "unnatural" role of an intermediate language in machine translation. Extremely simplifying the argument for Esperanto in this function (cf. Schubert 1988a,b,c) I can say that, on the one hand, an intermediate language in machine translation, being the one and only link between the source and the target languages, cannot make do with less than the entire and unrestricted expressive power of a human language, whereas, on the other hand, the specific needs of multilingual machine translation allow for human assistance in the first half of the translation process (source → intermediate language), but not in the second half (intermediate → target languages), so that the translation **from** the intermediate language should produce high-quality output fully automatically, without post-editing. Since a generally agreed-upon dogma says that fully automatic high-quality translation between ordinary human languages is impossible, the conclusion is a language which has acquired full expressiveness and at the same time is suited for translation to such an extraordinary degree that fully automatic translation from it is possible. DLT's solution to this is Esperanto. But because Esperanto is a language for people, it does not completely meet the needs of extreme translatability. For use in DLT, an intermediate language has therefore been designed. This is Esperanto with the additional condition that it should be **syntactically unambiguous.**

The required suitability for translation of an intermediate language has its semantic aspects as well, but there is no such thing as semantic unambiguousness. By contrast, syntactic unambiguousness can be achieved by relatively slight modifications. I take the term *syntax* to cover the entire form side of the linguistic sign (Schubert 1987: 14f.). DLT's intermediate language should accordingly be syntactically unambiguous not only at the sentence level, but also at the word level. Making Esperanto syntax unambiguous means making distinctions in form for the different syntactic analyses of any sentence (or word). At the sentence level this is achieved by an end-of-syntagma mark to be used when necessary (thus not at the end of every syntagma, but only when a different reading is possible as well). Witkam (1983: IV-92ff.) introduced an extra space in this function. For better visibility in printing, I use an underscore here:

> Ni vidas la viron en la parko.
> Ni vidas la viron _en la parko.

These are the two readings of the too well-known sample sentence 'We see the man in the park'. In the second instance, the extra space (here, underscore) signals the fact that the preceding noun syntagma (*la viron*) is finished, so that the subsequent syntagma cannot be a dependent of *viron*. A parser which encounters this disambiguating symbol must look for another possible governor for *en la parko* and will in this case find the verb, *vidas*.

In a similar way DLT's intermediate language is disambiguated at the word level. It is totally agglutinative, and the morpheme boundaries are marked by means of a special morpheme token ('). The sentence above thus reads

Ni vid'as la vir'o'n en la park'o.

Word level ambiguities – resolved by Esperanto speakers by understanding the context – are impossible in the intermediate language:

Esp. *la sendata letero*
IL *la send'at'a leter'o* 'the letter being sent'
IL *la sen'dat'a leter'o* 'the undated letter'

These modifications – morpheme token and extra space – are unobtrusive. DLT's intermediate language is in fact very close to common Esperanto. It is worth noting that this closeness is a feature essential to the functioning of the language in machine translation. At first sight one might feel tempted to think that the intermediate language, which always remains within the system and never functions as an input or output language for the users, is completely in the system designers' hands and can be modified in whatever way they find appropriate. At first glance this is so indeed. But as is confirmed by both theoretical reasoning and practical experience, it is of utmost importance to a machine translation system that its intermediate language possess a well-established, autonomous **norm**. It is needed for several purposes, each of which is crucial to the translation capacity of the system. First, the intermediate language should be independent of reference languages. It should not be defined by means of an explicit definition in, say, English, because it in that case could not be more than a subset of its reference language. In addition, it would lack the specific preciseness and clarity that is characteristic for a language used primarily for international, transethnic and cross-cultural communication. (For an ethnic language such as English, the international function is at best a secondary function which has no major impact on the language itself. For Esperanto, by contrast, the need of making oneself understood to members of different language communities and cultures in international communication is the main function which constitutes the language and is reflected in all elements of its structure.) Second, the intermediate language should be learnable. The Chinese-IL lexicographer and the French-IL lexicographer should be sure about the precise meaning of the word without having to look up an explicit definition which might be given in English or any other reference language or in translated (and thus, inevitably, not fully congruent) forms in French and Chinese. Third, regardless of the benefits of syntactic flexibility, the intermediate language should not copy or imitate the constructions found in the source language, but have its own preferred norm. Otherwise the translation system would produce English-like, French-like, Chinese-like and other source-like intermediate texts and the intermediate-to-target modules would have to be prepared for each of these varieties. The intermediate language was introduced among other things to solve the problem of combinatorial explosiveness, but if such translations were allowed, the combinatorial explosiveness of a system based on language pairs would be re-introduced in the system. It goes without saying that this consequence should be avoided at any cost.

As a conclusion it can be said, that although the intermediate language does not leave the translation system, it necessarily must be very close to a language spoken in a language community. This is why the inevitable modifications in DLT's intermediate language have been kept as small and unobtrusive as possible.

There is an additional argument for this, whose motivation is of a mainly practical nature. Its importance cannot be overestimated. This is the insight that machine translation presupposes the existence of huge dictionaries, knowledge banks etc. and that these enormous amounts of data cannot be collected and arranged in a processable form by lexicographic handwork only. If the scope of machine translation is to exceed the limits of highly restricted thematic fields (so-called domains or sublanguages), computational lexicography is impossible without a relatively high degree of automation. A prerequisite for (semi-)automatic lexicography, however, is the existence of substantial quantities of texts written in the language in question. DLT's intermediate language should also for this reason keep close to the language of available corpora, that is, to common Esperanto.

For all these reasons, the present description covers both DLT's intermediate language and common Esperanto. It replaces a description published earlier (Schubert 1986).

2. The syntactic system

This section presents first the elements of the syntactic system of Esperanto, the word classes, and then how they combine (dependent types).

2.1. Word classes

I distinguish twelve word classes. They are defined by syntactic distribution (Schubert 1987: 33), but most of them are more easily recognized by their word class markers. In the following list I therefore give these formal characteristics where appropriate.

As was stated in 1.2., the difference between common Esperanton and DLT's IL consists in the syntactic unambiguousness of the latter. That no more radical modifications are required is an insight gained not at the very beginning of the DLT project, but in the course of experimental system design. In the DLT feasibility study from the pre-implementation phase of the project (Witkam 1983: IV) a series of modifications is described which were then thought to be necessary or useful for Esperanto's function as a intermediate language. Some of these modifications came down to disambiguating certain function words by adding more specific ones to the list. These new function words were suggested to resolve various ambiguities, mainly semantic ones. In the implementation phase of the DLT project (since the beginning of 1985) the 1983 version of the IL was used, discussed, tested and revised. As a result it turned out that the requirement of unambiguousness at all levels of syntax is sufficient to delimit the modifications needed in Esperanto. At the same time the insight was gained that crucial needs of machine translation made it extremely desirable to keep the IL as close to the actually spoken form of Esperanto as ever possible. Because of all this, the present version of the IL uses only a few of the non-Esperanto function words. These have not been abolished, however, but rather declared optional, so that they remain part of the dictionary and might be used if an unforeseen need occurs (which has not been the case from 1985 until the time of writing, summer 1989). I include the IL-specific function words in this list, marking them with an "IL".

The "correlative table", referred to below, contains the correlatives of Esperanto. The words are made up of two parts, viz. the stems *i-* '[indefinite]', *ki-* '[interrogative]', *ti-* '[demonstrative]', *ĉi-* '[universal quantifier], *neni-* '[negator]' and *ali-* 'other' and the endings *-u* '[determiner]', *-o* '[impersonal pronoun]', *-a* '[quality]', *-e* '[place]', *-al* '[reason]', *-el* '[manner]', *-am* '[time]', *-om* '[quantity]' and *-es* '[possessor]'. Each of the stems can be combined with any of the endings so that one gets, e.g., *iu* 'someone', *nenial* 'of no reason' or *ĉiam* 'always'. The parts of the words are not considered independent morphemes in the IL, since not all of them have the meaning the morpheme has in other constructions (and homonymy in IL morphemes is undesirable). An example is the *-u* of *kiu* 'who' etc. which does not have the imperative meaning of the *'u* morpheme in *manĝ'u* 'eat' and similar forms. The *ali-* forms are not considered to be part of the table in traditional Esperanto grammars, although the community has begun to use many of the *ali-* forms. The grammarians are reluctant to add these forms due to a clash between *alie* interpreted as a deadjectival adverb 'otherwise, in another way' (< *alia* 'other') and *alie* interpreted as a table word 'elsewhere'. In DLT's IL an adjectival morpheme *ali'* is considered to exist in parallel with the *ali-* table words, so that all required forms can be made and (thanks to the morpheme tokens) be recognised unambiguously (*ali'e* vs. *alie*).

The words given literally below are mostly function words. For this category of words it is often difficult or even impossible to give a concise gloss in a meaningful way. I therefore omit glosses in most cases.

The word classes are:

Verb (VRB). All words with any of the endings *'i* (infinitive) and *'is, 'as, 'os, 'us, 'u* (finite forms: past, present, future tense, conditional, imperative).

Noun (SUB). All words with the ending *'o.*

Pronoun (PRN). The personal pronouns *mi* etc., the *iu, io* and *ies* series from the correlative table, *ambaŭ* and the word *lo* IL.

Adjective (ADJ). All words with the ending *'a* and the *ia* series from the correlative table.

Adverb (ADV). All words with the ending *'e,* the *ie, ial, iam, iel* and *iom* series from the correlative table and the words *almenaŭ, ankaŭ, ankoraŭ, apenaŭ, baldaŭ, des, eĉ, for, hieraŭ, hodiaŭ, ja, jam, jen, jes, ju, ĵe* IL, *ĵus, mem, morgaŭ, ne, nun, nur, plej, pli, plu, po, preskaŭ, tre, tro, tuj,* including compounds with one of these as the rightmost morpheme, e.g. *mal'tro.*

Numeral (NUM). *Nul, unu, du, tri, kvar, kvin, ses, sep, ok, naŭ, dek, cent, mil* and compounds ending in one of these, e.g. *du'mil.* Numbers expressed in digits belong to this word class, too.

Article (ART). *La, le* IL.

Preposition (PRP). *Al, anstataŭ, antaŭ, apud, ĉe, ĉirkaŭ, da, de, den*[IL], *dum, ekster, el, en, estiel*[IL], *ĝis, inter, je, kontraŭ, krom, kromaŭ*[IL], *kun, kvazaŭ, laŭ, malgraŭ, pe*[IL], *per, por, post, preter, pri, pro, sen, sub, super, sur, tra, trans* and compounds with one of these as the rightmost morpheme, e.g. *mal'antaŭ.*

Interjection (INT). *Nu* etc.

Bound function morpheme (FKC). This word class was introduced for the IL only. It contains two morphemes which in the IL cannot occur unless linked to another word by a hyphen (they are words of their own right in common Esperanto): *-ajn*[IL] and *ĉi-*[IL].

Subordinating conjunction (SBK). *Ĉar, ĉu, do, dum'kiel*[IL], *ke, kvankam, se, tamen.*

Coordinating conjunction (KON). *Aŭ, aŭnome*[IL], *kaj, kaŭ*[IL], *minus, nek, ol, plus, sed.*

2.3. Dependent types

The syntactic relations among the words categorised in the way shown above (2.2.) are described as dependency relations each between a governing and a dependent word. The dependents can be classified on distributional grounds (Schubert 1987: 52). In the present description, the following dependent types are distinguished:

subject	=	SUBJ
object	=	OBJ
predicative	=	PRED
infinitival complement	=	INFC
propositional complement	=	PROC
preposition argument	=	PARG
subordinate clause	=	SUBC
adverbial complement	=	ADVC
propositional adjunct	=	PROA
modal adjunct	=	MODA
linking adjunct	=	LIA
determiner	=	DET
attribute	=	ATR1
epithet	=	EPI
apposition	=	APO
numeral adjunct	=	NUMA
free adjunct	=	ADJU
relative clause	=	REL

In the tree structures actually processed in DLT programs, two additional dependent type labels are encountered. One is the label "GOV" on a branch above the main governor of a sentence (which is needed to avoid a distinction between labelled and unlabelled nodes, but has no linguistic content, since the main governor does not depend on anything), and the other is the "PCT" label on a branch on which the punctuation mark that marks the end of the sentence depends on the main governor (used for distinguishing incomplete sentences, processed in advance in order to speed up the process, from complete ones).

The classification of words in word classes is a generalisation which deliberately overlooks some particular characteristics of individual words. For example, not all verbs can govern each of the dependents listed in the relevant table below. Traditionally transitive and intransitive verbs are distinguished, which is, in terms of dependency syntax, a distinction as to the capacity of governing an object. In addition to the transitivity distinction, whose prominent place in traditional grammar does not seem to be very well motivated, a number of similar distinctions can be made with respect to the capacity of governing other dependents. Obviously these subcategorising distinctions are possible for word classes other than verbs as well. As long as the similarities between members of a word class are more important than their distinguishing characteristics, it is not advisable to split up word classes. Because of this, a different way to indicate the individual governing capacities of words is needed. In dependency syntax it is therefore common to distinguish dependents that can be governed by any member of the governing word class from dependents that can be governed only by a subclass. Subclass-specific dependents are called **complements**, the others **adjuncts**. Subclass-specific governing capacity is called **valency**. The valency of individual words or subclasses of words have to be entered in a dictionary. In contrast to other languages, Esperanto does not have a distinction between compulsory and optional complements. In principle, all dependents are syntactically optional. The tables in section 2.5. show complements above the double line and adjuncts below it.

The present description is not meant as an introduction to writing dependency syntaxes. I therefore refrain from motivating the classification of dependent types. An introduction for those who wish to apply this model of dependency syntax to any given language has been given earlier together with a comprehensive account of the decision process that motivates the choices to be made (Schubert 1987: 52-57).

2.4. Conditions

In order to function as a certain type of governor or dependent a word must meet a number of conditions. The tables give the essential conditions in an implicit way, that is, the conditions are expressed in the set-up of the tables. The conditions expressed in this way are the word class membership of the governor and the dependent, and the fact that the governing capacity with respect to certain dependents is subject to valency information contained in a syntactic dictionary. The latter fact is expressed in the distinction of dependent types that are complements (valency-bound dependents) and others that are adjuncts.

Moreover, words in some cases have to conform to additional conditions. These special conditions are referred to in the tables in two ways: First, the symbol found in the relevant table square refers to a so-called tree condition, and second, the comment in the rightmost column of the table refers to so-called feature conditions. The two types of condition are explained here.

Tree conditions

In the tables the cross (×) denotes that a word from the word class given in the relevant column without any additional conditions is able to function as a dependent of the type stated in the relevant line of the table.

The symbol "E" denotes that the dependent occurs in elliptic constructions only.

The symbols "da", "keĉu", "kiel", "kio", "ĝis" and "ol" denote that the dependency relation in question is possible, only f the word concerned is part of the structure in the way indicated in the example. The six tree conditions are presented in the form of tree structures which restrict the surrounding tree pattern which is a prerequisite for the dependency relation in question to be admissible. In the tree structures given below, "[GOV]" denotes the governor (given in the headline above the table), "[L]" the label or dependent type (given in the table line and "X" an arbitrary word allowed by the general conditions of the table. The asterisk (*) denotes a dependent which must not occur in the pattern.

"da"

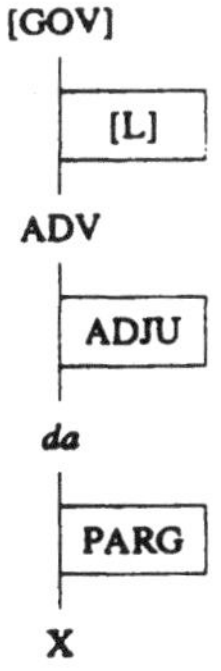

"keĉu"

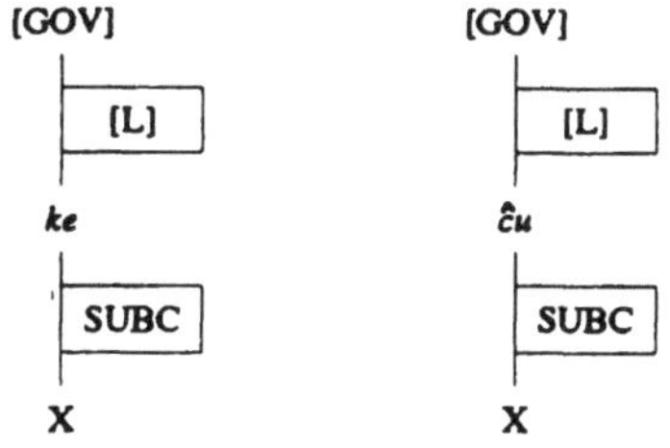

"kiel"

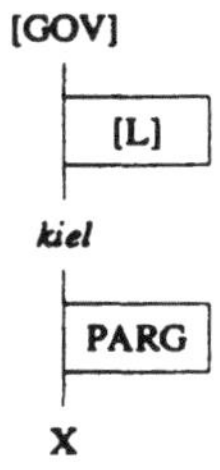

"kio"

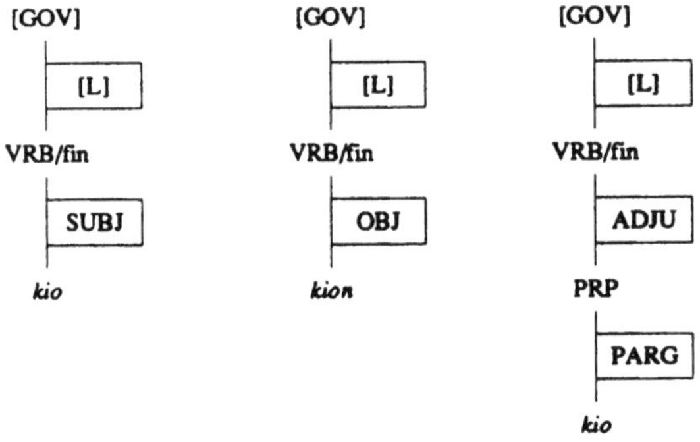

"ĝis"

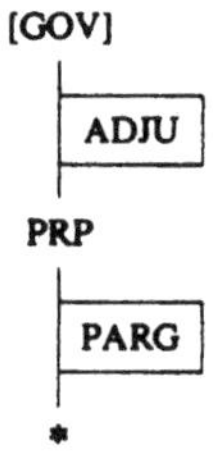

"ol"

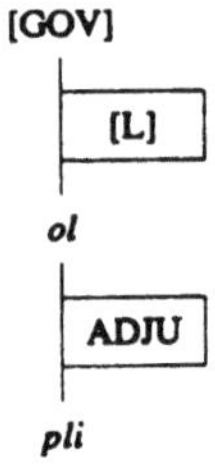

"ki"

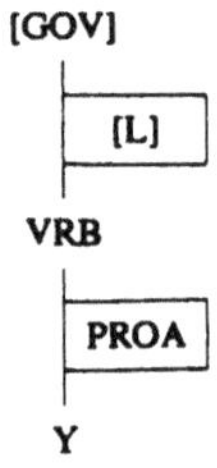

Y = ***kial, kiam, kie, kiel, kiom***

Feature conditions

In the rightmost column of the tables the following abbreviations for feature conditions are used. While tree conditions concern a larger part of the overall tree structure, feature conditions concern only a governor-dependent pair with a labelled branch between the two. The governor is a word of the word class given in the headline above the table. The label (dependent type) is given in the leftmost column of the table line in which it is relevant. The dependent may belong to any of the word classes in whose columns the table line in question has symbols. The feature conditions are not valid for words that cannot carry the feature in question. For example, the condition "acc" 'accusative' concerns nouns, adjectives and pronouns, but neither verbs, nor the invariable pronoun *ambaŭ*. So a feature condition does not forbid a word which cannot meet it, but rather forbids only those words which could, but do not, meet the condition.

G = The condition constrains the governor.

D = The condition constrains the dependent.

fin = The verb must be finite. This includes the tense and mood forms and the imperative (see 2.2.).

inf = The verb must be an infinitive.

nom = The word must be in the nominative case.

acc = The noun, adjective or pronoun must be in the accusative case. The adverb, even if it can carry the *'n* ending of the accusative, must be in the nominative case.

ptc = The adjective or adverb must be a participle.

agr = Agreement. In Esperanto there is agreement in two syntactic features: case and number. The agreement rules mainly concern nouns and their dependents.
Case agreement plays an important role in the identification of syntactic functions (= dependent types). The condition "agr" indicates that the dependent agrees in case with its governor, that is, it should have the same case form (nominative or accusative).
Number agreement does not directly serve as a means of recognizing dependent types, but it may function as a criterion for recognizing the presence of a dependency relation. The condition "agr" in this respect indicates that the dependent agrees in number with its governor. This constraint cannot be spelled out in such a simple way as the case agreement part of the condition. For number agreement, it is noteworthy that coordinated singular words or syntagmata may function as a single plural syntagma (cf. *ruĝa kaj blanka flago* 'a red and white flag' [one flag] vs. *nederlanda kaj belga aŭtoj* 'a Dutch and a Belgian car' [two cars]). DLT's IL, but not common Esperanto, has a special conjunction which coordinates co-referent nouns (*bona amiko kaŭ kolego* 'a good friend and colleague' [one person]). The special IL conjunction *aŭnome*, which means approximately 'which is also called', functions in a similar way. The common Esperanto conjunction *aŭ* 'or' is in the IL restricted to coordinating words for non-identical objects (cf. *Persujo aŭnome Irano* 'Persia or Iran' vs. *Irano aŭ Nederlando* 'Iran or the Netherlands').
In this connection it should also be noted that the numerals, except *unu* 'one' and *nul* 'zero', function as plural words. As in the case of personal pronouns like *ni* 'we', this is strictly speaking not a syntactic, but a semantic feature of the words concerned. Due to the hard regularness of the phenomenon, however, it can easily be handled together with syntactic rules. This facilitates the process in many ways.

lbl = Agreement with the label. This is perhaps a somewhat uncommon way of expressing the fact that in elliptic constructions where a numeral functions in a way normally reserved for nouns, any adjectives or pronouns that depend on it should carry the case required by the label of the numeral, while the numeral itself cannot be inflected: in *Ili aĉetis du domojn en sia hejmurbo kaj pliajn tri en ripozloko* the word *tri* 'three' carries above it the label "OBJ". Because of that label *pliajn*, the attribute of *tri*, carries the accusative form, whereas *tri* itself cannot express case.

casegov = The governing preposition controls the case of its dependent. In the occasion of prepositions which allow both cases, the choice of case is often determined not by syntactic criteria, but by the meaning of the verb or by a free (semantic) choice of the speaker/writer (cf. *en la ĝardeno* 'in the garden' vs. *en la ĝardenon* 'into the garden').

IL = The form in question does not exist or is incorrect in common Esperanto. It is correct in DLT's IL. This symbol marks only words and syntactic combinations that are incorrect in Esperanto. It does not mark possible modifications in the meaning of words.

2.5. Tables and samples

In this section the tables, explained above, are given. Each table is followed by samples for every combination of a dependent type (left column) and its word class (upper line).

In the samples, the governor of the syntactic combination illustrated is given in *italics*, the dependent in **bold** face. The glosses are literal, in order to mirror the Esperanto construction.

To speakers of Esperanto, some of the samples may have a rather low degree of grammaticality. Since we are aiming at authentic texts, which are full of deviations from what is strictly "correct" according to prescriptive grammars, I have generally followed the guideline of accepting rather than rejecting marginal syntactic combinations. In machine translation it is advisable to be prepared to accept as broad a range of varieties as possible, although the generation side of the system would not profit from making use of as many possibilities. As an intermediate language, Esperanto in DLT is admittedly never in the position of a source language, in which ill-formed input has to be treated, but since an intermediate language in many respects needs to be directly linked to texts from real life, the door to authentic corpora should remain open. This is why I here interpret the notion of correctness quite broadly.

2.5.1. Dependents of the verb

	VRB	SUB	PRN	ADJ	ADV	NUM	ART	PRP	INT	FKC	SBK	KON	conditions
SUBJ	×	×	×	E	da	×					keĉu	×	G: fin D: nom
OBJ	×	×	×	E	da	×					keĉu	×	D: acc fin
PRED	×	×	×	×	da	×					keĉu	×	D: nom inf
INFC	×											×	D: inf
PROC											keĉu	×	
PARG													
SUBC													
ADVC													
PROA	ki				× kiel			×			×	×	
MODA					×							×	IL
LIA		×	×		×				×		×	×	some IL
DET													
ATR1													
EPI													
APO													
NUMA													
ADJU													
REL	kio											×	D: fin

SUBJ/Verb

Necesas **investi**. – 'is-necessary to-invest'
Kiu **deziras** **aliĝi**, *anoncu* sin tuj.
– 'who wishes to-join, should-announce him/herself immediately'

SUBJ/Noun

Fero *rustiĝas*. – 'iron rusts'

SUBJ/Pronoun

Ĝi *kolektiĝis*. – 'it gathered'

SUBJ/Adjective

La granda *rustiĝas*. [ellipsis] – 'the big-one rusts'

SUBJ/Adverb

Multe da sablo *kolektiĝis*. – 'a-lot of sand gathered'

SUBJ/Numeral

Dek *estas* kvin oble du. – 'ten is five times two'

SUBJ/Subordinating conjunction

Ĝenas min, **ke** vi ne skribas. – 'annoys me, that you not writes'.
Ĉu li venos, *estas* nesolvita demando. – 'whether he will-come, is unsolved a-question'

OBJ/Verb

Mi *demandis*, kiam-do vi **venos**. – 'I asked, when you will-come'

OBJ/Noun

Li *aĉetis* **aŭton**. – 'he bought a-car'

OBJ/Pronoun

Li *aĉetis* **ĝin**. – 'he bought it'

OBJ/Adjective

Li aĉetis unu aŭton kaj *vendis* la **alian**. [ellipsis]
– 'he bought one car and sold the other'

OBJ/Adverb

Li *aĉetis* **tiom** da aŭtoj. – 'he bought so-many [of] cars'

OBJ/Numeral
Li aĉetis unu aŭton kaj *vendis* **du**. [ellipsis] – 'he bought one car and sold two'
OBJ/Subordinating conjunction
Oni *diris* al mi, **ke** li venos. – 'one told [to] me, that he will-come'
Mi ne *aŭdis*, **ĉu** li venos. – 'I not heard, whether he will-come'
PRED/Verb
La demando *estas*, kiel-do **atingi** la celon. – 'the question is, how to-achieve the goal'
PRED/Noun
Li *estas* **prezidanto**. – 'he is a-chairman'
Oni *elektas* lin **prezidanto**. – 'one elects him chairman'
PRED/Pronoun
Tio *estas* **ĝi**. – 'that is it'
Ĉu oni ne *elektis* vin **io**? – 'did one not elect you something'
PRED/Adjective
Ĝi *estas* **blua**. – 'it is blue'
Oni *farbas* la muron **blua**. – 'one paints the wall blue'
Ili *manĝas* fiŝojn **krudaj**. – 'they eat fishes raw'
PRED/Adverb
Tio *estas* **multe** da sablo. – 'that is much [of] sand'
PRED/Numeral
Du oble kvin *estas* **dek**. – 'two times five is ten'
PRED/Subordinating conjunction
La instrukcio *estas*, **ke** ni vendu. – 'the instruction is, that we should-sell'
La demando *estas*, **ĉu** ni vendu. – 'the question is, whether we should-sell'
INFC/Verb
Ŝi *devas* **fari** tion. – 'she must do that'
Ŝi *aŭdas* lin **veni**. – 'she hears him come'
Ŝi *instruas* **programi**. – 'she teaches to-program'
PROC/Subordinating conjunction
Li *sciigis* ilin, **ke** ili vendu. – 'he told them, that they should-sell'
Li *demandis* ŝin, **ĉu** ili vendu. – 'he asked her, whether they should-sell'
PROA/Verb
Kiam ili **venis**, ni *foriros*. – 'when they have-arrived, we shall-leave'
PROA/Adverb
Li **longe** *dormis*. – 'he a-long-time slept'
Oni *elektis* lin **kiel** prezidanton. – 'one elected him [as] chairman'
PROA/Preposition
Li *dormis* **en** sia lito. – 'he slept in his bed'
PROA/Subordinating conjunction
Li ne *povis* veni, **do** li devis malaliĝi.
– 'he not could come, so he had-to cancel-application'
Mi *venos*, **ĉu** tio plaĉos al vi aŭ ne.
– 'I shall-come, whether that pleases [to] you or not'
Li *promesis* veni, **sed** li devis malaliĝi.
– 'he promised to-come, but he had-to cancel-application'
Li *malaliĝis*, **t.e.** li telegrafis, ke li ne venos.
– 'he cancelled-application, i.e. he cabled, that he not would-come'
MODA/Adverb
Pove, mi ne *venos* al vi. [IL only] – 'Maybe, I not shall-come to you'
LIA/Noun
Sinjoro, ĉu vi *venos*? – 'sir, do you will-come'
LIA/RPN
Vi, ĉu vi *venos*? – 'you, do you will-come'

LIA/Adverb

Sekve, li ne *venos*. – 'as-a-consequence, he not will-come'
[the distinction of LIA vs. PROA in this function is IL-specific]

LIA/Interjection

Nu, li ne *venos*. – 'well, he not will-come'
[the distinction of LIA vs. PROA in this function is IL-specific]

LIA/Subordinating conjunction

Tamen, li ne *venos*. – 'however, he not will-come'
[the distinction of LIA vs. PROA in this function is IL-specific]

REL/Verb

Li *vendis* mian aŭton, kio tre **mirigis** min.
– 'he sold my car, which very-much surprised me'

2.5.2. Dependents of the noun

	VRB	SUB	PRN	ADJ	ADV	NUM	ART	PRP	INT	FKC	SBK	KON	conditions
SUBJ													
OBJ													
PRED													
INFC	×											×	D: inf
PROC											keĉu	×	
PARG													
SUBC													
ADVC													
PROA	×										×	×	
MODA													
LIA													
DET							×						
ATR1			×	×		×						×	D: agr
EPI		×	×									×	D: nom
APO		×										×	D: agr
NUMA													
ADJU					×			×				×	
REL	×											×	D: fin

INFC/Verb

la *espero* **venki** – 'the hope to-overcome'

PROC/Subordinating conjunction

la *decido*, **ke** ni vendu, – 'the decision, that we shall-sell'
la *demando*, **ĉu** ni vendu, – 'the question, whether we should-sell,'

PROA/Verb

Riparo de motoro, kiam ĝi **estas** funkcianta, estas danĝera.
– 'Repair of motor, while it is working, is dangerous'

PROA/Subordinating conjunction

Temis pri *donacado* de varoj al rifuĝintoj, **ĉar** ili estas nevendeblaj.
– 'it-was about giving of goods to refugees, because they are unsellable'

DET/Article

la *domo* – 'the house'

ATR1/Pronoun

iu *domo* – 'some house'

ATR1/Adjective

blua *domo* – 'blue a-house'

ATR1/Numeral

unu *domo* – 'one house'

EPI/Noun

la *reĝlando* **Nederlando** – 'the kingdom of-the-Netherlands'
sinjoro **'Willmann''o** – 'Mr. Willmann'
[names and other non-IL words are adapted to IL syntax in this way]

EPI/Pronoun

Ni aĉetis tri *komputilojn*, **ĉiuj** tre multekostaj.
– 'we bought three computers, all very expensive'

APO/Noun

La malsanulejo aĉetis novan *elektrokardiografon*, komplikitan **aparaton** por registri la funkciadon de la koro. – 'the hospital bought new an-electrocardiograph, complicated a-machine for to-record the functioning of the heart'

ADJU/Adverb

la *homoj* ĉi-**tie** – 'the people here'

ADJU/Preposition

la *aŭto* **de** mia amiko – 'the car of my friend'

REL/Verb

domo, kiun oni **vendas**, – 'a-house, which one sells,'
la *domo*, kie ni **loĝas**, – 'the house, where we live,'

2.5.3. Dependents of the pronoun

	VRB	SUB	PRN	ADJ	ADV	NUM	ART	PRP	INT	FKC	SBK	KON	conditions
SUBJ													
OBJ													
PRED													
INFC													
PROC											keĉu	×	
PARG													
SUBC													
ADVC										×	×		
PROA													
MODA													
LIA													
DET													
ATR1			×	×		×						×	D: agr
EPI													
APO		×										×	D: agr
NUMA													
ADJU					×			×				×	
REL	×											×	D: fin

PROC/Subordinating conjunction

Tio, **ke** ili baldaŭ venos, estas problemo.
– 'this, that they soon will-come, is a-problem'
Tio, **ĉu** ni iru, estas nesolvita problemo.
– 'this, whether we should-go, is unsolved a-problem'

ADVC/Bound function morpheme

  ĉi-*tiu* – 'this'

ADVC/Subordinating conjunction

  kiu-**do** – 'who'

ATR1/Pronoun

  ĉies *io* – 'everyone's something'

  Ili renkontas *nin* **ĉiujn**. – 'they meet us all'

ATR1/Adjective

  io **blua** – 'something blue'

ATR1/Numeral

  tri *iuj* – 'three somebodies'

APO/Noun

  ili renkontas *nin* **eŭropanojn** – 'they meet us Europeans'

ADJU/Adverb

  ni ĉi-**tie** – 'we here'

ADJU/Preposition

  iu **el** miaj amikoj – 'somebody of my friends'

REL/Verb

  tio, kion ni ne **atendis**, – 'that, which we ne awaited'

  ni, kiuj tiom **investis**, – 'we, who so-much invested,'

2.5.4. Dependents of the adjective

	VRB	SUB	PRN	ADJ	ADV	NUM	ART	PRP	INT	FKC	SBK	KON	conditions
SUBJ													
OBJ	×	×	×	E	da	E					keĉu	×	G: ptc D: acc fin
PRED	×	×	×	×	da	×					keĉu	×	G: ptc D: nom
INFC	×											×	D: inf
PROC											keĉu	×	
PARG													
SUBC													
ADVC										×	×		
PROA	×										×	×	G: ptc
MODA													
LIA													
DET							E						
ATR1			E	E		E						×	D: agr
EPI													
APO													
NUMA													
ADJU					× kiel			×				× ol	
REL	×											×	

OBJ/Verb

  Eniris persono, *demandanta*, kiam-do vi **venos**.

  – 'entered a-person, asking, when we would-come'

OBJ/Noun

  aĉetanta **aŭton** – 'buying a-car'

OBJ/Pronoun

ĝin *aĉetanta* – 'it buying'

OBJ/Adjective

aĉetanta unu aŭton kaj *vendanta* la **alian** [ellipsis]
– 'buying one car and selling the other'

OBJ/Adverb

aĉetanta **tiom** da aŭtoj – 'buying so-many [of] cars'

OBJ/Numeral

aĉetanta unu aŭton kaj *vendanta* **du** [ellipsis] – 'buying one car and selling two'

OBJ/Subordinating conjunction

diranta, **ke** li venos – 'saying, that he will-come'
demandanta, **ĉu** li venos – 'asking, whether he will-come'

PRED/Verb

Okazis situacio, *iganta* la problemon kiel-do **atingi** la celon.
– 'occurred a-situation, making the problem how to-achieve the goal'

PRED/Noun

persono, jam *estanta* **prezidanto**, – 'a-person, already being a-chairman'
komisiono, *elektanta* lin **prezidanto**, – 'a-commission, electing him chairman'

PRED/Pronoun

estanta **ĝi** – 'being it'
Ĉu oni ne estis *elektantaj* vin **io**? – 'do one not was electing you something'

PRED/Adjective

muro, *estanta* **blua**, – 'a-wall, being blue,'
laboristaro, *farbanta* la muron **blua**, – 'a-group-of-workmen, painting the wall blue'

PRED/Adverb

vojbaraĵo, *estanta* **multe** da sablo, – 'a-boom, being much [of] sand'

PRED/Numeral

faktoro, *iganta* la solvon **mil** – 'a-factor, making the solution one-thousand'

PRED/Subordinating conjunction

estinta, **ke** ni vendu, – 'having-been, that we should-sell'
estanta, **ĉu** ni vendu, – 'being, whether we should-sell'

INFC/Verb

devanta **fari** tion – 'having-to do that'
aŭdinta lin **veni** – 'having-heard him come'
instruanta **programi** – 'teaching to-program'

PROC/Subordinating conjunction

sciiganta ilin, **ke** ili vendu, – 'telling them, that they should-sell'
demandanta ŝin, **ĉu** ili vendu, – 'asking her, whether they should-sell'

ADVC/Bound function morpheme

ĉi-*tia* – 'such-a'

ADVC/Subordinating conjunction

kia-**do** – 'what-kind-of'

PROA/Verb

persono, ĉiam *vojaĝanta*, kiam oni **ŝatus** telefoni kun li,
– 'a-person, always travelling, when one would-like to-talk-by-telephone with him'

PROA/Subordinating conjunction

persono, volonte *vojaĝanta*, **se** li povas tion pagi,
– 'a-person, liking-to-be travelling, if he can that afford'

DET/Article

Ni prenis ne malgrandan kukurbon, sed **la** *grandan*. [ellipsis]
– 'we took not little a-pumpkin, but the big'

ATR1/Pronoun

Ni prenis ne malgrandan kukurbon, sed **iun** *grandan*. [ellipsis]
– 'we took not little a-pumpkin, but some big'

ATR1/Adjective

Ni prenis ne malgrandan kukurbon, sed la **solan** *grandan*. [ellipsis]
– 'we took not little a-pumpkin, but the only big'

ATR1/Numeral

Ni prenis ne malgrandan kukurbon, sed **du** *grandajn*. [ellipsis]
– 'we took not little a-pumpkin, but two big'

ADJU/Adverb

longe *dormanta* – 'a-long-time sleeping'
komisiono, *elektanta* lin **kiel** prezidanton, – 'a-commission, electing him as chairman'

ADJU/Preposition

dormanta **en** sia lito – 'sleeping in his/her bed'

ADJU/Coordinating conjunction

La lingvo estas pli **ol** *facila*. – 'the language is more than easy'

REL/Verb

La domo estas *tia*, kia ĝi **devas** esti. – 'the house is such, as it should be'

2.5.5. Dependents of the adverb

	VRB	SUB	PRN	ADJ	ADV	NUM	ART	PRP	INT	FKC	SBK	KON	conditions
SUBJ													
OBJ	×	×	×	E	da	E					keĉu	×	G: ptc D: acc fin
PRED	×	×	×	×	da	×					keĉu	×	G: ptc D: nom fin
INFC	×											×	D: inf
PROC											keĉu	×	
PARG		×	×									×	G: *kiel* cf. tree cond. "kiel"
SUBC													
ADVC										×	×		
PROA	×										×	×	G: ptc
MODA													
LIA													
DET													
ATR1													
EPI													
APO													
NUMA													
ADJU					× kiel			×				× ol	
REL	×											×	

OBJ/Verb

Li eniris *demandante*, kiam-do vi **venos**. – 'he entered asking, when you will-come'

OBJ/Noun

aĉetante **aŭton** – 'buying a-car'

OBJ/Pronoun

aĉetante **ĝin** – 'buying it'

OBJ/Adjective

 ac̄etante unu aŭton kaj *vendante* la **alian** [ellipsis] – 'buying one car and selling the other'

OBJ/Adverb

 aĉetante **tiom** da aŭtoj – 'buying so-many [of] cars'

OBJ/Numeral

 aĉetante unu aŭton kaj *vendante* **du** [ellipsis] – 'buying one car and selling two'

OBJ/Subordinating conjunction

 dirante, **ke** li venos, – 'saying, that he will-come'
 demandante, **ĉu** li venos, – 'asking, whether he will-come'

PRED/Verb

 igante la problemon kiel-do **atingi** la celon
 – 'making the problem how to-achieve the goal'

PRED/Noun

 Estante **prezidanto**, ŝi ne rajtis dungiĝi ĉe la asocio.
 – 'being chairman, she not could be-employed with the association'
 Elektante lin **prezidanto**, la asocio honoris sian maljunan membron.
 – 'electing him chairman, the association honoured its old member'

PRED/Pronoun

 estante **ĝi** – 'being it'
 Ĉu ne, *elektante* lin **io**, oni povus flati lin?
 – 'does not, electing him something, one could flatter him'

PRED/Adjective

 Estante **blua**, la muro ne taŭgis kiel ekrano por diapozitivoj.
 – 'being blue, the wall not was-suitable as a-screen for slides'
 Farbante la muron **blua**, oni igis ĝin maltaŭga kiel ekrano.
 – 'painting the wall blue, one made it unsuitable as a-screen'

PRED/Adverb

 estante **multe** da sablo – 'being much [of] sand'

PRED/Numeral

 igante la solvon **mil** – 'making the solution one-thousand'

PRED/Subordinating conjunction

 estinte, **ke** ni vendu, – 'having-been, that we should-sell'
 estante, **ĉu** ni vendu, – 'being, whether we should-sell'

INFC/Verb

 devante **fari** tion – 'having-to do that'
 aŭdinte lin **veni** – 'hearing him come'
 instruante **programi** – 'teaching to-program'

PROC/Subordinating conjunction

 dirante, **ke** ili vendu, – 'saying, that they should-sell'
 demandante ŝin, **ĉu** ili vendu, – 'asking her, whether they should-sell'
 tiel, **ke** ne eblis ĝin trovi, – 'so, that ne was-possible it to-find'

PARG/Noun

 elekti iun *kiel* **prezidanton** – 'elect someone [as] chairman'

PARG/Pronoun

 elekti iun *kiel* **tion** – 'elect someone [as] that'

ADVC/Bound function morpheme

 ĉi-*tie* – 'here'

ADVC/Subordinating conjunction

 kie-**do** – 'where?'

PROA/Verb

 vojaĝante, kiam-ajn **eblas**, – 'travelling, whenever is-possible'

PROA/Subordinating conjunction

 vojaĝante, **se** nenio devigas lin resti, – 'travelling, if nothing forces him to-stay'

ADJU/Adverb

tre *multe* – 'very much'
longe *dormante* – 'a-long-time sleeping'
elektante lin **kiel** prezidanton, – 'electing him [as] chairman'

ADJU/Preposition

dormante **en** sia lito – 'sleeping in his/her bed'

ADJU/Coordinating conjunction

La lingvon vi lernos pli **ol** *facile.* – 'the language you will-learn more than easily'

REL/Verb

tiom, kiom vi **deziras,** – 'as-much, as you wish'

2.5.6. Dependents of the numeral

	VRB	SUB	PRN	ADJ	ADV	NUM	ART	PRP	INT	FKC	SBK	KON	conditions
SUBJ													
OBJ													
PRED													
INFC													
PROC													
PARG													
SUBC													
ADVC													
PROA													
MODA													
LIA													
DET							E						
ATR1			E	E								×	D: lbl
EPI													
APO													
NUMA						×							
ADJU					×			× ĝis				× ol	
REL	×											×	D: fin

DET/Article

la *du* [ellipsis] – 'the two'

ATR1/Pronoun

iuj *du* [ellipsis] – 'some two'

ATR1/Adjective

la **aliaj** *du* [ellipsis] – 'the other two'

NUMA/Numeral

mil *naŭcent* – 'one-thousand ninehundred'

ADJU/Adverb

preskaŭ *cent* – 'almost a-hundred'
Ni vendis al ili **po** *cent* librojn. – 'we sold to them each a-hundred books'

ADJU/Preposition

du **el** ili – 'two of them'
Ĉiu el la premiitoj rajtas ricevi **ĝis** *tri* librojn.
– 'each of the prize-winners is-entitled to-get up-to three books'

ADJU/Coordinating conjunction

Ni havas pli **ol** *cent* mendojn. – 'we have more than a-hundred orders'

REL/Verb

du, kiuj **alvenis** hieraŭ, [ellipsis] – 'two, that arrived yesterday,'

2.5.7. Dependents of the preposition

	VRB	SUB	PRN	ADJ	ADV	NUM	ART	PRP	INT	FKC	SBK	KON	conditions
SUBJ													
OBJ													
PRED													
INFC													
PROC													
PARG	×	×	×		× da	×		×			keĉu	×	casegov
SUBC													
ADVC					×								
PROA													
MODA													
LIA													
DET													
ATR1													
EPI													
APO													
NUMA													
ADJU					×							×	
REL													

PARG/Verb

pri **manĝi** 'about to-eat'

PARG/Noun

pri **domo** – 'about a-house'

PARG/Pronoun

pri **tio** – 'about that'

PARG/Adverb

pri **hieraŭ** – 'about yesterday'

pri **iom** da neĝo – 'about some [of] snow'

PARG/Preposition

de **sur** la ŝranko – 'from on the cupboard'

PARG/Subordinating conjunction

Li parolis *pri* **ke** ni dungu iun. – 'he spoke about that we should-employ someone'

Li parolis *pri* **ĉu** ni dungu iun. – 'he spoke about whether we should-employ someone'

Li rezervis sidlokon, *por* **ke** li ne devu stari.

– 'he reserved a seat, for that he not should-have-to stand'

ADVC/Adverb

ie-*en* – 'in [local meaning]'

ADJU/Adverb

profunde *en* la maro – 'deeply in the sea'

longe *post* lia morto – 'a-long-time after his death'

2.5.8. Dependents of the subordinating conjunction

	VRB	SUB	PRN	ADJ	ADV	NUM	ART	PRP	INT	FKC	SBK	KON	conditions
SUBJ													
OBJ													
PRED													
INFC													
PROC													
PARG													
SUBC	×											×	D: fin
ADVC													
PROA													
MODA													
LIA													
DET													
ATR1													
EPI													
APO													
NUMA													
ADJU													
REL													

SUBC/Verb

Ŝi diris, *ke* ni **telefonu** al ŝi. – 'she said, that we should-call-by-telephone to her';
Ŝi demandis, *ĉu* ni **telefonos** al ŝi. – 'she asked, whether we would-call-by-telephone to her'
Ŝi venos, *se* ŝi **ricevos** bileton. – 'she will-come, if she obtains a-ticket'

Note:
In some cases a subordinating conjunction may function in a way very similar to coordination. It then follows the table for a coordinating conjunction as the governor. If one would prefer to avoid such a violation of the strict disjunctness of word classes, the kind of construction in question might in some occasions be explained in terms of an ellipsis, but, especially for the coordination of short syntagmata, it is difficult to insist on such a solution with the subordinating conjunction in a normal subordinating function, and the subordinated item as an elliptic proposition:

Neuzebla *ĉar* tro **granda** ŝlosilo. – 'unusable since too big a-key'

2.5.9. Dependents of the coordinating conjunction

	VRB	SUB	PRN	ADJ	ADV	NUM	ART	PRP	INT	FKC	SBK	KON	conditions
SUBJ	×	×	×	×	×	×					×	×	
OBJ	×	×	×	×	×	×					×	×	
PRED	×	×	×	×	×	×					×	×	
INFC	×											×	
PROC											×	×	
PARG	×	×	×		×	×		×			×	×	
SUBC	×											×	
ADVC													
PROA					×			×			×	×	
MODA						×						×	
LIA		×	×		×				×		×	×	
DET													
ATR1			×	×		×						×	
EPI		×										×	
APO		×										×	
NUMA													
ADJU					×			×				×	
REL	×											×	

This table as it were sums up and makes explicit the columns of the previous tables for coordinating conjunctions. In addition it is an almost complete overview of all possible combinations of a word class and a dependent type – but not entirely, since in this table those combinations are missing that cannot be coordinated (DET, ADVC ...).

3. Sample sentence

On the next page a sample tree structure which conforms to the syntax described in this article is displayed. It is a real-life sentence from DLT's Esperanto corpus (originally from "Monato", a monthly news magazine):

> Laŭ Marcelino Oreja, la ĝenerala sekretario de l' Eŭropa Konsilio, kiu ĵus dissendis manifeston por savi la lingvan heredaĵon de Eŭropo, la uzo de lingvoj por komputiloj ne nur faras ilin pli gravaj, sed ankaŭ kreas riskon, ke normigita lingvo, kiu forigis ĉiujn specialajn diferencojn por ke komputiloj facile uzu ĝin, iom post iom uniformigos kaj malriĉigos la naciajn lingvojn.
>
> 'according-to Marcelino Oreja, the general secretary of the of-Europe Council, who just sent-out a-manifesto for saving the linguistic heritage of Europe, the use of languages for computers not only makes them more important, but also creates a-risk, that normalised language, which has-abolished all specific differences so that computers easily can-use it, step by step will-uniform and will-impoverish the national languages'

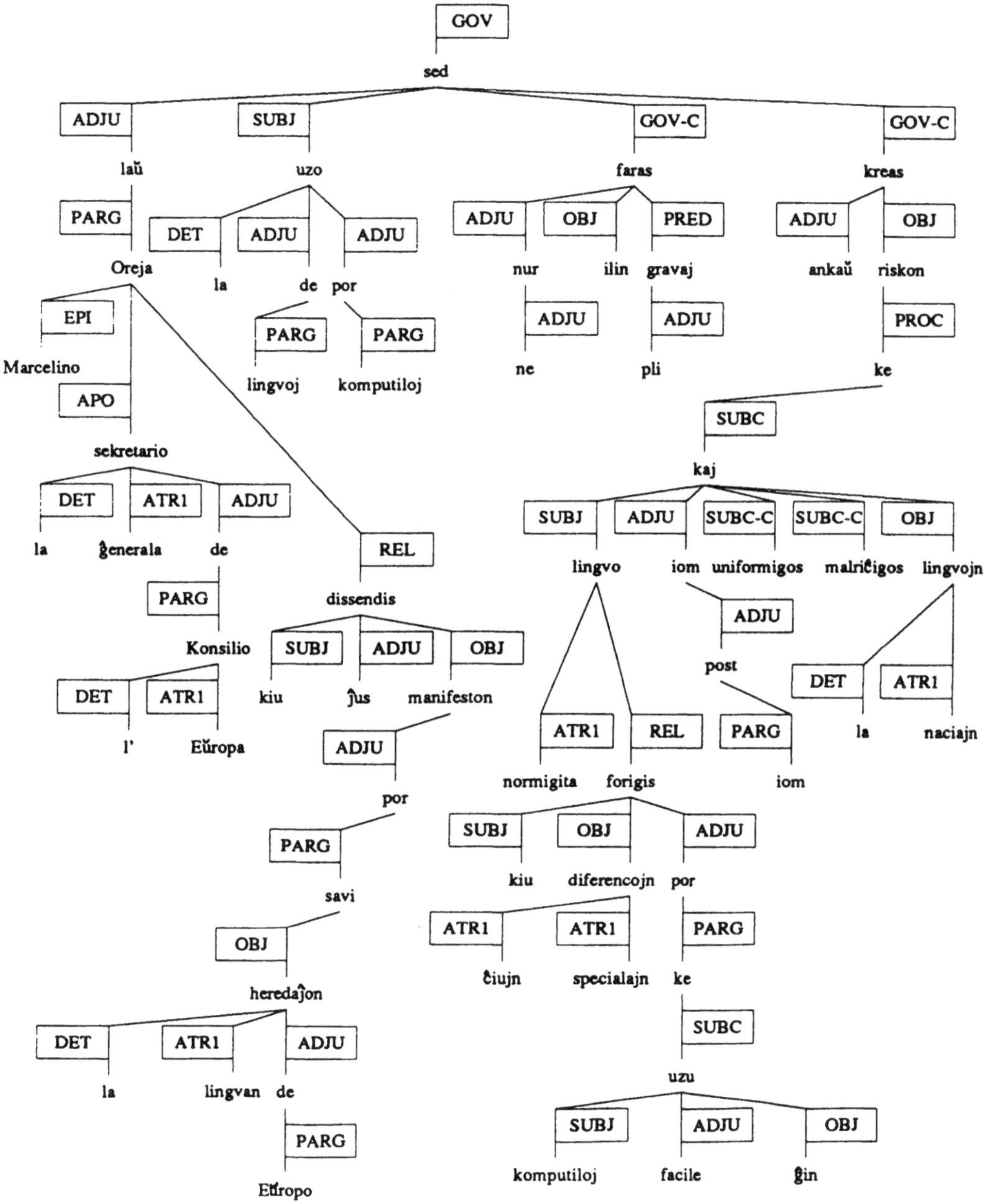
GOV
sed
ADJU
SUBJ
GOV-C
GOV-C
laŭ
uzo
faras
kreas
PARG
DET
ADJU
ADJU
ADJU
OBJ
PRED
ADJU
OBJ
Oreja
la
de
por
nur
ilin
gravaj
ankaŭ
riskon
EPI
PARG
PARG
ADJU
ADJU
PROC
Marcelino
lingvoj
komputiloj
ne
pli
ke
APO
SUBC
sekretario
kaj
DET
ATR1
ADJU
SUBJ
ADJU
SUBC-C
SUBC-C
OBJ
la
ĝenerala
de
REL
lingvo
iom
uniformigos
malriĉigos
lingvojn
PARG
dissendis
ADJU
Konsilio
SUBJ
ADJU
OBJ
post
DET
ATR1
DET
ATR1
kiu
ĵus
manifeston
la
naciajn
l'
Eŭropa
ADJU
ATR1
REL
PARG
normigita
forigis
iom
por
SUBJ
OBJ
ADJU
PARG
savi
kiu
diferencojn
por
OBJ
ATR1
ATR1
PARG
ĉiujn
specialajn
ke
heredaĵon
SUBC
DET
ATR1
ADJU
uzu
la
lingvan
de
SUBJ
ADJU
OBJ
PARG
komputiloj
facile
ĝin
Eŭropo

References

Blanke, Detlev (1985): *Internationale Plansprachen.*
Berlin: Akademie-Verlag

Duličenko, Aleksandr D. (1988): Proekty vseobščych i meždunarodnych jazykov (Chronologičeskij indeks so II po XX vv.).
In: *Interlingvističeskaja teorija i praktika meždunarodnogo vspomogatel'nogo jazyka.* = Interlinguistica Tartuensis 5. = Tartu Riikliku Ülikooli toimetised // Učenye zapiski Tartuskogo gosudarstvennogo universiteta // Acta et commentationes Universitatis Tartuensis 791, pp. 126-162

Reichenbach, Hans (1947): *Elements of symbolic logic.*
New York: Free Press

Schubert, Klaus (1986): *Syntactic tree structures in DLT.*
Utrecht: BSO/Research

Schubert, Klaus (1987): *Metataxis. Contrastive dependency syntax for machine translation.*
Dordrecht/Providence: Foris

Schubert, Klaus (1988a): Att knyta Nordens språk till ett mångspråkigt datoröversättningssystem.
In: *Nordiske Datalingivstikdage og Symposium for datamatstøttet leksikografi og terminologi 1987, Proceedings.* = Lambda 7. [København:] Institut for Datalingvistik, Handelshøjskolen i København, pp. 204-216

Schubert, Klaus (1988b): Ausdruckskraft und Regelmäßigkeit. Was Esperanto für automatische Übersetzung geeignet macht.
In: *Language Problems and Language Planning* 12, pp. 130-147

Schubert, Klaus (1988c): The architecture of DLT – interlingual or double direct?
In: *New directions in machine translation.* Ed. Dan Maxwell / Klaus Schubert / Toon Witkam. Dordrecht/Providence: Foris, p. 131-144

Schubert, Klaus (1989a): Interlinguistics – its aims, its achievements, and its place in language science.
In: *Interlinguistics – aspects of the science of planned languages.* Ed. Klaus Schubert (with Dan Maxwell). Berlin/New York: Mouton de Gruyter, pp. 7-44

Schubert, Klaus (1989b): An unplanned development in planned languages.
In: *Interlinguistics – aspects of the science of planned languages.* Ed. Klaus Schubert (with Dan Maxwell). Berlin/New York: Mouton de Gruyter, pp. 249-274

Wells, John C. (1978): *Lingvistikaj aspektoj de Esperanto.*
Rotterdam: Universala Esperanto-Asocio

Witkam, A. P. M. (1983): *Distributed Language Translation. Feasibility study of a multilingual facility for videotex information networks.*
Utrecht: BSO

[Zamenhof, L. L.; under the pseudonym:] Ėsperanto (1887): *Meždunarodnyj jazyk.*
Varšava: Kel'ter

The theory and practice of metataxis

Klaus Schubert

Utrecht, Netherlands

1. Introduction to the second part of this book

The Distributed Language Translation project was the first to make practical use of metataxis in machine translation. The idea was originally found in a seldom-read chapter of Lucien Tesnière's (1959/1982: 283-319) main work on dependency grammar, where he coins the term *métataxe* for the structural change that occurs during translation. Tesnière's model was introduced to the DLT machine translation system as a logical consequence of the insight that dependency syntax of a Tesnière'ian signature is particularly well suited for the purposes of multilingual machine translation (Schubert 1986: 166, also 1987b: 193-194). The idea was then adapted to the requirements of applied computational linguistics, worked out in detail and realized in a joint effort of the DLT team.

When I published the theory and some guidelines to the application of work on metataxis (Schubert 1987b), I could already base my account on experience gained in practical work with metataxis. After a series of dependency syntaxes had been written for structurally diverse languages (some of which are included in the first part of this book), the contrastive step had been taken. In the shape of a strictly form-oriented translation syntax of the dependency type, the model had been applied to the languages included in the first DLT prototype, viz. English and French, with Esperanto as the system's intermediate language. The two metataxis rule systems for English-to-Esperanto and Esperanto-to-French translation had been written by Dan Maxwell and Dorine Tamis, respectively. For the implementation a complex software system for dedicated tree transduction had been written in Prolog. The interfacing step between the purely grammatical work of the metataxis writers and the computational system provided by DLT's computer scientists, the formalization, had been carried out by Job van Zuijlen for both metataxes. At a later stage Dorine Tamis took over the Esperanto-French part.

This second part of the volume contains accounts by Dan Maxwell and Dorine Tamis of their metataxes. The versions published here have been revised and updated in the light of the experience gathered when working with the first DLT prototype, and its follow-up versions (Prototype 1: December 1987, Prototype 2: March 1988, selective demonstration version: August 1988, first shown at the 1988 Coling conference in Budapest). The two articles are meant to give the reader a detailed understanding of the solutions adopted for a series of everyday tasks and some of the more intricate problems in the translation syntax of the language pairs in question. They are not meant to cover the language pairs as comprehensively as the internal working versions of the metataxes (Maxwell 1987; Tamis 1987b and subsequent updates of both).

The most computer-oriented article in this book is Job van Zuijlen's contribution on the formalization of metataxis. In the same way as the other two articles, his account is based on the implementational experience gained when developing the subsequent prototype versions of the DLT system.

Section 2 describes metataxis in detail, section 3 places it in a more general perspective of system design and section 4 takes up prospects for further improvement.

2. Essential features of metataxis

I have earlier given a comprehensive account of what metataxis is and how it works (Schubert 1987b: 130-194). It may therefore be sufficient to now recall the main characteristics.

Translation is an extraordinarily complex process, so that both the design of a machine translation system and the system itself should be built up in a highly structured and thoroughly modular way. One of the main guidelines of modularity in this respect is the triple distinction of levels in grammar, formalism and implementation, which roughly correspond to the skills of theoretical linguists, computational linguists and computer scientists (Schubert 1987b: 209; 1988b). All I say about metataxis here is concerned with the grammar level unless otherwise stated.

2.1. A generator of alternative translations

A metataxis for a given pair of a source and a target language is a structured rule system for the syntactic part of the overall translation function. It works in combination with a bilingual dictionary. The general principle is to generate all syntactically possible alternative translations of a source language sentence with all alternative word translations provided in the dictionary. When these alternatives have been generated, a choice is made by semantic and pragmatic modules which are not part of the metataxis.

The metataxis rule system receives as its input a dependency tree of a piece of source language text. For the sake of simplicity I shall in the following call this piece a sentence, although there is no intrinsic need to limit metataxis to sentences. In principle, both sentential syntagmata and longer structures of interrelated sentences can be handled as well.

Since the above two paragraphs are a true picture of metataxis and a valid description at the grammar level, I shall keep using it throughout this account. It may nevertheless be appropriate to mention that the levels of formalism and implementation may look different. For example, the idea of generating all syntactically possible translations of a sentence is theoretically appealing, since it works with relatively simple structures. But if this is carried out in reality, the structural and lexical alternatives combine to produce enormous numbers of tree structures. It is therefore expedient to design more compact representations that express the ambiguity of the generated sentences in a more efficiently processable way. As long as these representations have exactly the same functionality as a set of simple but numerous alternative trees, there is no reason not to use the simple tree model for describing the involved functions at the grammar level. In a similar way the bilingual dictionary I mention here may in reality be replaced by some other source of word translations and contrastive syntactic knowledge derived from the system's knowledge bank that provides the same information (cf. 4.). My point is that whatever the implementational solution is, its functionality is in a valid way depicted by the image of a dependency tree being transformed into a multitude of syntactically correct alternative translations by means of a rule system and a dictionary.

The metataxis rule system transforms a given dependency tree from source into target language. In DLT, a complete transition of the system comprises two subsequent metataxis processes, viz. source to intermediate language and intermediate to target language. The whole discussion in this article deals with only one of these halves of the translation system, no matter which. Speaking about the source and the target language, I thus mean source and target of a single half. It is obvious that one of the two languages connected through metataxis in DLT is always Esperanto.

Metataxis is a model for syntactic translation procedures. In the subsections to follow I discuss its way of breaking down the complex translation process into smaller portions. In particular, I take up the following questions: What is a metataxis rule? How does it make use of the dictionary? How does it interact with the sentence being translated? Which rule is applied when? What is the relation between the source and the target language sentence during the metataxis process?

2.2. The structure of metataxis rules and dictionary entries

A metataxis rule is a rule that transforms a certain piece of a source language tree into a piece of a target language tree. A dependency tree consists of nodes and labelled branches (for details see Schubert: *Dependency syntax for parsing and generation*, this volume). Each node carries a word with accompanying syntactic information in the form of a feature list. (It is again for the sake of simplicity that I always call the content of a node a word. As the morpheme-based Hungarian syntax in this volume shows, it is sometimes useful to choose a smaller unit.) With the exception of the main internal governor of the sentence, each word in a sentence has exactly one governor. The kinds of possible syntactic relations of dependents to their governors are classified. They are called dependent types. The dependent type is indicated in the label on the branch between the dependent and its governor. Dependency trees differ greatly in size and shape, but they are always instances of a well-defined structure which is made up of words that belong to a limited set of word classes and labels from an equally enumerable set of dependent types. However different dependency trees may look, they are all built up of recursively combined patterns, and it is therefore a straightforward idea to let metataxis rules work on these patterns.

A metataxis rule can be described in terms of two patterns. It contains a target language output pattern which is generated if a given source language input pattern is encountered in the tree being translated. Since the structure being transformed is a dependency tree, this is true of the two patterns in a metataxis rule as well. From the point of view of computational formalization it would be ideal, if each node and each label of the tree could be transformed separatedly in a context-free manner, but it goes without saying that contrastive syntax is not that simple. Still it is a good general guideline to keep the two patterns of metataxis rules as small as possible. The smaller the patterns, the more general are the rules, and the more general they are, the smaller the number of rules needed. There is, however, a trade-off between the preference for a small rule set and for a small dictionary.

The smallest possible input pattern of a metataxis rule is a single node or a single label. A rule that translates a single node with a specific word literally given is in fact a dictionary entry. Often, however, dictionaries do not translate word by word, but have to resort to larger units. As soon as a bilingual dictionary of the metataxis type contains such multi-word units, these cannot be given simply as word strings but have to appear in the form of a small tree structure with the dependency relations between the words given as branch labels. Metataxis thus requires the entries of its bilingual dictionary to be tree-structured. Even a single-word entry is in this sense a tree – one which consists of a single node without any branches.

Metataxis rules and dictionary entries both consist of two corresponding dependency trees, an input pattern and an output pattern. In principle, there is accordingly no difference between the rules and the dictionary in metataxis. It would theoretically be possible to include all the information required for syntactic transfer in the dictionary. Such a dictionary, however, which gave the transfer information for every word or multi-word unit separately, would in many respects contain a prohibitively high degree of redundancy. The metataxis rule system removes this redundancy from the dictionary. In this sense the metataxis rule system can be considered to be a set of redundancy rules over the bilingual dictionary.

As a consequence, the tree structures that function as input and output patterns in a metataxis rule are in most cases of a more general nature than the trees made from sentences or found in the dictionary. Metataxis rules therefore normally contain variables. Instead of a word, a node in a rule pattern may carry a variable that ranges over a given list of words, over a word class or over the entire vocabulary. Also the feature lists of the nodes may at least in part consist of variables.

2.3. Interaction of rule and tree

The insight that trees consist of repeated patterns which can be catered for in separate metataxis rules is not enough to devise an efficient system of transformation rules. Before any rules can be written, a closer look should be directed at the question how the rules interact with the tree to be translated. For being able to write a metataxis rule system, it is important to know what is transformed when and which rule transforms which part of the tree.

The transformation procedure carried out by means of a number of metataxis rules and dictionary entries could in principle step through the tree structure to be translated in a variety of different ways. For the metataxis model one particular possibility has been chosen which seems to be linguistically well motivated. The dependency relation is a directed relation. It is therefore natural that dependency-syntactic descriptions follow this notion of directed syntactic relationships. Normally the link between two words is thus presented in terms of the governing word's capacity to have certain dependents. Only in an implicit way do these descriptions give information about the dependent's capacity to be governed by certain governors. Accordingly, the metataxis process moves through the tree in the direction from a governor to its dependents. Metataxis thus proceeds from the top of the tree downwards. The first metataxis rule applied transforms the main internal governor of the sentence. If the rule contains variables for words, it invokes dictionary entries for the encountered word to transform it and insert one of its target language counterparts in the appropriate slot indicated by the variable in the output pattern of the rule. When this is done, the mechanism steps on to the next source language symbol to be translated. A symbol in this sense is either a word or a dependent type label. In this way the process works its way through the whole tree until everything has been transformed into target language forms.

During this procedure, the tree changes. Words and labels are replaced by target language ones, but also the graphical structure of the tree itself can change through the addition, deletion or any other rearrangement of nodes and branches. These rearrangements can be brought about by metataxis rules or by dictionary entries. A rearrangement takes place every time the input pattern of the rule or entry in question differs from the output pattern. This accounts for the fact that a single word may be translated by several ones or vice versa, that for example an object may be translated into a prepositional construction, that auxiliaries may be merged into morphological features and many other restructuring phenomena of this kind.

As the wording in different parts of the discussion above indicates, is has been found to be expedient to let the entire metataxis process take place in a isngle tree where forms of the two involved languages temporarily meet. At first sight, one might without hesitation opt for an approach with two separate trees: the source language tree which is read and interpreted and the target language tree which is built up. However, the process is freed from much bookkeeping and tracemarking if the pieces of tree already translated are actually removed from the tree and replaced by their target language counterparts. The metataxis process thus takes place in a hybrid tree. As the process moves through the tree from the top downwards and from left to right, the tree is transformed from a source into a target language structure. The process has been devised in such a way that the part of the tree already translated always remains a coherent unit. This means that the next symbol to be transformed is always a symbol adjacent to already transformed labels or nodes. In this way target language "islands" in source language structure are excluded, whereby an unnecessary complication in the metataxis rules is avoided which would be inevitable if the rules had to foresee whether or not a certain symbol already encountered has been transformed. This feature of the hybrid tree implies that if the tree is graphically drawn during the metataxis process, there is a borderline between the symbols of the two languages, and this line is more or less straight without crossings or loops.

In section 2.4. I say a few more words about the size of the portions transformed by one rule. But it is clear already now that handling the tree in portions might entail the risk of not covering all the possible elements and structures of an arbitrary tree. Some portion might happen not to be covered by any rule. Since it is the function of the metataxis rule system to transform all well-formed input, this must not happen. Therefore, there has to be a guarantee that metataxis handles whatever well-formed input is submitted to it. The solution adopted in the DLT metataxes ensures coverage by an uncomplicated means. I said above (2.2.) that writing a metataxis rule system would be easiest, if one could translate word by word and label by label. Of course such an approach yields "translations" that are not much better than the word-by-word translations discussed by machine translators in the fifties (examples in Hutchins 1986: 36). However, such a rule system has the advantage that it can easily be made complete: Given a dictionary that translates all the words encountered in the sentence, all one needs is a metataxis rule for each possible dependent type label of the source language. Such a system "translates" every sentence whose words are found in the dictionary and whose labels belong to the pre-defined set. In order to ensure that the rule system cope with all input that is well-formed in this sense, the DLT metataxes contain a set of label-to-label rules. These are called the unmarked metataxis rules (the name refers to their hierarchical position, see 2.4.).

Once one has adopted this simple but efficient measure, one can make a virtue of the need. The more similar the two languages (more precisely, their syntax descriptions) are to one another, the more cases are transformed correctly by the unmarked rules alone. This reduces the need for metataxis rule writing in a welcome way, since now only such rules have to be written which account for "deviations" from the unmarked rules. Once you have a rule that states that an English subject becomes an Esperanto subject, you need other subject rules only for the cases when this is not so, as for example in the constructions of the type *She was given a book*, which cannot be translated in the same syntactic shape into Esperanto (nor to most other languages). In Esperanto, it becomes *Al ŝi estis donita libro* 'to her [prepositional adjunct] was given a book [subject]'. The next section takes up the question how the rule system can decide when to use the special rule and when to apply the unmarked one.

What at first sight looks as a simple safety measure at the level of formalism, turns out to render a distinction which has long been in the focus of linguistic discussion: There has been a debate about the status of contrastive linguistics in which the main issue was whether the discipline should be concerned only with the differences among languages or with the entire systems of the languages compared. In metataxis the correspondences are accounted for by unmarked and the differences by marked rules.

2.4. Applicable rules and the hierarchy of specificity

In the description above I showed how the metataxis rule system step by step transforms a source language dependency tree into a set of equivalent target language trees, moving the borderline through the hybrid tree from its top downwards. I have not yet said how the one rule to be applied in a given context is chosen from the total number of available rules. The procedure for this is twofold. First, all rules are selected that are applicable at all and then from this subset of the entire rule system, one rule is chosen and applied.

The first part of the procedure, the selection of applicable rules, is done by pattern matching. Since both the tree being translated and the input patterns of the metataxis rules are dependency trees, they can be compared straightforwardly. At any given moment in the metataxis process, the next symbol (word or label) to be tackled is the leftmost one of those that are situated immediately below the borderline. Applicable rules are all rules that match with that symbol and some part of the tree below it. This means that the input pattern of a given rule is, as it were, laid onto the hybrid tree with the top symbol of the input pattern on the "next" symbol of the tree. They match if the tree contains nodes and labels that coincide with those in the input pattern. Nodes and labels coincide if they are literally equal or if the item given in the tree being translated is within the range of the variable in the input pattern. If there are more branches and nodes in the tree than in the input pattern, this does not disturb the match, unless the input pattern contains a so-called negative condition, that is, a condition which explicitly forbids a certain node or label to be present in the tree. When the rule later on is chosen for actually being applied, it replaces the bit of the tree with which it matches, leaving any additional symbols below the borderline to be handled in a later step.

In this way all the applicable rules are selected. Unless only a single rule has been found to be applicable, a choice has to be made among the applicable rules. The unmarked metataxis rules discussed above (cf. 2.3.) can be used as an illustration for this. They are applicable very often, but for obvious reasons they should not always be used. The unmarked rules not only fulfil the mechanical task of guaranteeing that the process never stops before the whole tree has been transformed; their output can in many cases be used as correct portions of the target language tree. For many structures, however, more specific rules have to be devised. It would not be expedient if this implied the need of equipping the unmarked rules with some sort of condition which would explicitly exclude their use in these cases. Such conditions would have to be adapted each time the metataxis writer adds a new marked rule and they would in addition be redundant in the sense that they would contain a description of the structure covered by a different, more specific rule, which is also described there. A more versatile solution has therefore been adopted. The metataxis rules are arranged in a hierarchy, so that the more specific rules prevail over the less specific ones. This is not only a two-level hierarchy of superior and inferior rules, but rather a many-layered hierarchy. The criterion for letting a rule prevail over another rule is simple: the more specific rule has priority. Specificity is in this respect measured in a straightforward way: The input patterns of the rules are compared. The rule that has more symbols (nodes or labels) is more specific than the rule with less symbols. In the case of equal numbers, the rule whose internal governor is more precisely specified prevails. Thus a word literally given with all features specified prevails over a word with variables or empty slots in the feature list, a word prevails over a variable, a variable that ranges over a small word list prevails over a word class variable etc. As Job van Zuijlen's contribution shows, it is not necessarily inevitable to implement a mechanism for measuring the specificness of rules. Rule ordering at the implementation level will suffice in most cases. The only requirement of modularity in this respect is that the solution adopted at the implementation level should by no means restrict the expressive power defined in the linguistic design of the system.

In this way the metataxis rules are ordered in a suitable and, as experience shows, linguistically well-motivated way. Yet, one more refinement is needed to obtain as powerful and versatile an instrument as is required for machine translation. The idea of priority is only applicable, if it is the metataxis writer's intention that only a single rule be chosen, as I have tacitly assumed so far. In some cases, however, it may be desirable to generate parallel alternatives in order to submit them to a (possibly semantic or pragmatic) choice to be made later on in the overall translation process. It is no problem to write two different rules which match the same input, but a special means is needed to prevent these rules from overriding each other by hierarchical priority. To this end the metataxis writer can mark a rule as "parallel", which means that, when it is chosen, it will be carried out and the same input will be submitted to other applicable rules that hold a lower hierarchical position than the rule applied first. It is an interesting feature of the specificity criterion, which illustrates its linguistic motivation, that there is no need to indicate to which particular rule a given rule is parallel. It is sufficient to say that it is parallel. The next highest rule in the hierarchy will then be looked for and applied.

2.5. Monolingual processings and transformation proper

The metataxis process is a complicated sequence of rule applications. In order to restrict its complexity, it has been provided with the possibility of removing certain steps from the main part of the process. The transformation phase of the metataxis process, in which the transfer step from the source to the target language is carried out, is surrounded by a pre-processing and a post-processing phase. This subdivision of working steps is built on a linguistically motivated distinction of functions.

Since the power of metataxis rules is higher the more the trees to be handled consist of repeated patterns, it is useful to increase their similarity before handling, if this can be done without afflicting the linguistic functionality of the translation procedure and the quality of its outcome. For example, English verb constructions comprise varying numbers of (auxiliary and finite) verbs which in the trees are reflected by equally varying numbers of nodes. This would make it necessary to devise metataxis rules for transforming one-, two-, three- and four-verb constructions, although most of the contents of these different rules, like for example information about what to do with an indirect object, is the same. In such a case, the transformation into the target language becomes much simpler, if the variety of source language forms is first reduced to a uniform representation. In the case of English verb constructions, this is a tree with a single governing verb (the content verb of the construction) with features like tense, mood and aspect expressed in its feature list. Thus *would have been coming* becomes something like "*come* [tense: perfect, mood: conditional, aspect: progressive]".

Many other preparatory rules can be imagined. What is common to all of them is that they do not yet carry out the transfer step, i.e., they are monolingual. The same holds for rules that follow the transformations rules, carrying out modifications within the target language tree. The post-processing rules are mainly used to adjust structures preliminarily generated by the transformation rules in a deliberately "incorrect" shape. This can be a welcome device since it allows the transformation rules to be overgeneral (and thus simpler). Such adjusting post-processing rules can be used whenever the "incorrectness" can be repaired on a monolingual basis. The linguistic motivation of the tripartition of metataxis rules thus lies in the distinction between monolingual source language rules, bilingual transformation rules and monolingual target language rules.

The latter type of rules is functionally very close to target language synthesis rules, since both carry out monolingual modifications in target language trees. From an implementational point of view there may not even be a need to keep them apart. For the linguist, however, there is a distinction: The post-processing rules belong to the metataxis complex, since they rely on knowledge of the source language, even though they do not use source language elements in the trees they handle. The synthesis rules, by contrast, carry out purely language-specific generation tasks such as form government and agreement, morphological synthesis and elision and contraction. These functions can be fulfilled without reference to the source sentence. They add information to the target sentence which is redundant as long as the sentence is represented in the form of a labelled dependency tree, but which is needed when the tree structure, the labels and the feature lists are dropped and the tree is linearized. (Monolingual synthesis rules for DLT's first target language, French, have been written and formalized along these lines by Dorine Tamis 1987a.)

A word about terms. In earlier work (Schubert 1987b: 168), I called the monolingual pre- and post-processing rules filters. The term has turned out to be misleading, since it could suggest that the rules might filter out and discard some of the structures submitted to them, which is not the case. In contrast to recognizing or parsing rules, the monolingual rules discussed here are part of metataxis and share this rule system's property of not rejecting anything.

3. Metataxis and the implicitness principle

Having seen in section 2. how metataxis rules are designed, grouped, ordered, selected and applied, we can now step back a bit and look at metataxis in a more general way.

Opting for metataxis means choosing to carry out the transfer step in translation at the syntactic level. This is not a self-evident choice, nor a generally preferred one in today's machine translation landscape. A few explanatory words may therefore be in order.

It is generally agreed that the experience acquired in early machine translation experiments shows that purely syntactic translation is impossible. And of course metataxis is by no means an attempt to reach the goal along paths that led astray in the fifties. Metataxis is an instrument to make use of the syntactic regularity in the translation correspondences between languages in a highly efficient way. It should be kept in mind that metataxis is not meant to carry out the entire translation function, but just its syntactic part. As soon as a metataxis process has delivered all the syntactically possible alternative translations, the semantic and pragmatic components of the machine translation system make a choice among them. It is therefore evident that translation is done by neither syntax nor semantics alone, but only by the joint and coordinated functions of metataxis and the mechanisms for semantic-pragmatic choice, and one should not be judged without reference to the other.

Given its role as one of two partners in the interplay of form- and content-related translation mechanisms, metataxis can be seen as a realization of the **implicitness principle** in machine translation. There are approaches to machine translation that gear source language analysis and target language synthesis towards an interface at a level of isomorphic syntactic structures. Other approaches appeal to some sort of semantic isomorphism in the form of frames of deep cases or semantic roles. By contrast, the metataxis approach does not rely on isomorphism of any such kind. In metataxis the transfer step is done between non-congruent, non-isomorphic, language-specific structures. From a theoretical point of view, such a step is of course possible because of the existence of a common meaning of the structures considered to be corresponding. The implicitness principle used in the metataxis approach, however, implies that, although there is a semantic *tertium comparationis*, there is no need to spell it out; it can be kept implicit (Schubert 1987a: 116, 1988a).

In this way the metataxis approach avoids a problem which has been noticed by various machine translation specialists. Although deep cases are a very popular instrument in machine translation, the (often tacit) assumption that they are a language-independent representation of semantic dependency relations is erroneous. Not only are deep cases difficult to define and to delimit, they can also be shown to be language-specific (Pleines 1978; Engel 1980; Tsujii 1986). Instead of looking for another, truly language-independent representation for the common meaning of corresponding syntactic forms in the source and the target language (which ultimately may not exist), the metataxis approach prefers to make use of the fact that two corresponding forms have a common meaning and tacitly to account for the mapping between the two forms without providing a third form for making explicit what that common meaning is.

4. Prospects

The three articles to follow describe the first approaches to a realization of the metataxis model. Their authors have entered a new field and now relate the solutions found and problems encountered during the first years of application in practice. In step with the accumulation of more practical experience as well as new and deeper theoretical insights, various aspects of the overall set-up of metataxis may be built out and improved. A number of possible directions of development can be suggested already now. The overview is of course not complete.

The first of these development directions is something metataxis shares with grammar in general: an extension of scope. According to a tradition with a very long standing in grammatical thinking, the metataxes contained in this volume mainly focus on syntagmata and sentences. A number of word level rules is taken up, especially in Dorine Tamis's contribution, but as a whole metataxis needs to be extended from the sentence level both downwards to the word level and upwards to the text level.

Word level metataxis is required in particular for languages with productive word formation processes or with virtually unenumerable morphological forms. From the languages represented in the first part of this volume, Finnish and Hungarian may be taken as examples for morphological productivity, whereas German is an instance of a language with productive word formation. But also languages not traditionally held to be especially productive in word formation such as French or Italian may well be so in technical language and terminology, areas that are marginal in most grammatical accounts, but crucial for machine translation. Moreover, it should not be forgotten that productive word formation is not only a feature of one or other prospective source or target language but to a particular degree also of DLT's intermediate language Esperanto. This is by no means an accidental feature, but one of the characteristics of Esperanto that have brought about its prominent privileged position among the candidates for an intermediate structure. Productive and well-described word formation is an extremely expedient feature for a language used in knowledge representation, inferencing, machine learning and other translation-oriented techniques of Artificial Intelligence.

Text level metataxis is the other side of this development direction, that should be promoted in the future. There are syntactic elements in the phenomena that constitute the difference between unrelated sentences and a coherent text, and these should not be omitted in translation. Failure to include them may destroy the message of the text. The rules for translating these text-structuring phenomena should be studied, described and made applicable within a framework of text level metataxis.

The second direction that should be paid attention to is the acquisition and updating of knowledge about metatactic relations between two languages. The two metataxes accounted for in this volume were entirely written "by hand" and the relevant metataxis information in the bilingual dictionary entries was likewise encoded by lexicographers. In the future, when work will be done on a larger scale than what was needed for the DLT prototypes, it will become increasingly interesting to consider various aspects of semi-automatical rule and entry generation. While corpora of authentic text were until now used only to inspire the grammarians' and lexicographers' intuition and to provide sample material, they should in the future be linked to the improvement of metataxes more directly (Schubert, forthc.). Corpora can no doubt become valuable sources for automatically deriving regularities in structural correspondence, which may then be edited by a linguist. In a more distant future, one may even consider possibilities of including corpora directly in the translation system as sort of an implicit contextual dictionary.

A scheme for the acquisition, representation and processing of language-related knowledge is at present being worked out for the DLT system. Victor Sadler's design (cf. Sadler, forthc.) is based on a **bilingual knowledge bank**. The knowledge bank contains texts with their translations. It is derived from a parallel corpus of texts in a source or target language of the system and the intermediate language (e.g., English-Esperanto, French-Esperanto etc.). The texts are represented in an analysed and syntactically disambiguated form with syntactic, textual and translational correspondences marked. In an architecture where the one and only knowledge source is such a knowledge representation that is fairly close to plain texts, metataxis acquires a new quality. Whereas the present metataxis rule systems in the DLT prototype versions are seen as an independent mechanism, it will in the new system configuration get the character of a set of **generalization rules**, by means of which the specimen knowledge contained in the knowledge bank can be made applicable to new and unforeseen texts.

The content of the rule sets will essentially remain unchanged, but their function will shift: Metataxis becomes a higher-level grammar that makes available the knowledge implicitly contained in a textual representation.

References

Engel, Ulrich (1980): Fügungspotenz und Sprachvergleich. Vom Nutzen eines semantisch erweiterten Valenzbegriffs für die kontrastive Linguistik. In: *Wirkendes Wort* 30, pp. 1-22

Hutchins, William John (1986): *Machine translation: past, present, future.* Chichester: Horwood / New York etc.: Wiley

Maxwell, Dan (1987): Metataxis English-IL. Unpublished report. Utrecht: BSO/Research

Pleines, Jochen (1978): Ist der Universalitätsanspruch der Kasusgrammatik berechtigt? In: *Valence, semantic case, and grammatical relations.* Ed. Werner Abraham. Amsterdam: Benjamins, pp. 335-376

Sadler, Victor (forthcoming): *Working with analogical semantics. An assessment of current disambiguation techniques in DLT.*
Dordrecht/Providence: Foris [autumn 1989]

Schubert, Klaus (1986): *Syntactic tree structures in DLT.*
Utrecht: BSO/Research

Schubert, Klaus (1987a): Wann bedeuten zwei Wörter dasselbe? Über Tiefenkasus als Tertium comparationis.
In: *Linguistik in Deutschland.* Ed. Werner Abraham / Ritva Århammar. Tübingen: Niemeyer, pp. 109-117

Schubert, Klaus (1987b): *Metataxis. Contrastive dependency syntax for machine translation.*
Dordrecht/Providence: Foris

Schubert, Klaus (1988a): Implicitness as a guiding principle in machine translation.
In: *Coling Budapest. Proceedings of the 12th International Conference on Computational Linguistics.* Ed. Dénes Vargha. Budapest: John von Neumann Society for Computing Sciences, pp. 599-601

Schubert, Klaus (1988b): Modularity in linguistic system design.
In: *Zbornik IV. konference Računalniška obdelava jezikovnih podatkov // Proceedings of the IV-th Conference Computational Processing of Language Data.* [Ljubljana]: Institut "Jožef Stefan" / Društvo za uporabno jezikoslovje Slovenije, pp. 91-106

Schubert, Klaus (forthcoming): Kunskap om världen eller kunskap om texten?
In: [Proceedings of: Nordiske Datalingvistikdage og Symposium for datamatstøttet lexikografi og terminologi. Reykjavík, June 1989]

Tamis, Dorine (1987a): Contribution à la synthèse automatique du français.
Unpublished report. Utrecht: BSO/Research / Unpublished doctorandus thesis. Amsterdam: Vrije Universiteit

Tamis, Dorine (1987b): La métataxe IL-français.
Unpublished report. Utrecht: BSO/Research

Tesnière, Lucien (1959): *Éléments de syntaxe structurale.*
Paris: Klincksieck, 2nd ed., 4th print. 1982

Tsujii, Jun-ichi (1986): Future directions of machine translation.
In: *11th International Conference on Computational Linguistics. Proceedings of Coling 86.* Bonn: Institut für angewandte Kommunikations- und Sprachforschung, pp. 655-668

Esperanto-French metataxis

Dorine Tamis

Utrecht, Netherlands

1. Introduction

The aim of the present paper is to give an overview of the metataxis rule system for IL-French, which describes the syntactic relationships between the two languages IL (the Esperanto-based Intermediate Language) and French. This metataxis rule system has been designed for implementation in the first target language module of the semi-automatic machine translation system DLT (Distributed Language Translation).

Metataxis treats the syntactic relationships between two languages. For a given source language, metataxis tries to find all syntactically possible translation alternatives in a given target language. This set of syntactic transformations includes both structural changes and word translation, which means that all possible structural and lexical translations are generated in a given target language for a given source language input pattern. To represent the contrastive knowledge about these syntactic relationships, so-called metataxis rules are used. The contrastive rules must be able to deal with all these possible structural and lexical translations between two languages. The input language is found on the left hand side of the rule and the output language on the right hand side.

Metataxis is based on dependency syntax and is therefore a form of contrastive dependency syntax. Consequently, before the linguist can write this contrastive rule system, both the input and the output language must have been described according to the dependency model. Both dependency syntaxes must be available. "A metataxis rule system thus establishes a link between the dependency syntaxes of two languages" (Schubert 1987b: 132). The input must be in accordance with the dependency syntax of the input language, whereas the output must be well-formed according to the dependency syntax of the output language. DLT's dependency syntax model is based on Tesnière (1959) and is elaborated in Schubert (1986a, 1987b).

The aim of the present paper is to give an overview of the metataxis rule system between the Intermediate Language (IL) of the semi-automatic machine translation system DLT (Distributed Language Translation) and French (FR). The Intermediate Language is a slightly modified form of Esperanto, of which the differences are described by Schubert (1987a). As French is the first target language of the DLT system, the rule system described here has its practical application in the form of implementation in the first target language module of the DLT system. For a more detailed description of the rule system I refer to Tamis (1987b). In this paper, I will focus on the various types of rules which are at the disposal of the metataxis writer for representing his or her knowledge of the contrastive syntax. Since the form of the rules have a general scope, they can be used for other languages as well. In general, for metataxis rules, one of the main distinctions is between unmarked rules, described in section 2., and marked metataxis rules, treated in section 3. Finally, in section 4. a summary will be given.

Before taking a closer look at the rules, let us consider the overall IL-French metataxis process. The input to the IL-French metataxis is an IL dependency tree according to the autonomous description of the IL dependency syntax in this volume. The output of the IL-French metataxis is a set of its target language equivalents, which are French dependency trees according to the French dependency syntax as described in Tamis (1987a). The IL dependency tree is a syntactic tree which represents the syntactic interpretation of the IL input sentence to be translated into French. Since the intermediate language is a syntactically unambiguous language, every IL sentence delivers only one syntactic tree as input to the IL-French metataxis. This input IL tree may result in several French trees because of two phenomena. Firstly, an IL structure can be translated into different French structures (the meaning of those alternatives can be similar or different depending on the context). For instance, the IL sentence *anstataŭigu la valvon* 'replace the valve' has a number of possible French translation structures (the list is not exhaustive):

Remplace le clapet.	Il est nécessaire de remplacer le clapet.
Remplacez le clapet.	Le clapet est à remplacer.
Remplacer le clapet.	Le remplacement du clapet s'impose.
Il faut remplacer le clapet.	Le clapet doit être remplacé.

On the other hand, an IL word can have more than one possible French translation, due to the phenomenon of lexical ambiguity. The IL word *lando* 'country', for example, can be translated as *pays*, *région* or *contrée*, each of which is used in a different context. Figure 1 provides an overview of the IL-French metataxis process.

Fig. 1: IL-French metataxis

2. Unmarked rules

2.1. Introduction

The IL-French metataxis writer has the task of establishing the syntactic relationships between IL and French. The general similarities between the two languages are likely to be the first phenomena discovered. These general relationships in terms of general metataxis rules take care of the transformation of each element in the input dependency tree, so that nothing remains unchanged during the translation process. There must be a list of exceptionless general rules which can take care of the translation of every IL word and of every IL syntactic structure into French. These general rules are called unmarked rules. There are no restrictions on their transformations from the IL into French. Once this list is available, there is a basis for the further development of the contrastive rule system. Extensions can be made on this base ranging from the more general level towards the more specific metataxis rules, which are called marked rules (section 3.).

Schubert (1987b: 136) notes that metataxis rules are effective on all levels of syntax: word, sentence and text level. Rules involving more than one sentence, i.e. metataxis at the text level, presuppose a text grammar and will not be treated here. The IL-French metataxis rule system, including both unmarked and marked rules, will be described in the next sections at the word and the sentence level.

2.2. Word level

Metataxis at the word level transforms words and can be called lexical transformation. The word level rules treat the syntactic form of the words. In general, the dictionary takes care of word translation. A list of general rules, however, can be made for the transformation of word classes and of features which are part of the syntactic word form. The rules are described in the following subsections.

2.2.1. Word classes

For the IL, twelve major word classes are distinguished by Schubert in this volume: verb (VRB), noun (SUB), pronoun (PRN), adjective (ADJ), adverb (ADV), numeral (NUM), article (ART), preposition (PRP), interjection (INT), bound function morpheme (FKC), coordinating conjunction (KON) and subordinating conjunction (SBK). For French, eleven word classes are distinguished: verb (VRB), noun (SUB), pronoun (PRN), adjective (ADJ), adverb (ADV), numeral (NUM), determiner (DET), preposition (prp), interjection (INT), coordinator (CON) and subordinating conjunction (SBK). Every IL word has only one word class. IL content words bear morphemes which identify their word class. For example, an IL word ending in the morpheme '*o* is always a noun. On the other hand, IL function words must be listed explicitly in the dictionary with their appropriate word class. In French, the syntactic category of every word must be made explicit, because it is usually not the case that the word class of a French word can be determined on the basis of its form. Moreover, a French word often has more than one word class. An example is the French word *manuel* 'manual', which belongs to the word classes of the nouns and the adjectives. The translation of the IL noun *manlibro* in French is *manuel*. The proper word class of *manuel* is found by examining the word class of the IL origin word, which in this case is a noun. *Manuel* as an adjective is a translation of the IL *permana* 'by hand'. Finally, the word class of the French word is needed in order to deal with further treatments of the French dependency tree after the metataxis process.

An unmarked metataxis rule is written for each word class in the IL in order to have at least one word class for each French translation equivalent. Such unmarked rules can be seen as redundancy rules which overlie the bilingual IL-French lexicon. In this way, not all dictionary entries from the bilingual lexicon need to include the word class of the words they treat. Two types of general rules are found: either an IL morpheme (1) or an IL word class (2) is transformed into the appropriate word class of the French translation. Before showing both rules, a few remarks about the rule formalism need to be made. The IL input structure is on the left hand side of the transformation arrow and the French output on the right hand side. The variable <X> is used to indicate a word or a stem and the back quote (') is used for marking the morpheme boundary in the IL word. For reasons of readability, this morpheme division is omitted in some cases. A word will be represented by the following list: **[word/word class/[feature list]]**. Not all the list elements are always mentioned in the examples. The first rule illustrates the transformation of the IL morpheme '*a* into a French adjective, for example, the IL adjective *aera* 'air [attributive]' is translated as the French adjective *aérien*:

IL		**FR**
[<X>'**a**]	⇒	[<X>/**ADJ**]

The next rule transforms IL adverbs into French adverbs, for example, the IL adverb *morgaŭ* 'tomorrow' is translated as the French adverb *demain*:

IL		**FR**
[<X>/**ADV**]	⇒	[<X>/**ADV**]

2.2.2. Syntactic features

General rules are established not only for the word classes but also for the syntactic features of the words. All the IL syntactic features necessary for our translation purpose can be detected from specific morphemes of the words. This is not the case in French. The first step to be made is to look at the translation relevant syntactic features of both languages (Schubert 1987b: 153). The number feature ([f_num]) of the noun is an example of a translation relevant feature, since in general, the noun in the French translation preserves the same number feature as the noun in the IL source language. Within the metataxis rules, each feature has a name and a value. The IL inflexion morpheme *'j* identifies the plural (pl) value of the number feature (the plural number feature). When this IL morpheme is part of a noun, it is transformed into the appropriate French feature by means of the following unmarked IL-French metataxis rule:

IL		**FR**
[<X>'o'**j**]	⇒	[<X>/[**f_num,pl**]]

For instance, the IL noun *pilotoj* 'pilots' is translated into the French *pilotes* by means of the following dictionary entry:

IL	**FR**
[pilot'o]	[pilote]

followed by the above-mentioned general metataxis rule which adds the plural number feature to the French translation, of which the final form becomes [pilote/[f_num,pl]]. In the French tree, the French morphology will transform the word form *pilote* together with its syntactic feature into the correct syntactic form *pilotes* (see Tamis 1988). As is shown above, this unmarked metataxis rule can derive regular plural noun forms. Consequently, only the singular form of a noun with a regular plural has to be put in the dictionary. A "raw" dictionary entry without syntactic features would contain the complete syntactic word forms of both nouns:

IL	**FR**
[pilot'o'j]	[pilotes]

Syntactic features comprise tense and mood features as well. This means that all the IL verb endings must be transformed into the appropriate French tense and mood forms. But of course, the forthcoming sentence and text level metataxis must have the opportunity to change these features when necessary under the influence of a larger context. The following metataxis rule is intended to illustrate a verb transformation rule. It transforms the IL inflexion morpheme *'as* into a French verb with the indicative value of the mood feature ([f_mood,ind]) and the present value of the tense feature ([f_tns,pr]).

IL		**FR**
[<X>'**as**]	⇒	[<X>/**VRB**/[**f_mood,ind, f_tns,pr**]]

An example of the rule is *legas* 'read(s)':

IL	**FR**
[leg'as]	[lire/VRB/[f_mood,ind, f_tns,pr]]

2.3. Sentence level

Dependency trees do not only contain words but they also indicate the syntactic relations between the words: the dependency relations. Metataxis at the sentence level transforms these dependency relations and can, therefore, be called structural translation. The dependency relations found in the input dependency tree are transformed into equivalent dependency relations in the output tree. For the IL, eighteen dependency relations are distinguished by Schubert in the syntax description in this volume (without the top label [GOV]), whereas Tamis (1987a) distinguished twenty two relations for French. A list of unmarked metataxis rules is written in order to include each possible IL dependency relation: the rules transform labeled trees by changing an IL label into a French label without any restriction on the word, word class or feature depending on this label or elsewhere in the tree. The dependency relations of the following example sentence *la komputilo tradukas la manlibron* 'the computer translates the manual' can be transformed by means of four unmarked rules into the correct dependency relations of the French translation *l'ordinateur traduit le manuel*. These rules treat the following dependency relations: the subject dependent ([SUBJ]), the object dependent ([OBJ]), the attribute dependent ([DET]/[F-ATR1]) and the top label of every sentence ([GOV]). The label prefix "F-" is used to indicate that French is the language concerned in the dependency relations. The unmarked structural rules are:

	IL		**FR**
1.	[GOV]	⇒	[F-GOV]
2.	[SUBJ]	⇒	[F-SUBJ]
3.	[OBJ]	⇒	[F-OBJ]
4.	[DET]	⇒	[F-ATR1]

The IL and French dependency trees of the example sentences are:

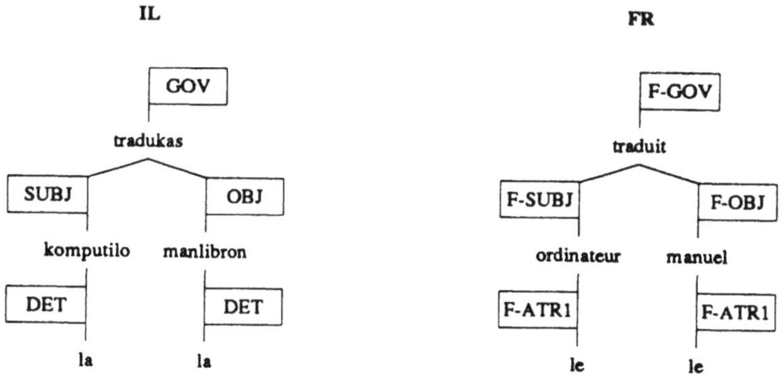

Fig. 2: Graphical IL and French dependency trees

The above graphical representation of dependency trees will be replaced in the rest of this paper by a square bracket representation. As we have already seen (cf. 2.2.1.), a word is represented by the following list: **[word/word class/[feature list]]**. To represent an entire dependency tree node, the label of the word and a list of depending words are added to the above-mentioned list. This results in the following notation: **[label, word, list of dependents]**. The list of dependents can be empty (i.e. there are no dependents) or can be a new list of the dependency tree type: **[label, word, list of dependents]**. Each IL word is divided into morphemes by means of the back quote (cf. 2.2.1.). As an illustration, figure 3 shows the bracket representation of the above-mentioned IL and French dependency tree:

IL	**FR**
[GOV, traduk'as,	[F-GOV, traduit,
[SUBJ, komput'il'o,	[F-SUBJ, ordinateur,
[DET, la]],	[F-ATR1, le]],
[OBJ, man'libr'o'n,	[F-OBJ, manuel,
[DET, la]]]	[F-ATR1, le]]]

Fig. 3: Bracket IL and French dependency trees

3. Marked rules

3.1. Introduction

In a lot of cases, the unmarked rules will give a result that is not desirable. To limit the scope of the general rules, restrictions and conditions on the rules seem to be necessary. The presence or even absence of a specific word requires a modification of the established general metataxis rules. Besides these general rules, more specific rules are needed to take these kinds of dependency tree transformations into account. This leads us to the marked metataxis rules. This section will give an overview of the marked rules which are part of the IL-French metataxis rule system (although without trying to be complete). With the formalisation of the metataxis rules in mind (see Van Zuijlen, this volume), it is important for the metataxis writer to clearly define all the restrictions and conditions on the rules.

3.2. Word level

In this section, the marked metataxis rules at the word level will be treated. Mainly, these rules modify word classes and syntactic features without the influence of any syntactic sentence context. Moreover, the use of redundancy rules will be explained.

3.2.1. Word classes

It is sometimes necessary to change an IL word class into a French word class other than the one which the general rule would change it into. In principal, all types of metataxis rules can make this transformation. Metataxis rules which treat a certain transformation on sentence level can cause the modification of a specific word class of one of the parts of the construction as well. Mostly, this modification occurs under the influence of the context of the word. An entry in the IL-French dictionary illustrates this phenomenon at the word level: it changes the IL adverb *krajone* 'with a pen' independently of any syntactic context into a French construction whose internal governor *avec* belongs to a different word class:

```
IL           FR
[krajon'e]   [avec/PRP,
               [F-PARG, crayon/SUB,
                 [F-ATR1, un/DET]]]
```

3.2.2. Syntactic features

Also syntactic features can be modified by metataxis rules on all levels. As an example at the word level, the number feature is elaborated here. As mentioned earlier (cf. 2.2.2.), the number feature is generally preserved in the translation of an IL noun into its French equivalent. There are some specific cases, however, which require a fixed number feature in the target language, no matter what the number feature in the source language is. In this case, the general metataxis rule "preserve the number feature" must be replaced by two marked rules, the first of which changes an IL singular noun into a French noun with a plural number feature ([f_num,pl]) and the second works the other way round, i.e. it changes a plural IL noun into a singular French noun ([f_num,sg]). These rules can not be applied in the general form in which they are represented below. The restriction is that they are only valid for a certain number of words which must be considered as different values of the variable <X>.

	IL		FR
1.	[<X>'o]	⇒	[<X>/[**f_num,pl**]]
2.	[<X>'o'j]	⇒	[<X>/[**f_num,sg**]]

An example of the first rule is the IL word *mono* 'money' which has four different possible French translations, of which two, *espèce* and *devise*, require a plural number feature, as can be seen in the next dictionary entry:

IL	FR
[mon'o]	[argent]
[mon'o]	[espèce/[f_num,pl]]
[mon'o]	[devise/[f_num,pl]]
[mon'o]	[monnaie]

The IL word *informoj* 'information' is an illustration of the second rule. The IL plural form *informoj* must be translated as the singular French noun *information*. The IL singular counterpart *informo* has, in addition, the alternative translation *renseignement*, as is shown in the following dictionary entry:

IL	FR
[inform'o'j]	[information/[f_num,sg]]
[inform'o]	[information]
[inform'o]	[renseignement]

A number of French words always have a fixed syntactic feature, i.e. they can only be used with a particular value of a given syntactic feature. For example, some French adjectives can only be used in a masculine form, such as *ouvrable* 'open'. Consequently, whatever the original IL word is, the French translation contains this specific syntactic feature. It is not necessary to add this feature each time the word in question appears in the bilingual dictionary. This leads to a specific target language dictionary, where these inherent word features can be included. The word *alentours* 'environment', for example, has only a plural syntactic form and is represented in this syntactic target dictionary as: [alentours/SUB/[f_num,pl]].

3.2.3. Redundancy rules

If some regular change in word or morpheme transformation is examined, so-called redundancy rules can be written. These redundancy rules behave like generalized dictionary entries and are part of the metataxis rule system. If an IL word is not found in the dictionary, a translation may be generated by these redundancy rules when all the morphemes of the unknown IL word are known to the system. Since the word formation process is very productive in the IL, the dictionary will never be able to contain all complex IL words. The solution consists of the redundancy rules which enable the generation of new French translations (but only when they can be generated in a regular way). On the other hand, the size of the dictionary can be reduced by removing the regular word formations and translations and replacing them with redundancy rules. No equivalent should be added to the bilingual dictionary if it can be derived from the application of redundancy rules (or other metataxis rules). The redundancy rules can also apply in parallel to any specific dictionary entry. Some translations can be derived in a regular way, whereas other translation equivalents do not correspond to any redundancy rule. This parallel translation takes into account all possible syntactic translations of an IL word, the main objective of metataxis. However, it must also be possible to indicate for any given dictionary entry, that this entry prohibits parallel translation based on redundancy rules.

The following metataxis rule shows the alternative translations for the IL derivational morpheme *'ig*. The rule is not unmarked because there is a restriction: the word class of the stem is limited. In the case of a verb stem preceding the morpheme *'ig*, the French construction *faire* 'to do' with the infinitive form ([f_mood,inf]) of the stem (<X>) can be made (1a) and in the case of an adjective or noun stem, the other construction, the verb *rendre* 'to make' plus the infinitive form of the stem (<Y>), must be chosen (1b).

	IL		**FR**
1a	[<X>**'ig'**i]	⇒	[rendre/VRB, [F-PRED, <X>]]
1b	[<Y>**'ig'**i]	⇒	[faire/VRB, [F-INF, <Y>/VRB/[f_mood,inf]]]

Conditions on the rules:
(1a) <X> = ADJ or SUB (ADJvSUB)
(1b) <Y> = VRB

When the IL complex word *pur'ig'i* 'to clean' is not found in the dictionary, the entry for the adjectival stem *pur'a* 'clean' is looked for and is used according to this redundancy rule which changes the verb with suffix *'ig* into the French construction *rendre* plus the translation of the stem which in this case is *propre*. Example 1a below shows the result: the French construction *rendre propre*. The IL word *manĝigi* 'to make eat' is translated into *faire manger* (example 1b).

	IL	**FR**
1a	[pur'ig'i]	[rendre/VRB, [F-PRED, propre/ADJ]]
1b	[manĝ'ig'i]	[faire/VRB, [F-INF, manger/VRB/[f_mood,inf]]]

In these above-mentioned cases, the variables <X> and <Y> have other possible translations in the bilingual dictionary. The stem *pura*, for example, still has three alternative translations: *pur, net* and *nu*. Consequently, the results of the redundancy rule must be: *rendre propre*, *rendre pur*, *rendre net* and *rendre nu*. As mentioned earlier, a number of words can be translated both by a redundancy rule and an entry in the dictionary. This is also illustrated in the above-mentioned IL examples. For instance, *purigi* does have an alternative French translation in the dictionary, namely *nettoyer*.

A problem arises when the word translated by the redundancy rule has dependents. When a composite word is translated into a construction of several words in the target language, all possible dependents in the input structure must find a place in the output structure. The translation of the dependents concerned is not necessarily done in the same rule, but the metataxis writer must determine their appropriate place in the output tree. The following redundancy rule illustrates this phenomenon. It treats the transformation of the IL prefix *ek'* 'to begin to' into the French construction *commencer à*. A possibly occurring object dependent does not depend on the governor in the French tree, but on the infinitive verb <X>. To indicate that it concerns an optional dependent, parentheses are used in the rule.

```
IL                      FR
[ek'<X>'i,         ⇒    [commencer,
  ([OBJ, <Y>])]           [F-OBJ, à/PRP,
                            [F-PARG, <X>/VRB/[f_mood,inf],
                              ([F-OBJ, <Y>])]]]
```

Consequently, the IL structure *ekkompreni la problemon* 'to begin to understand the problem' is transformed by this redundancy rule into the French *commencer à comprendre le problème*, as is shown in the following scheme:

```
IL                      FR
[ek'kompren'i,          [commencer,
  [OBJ, problem'o'n,      [F-OBJ, à/PRP,
    [DET, la]]]             [F-PARG, comprendre/VRB/[f_mood,inf],
                              [F-OBJ, problème,
                                [F-ATR1, le]]]]]
```

3.3. Sentence level

In this section, the marked metataxis rules at the sentence level will be described. Every structural change influenced by restrictions on the input pattern is treated by marked rules at this level. These marked metataxis rules take into account the **syntactic sentence context** of a specific word or construction and, consequently, the input pattern is always larger than a single word (as we saw earlier for the marked rules on word level). The top node of the rule can be a word, a variable or a label. In principle, every change of the governor and its dependents is possible. The rules check the obligatory or optional presence or absence of specific elements in the input tree and in the output tree. These elements influence the transformation described, so the rule is only applied when the input tree corresponds to the input pattern and when the input tree satisfies all the conditions. Four types of rules are distinguished, in order of generality ranging from the more specific to the more general one:

(1) word-specific rules;
(2) subclass-specific rules;
(3) word class-specific rules;
(4) label-specific rules.

3.3.1. Word-specific rules

The word-specific rules are rules whose governor is a **word**. They translate a given word within a certain syntactic context. This specific syntactic context is expressed by words, labels, features and variables. Not only the governor, but also the dependent(s) can be modified by these rules. Word-specific rules are found in the bilingual IL-French dictionary (examples A and B) and in the form of lexical metataxis rules (example C).

Example A. Word-specific rule: dictionary / small context

The following entry from the bilingual dictionary gives a small syntactic context for the translation of the IL adverb *acide* 'acid' and the IL verb *gusti* 'to taste'. When *acide* has an [ADJU] dependency relation with the verb *gusti*, it is translated into an [F-ATR2] adjective *acide*, as part of the French construction *avoir un goût acide.*

```
IL                      FR
[gust'i,           ⇒    [avoir,
  [ADJU, acid'e]]         [F-OBJ, goût,
                            [F-ATR1, un],
                            [F-ATR2, acide/ADJ]]]
```

Example B. Word-specific rule: dictionary / large context

The syntactic context in the bilingual dictionary can be larger than the one mentioned in the previous example. The information present about the syntactic context of a word can enable the word-specific metataxis rule in the bilingual dictionary to choose a translation on syntactic grounds. Let's take the IL verb *kalkuli* 'to count' as an example. It can be translated into several French constructions: *imputer à, compter sur, mettre au nombre de, tenir compte de, calculer, compter, faire des calculs* and *dénombrer.* As is shown below, the dictionary entry of *kalkuli* contains two variables <X> and <Y>, whose dependency relation is clearly specified, respectively [OBJ] and [PARG]. The French verb *imputer* is chosen if both dependents are present in the input tree.

```
IL                      FR
[kalkul'i,         ⇒    [imputer,
  [OBJ, <X>],             [F-OBJ, <X>],
  [ADJU, al,              [F-APREP, à/PRP,
    [PARG, <Y>]]]           [F-PARG, <Y>]]]
```

The following conditions are imposed on the input structure:
(1) the presence of the verb *kalkuli* as a governor;
(2) the presence of an [OBJ] dependent of any word class type;
(3) the presence of a [ADJU] dependent with the word *al*;
(4) the presence of a [PARG] dependent of any word class type.

For instance, the example sentence *mi kalkulas viajn erarojn al via sensperteco* 'I attribute your mistakes to your inexperience' is translated as *j'impute vos erreurs à votre manque d'expérience.* Figure 4 shows the bracket representation of both sentences.

IL	**FR**
[kalkul'as,	[impute,
[SUBJ, mi],	[F-SUBJ, je],
[OBJ, erar'o'j'n,	[F-OBJ, erreurs,
[ATR1, via'j'n]],	[F-ATR1, vos]],
[ADJU, al,	[F-APREP, à,
[PARG, sen'spert'ec'o,	[F-PARG, manque,
[ATR1, via]]]]	[F-ATR1, votre],
	[F-ATR2, de,
	[F-PARG, expérience]]]]]

Fig. 4: Bracket IL and French dependency trees

Example C. Word-specific rule: lexical metataxis rule

In contrast with the above-mentioned rules, the following word-specific rule is not part of the bilingual dictionary. The governor certainly is a word (in this case: *esti* 'to be') similar to all the dictionary entries, but the rule has a remarkable condition. The translation is only correct in the case of a subjectless IL sentence. This condition can be considered as a negative condition to the rule: the absence of a subject dependent is required. Consequently, the rule is part of the metataxis rule system and is called a lexical metataxis rule. The negative condition is represented by a dependent preceded by an asterisk (in this case: *[SUBJ]). The French verb, however, requires a subject, and the metataxis rule accordingly introduces the pronoun *ce* 'it' as the new subject of the French construction.

IL		**FR**
[est'i,	⇒	[être,
[PRED, <X>'a],		[F-SUBJ, ce/PRN],
*[SUBJ]]		[F-PRED, <X>/ADJ]]

The following conditions are imposed on the input structure:
(1) the presence of *esti* as a governor;
(2) the presence of a [PRED] dependent with the final morpheme '*a*;
(3) the absence of a [SUBJ] dependent.

Example:
IL: Estas simpla. 'It is simple.'
FR: C'est simple.

3.3.2. Subclass-specific rules

The so-called subclass-specific rules transform a word which belongs to a **group of words**. The members of this group do not necessarily belong to the same word class, but they do have the same syntactic behavior. The rules are part of the lexical metataxis rules. The governor is a variable which represents the subclass for which the rule is valid. For instance, the following contrastive construction is often seen: an

IL verb which governs an object ([OBJ, <Y>]) is often translated as a French verb governing a specific preposition ([F-APREP, <Z>/PRP]):

```
IL                    FR
[<X>'i,          ⇒    [<X>,
  [OBJ, <Y>]]           [F-APREP, <Z>/PRP,
                          [F-PARG, <Y>]]]
```

The following conditions are imposed on the input pattern:
(1) presence of a VRB governor;
(2) presence of an [OBJ] dependent of any word class type.

The following conditions are imposed on the output structure:
(1) presence of a French verb which can govern a preposition;
(2) <Z> is the preposition generally used with this French verb <X>.

Figure 5 shows the dependency trees of the following example sentence:
IL: Li ĉeestas la kunvenon. 'He is present at the meeting.'
FR: Il assiste à la réunion.

```
IL                          FR
[ĉe'est'as,                 [assiste,
  [SUBJ, li],                 [F-SUBJ, il],
  [OBJ, kun'ven'o'n,          [F-APREP, à,
    [DET, la]]]                 [F-PARG, réunion,
                                  [F-ATR1, la]]]]
```

Fig. 5: Bracket IL and French dependency trees

It is very difficult to specify exactly in which cases the general rule must be used and which verbs it concerns. A solution would be to list all possible appropriate IL or French verbs for which the rule is valid and to mention them explicitly, but this is not always the most economic solution. The size of the subclass can vary enormously, ranging from a small number of possible words, as will be shown below in example A, to a larger number of applicable words, as will be shown in the examples B and C.

Example A. Subclass-specific rule: list

The next lexical metataxis rule makes use of a list which consists of three verbs *esti* 'to be', *stari* 'to stand' and *ekzisti* 'to exist'. They form the subclass for which the rule is only valid. The rule transforms these verbs when they occur in a construction without object or predicative dependent into the French impersonal verb construction *il y a*. So, the IL sentence *multaj lernantoj estas en la lernejo* 'there are a lot of students in the school' is translated as *il y a beaucoup d'élèves à l'école*. An alternative to this rule consists of three separate dictionary entries for the three different verbs. The metataxis writer must be aware of this additional possibility and choose whether to put the information in the dictionary or in the metataxis. A lexical metataxis rule can go beyond the information in a dictionary entry by indicating specific word class requirements for the dependents by putting them together in a list. As is shown below, the metataxis rule indicates a list of 4 possible word classes for the subject position (i.e. noun, pronoun, numeral and adverb). Consequently, in the case of the above-mentioned transformation, the preference is given to a metataxis rule instead of several dictionary entries, although the list of qualified verbs is very small.

```
IL                                        FR
[<X>'i,                              ⇒   [avoir/VRB,
 [SUBJ, <Y>/(SUBvPRNvNUMvADV)],            [F-SUBJ, il],
 *[PRED],                                  [F-ADVC, y],
 *[OBJ]]                                   [F-PSUBJ, <Y>]]
```

The following conditions are imposed on the input structure:
(1) presence of a VRB governor from the list *esti, stari* and *ekzisti*;
(2) presence of a [SUBJ] dependent of one of the following word classes: SUB, PRN, NUM or ADV;
(3) absence of a [PRED] dependent;
(4) absence of an [OBJ] dependent.

Example B. Subclass-specific rule: large subclass

A subclass of words which may be needed for a certain rule is often larger than in the above-mentioned metataxis rule. The next rule, for instance, is valid for a larger subclass, namely the subclass of IL adverbs ending in '*e* which carry the verb ending '*ant* and which govern an [ADJU] dependent with the word *ne* 'not'. No explicit list is needed in this case, because the subclass is explicitly defined by the suffix '*ant*. The adverbs are changed into a French prepositional construction with *sans* 'without' governing the infinitive form ([f_mood,inf]) of the variable <X>. For instance, *ne parolante* 'without talking' is translated as *sans parler* by the following rule:

```
IL                 FR
[<X>'ant'e,   ⇒   [sans/PRP,
 [ADJU, ne]]        [F-PARG, <X>/VRB/[f_mood,inf]]]
```

The following conditions are imposed on the input tree:
(1) presence of an ADV governor with '*ant* morpheme;
(2) presence of the [ADJU] dependent with the word *ne*.

Example C. Subclass-specific rule: large subclass

As a final example of a subclass-specific rule, consider a metataxis rule valid for a larger subclass than the previous rule. In fact, it is valid for the entire word class of the verbs, but the verbs have to satisfy a particular condition: they must be constructed with the past tense inflectional morpheme '*is* and they must govern the adverb *ĵus* 'just'. In this case, they can be translated into a particular French tense form with the verb construction *venir de*, which expresses the recent past tense. The main French verb *venir* receives the following syntactic features: the present value (pr) of the tense feature ([f_tns]) and the indicative value (ind) of the mood feature ([f_mood]). The dependent of the preposition *de* is a translation of the IL stem and has the infinitive form. Text grammar must of course have the opportunity to change these tense and mood features whenever necessary under the influence of a larger context. The subclass-specific metataxis rule needed is accordingly as follows:

IL		FR
[<X>'is,	⇒	[venir/VRB/[f_mood,ind, f_tns,pr],
[ADJU, ĵus]]		[F-APREP, de/PRP,
		[F-PARG, <X>/VRB/[f_mood,inf]]]]

The following conditions are imposed on the input tree:
(1) presence of a VRB governor with '*is* morpheme;
(2) presence of the [ADJU] dependent *ĵus*.

Example:
IL: Li ĵus eliris. 'He just left.'
FR: Il vient de sortir.

3.3.3. Word class-specific rules

A number of transformations can be observed for an entire **word class**. The governor of these word class-specific rules is a variable which represents the word class which has to be present in the input tree for the rule to be applicable. This variable can indicate a combination of different word classes as well, as long as they have the same syntactic behavior in the sentence. The word class-specific rules are part of the lexical metataxis rules. The syntactic sentence context in terms of dependents can vary enormously. Rules A and B below treat the word class of the nouns with one specific dependent, namely *tia* 'such' and *multa* 'many' respectively, whereas rule C illustrates the case of a more general dependent for a noun and a verb.

Rule A. Word class-specific rule: one dependent

The following metataxis rule is valid for the entire word class of nouns, as is shown by the variable governor <X> with noun ending '*o*. One IL dependent is explicitly given in the rule: *tia*. This IL word can not be treated in the IL-French dictionary, because the noun which governs *tia* in the input tree receives a new dependent during the translation into French, namely a determiner in basic form *un*. The IL *tia donaco* 'such a present' is translated as *un tel cadeau* by the following metataxis rule:

IL		FR
[<X>'o,	⇒	[<X>,
[ATR1, tia]]		[F-ATR1, un/DET],
		[F-ATR1, tel/ADJ]]

The following conditions in the input tree:
(1) presence of a SUB governor;
(2) presence of the [ATR1] dependent with the word *tia*.

Rule B. Word class-specific rule: inversion

A number of IL adjectives can be translated into French adverbs which can govern a prepositional complement with the preposition *de*. This preposition governs the noun which in the IL is the governor of the adjective. For example, *multaj homoj* 'a lot of people' will be translated as *beaucoup de gens*. The word *homoj* governs *multaj*, but in French the dependency relation is inverted: *beaucoup* governs *de*, which in turn governs *gens*. This inversion is dealt with by the following word class-specific rule for nouns:

```
IL                          FR
[<X>'o,               ⇒     [beaucoup/ADV,
  [ATR1, mult'a]]             [F-APREP, de/PRP,
                                [F-PARG, <X>]]]
```

Conditions in the input tree:
(1) presence of a SUB governor;
(2) presence of the [ATR1] dependent *multa*.

Rule C. Word class-specific rule: two variables

The above-mentioned word class-specific rules contain a fixed dependent, such as *tia* or *multa*, with a well defined dependency relation. The following metataxis rule introduces not only a variable for the governor, but also one for the dependent, which consequently can be of any word class (<Y>). But the IL dependency syntax only allows for an infinitive complement ([INFC]) which is directly dependent on the governing noun. The dependency label of the second variable remains well defined: [INFC, <Y>]. The rule transforms an IL infinitive complement depending on a noun into a French prepositional complement with the preposition *de*, for example *la neceso investi* 'the need for investment' is translated as *la necessité d'investir*.

```
IL                          FR
[<X>'o,               ⇒     [<X>,
  [INFC, <Y>]]                [F-APREP, de/PRP,
                                [F-PARG, <Y>]]]
```

Conditions in the input tree:
(1) presence of a SUB governor;
(2) presence of an [INFC] dependent of any word class type.

3.3.4. Label-specific rules

The unmarked general label rules transform labeled trees without any kind of restriction (cf. 2.3.). Marked label rules, on the other hand, translate labeled trees under specific conditions. The described transformation is only possible when the governor fulfills a specific dependency relation in the text: the transformation is label-specific. Consequently, this determining dependency relation must be part of the rule. The governor of the marked rules is not a labelless word or word class, but it has a clearly defined label (or can even have a combination of several labels). The examples A and B give different types of label-specific rules. They are called structural metataxis rules.

Example A. Label-specific rule: relative clause

One of the alternative translations for an IL adjective with the verb ending *'ant* is a relative clause ([F-ATR2]) in French. The main verb of the relative clause is the translation of the IL stem into a verb in the present tense and the subject of the relative clause is the pronoun *qui*. The IL adjective *ridanta* from the sentence *la* *ridanta viro* 'the laughing man', thus, can be translated as *l'homme qui rit* 'the man who laughs'. This translation, however, is restricted to IL adjectives which fulfill an [ATR1] dependency relation. In the case of a predicative adjective ([PRED]), such as in *la viro estas ridanta*, the French relative clause translation is incorrect: **l'homme est qui rit*. The following metataxis rule requires a tree with the label [ATR1] as part of the input pattern to deal with the above mentioned difference.

IL		**FR**
[ATR1, <X>'ant'a]	⇒	[F-ATR2, <X>/VRB/[f_mood,ind,f_tns,pr], [F-SUBJ, qui/PRN]]

Conditions in the input tree:
(1) presence of an [ATR1] dependency relation;
(2) presence of an ADJ with '*ant* morpheme.

Example B. Label-specific rule: coordination

In the IL coordinate structures with one determiner such as *la domoj kaj arboj* 'the houses and the trees', the determiner depends on the coordinator *kaj* to indicate that it relates to both IL nouns *domoj* and *arboj*. This construction is translated into French by a coordinate structure with two determiners depending each on the nouns which the coordinating conjunction *et* governs: *les maisons et les arbres*. The corresponding IL and French dependency trees are shown in figure 6, followed by figure 7 with the bracket representation to illustrate the representation of coordination in dependency grammar. The label suffix "-C" is used to indicate the coordinated dependents. In this example, the coordinating conjunction *kaj* has a subject dependency relation.

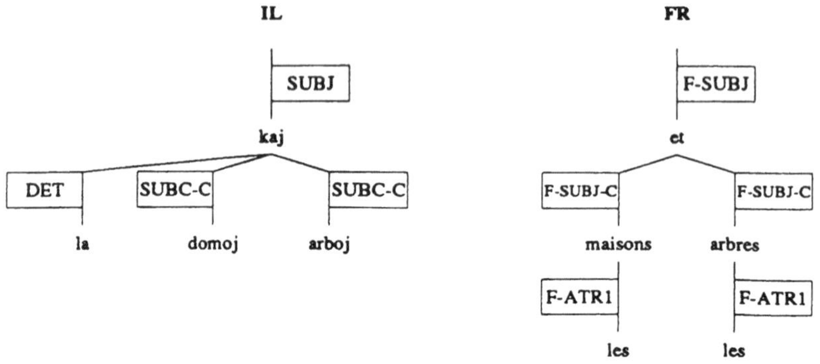

Fig. 6: IL and French dependency trees

```
IL                          FR
[SUBJ, kaj,                 [F-SUBJ, et,
  [DET, la],                  [F-SUBJ-C, maisons,
  [SUBJ-C, dom'o'j],            [F-ATR1, les]],
  [SUBJ-C, arb'o'j]]          [F-SUBJ-C, arbres,
                                [F-ATR1, les]]]
```

Fig. 7: Bracket IL and French dependency trees

Some French constructions do not require this determiner repetition, but they are very specific and both nouns are considered to be very closely related. The following structural metataxis rule takes care of the doubling phenomenon. It does start with a label, like the previous structural metataxis rule, but the identity of this label is now uncertain and a variable is used (<LAB>). The label of the depending nouns, in the input pattern (<A>'o and <B>'o), however, are clear in some respect, i.e. they must be similar to the label of the coordinator (<LAB-C>). The determiner <Y> has been doubled in the output of the rule.

```
IL                               ⇒    FR
[<LAB>, <X>/CON,                      [<F-LAB>, <X>/CON,
  [DET, <Y>],                           [<F-LAB-C>, <A>,
  [<LAB-C>, <A>'o,                        [F-ATR1, <Y>]],
    *[ATR1, (DETvNUM)],                 [<F-LAB-C>, <B>,
    *[DET, (DETvNUM)]],                   [F-ATR1, <Y>]]]
  [<LAB-C>, <B>'o,
    *[ATR1, (DETvNUM)],
    *[DET, (DETvNUM)]]]
```

Conditions in the input tree:
(1) presence of a CON governor with a certain label <LAB>;
(2) presence of a [DET] dependent;
(3) presence of two SUBs with coordinated <LAB> label;
(4) both SUBs do not have [ATR1] dependent of the word class DET or NUM.
(5) both SUBs do not have [DET] dependent of the word class DET or NUM.

4. Summary

To represent syntactic knowledge about the syntactic relationships between two languages, the metataxis writer has a number of possible rules at his or her disposal. Several types of rules have been discussed in this paper. The rules transform an input pattern in a given source language into a pattern in a given target language. In the DLT system, the rules can be part of both the bilingual dictionary and the metataxis rule system. As we have seen, the metataxis rules can be divided into the unmarked rules and the marked rules. The former type can be applied quite generally, but the latter has a number of restrictions on its application. The metataxis writer must clearly define whatever restrictions are found.

The examples given are from the IL-French metataxis rule system which has been written for the first target language of the DLT system and its intermediate language. The form of the metataxis rules discussed has a more general scope. It can be applied to the contrastive syntax between other languages as well and, thus, serves as a framework for the development of subsequent metataxis rule systems.

References

Grevisse, Maurice (1986): *Le bon usage. Grammaire française.*
Paris-Gembloux: Duculot

Maxwell, Dan (1987): Metataxis English-IL.
Unpublished report. Utrecht: BSO/Research

Kalocsay, Kálmán / Gaston Waringhien (1980): *Plena analiza gramatiko de Esperanto.*
Rotterdam: Universala Esperanto-Asocio, 4th ed.

Schubert, Klaus (1986a): *Syntactic tree structures in DLT.*
Utrecht: BSO/Research

Schubert, Klaus (1986b): Kiel verki regularon pri metatakso inter etna lingvo kaj la IL.
Unpublished report. Utrecht: BSO/Research

Schubert, Klaus (1987a): Reviziita difino de la diferencoj inter la IL de DLT kaj Esperanto.
Unpublished report. Utrecht: BSO/Research

Schubert, Klaus (1987b): *Metataxis. Contrastive dependency syntax for machine translation.*
Dordrecht/Providence: Foris

Tamis, Dorine (1987a): Syntaxe dépendantielle du français pour DLT.
Unpublished report. Utrecht: BSO/Research

Tamis, Dorine (1987b): La métataxe IL-français.
Unpublished report. Utrecht: BSO/Research

Tamis, Dorine (1988): The treatment of form determination for French in DLT.
In: *Interface, Tijdschrift voor Toegepaste Linguïstiek // Journal of Applied Linguistics* 3, pp. 45-56

Tesnière, Lucien (1959): *Éléments de syntaxe structurale.*
Paris: Klincksieck, 2nd ed, 4th print. 1982

English-Esperanto metataxis

Dan Maxwell

Utrecht, Netherlands

1. Introduction

This article surveys and discusses some of the more important and interesting metataxis rules devised for the DLT-module with English as a source language. Presentation and discussion of all rules created so far is given in Maxwell (1987). Many of these have been implemented in the DLT prototype, which translates **Simplified English** (SE), as defined in van der Korst (1987), to DLT's slightly modified Esperanto. Rules included in SE and dealt with in this article are marked as *SE* in the text.

This article also discusses the ideas underlying the notation in the rules and how the rules interact with each other in sentences in which a choice must be made among more than one of them. Tree diagrams will be given, but a general familiarity with dependency syntax is assumed, since it is the basis for all the articles in this book. The alternative representation of rules by means of labelled bracketing is not given here, although it is used exclusively in the complete version cited above. The reason for this divergence is that trees are the more familiar kind of representation for most linguists, but labelled bracketing is more helpful for someone who has to transform the rules into computer code.

A few comments about the representation of English syntax in the rules given are desirable at the beginning, since there is no other article in this volume which deals specifically with English dependency syntax. These rules generally present portions of English trees in the form that is provided by the parser for English used in DLT. There is precisely one dictionary form for each word, but the entry associated with this form provides the other forms and information about them. Information in the tree, specifically the label on the branch above the word and, if necessary, features written together with the word provide additional information which makes it possible to determine which form of the word has actually been used in the sentence. Since there are relatively few inflectional forms in English, the more radical solution to this problem taken for Hungarian and Japanese (See the articles in this volume by Prószéky/Koutny/Wacha and Sato, respectively) of associating a morpheme rather than a word with each node of the tree is not necessary. On the other hand, the approach used in the Esperanto syntax of writing morphemes directly in both rules and trees is unfeasible, since the several inflectional English morphemes have a variety of generally unrelated graphemic shapes and are in fact not analyzable as a segment of the whole word, e.g. *write, wrote*, but *run, ran*, or *go, went*. It is left to the parser to transform these graphemic differences into the appropriate more general feature such as **pst** (past), **prf** (perfect), etc.

Although specific trees make use of specific words, syntactic rules need to be more general. A given syntactic rule can transform a feature, word, or label, some combination of these diverse parts of a syntactic tree, or several related features, words, or labels within a given tree. More general rules will of course be applicable to more than one specific tree structure. This generality is achieved by making reference to syntactic categories in the rules. These categories can be viewed in mathematical terms as variables which range over a set of words. Precisely which words are in the range of a given variable is determined by restrictions in the rule, such as the variable's syntactic category, and a list of associated words. The omission of such a list for any given category means that there is no restriction for the given variable. The rule is applicable for any word of that category in the language.

Metataxis rules for a given language pair make reference to the categories used in the dependency syntaxes of the two languages concerned, in this case English and Esperanto. Sometimes it is necessary to refer to some subset of the words in a given category. This subset may in some cases coincide with the subcategorization provided by the authors of the dependency syntaxes concerned, but this will not always be the case, since the decisions made in constructing these dependency grammars must be based on language-internal considerations rather than correlations with another language, and quite often the author(s) of one dependency syntax has (have) little or no knowledge of the other language concerned. If the subset does not so coincide, a list of the words concerned must be provided and in some way be associated with the appropriate part of the rule. The first example of a rule of this sort is found in section 4.

There are of course other ways in which any two languages do not precisely correlate with each other. The set of syntactic categories will probably vary at least slightly, and even when the two languages both have a particular category, the usage of members of this category in one language will probably not coincide precisely with the usage of the members of the other. Whenever coincidence of this sort is lacking, it is necessary to translate from one language to the other by what in DLT is referred to as a "marked" metataxis rule, that is, a rule which performs some structural change other than that of preparing that part of the tree for lexical transfer. An "unmarked" rule simply removes the language label when going from any source language to the intermediate language or adds the appropriate language label when going from the intermediate language to any target language. This amounts schematically to the following operation:

$$\text{L-LABEL} \rightarrow \text{LABEL}$$

or

$$\text{LABEL} \rightarrow \text{L-LABEL}$$

where L and LABEL are variables referring respectively to the language and dependency label concerned.

A rule which translates a prepositional phrase as a case-marked noun, or perhaps as a noun without any overt indication of its relationship to the rest of the sentence, is one example of a marked rule.

Most of the rules in the English-Esperanto metataxis are marked rules. There are also unmarked rules, of course, to cover the cases in which word-for-word translation is possible. The unmarked rules are less numerous than the marked rules, but it is probably true that any one of them will be applied more frequently than any one marked rule, since cases of literal translation between English and Esperanto are fairly common. In this article, however, I will be exclusively concerned with marked rules.

In addition to the distinction between marked and unmarked rules, DLT makes a distinction between rules which actually translate from one language to another and rules which are linked to the translation process, but do not themselves change the language of the tree. There are two groups of the latter: one group prepares the source language tree for translation by adjusting certain structures for which it would be difficult to write a direct transformation rule (pre-processing rule); the other type takes the output of the transformation rules and carries out various small but essential changes in the new tree, which are dependent on other properties of the language in this tree for the way in which they are realized (post-processing rule). I deal with specific examples of these two latter rule-types in sections 7 and 5, respectively.

The input to a given translation rule can deal with a specific node or several linked nodes in a tree. The output can have the same variation and is in principle not dependent on the form of its input. The range of a given node is similarly flexible: it may be a single word, a group of words in a specific syntactic category or all words of that category.

2. A complex word level metataxis rule: Zamenhof's tabelo

One of the most striking series of regularities in Esperanto involves a set of precisely 54 words, including pronouns and adverbs which in other languages are sometimes a single word, sometimes a phrase. The interrelationships between these words are considerably more transparent than the relationships between the corresponding words and phrases in other languages, since in the latter various irregularities and formation methods become intertwined in unpredictable ways. This will become evident in the following discussion of the metataxis rules for this set of words, which taken together are known to Esperantists as Zamenhof's "tabelo" (table).

The table in the form used by DLT consists of 6 rows and 9 columns of words. One of the rows consists of question words beginning with *k-*, one of demonstrative words beginning with *t-*, one of indefinites beginning with *Ø*, one of universal quantifiers beginning with *ĉ-*, and one of negators beginning with *nen-*. To these five traditionally accepted rows, DLT has added a sixth row *ali-* meaning 'other' (See Schubert's article in this volume on Esperanto syntax for a discussion of this). The columns are equally systematic, each one having a specific ending with a specific meaning. They are as follows: *-u* (determiner), *-o* (pronoun), *-a* (quality), *-al* (reason), *-am* (time), *-e* (place), *-el* (manner), *-es* (possessor), *-om* (amount)[1]. *-i-* is the core of all fifty-four words.

		-u
ki-		-o
t-		-a
-		-am
	-i-	
ĉ-		-e
nen-		-el
ali-		-es
		-om

In English, many of the notions expressed by the words in the table can be translated as a single word (*why* = *kial, this* = *tio*), but some require several words (*so much* = *tiom*, (*for every reason* = *ĉial*). If there is a preposition in the English, as in the last example, it has no corresponding morpheme in the Esperanto translation.

One of the metataxis rules for generating this table translates various combinations of preposition + determiner + noun. In essence, the determiner is translated by the first part of the word (constant in a given row) and the noun by the last part (constant in a given column).

Phrasal translation to the "tabelo", SE

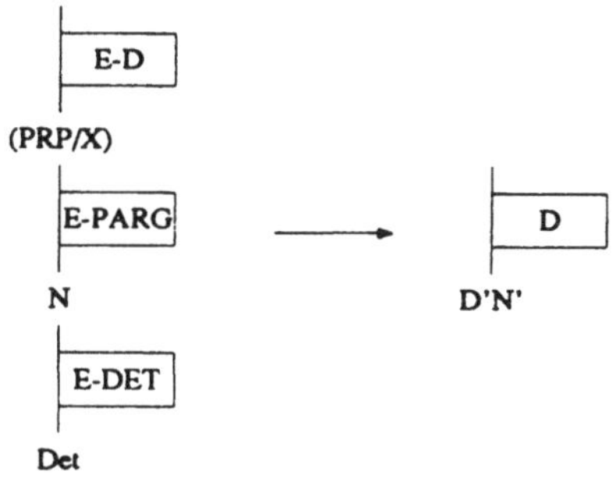

P = {for/in/Ø/at/at; in}
N = {reason/way; manner/amount; quantity/time/place}
Det = {what; which/this; that/some; any/each; every; all/other/no}
D′ = {ki -do/ti/i/ĉi/ali/neni}
N′ = {al/el/om/am/e}

This rule is actually an abbreviated way of writing a large number of simpler rules. It links no less than 5 lists of meaning-units[2], three with English and two with Esperanto. The first of these groups appears in the input and the other in the output. The list with input N is translated by the list with input N′; the list with input Det is translated by the list with input D′; the list with input P is not translated. Positions within each list are separated by a slash (/). When a member of an output list corresponds with a member of an input list, the former will also translate the latter. In some cases, there is more than one member in a given position; the choice between these seems to be absolutely free, and they are accordingly linked by the semi-colon (;), used as a logical disjunctor in the computer language Prolog. Disjunction is of course exclusive in this case.

This rule will accordingly translate certain adverbials and prepositional phrases from English into a single Esperanto word. In some of these cases, there is a single English word with the same meaning. For example, *kial* is produced by the above rule as the translation of *for what (which) reason*, but must also be allowed to translate the word *why*. This can be taken care of by having a dictionary entry *why = ial*.

This sort of situation, in which a word or expression in one language has more than one possibility in the other language also occurs in the opposite direction. The expression *of this sort* can be translated either by the tabelo-word *tia* or by the expression *de tiu speco*. The former translation will be generated by a rule similar to the one above, but some parts of it will be marked as **parallel**, meaning that the system should produce a copy of this portion of the tree, to be translated by different rules. In this case, simple word-for-word translation suffices to produce the second possiblity.

3. A pre-processing rule: Valency and auxiliaries

Any verb of a language has a particular valency, but it is not easy to find a method of consistently representing this valency in the trees of dependency syntax which does not cause other problems. In DLT, the choice has been made to let the subject in English and other European languages be governed by the finite verb, whether this is the main verb or an auxiliary. This obviously has the advantage of making rules concerning subject-verb agreement easier to state, since in these languages it is always the finite verb which agrees with the subject. Linearization rules are also presumably easier to deal with by virtue of this decision, since it is always the finite verb rather than any other which follows the subject in declarative sentences or precedes it in questions. But this does cause a problem with respect to rules which mention both the subject and the lexical verb in the input, since it means that the hierarchichal relationship between them varies according to the combination of auxiliaries present in the clause, if any. It would appear to be unsatisfactory to have to restate each such rule for each different configuration of this sort.

The solution to this problem within the metataxis, derived from the corresponding programming solution created by Job van Zuijlen, is to have an iterative preparatory English-to-English rule which transforms each auxiliary node and label combination into a feature associated with the main verb. Thanks to this preparation, it is necessary to state each of the above problematic rules precisely once. Here is the preparatory rule:

Aux = feature, SE

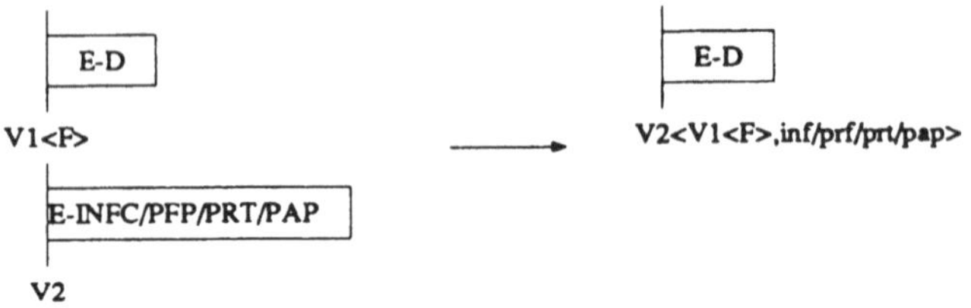

Restated verbally, this says:

> Rewrite V1, along with all of its features F and the label under it (if it is one of the four given) as the corresponding feature of V2.

The formulation of this rule ensures that it can apply several times within the same clause, depending on how many auxiliary verbs are present.

This rule provides new input for certain rules in the next section.

4. Complicated transformation ruiles: Relative clauses, questions, and related

The sentences in [1a-c] do not fall under the same traditional heading, but have a property in common which has caused them to be treated in essentially the same way in recent constituency structure literature.

[1a] *Which student* did you say that the teacher thought _would succeed?
[1b] The professor asked *which student* you said the teacher thought _ would succeed?
[1c] The student *that* you said the teacher thought _ would succeed has dropped out.
[1d] *That student* you said the teacher thought _ would succeed.

The relationship between the word or phrase in italics and the subsequent dash comes about as a result of a direct question in [1a]; an indirect question in [1b]; a relative clause in [1c]; and topicalization in [1d]. All four sentences have in common that the word or phrase in italics is in some sense the missing subject. The only limits in the distance between such a noun and its "understood position" (also known as its "deep structure position" in some kinds of syntactic description), are those imposed by the short-term memory of the speaker and perhaps the hearer (insofar as the speaker takes these into consideration).

Since trees of dependency syntax, as used in DLT, do not directly indicate the order of words, the representations of the above sentences are quite straightforward, at least as treated in DLT. *Which student*, *that*, and *that student* will all be dependents of the finite verb in the clauses in which they are the understood subject.

The translation of these sentences into Esperanto will also be straightforward, since Esperanto has long-distance dependencies which have the same essential characteristics. There would be a difficult problem, if it were necessary to mention the antecedent of the relative pronoun in sentences like [1c] or the governing verb of the entire clause, since there is no theoretical limit on the number of clauses that can occur between the relative pronoun and its antecedent. Since this is not necessary, the differences between English and Esperanto in these structures can be dealt with in a series of fairly simple rules. In other words, the property of unboundedness is for the purposes of DLT mainly a property of word order to be dealt with by linearization rules.

One of the differences deals with the case in which the English relative clause lacks any relative pronoun at all. Since Esperanto cannot omit the relative pronoun in this way, it is necessary to have a rule which inserts such a pronoun:

Relative pronoun insertion

The asterisk in this rule refers to an explicit empty node which appears at the end of certain branches in the English tree. This is then filled by the Esperanto relative pronoun. It is of course conceivable that the parser will not create an explicit empty category, since the job of indicating to the parser where to put this category is not trivial, but in that case the task of indicating where the relative pronoun should be inserted is more difficult. It is also possible that our trees will need to deal with empty categories which do not involve relative clauses and which accordingly should not be filled in this way. In order to deal with such a situation, it appears that a distinction between different kinds of empty categories is sufficient.

Decision questions in Esperanto differ from those in English by being introduced by the word *ĉu*. The metataxis must specify the structures in which this word is to be introduced. But the precise details of what must be specified depend in turn on what is available from the parser. Since questions are not found in the type of texts that the DLT-prototype translates, it is not yet clear what kind of structure the English parser will provide. In particular, it is not clear whether the governing label for the entire sentence will itself make a distinction between information questions and decision questions.

The following rule uses the label QD to mean "decision question".

Decision questions 1

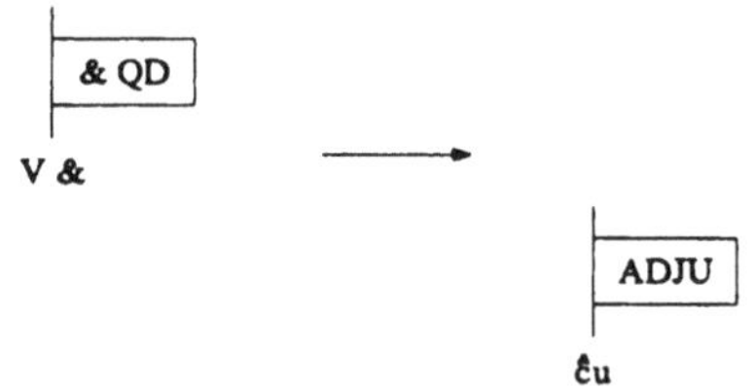

This notation is to be interpreted that the branch on the right side of the rule must be inserted as a dependent of the node on the left side.

If the decision is made not to distinguish between a decision question and information question in the parser, then the metataxis rule must be made more complicated by including a "negative condition". This stipulates that the rule applies only if there is no information question word in the same clause. This word does not involve a case of an unbounded gap, since the question word must be in the same clause as the question label. If it is not, but is rather further down in the tree, then it must indicate an indirect question in the clause concerned. Here is this version of the rule:

Decision questions 2

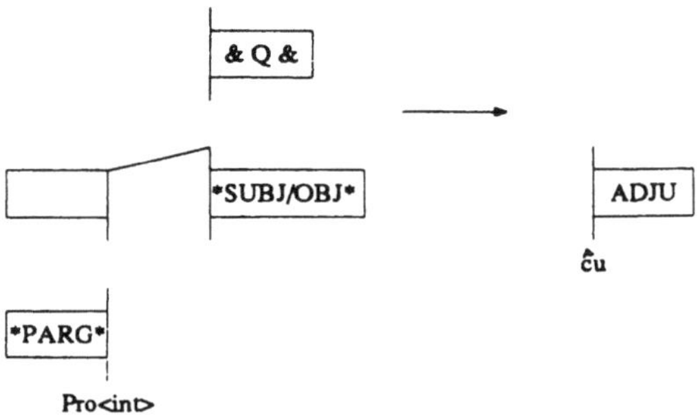

Pro<int> = how, what, why, who, when, where, when,

Q is a dependency label for both types of questions, created by the parser presumably on the basis of a question mark at the end of the sentence. The asterisks * are used to surround negative conditions. The three labels subsumed in this rule are not necessarily at a given fixed distance in the tree from the top node, since the clause concerned may or may not have auxiliaries and only the first two of these labels can be directly governed by the verb.

5. Post-processing rules: Case and agreement

The pre-processing rule in section 3 provides preparation for later rules which actually perform the translation. In this section we will examine several rules which operate on the **output** of the translation to carry out several small but essential changes, which are necessary to make the sentence acceptable input for the target language metataxis.

Case and agreement are widespread linguistic phenomena, but the details vary considerably from one language to the next. Even within European languages, in which there is widespread unanimity about which morphemes are casemarkers and which are something else such as adpositions, there is considerable variation as to which cases are used and as to which parts of speech and which syntactic functions are marked by which case. The situation in English and Esperanto is summarized in the following table:

	English		**Esperanto**	
categories	Pro<pers>+who			
cases	nominative	accusative	nominative	accusative
functions	SUBJ	OBJ PARG	SUBJ PARG (lo-cation)	OBJ PARG (di-rection)

It is easy to see that mapping the cases of one language onto those of the other would be no easy matter. But if we formulate casemarking rules in such a way that they apply only to the output of translation rules, the task becomes much easier. All the information is available in the Esperanto tree to make a determination of cases straightforward. Here is the case rule for direct objects:

Object case assignment, SE

The one other rule which I give for case-marking is a little bit more difficult to formulate, since it involves referring to several subcategories

Adverbial case assignment, p, SE

V = {ir'i, met'i...}
Adv = {ie, tie, kie...}

It is notable that neither of these rules change anything in the existing structure. They merely add the accusative suffix *'n*. The second rule is marked as parallel (p), since it seems to be possible to use any verb + adverb combination in a locative rather than directional sense.

The situation for agreement phenomena is similar in that all the information needed to determine agreement is available in the Esperanto tree. Attributive adjectives and determiners agree with their governing nouns in both number and case.

Attributive agreement, SE

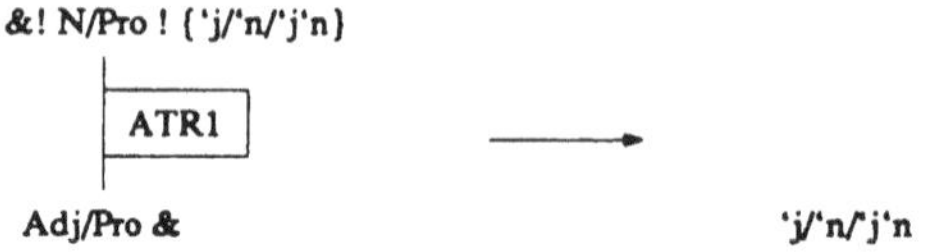

Many words which can have a determining function can also be used independently of any substantive. They are considered to be pronouns in DLT's Esperanto. This rule simply writes whatever combination of *'j* (plural) and *'n* (accusative) is found in the governing noun to the dependent attributive adjective or determining pronoun. This rule also covers participles which function attributively, since these are treated as adjectives in DLT. If a given noun has several such dependents, the rule will apply several times. The two double slashes (//) correlate with each other, but not with the items separated by single slashes.

Agreement rules become more tricky in coordinate structures. The conjunction of two or more things inevitably results in a plural concept, even if the individual items in question are all singular. This has as a consequence that whatever agrees with the entire construction will be plural, as [1] exemplifies:

[1a] interes'a'j libr'o kaj gazet'o
interesting book and newspaper
[1b] interes'a'j libr'o'j kaj gazet'o
[1c] interes'a'j libr'o'j kaj gazet'o'j

The examples with determiners in [2b] seem a bit odder but are considered acceptable.

[2a] iu'j amik'o kaj kon'at'o
some friend and acquaintance
[2b] iu'j amik'o'j kaj kon'at'o
[2c] iu'j amik'o'j kaj kon'at'o'j

The modifiers in the above sentences take scope over all coordinates of a coordinate structure. In DLT's dependency grammars for both English and Esperanto, such structures are treated as sisters of these coordinates.

This relationship is assumed in the following rule, which simply adds the plural morph *'j* to the dependent modifier in all these structures.

Coordinate agreement with adjectives and determiners

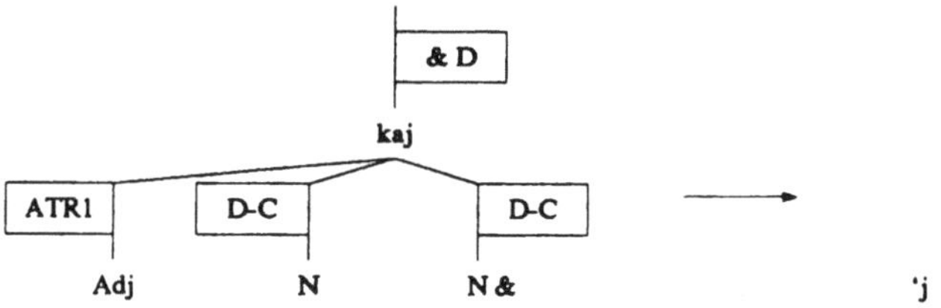

6. Noun chains

In English it is possible, especially in specialized texts, to have a series of two or more nouns which are linked together as a single unit. Examples of normal size are *stall warning system* and *flight compartment circulation*. A more extreme case is *entry age normal level dollar actuarial dollar cost method*, although this example does apparently have two adjectives thrown in.

The first and biggest problem of a translation procedure for such constructions is to determine the proper syntactic relationship between the individual parts of the construction. But this problem does not concern metataxis and will accordingly not be dealt with here. Instead, I shall describe the translation process for a given tree structure of this sort. It is furthermore necessary to keep in mind that this process applies only for noun chains which are not translated as a whole in the bilingual dictionary. The two word chain *wood alcohol*, for example, will be translated as *metanol'o* rather than as a combination of the translation of *wood* and the translation of *alcohol*. The hierarchy described briefly in the introductory section of this article ensures that specific dictionary entries will always take precedence over constructions created by metataxis rules like those described in this article.

This process deals recursively with a pair of such nouns at a time. The only further requirement is that they be in a governor-dependent relationship according to the tree structure created by the parser. There are three ways to translate such a pair into Esperanto:

(i) W2 can be made part of a compound with the governing noun W1 as the final part: W2'(*o'*)W1.

(ii) W2 can be translated as an adjective: W2*'a* W1

(iii) W2 can be translated as a noun which is the object of a preposition which in turn depends on W1: W1 Prp W2.

It is not always possible to choose freely between these three possibilities. Various factors conspire to eliminate some possibilities and to make some of the remaining possibilities preferable to others. For example:

(a) Any word which itself becomes part of its governor (solution (i)) cannot itself have an adjectival or prepositional dependent.

(b) If solution (ii) is chosen for a given word W, then any specifying preposition with this adjective must be directly prefixed to it.

It seems that solution (iii) is possible under all circumstances. It is also the most explicit concerning the nature of the relationship between the two nouns and for this reason is probably the most useful for the purpose of target-language directed metataxis. But making the intermediate translation this explicit may not be easy, given the indefinite nature of the source language construction. More specificly, solution (iii) requires picking the appropriate preposition, even though no preposition is available in the source language, deciding whether to add the definite article as a dependent of W2, and deciding whether or not to pluralize W2. All of these features are excluded in the source language by the nature of the English construction.

7. Valency changes

In this section I will be concerned with constructions in which the valency of the English verb is slightly different from that of the Esperanto verb which translates it. It is necessary to have metataxis rules to deal with these cases. I will further show that this causes a problem for certain passive constructions and suggest that the best solution for this is to modify the input structure before it is translated.

A fairly simple case of valency difference is found with so-called bitransitive verbs like *give, buy,* .... This is demonstrated in [1-2]:

[1a] They gave the money to the teacher.
[1b] They gave the teacher the money.

[2a] Ili don'is la mon'o'n al la instru'ist'o.
[2b] *Ili don'is la instru'ist'o la mon'o'n.

The point of these sentences is that the possibility of two objects, neither of which is governed by a preposition, exists in English, but not in Esperanto.

Furthermore, bitransitive sentences in English can be split into two groups, those which require *to* and those which require *for* as the prepositional governor of the second object. In such sentences *por* is required in Esperanto. This is demonstrated in [3-4]:

[3a] They bought the flowers for the secretary.
[3b] They bought the secretary the flowers.

[4a] Ili aĉet'is la flor'o'j'n por la sekretari'o.
[4b] *Ili aĉet'is la sekretario la flor'o'j'n.

In order to deal with the structure in sentences like [1b] and [3b], the following metataxis rule is necessary:

Prepositional objects with bitransitives

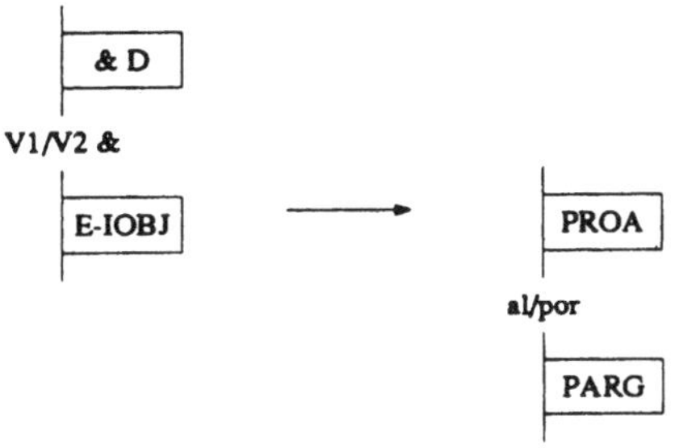

V1 = don'i, dir'i ...
V2 = aĉet'i, plan'i ...

A structurally somewhat more complicated case of valency difference is found in sentences involving accusative with infinitive (aci). This structure is found in both English and Esperanto, but not for precisely the same group of verbs. The complements of a subclass of the aci verbs in English must be translated by a dependent clause in Esperanto:

[5] I expected **them to come to the party.**
Mi atend'is, **ke ili ven'os** al la fest'o.
I expect-PAST that they come-FUT to the party
'I expect that they will come to the party.'

The Esperanto verbs which differ in this way can be further subclassified according to whether they themselves require the subordinate verb to be in the future tense, as in [6], the generic tense [7], or the volitive mood [8].

Mi kred'as, ke ili feliĉ'as.
I believe-PRES that they be-happy-PRES
'I believe that they are happy.'
[8] Mi pet'is, ke ili help'u.
'I request-PST that they help-VOL.'

The following rule deals with these constructions. The "+" means that any dependents of the category concerned must continue to depend on this category in the new tree, in which the category itself has a different function and perhaps a new governor. **S** is itself a metavariable standing for **Noun, Pronoun,** or **Numeral.**

Aci becomes a clause

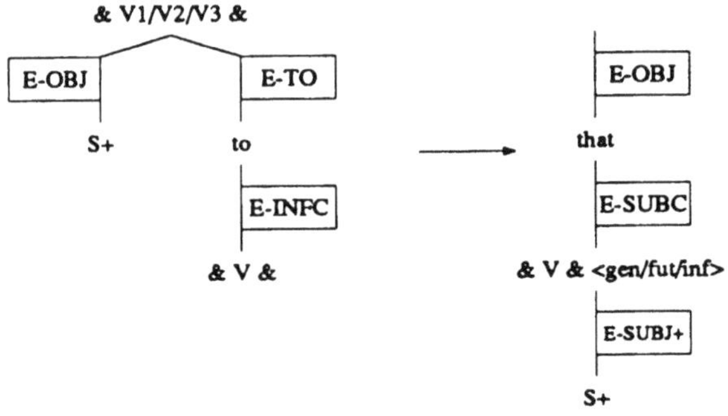

Now note that the English sentences in [1b], [3b], and [5] can be passivized as [9a], [9b], and [9c], respectively:

[9a] Mary was given the money (by the professor).
[9b] Mary was bought some flowers (by the professor).
[9c] They were expected to come (by the professor).

But the direct translations of these sentences into Esperanto, as shown in [10a-c], are ungrammatical.

[10a] *Maria don'at'is la mon'o'n (far la profesor'o).
[10b] *Maria aĉet'at'is flor'o'j'n (far la profesor'o).
[10c] *Ili atend'at'is ven'i (far la profesor'o).

These sentences suggest that Esperanto has less flexibility in grammatical relations than English, although this is of course more than compensated by greater freedom in word order.

In order to deal with the structures in [9], it is necessary to introduce a rule which transforms the passive voice into the active voice, just in case the verb belongs to one of the groups mentioned in the rules already discussed in this section. The following rule accomplishes this.

Passive to active

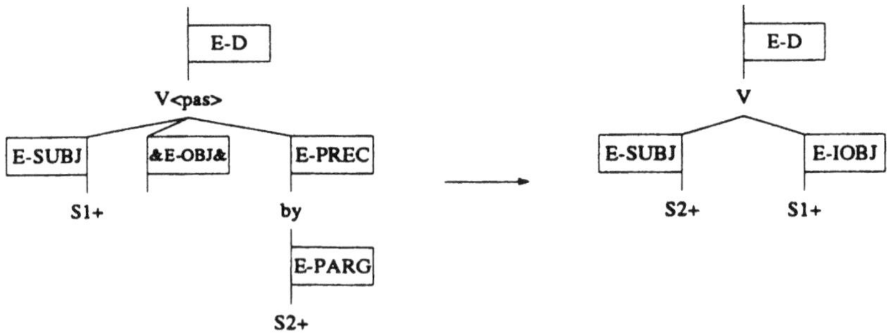

V = give, ... buy, ... expect ...

Note that the above rule does not deal with cases in which the passive agent introduced by *by* is omitted. A separate rule, not given here, is necessary to deal with these cases. This rule must introduce a dummy subject such as *one* in the output.

The above rule is another example of a preparatory English-to-English or **pre-processing** rule. It provides input for other rules discussed in this section. It might be possible to directly translate the structures which have been discussed here without any preparatory English-to-English rules, but closer examination shows that this would be difficult, since it would be necessary to specify details of several interacting structural changes in the same rule.

8. Tense

Both English and DLT's Esperanto have a fairly large number of tenses, but probably in no case is a specific tense in one language used in precisely the same situations as a specific tense in the other. (I use *tense* for the phenomenon that some linguists call *tense-aspect.*)

It is important to note that if a particular tense in English is **sometimes** translatable as a specific tense in Esperanto, this is sufficient to require a rule which specifies the necessary structural change from that tense in English to the corresponding tense in Esperanto. The fact that the same English tense is sometimes translated by a different Esperanto tense will be treated by a different rule.

The problem then remains of providing the translation system with a way of making a choice between these different syntactic possibilities. If possible, this will be done by making reference in one of these rules to some other aspect of the tree, such as an adverb, which determines the choice. If such a formal distinction is available in even some of the cases dealt with by one of the two rules, it should and will be exploited. In cases where no such formal distinction is available, we must rely on other features of the translation process outside of metataxis to make this choice. In DLT, we prefer to avoid relying on such factors wherever possible, not only because they are generally less well understood than formal sentence-level syntactic properties, but also because non-formal factors seem to be intrinsically more difficult to transform into computer algorithms.

The following two rules illustrate some of these points by giving two different rules to translate the English perfect tense: **V<prf>**:

Present perfect

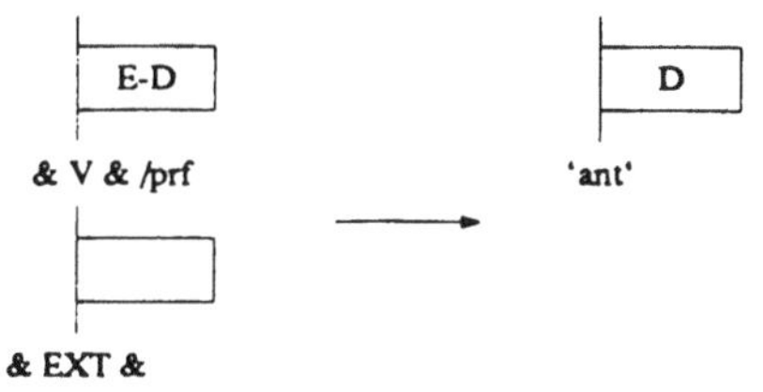

Perfect

The first of these rules would be used in [1], the second in [2]; The difference is that the activity specified by the verb is still continuing at the time of speech in [1] only.

[1] Sam **has worked** here since January.
[2] The demonstrators **have destroyed** all the barriers.

"D" is a variable label which ranges over GOV, SUBC, and ATR. Both of these rules translate the same English structure, given in the rule as *have*, but in the initial tree *have* + **past participle of the verb**. What distinguishes one from the other is the condition EXT (extent) in the first rule, which indicates a large group of adverbial expressions which have in common that all indicate an extent of time, during which the activity named takes place. These can be summarized by saying that EXT can be realized by a single word, a noun phrase, a prepositional phrase, or a clause. The actual implementation must of course specify these more precisely, but I omit these details here. In all these cases, the construction is translated by the Esperanto present participial suffix *'ant'*. If no such extent adverbial is in the tree as a dependent of the main verb, then the Esperanto past participial suffix *'int'* is chosen to translate the construction.

The symbols &...& are placed around the part of the rule which serves as a condition of this sort. Note that this condition is part of the form of the sentence. DLT's metataxis rules are in no way based on "understanding" anything which is not explicitly mentioned.

Conditions like the one above are not translated by the rule in which they occur. This causes a problem when the condition occurs higher in the tree than the part to be translated, since the translation program works essentially from the top of the tree downward. One feasible solution seems to be to assume that the condition of the rule has already been translated at the time that the rule concerned is encountered and accordingly to write this part of the rule as part of an Esperanto tree rather than as an English tree. We encounter examples of this situation in section 7.

Note that the lexical verb is itself not in the translated part of the rule. This is because this verb may belong any one of several different classes, each of which requires a rule of its own. I thus follow a policy of translating only one well-defined part of a given tree in a given rule. This presupposes that the nodes specified in the rule will be syntactically linked. The alternative would involve more complex rules which often repeated the same structures as parts of several different rules. This seems less economical and misses linguistic generalizations.

Of the two rules, **present perfect** is clearly more complex than **perfect**. This fact is the sort of structural property which is used to ensure the proper interaction whenever two or more rules translate the same structure. By virtue of its greater complexity,

present perfect is also more specific than **perfect**. DLT rules operate according to a **hierarchy of specificity**. In case of conflict, the more specific rule always takes precedence over the less specific rule.

This principle is not entirely new in linguistics. Koutsoudas, Sanders, and Noll (1974) describe a very similar principle to deal with phonological rules in a so-called "bleeding relationship". This also involves choosing between two rules which both seem to be applicable. Some linguists have traced the idea of this sort of relationship all the way back to the work of the famous Indian linguist Pāṇini (Schubert 1988: 164, citing Hudson 1984: 16). But the application of such a principle in DLT is, as far as I know, the first time it has been explicitly used in a machine translation project.

We have just seen a case of a specific English structure being translated in two different ways depending on the presence or absence of an adverbial dependent. It may be helpful to see the other rule which is necessary to translate the verbal construction in the above sentences. This rule is considerably simpler than the ones already presented:

Generic, SE

The feature **gen** (generic) refers to the tense of the verb. This tense has traditionally been called the present tense. But in English this tense typically does not indicate present time, but rather that the event concerned is true without reference to any specific time (cf. Bailey 1985).

This rule simply translates the feature <gen>, which specifies the form of the verb, as the Esperanto finite present tense suffix *'as*. The label above the word concerned is transformed into its corresponding label in Esperanto, which in this case happens to have the same name, except that the language prefix E- is dropped.

Now let us look at a tree to see the combined effect of two related rules. For the sake of simplicity, I will assume that the system is here concerned with a tree with no extent adverbial and that we have a specific verb *work* and a specific governing label E-GOV, rather than the variables given in the above associated rules. And lexical transfer is assumed without further discussion to translate *work* as *labor'i* (the infinitive form given in the bilingual dictionary), even though how this translation is chosen among the several possibilities for this particular English word involves an entirely different area of machine translation not dealt with in this volume. See Papegaaij (1986) and Sadler (forthc.) for the DLT treatment of this problem.

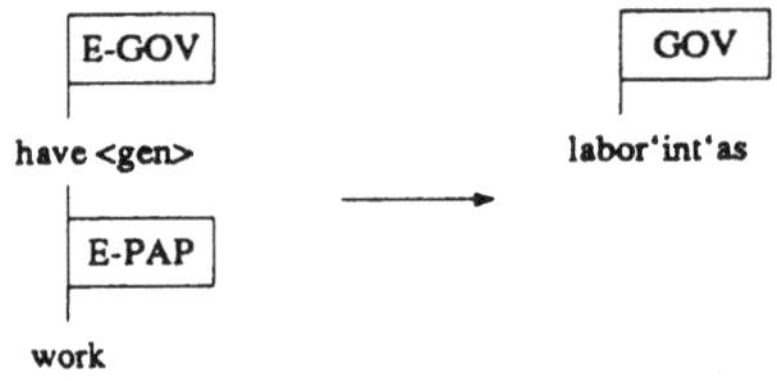

I have not dealt with a few details: how does the system know that *'ant'* and *'as* form a single word with the verbal root *labor'*? How does the system know the proper order of these morphemes?

Part of the answer to these questions lies in an essential difference between normal Esperanto and DLT's Esperanto – the morpheme marker ('). Any lexical formative mentioned in a rule which begins or ends in this marker is defined as a morpheme which cannot by itself form a word. Such morphemes in syntactically linked nodes can accordingly be required to combine in a way to form a possible word, which is defined as a combination of morphemes with a marker at neither the beginning nor the end. The markers also determine the order of morphemes, except in cases when there its more than one morpheme with markers at both the beginning and the end. Separate linearization rules are necessary in such cases, but they do not concern us here.

9. Voice

The analysis in this section does not choose between the active and passive voices, but merely translates an English passive into an Esperanto passive. The passive voice in both English and Esperanto can for any tense be derived in quite regular ways from the corresponding active tense. In English, one of the two helping verbs *be* or *get* is inserted as the governor of the main verb and requires this verb to be in the passive form. Thus the passive of *saw*, which in the English dependency tree appears as *see*/**pst**, is *see*/**pst,pas**, the passive of *will have seen*, which in the tree appears as *see*/**fut**/**prf**, becomes *see*/**fut**/**prf**/**pas**, and so on. In the Esperanto passive, the participial tense suffixes *'ant'*, *'int'* and *'ont'* (present, past, and future) become *'at'*, *'it'*, and *'ot'*, respectively. In other words, the loss of the *n* changes an active participle into a passive participle, while maintaining the same tense.

The regularities of the English structure have been captured by the rule in section 2 transforms the auxiliaries *be* and *get* into the feature **pas**. This feature will subsequently be transformed into *'at'*, *'it'*, or *'ot'*, depending on which of the three IL participial suffixes is generated by tense rules of the sort already discussed in section 8.

In spite of these evident regularities, the two different language systems in many cases do not directly correlate with each other. In the simple passive tenses *is seen*, *was seen*, and *will be seen*, the information about tense suffices to derive one of the three finite suffixes (one of the three rules has already been given in section 8 as **generic**), but not one of the participial suffixes. This is not enough, since Esperanto passive forms, as used in DLT, can always include one of these suffixes. We accordingly need additional rules to determine which of these is necessary in such cases.

It seems that the future participial suffix (*'ont'*) is used mainly to translate expressions *about to* V, and *going to* V. So there is a direct correlation with form, and this in turn makes it possible to write a metataxis rule to produce the proper translation in these cases. So the problem remains how to choose between the *'at'* and the *'it'* forms in those cases which the English syntax does not force a choice. It is not surprising that this is a difficult problem for the English-IL metataxis; Esperantists have for several decades discussed the choice between these two possibilities (See Kalocsay/Waringhien 1980: 151ff. for a full discussion and proposed solutions). Note that most western European languages, at least, present the same problem as English for this construction. In this particular instance, Esperanto is richer than the native languages of most speakers of Esperanto, and these languages clearly have some influence on their speakers thinking about this construction.

The solution at present taken in DLT has been to allow the lexical properties of the verb to determine the choice (Schubert 1987b). Verbs which by their nature indicate an activity with an internal boundary take the past tense suffix *'it'* in such cases, and the others take *'at'*. This is handled formally by listing one of these groups of verbs and writing a rule which transforms the feature <pas> into the appropriate suffix when the verb concerned is one of those in this list. If the verb concerned is not in this list, this transformation produces the other suffix.

Passive translation 2

V <pas> ⟶ V'it'

if V = {detru'i, fin'i,..}
otherwise V <pas> → V'at'

The above list of verbs needs to be fully specified, either as part of a single rule such as the above, or in the dictionary with the individual words concerned.

Note that the rules discussed in this section both have an input in Esperanto. In section 5 we have seen other cases of rules of this sort.

The use of relatively simple rules to translate syntactically linked nodes forming part of a larger structure has the further advantage of dealing with both tensed and participial constructions by means of the same rules.

The rule **perfect**, discussed in section 8, produces the desired result in verbal constructions with the combination **modal verb +INFC** *have* **+PFP V**, such as *would have finished*, for which the translation is V*'int'us*. Likewise the following rule to translate the construction *about to* V can be used in constructions with a tensed verb, such as *I was about to leave*, and also in participial constructions such as *Being about to leave, they got up*.

about to V

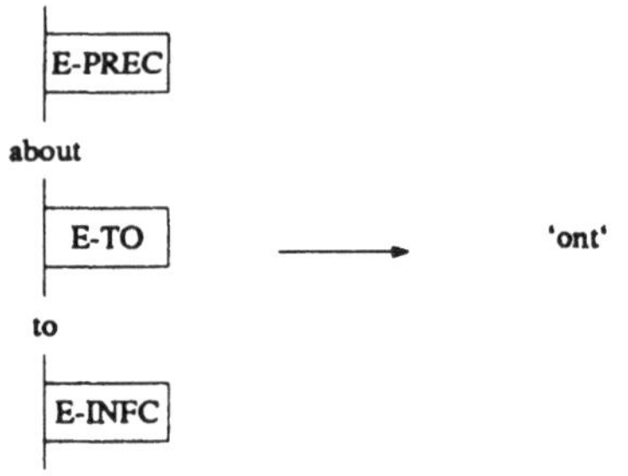

10. Reflexive determiners

Sentence-based metataxis rules are by themselves clearly inadequate for the purpose of consistently making a selection among alternative translations, since the correct choice often depends on factors outside the sentence. DLT of course has other ways of dealing with this sort of problem, though they are not treated in this book. What metataxis does is produce the various alternative translations which provide a basis for a later selection process. I am concerned in this section with a situation of this sort, specifically reflexive determiners. *His*, for example, can be translated in some contexts as *li'a*, in other contexts, as *hi'a*, and in still a third group as *si'a*. The first choice is correct if the antecedent of the pronoun is indefinite, or if its sex is unknown. The second choice is correct if its sex is understood to be male. The third choice is correct irrespective of the sex of the antecedent if the English determiner is coreferential with the subject of the same clause, infinitival, or participial phrase.

In most cases, there is nothing in the syntax of these structures which will indicate which of these conditions applies. The best that can be done within the format of metataxis rules presented in this article is to assume that the antecedent of *his* has in some way been determined and to write a rule or rules which show how this information is to be used in choosing the proper translation. In other words, I am not concerned here with the solution to the problem just outlined, but with exploiting this solution. A further limitation is that I will be concerned merely with the rules for *si'a*.

The following rule makes use of indexes **i, j** as a notation for indicating the specific reference of the nominal in question.

Reflexive determiners in objects

This says that any third person possessive determiner governed by an object noun should be translated by *si'a* if it has the same index, given here as **i**, as the verb or participle which governs this object.

It is accordingly evident that the index is given not with a specific nominal coreferent of *si'a*, but with the verb or adjective of which this nominal coreferent is the understood semantic "controller". This will be the nominal that is modified by the adjective or participle concerned or that is the subject of the finite verb concerned.

Reflexive determiners in prepositional arguments

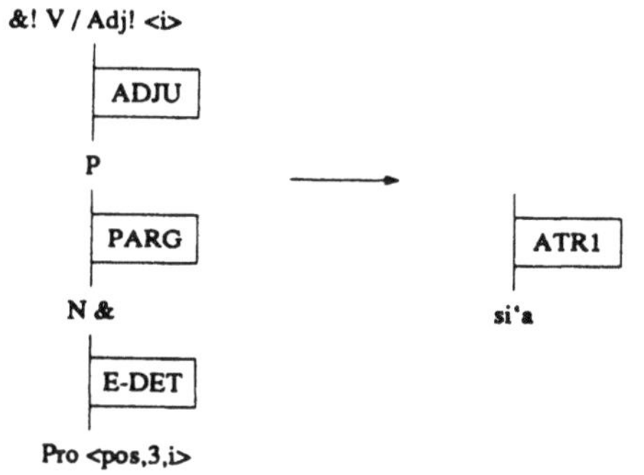

This rule is identical to the first one, except that the target of the rule is the object of a preposition rather than a direct object.

Reflexive determiners dependent on deverbal nouns

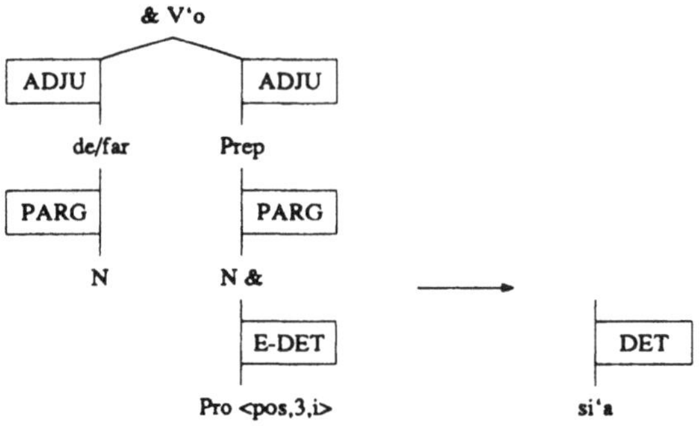

It is interesting to note the different syntactic contexts in which these indices can be identical. These are shown in the following sentences. In each case, the indices show one way, though not the only way, to understand the reference of the determiner. The interpretation indicated in the indices is assumed in the subsequent discussion.

[1] She$_i$ dressed her$_i$ children.

This is the most common and straightforward case. The verb takes its index from an overtly expressed subject.

[2] She ordered the butler$_i$ to dress his$_i$ children.

The governor of the object with the possessive determiner is *dress*. This verb takes its index from its controller *the butler*. Only in this case is *his* translated as *si'a*. If the determiner were changed to *her*, it would evidently take its index from the subject of the sentence (or some previous sentence). If it were *their*, one would have to look at preceding sentences to determine the source of the index. But in these cases the proper translations would be *ŝi'a* and *ili'a* respectively.

[3] They heard someone$_i$ talking to his$_i$ computer.

In this case, the governor of the determiner's noun is a preposition which is itself governed by a participial form of the verb. The controller of *talking* is *someone*, but whether or not *someone* is co-indexed with *his* depends on the larger context of this sentence. If and only if these two words are co-referential should *his* be translated as *si'a*.

[4] Martha$_i$'s love for her$_i$ children is understandable.

Here we see the need for the third of the above rules. The determiner *her* should be translated by *si'a*, if *her* is coreferential with *Martha*, even though the latter is the subject not of the sentence but only of the verbal noun *am'o* 'love'.

These syntactic contexts are all covered by the above rules. This shows that sentence-based metataxis is able to produce the right translation as well as some alternatives which are not correct. If the text grammar is also able to assign indexes correctly, then the correct choice can be made among these alternatives.

11. Paraphrase

Every human language has a certain amount of flexibility in the sentence structure which makes it possible to express a given idea in more than one way. These alternatives are not strictly equivalent; that is, it is not always possible to put one of them in the place of another and get a text that is equally well-structured and stylistically felicitous. But they have the same "truth conditions"; in other words, they are true in the same set of circumstances. A metataxis module should strive not only to provide an acceptable structure for use in translation of any given sentence, but also to provide these alternatives. It could then be left to an additional part of the translation process, presumably text grammar, to determine which of these is best in specific texts.

One way of dealing with paraphrase has been mentioned briefly in sections 2 and 5: a given rule can be marked as "parallel". This allows one or more other rules further down in the hierarchy of specificity to provide one or more alternative translations. But not all cases of paraphrase can be dealt with this way, simply because paraphrase sometimes involves rather radical restructuring of the syntax and accordingly cannot be formulated as a more or less specific way of dealing with a particular input structure. This section will deal with rules of this sort by means of English-to-English metataxis rules.

Although it is not clear that all the different kinds of paraphrase discussed here are useful for the English-IL metataxis, it seems desirable to make the plausible assumption that they at least might be useful.

I start by dealing with passive paraphrases of active sentences. Consider the following pairs:

[1a] The students enjoyed *Wind in the Willows.*
[1b] *Wind in the willows* was enjoyed by the students.

[2a] Carpenters hired by city hall are building a house.
[2b] A house is being built by carpenters hired by city hall.

[3a] Goldilocks was sleeping in this bed.
[3b] This bed was being slept in by Goldilocks.

[4a] Snow is falling in Utrecht.
[4b] *Utrecht is being fallen in by snow.

[5a] Jill snored all night long.
[5b] *All night long was snored by Jill.

[1-2] show cases in which the passive voice can used to paraphrase the active. The active object with any dependents becomes the passive subject, and the active subject becomes a *by* phrase. [3] shows an example in which the combination **Verb + preposition** functions as a single unit for the purpose of passivization. The object of the preposition accordingly seems to have the function of the direct object and the same sort of paraphrase is possible. [4] shows that this paraphrase possibility does not always exist with prepositional objects. [3] is in fact probably an exception which can be dealt with by marking the verb "sleep" in the dictionary as being subject to passivization. [5] shows that this type of paraphrase is not possible for intransitive verbs, even when modified by substantives functioning adverbially.

The following rule transforms the above [a] sentences into the [b] sentences, ignoring details like agreement and case, since the information necessary to translate these into DLT's Esperanto is provided by the labels.

Active to passive, p

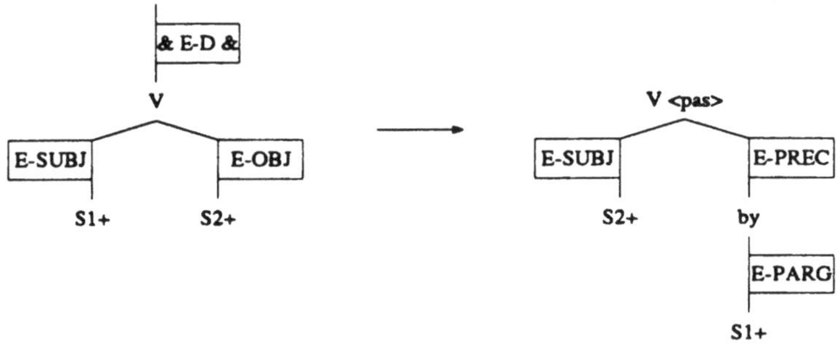

A metataxis rule in the other direction (passive to active) is discussed in section 7. That was a case of a syntactically necessary paraphrase because of interacting valency differences between English and Esperanto, and the rule was accordingly restricted to the groups of verbs concerned. A more general version of that rule could also be used like the above active to passive rule for more general cases of stylistically desirable paraphrase.

We now turn to paraphrase involving so-called clefted constructions, demonstrated in [6-7]:

[6a] The electrical power supplies the main power supply of the aircraft.
[6b] It is the main power of the aircraft that the electrical power supplies.
[6c] The main power of the aircraft is what the electrical power supplies.

[7a] The water drains through the drain pipe.
[7b] It is the drain pipe that the water drains through.
[7c] The drain pipe is what the water drains through.

The [a] sentences serve as the input structure for two types of clefting. The [b] sentences emphasize a particular noun phrase of the original sentence by moving it in front of the rest of the sentence and introducing it with the words *it is* and following it with *that*. In the [c] sentences, which involve what is sometimes known as **pseudoclefting**, the words 2s what rather than *it is...that* are introduced to set off the preposed noun phrase. Here are the two rules concerned:

Clefting, p

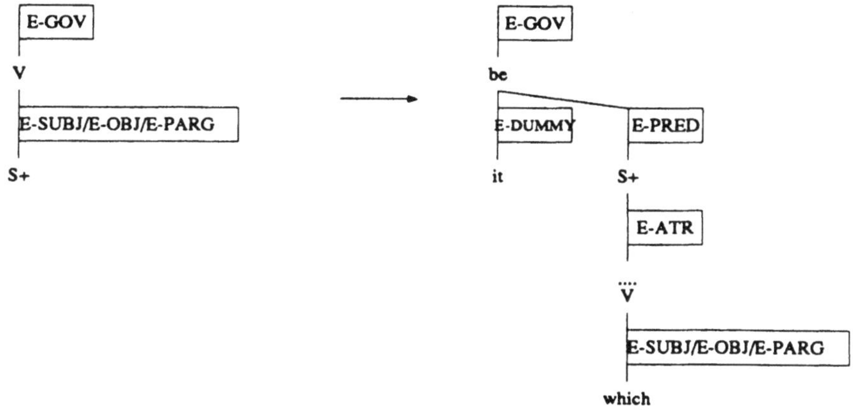

Pseudo-clefting, p

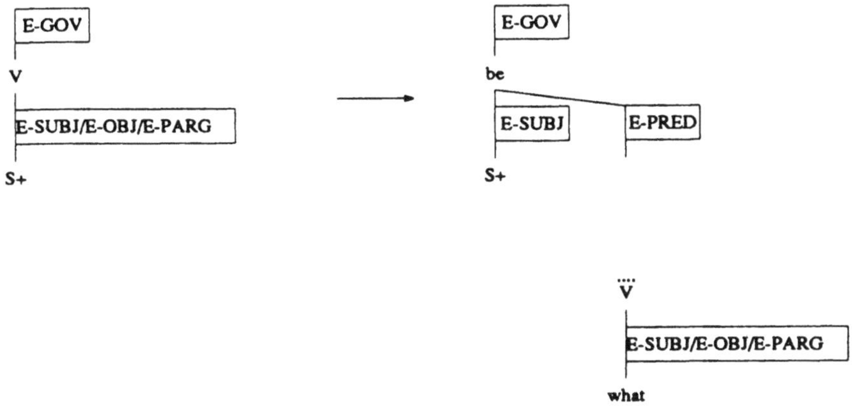

The dots in the output of both these rules indicate that the distance between the new structure and the old can be indefinitely large. These involve unbounded structures of the sort discussed in section 4.

12. A sample sentence

The following sentence has been constructed with the intention of demonstrating the interaction of some of the metataxis rules discussed in this article. I think that it nevertheless is a fairly natural sentence:

The students who expect the professor to be granted new
funds at that time by the government have lived here since January.

The parser produces the following tree:

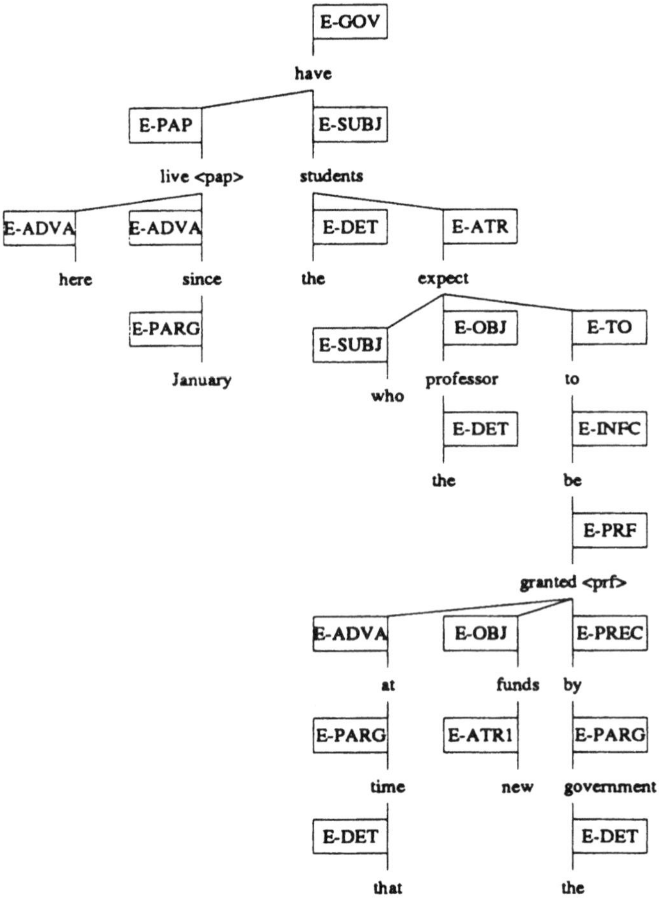

Starting from the top of the tree, we see that there are two verb complexes which need to be rewritten as a single verb with features. This produces the following tree:

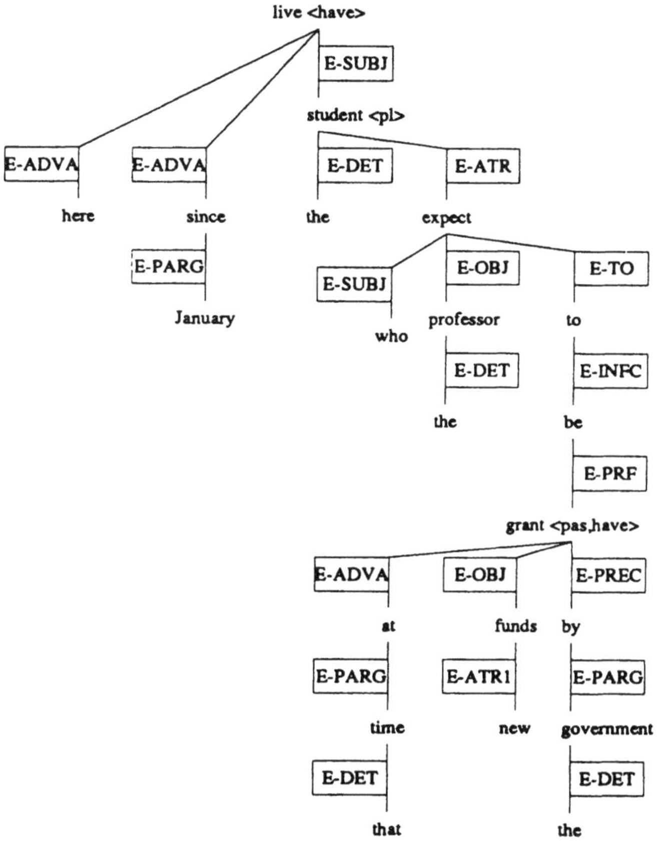

The feature <have> in the main verb complex will be translated as *'ant'* rather than *'int'* because of the temporal extent adverbial *since January*. Lexical transfer makes the first part of the sentence *viv'ant'as ĉi-tie ek'de januar'o*. The are no rules involving structural changes for *students*, which accordingly becomes *student'o'j*. The main verb of the relative clause can also be translated by unmarked rules, but then introduces an accusative plus infinitive construction of the sort discussed in section 7. In this case, this construction cannot be translated by the corresponding structure in Esperanto. The rule **accusative plus infinitive** makes *professor* into the subject of a finite subordinate clause dependent on *atend'as*:

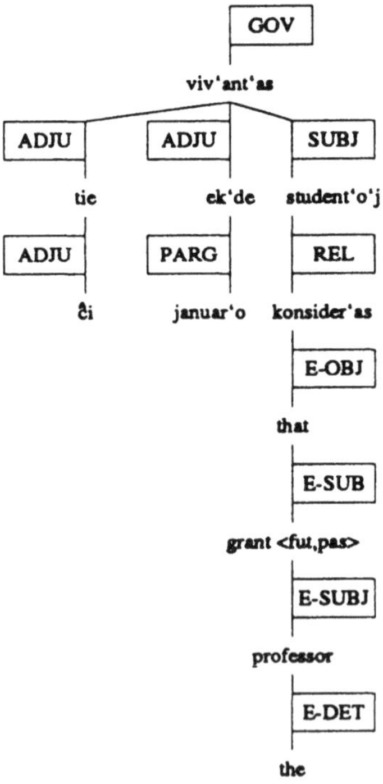

Moving into the newly created subordinate clause, we see that there is an object in a passive clause and the verb is in the first of the two groups in the rule **passive becomes active** treated in section 7. This rule is accordingly applicable. In the following tree, I omit *la student'o'j, kiu'j konsider'as, ke...viv'ant'as ĉi-tie ek'de januar'o*, which naturally remains unchanged.

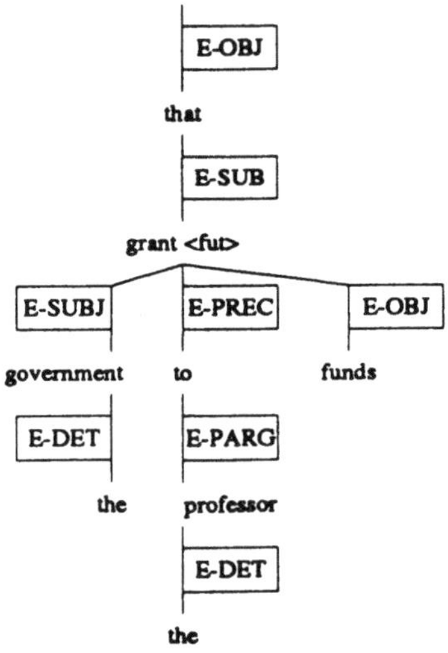

After two pre-processing (English-to-English) rules to rewrite the accusative + passive infinitive construction as an active subordinate clause which is the object of *atend'as*, the construction can now be translated to Esperanto. This will be done by unmarked rules, except that a rule not dealt with in this article, but similar to the rule which translates <gen> to *'as*, translates the feature <fut> to *'os*.

The one remaining rule is the one given in section 4 for Zamenhof's tabelo. This translates *at that time* as *tiam*. The overall result of the metataxis process is the following tree:

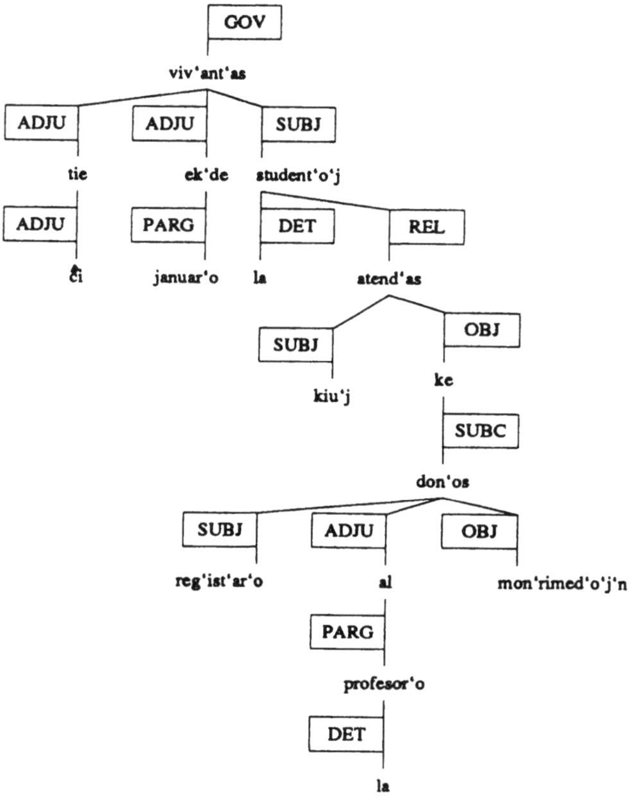

It would actually be somewhat more elegant to translate this subordinate clause by making use of the word *subvenci'i* to translate *grants funds to*. This translation does not require transforming the passive of the English original to the active, although this would be an option via the paraphrase rules. If this option is chosen, the translation becomes *la regist'aro subvenci'os la profesor'o'n*, with a considerably simpler tree structure. If this option is not chosen, then there is the problem of recognizing the passive form of the unit to be translated by a form of *subvenci'i*, which can be used to translate the appropriate part of either *funds will be granted to the professor* or *the professor will be granted funds*. It seems that a "metarule", by which the existence of a specific rule implies the presence of another structurally related one, will solve this problem. This might be stated schematically as follows:

$$A \rightarrow B \Rightarrow A' \rightarrow B'$$

where in this case A′ is the passive version of A and B′ the passive version of B. In this case the metarule must also eliminate the word *to* of the active version and make the corresponding adjustment of the dependency label that would be governed by *to*. The following metarule does this:

Passive for lexical collocations

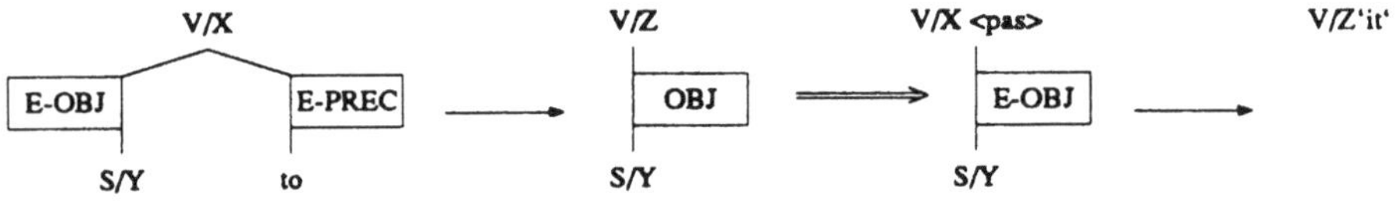

X = give
Y = funds
Z = subvenci'i

The structure in the second part of the rule is, in English, exceptional in that it combines a passive verb and an object. It might be desirable to draw attention to this situation with a special label, but I have not done that here.

Notes:

(1) Many Esperantists would put the meaning unit *-e'n* here as well, meaning 'place to which'. But as the morpheme divider shows, this is a combination of two meaning units: *e* and the accusative morpheme *'n*, which can be added to all nouns and pronouns as well. If words of this sort are to be added to the table, then there would seem to be no principled reason not to do the same for certain other suffixes.

(2) The Esperanto units of meaning would traditionally be considered morphemes, but in the definition of the DLT interlingua this is not the case. This decision has been made to avoid confusion in the parser between these words and verb forms with the same endings. e.g. *ki'u* (who, which) would be confused with *manĝ'u* (imperative form of 'eat'). This decision enables the generalization to be maintained that any word ending in *'u* is a particular form of the verb.

References

Bailey, Charles-James N. (1985): Irrealis modalities: the misnamed 'simple present tense' in English.
In: *Language and Communication* 5, pp. 297-314

Hudson, Richard (1984): *Word grammar.*
New York/Oxford: Blackwell

Kalocsay, Kálmán / Gaston Waringhien (1980): *Plena analiza gramatiko de Esperanto.*
Rotterdam: Universala Esperanto-Asocio, 4th ed.

Korst, Bieke van der (1986): A dependency syntax for English.
Unpublished Report. Utrecht: BSO/Research

Koutsoudas, Andreas / Gerald Sanders / Craig Noll (1974): The application of phonological rules.
In: *Language* 50, pp. 1-28

Maxwell, Dan (1987): English-IL metataxis.
Unpublished Report. Utrecht: BSO/Research

Papegaaij, B. C. (1986): *Word expert semantics: an interlingual knowledge-based approach.*
Dordrecht/Riverton: Foris

Sadler, Victor (forthcoming): *Working with analogical semantics. An assessment of current disambiguation techniques in DLT.*
Dordrecht/Providence: Foris [autumn 1989]

Schubert, Klaus (1987a): *Metataxis. Contrastive dependency syntax for machine translation.*
Dordrecht/Providence: Foris

Schubert, Klaus (1987b): Reviziita difino de la diferencoj inter Esperanto kaj la IL.
Unpublished report. Utrecht: BSO/Research

Aspects of metataxis formalization

Job M. van Zuijlen
Utrecht, Netherlands

1. Introduction

In this article, we will discuss various aspects of the formalization of contrastive dependency grammar or metataxis. Metataxis is the linguistic description of a dependency tree transformation process that brings about the syntactic changes which are necessary to translate one language into another. The linguist decomposes the transformation of dependency trees at sentence level into transformations that apply to subtrees, much in the same way as a sentence grammar is composed of a set of rules applying to the syntagms which the sentence is built from. For each transformation, the linguist formulates a rule that specifies the input tree that the rule applies to and the tree that is the result after successful application of the rule. If necessary, conditions may be added that stipulate under which conditions the transformation is allowed.

The metataxis "on paper" is written from a linguistic point of view. That is, it is still close to the contrastive grammar it intends to describe and, as a consequence, the transformations are not always performable in one go in the actual translation system. Moreover, the linguist may use a compact notation that has to be expanded to obtain proper transformation rules. For this reason, the linguist's metataxis undergoes **formalization**, i.e. the rules are reformulated in a formal language (e.g. a high-level programming language such as Prolog) and, at the same time, they are checked with respect to the restrictions and well-formedness conditions imposed by the translation system.

An interesting feature of the DLT-system is, that it is **interlingual** and uses a **natural language** (slightly modified Esperanto) as intermediate language (IL). As a result, the translation from source language (SL) into target language (TL) involves two natural language translation processes: one from the SL into the IL, the second from the IL into the TL. In both cases the the same metataxis process is used, only the language pairs involved are different. Therefore, it is convenient to speak in general terms of the metataxis process as being the transformation of SL-trees into TL-trees, but one should keep in mind that in this case SL and TL refer to the language pair involved in only one half of the translation process and that either the SL or the TL is the IL.

What is presented here should not be considered a guideline for metataxis formalization but rather a compilation of remarks and observations based on the experience gained from the formalization of the English-IL and the IL-French metataxis as used in the DLT prototype. In particular, our concern will be the needs of the metataxis developer on the one hand, and the restrictions imposed on the metataxis formalizer on the other.

The contrastive syntax developed by the linguist is not a complete description of the syntactic SL-TL translation process. Part of the transformation is performed by the bilingual dictionary that is responsible for the translation of single SL-words or the combination of an SL-word and one or more SL-subtrees (*kick the bucket*, for example) that require a special translation. The result of the translation may be a TL-word or a TL-tree. For this reason, Schubert (1987: 135ff) views metataxis rules as **contrastive lexical redundancy rules**, thus emphasizing that the bilingual dictionary and metataxis behave as a single set of transformation rules.

The metataxis rules as specified by the linguist are, for the most part, formulated as SL-TL transformation rules. That is why they transform an input tree that is correct according to the source language grammar into an output tree that is correct according to the target language grammar. This presupposes that in the actual translation system the SL-tree representing the input sentence and delivered by the SL-parser can be transformed by just applying the appropriate metataxis rules and consulting the bilingual dictionary, into a TL-tree that can be converted directly into a target language sentence. It turns out that this is not always possible, so a **pre-processing** and a **post-processing** stage have been added to the metataxis process.

Pre- and post-processing are monolingual processes, but to formulate the rules, knowledge of the other language is necessary and for this reason they are viewed as part of the metataxis. However, the distinction between the processes is significant for formalization, since the rules for each process are included in a separate rule base. Together with the bilingual dictionary they constitute the formalized linguistic knowledge sources necessary to transform a source language tree into a target language tree.

During the execution of the metataxis process, a source language tree is transformed step-by-step into a target language tree. Therefore, we distinguish not just SL- and TL-trees, but also the so-called **hybrid** dependency tree, characterized by the fact that it contains SL as well as TL elements. The part of the tree that is translated comprises one complete substructure dominating all parts of the tree that are not yet translated. In other words, there is a **single borderline** that separates the translated part from the untranslated parts of the tree. As a result, it is not necessary to keep a separate record of what has been translated.

Our treatment of metataxis formalization will focus on a number of significant issues. First we will have a look at the metataxis process, which gives us an opportunity to see how metataxis rules are formalized and put to work. Then, we will compare linguistic and formal expressiveness in the light of the question: is it always possible to write a formal rule that does the same as the rule "on paper". We conclude that in order to achieve this an alternative control strategy for the metataxis process is necessary. Finally, we discuss the tripartition of the metataxis and its relation to the borderline between parser and pre-processing and the interaction between the metataxis and the bilingual dictionary. We proceed by proposing an alternative view of the tripartition leading to a metataxis process which is based on normalized constructions with associated operators.

(a)
```
[E-GOV, walk
        [E-SUBJ, we],
        [E-CIRC, in,
                [E-PARG, garden,
                        [E-DET, the]]]
]
```

(b)

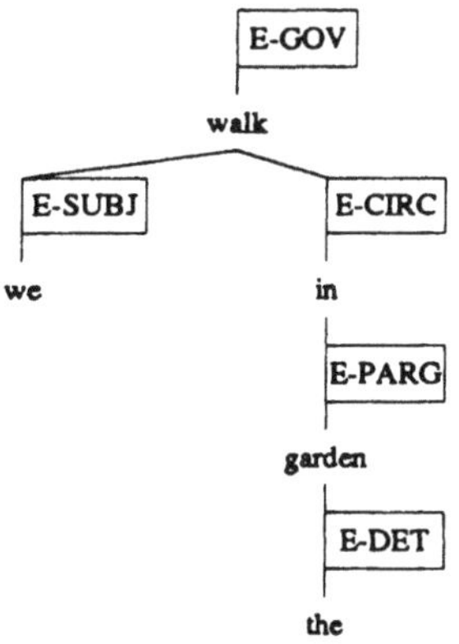

Figure 1: Two alternative ways to represent the dependency tree for We walk in the garden. *(a) shows the pretty-printed list notation, resembling the representation used for formalization; (b) is the graphic representation used for inspection purposes by the linguist.*

In this article we will use a simplified formal notation. Dependency trees (see Figure 1) will be represented as lists (Schubert 1986: 99). The elements of the lists are labels, nodes and subtrees, which are lists themselves. A label contains the name of a dependency type and a prefix identifier to indicate a natural language other than the IL. A node contains the basic form of a word and, possibly, further syntactic information. Labels, nodes and subtrees may be represented by variables, usually indicating that those parts of the tree are translated by other rules or by calling the bilingual dictionary. A tree may start with a label or a node. A rule consists of two tree structures separated by an ⇒. Dictionary entries are considered rules as well.

Some examples of the notation are given in the following overview:

E-SUBJ	*"SUBJ"-label with prefix identifier "E"*
[walk, [SUBJ, we]]	*dependency tree for "we walk"*
[walk/VRB/[tns=pres],	*node with syntactic information about "walk"*
[<Label>, <Word>]	*tree with variables*
{Subtrees}	*variable matching with zero or more elements of a list*
{Subtrees1}+{Subtrees2}	*concatenation of list elements*
<Tree1> ⇒ <Tree2>	*notation of transformation rules*

As may be seen from the dependency tree for *we walk*, trees are presented in a "pretty-printed" format. For each dependency level the subtrees are preceded by one tab space. This facilitates visualizing the graphical representation of the tree on the basis of the list representation.

2. The metataxis process

The metataxis process transforms SL-trees into TL-trees according to the rules present in the rule bases and the entries in the bilingual dictionary. Transformation starts at the top of the tree and as much as possible is translated in one go. A rule or a dictionary entry is selected by comparing patterns present in the tree with the left-hand side of the rules and the dictionary. If a rule or an entry that matches is found, it is applied to the tree resulting in a partly transformed tree.

As an example, we will look at the translation into the IL of *We didn't see a single man yesterday*, which has the following dependency tree:

Initial SL dependency tree

```
[E-GOV, do/[tns=past],
    [E-ADVA, not],
    [E-SUBJ, we],
    [E-INFC, see,
        [E-OBJ, man,
            [E-DET, a],
            [E-ATR1, single]]
    ],
    [E-CIRC, yesterday]
]
```

Notice, that the form *didn't* does not appear in the tree. The parser performs morphological analysis and converts contracted forms into separate words: *didn't* becomes *did not*. Also, each word is converted into a **basic form** and a list of **syntactic features**: *did* becomes *do* with **tns=past**, a tense feature.

It is common practice for the tensed verb to be the **internal governor** (positioned at the top node) of the dependency tree of a sentence. However, most auxiliary verbs in English are translated into the IL as affixes, attached to the basic form of the main verb. Some of them, such as *do* in combination with negation are not translated at all, but transfer their features to the verb they govern. In such cases, the metataxis writer may formulate a rule which deletes one or more SL words:

"do"-deletion metataxis rule 1

```
[E-GOV, do/[tns=<Tense>,frm=fin],       ⇒    [GOV, <Verb>/[tns=<Tense>,frm=fin]
    [E-ADVA, not],                                [ADJU, ne]]
    [E-INFC, <Verb>/[frm=inf]]]
```

The word *do* is deleted and its features are inherited by the main verb. The adverb *not* is translated into IL as *ne* and becomes a dependent of the main verb. The result is a construction in which an untranslated part (the main verb) governs a part already translated. This violates the well-formedness condition for hybrid trees which states that the translated part of the tree should form a single structure. Moreover, the rule does not say where other dependents of the verb *do* should be attached. This is a problem of contrastive syntax and should be documented by the metataxis writer.

A revised rule would delete *do* and reconfigure the tree, but it would not perform any translation apart from the top label:

"do"-deletion metataxis rule 2

```
[E-GOV, do/[tns=<Tense>,frm=fin],       ⇒    [GOV, <Verb>/[tns=<Tense>,frm=fin],
    [E-ADVA, not],                                [E-ADVA, not],
    [E-INFC, <Verb>/[frm=inf],                    {Subtrees1}+{Subtrees2}]
        {Subtrees2}],
    {Subtrees1}]
```

Since the only part of the input tree that is translated is the top label, it seems a better idea to formulate the rule as a pre-processing rule. Indeed, in the formalized version of the English-IL metataxis all rules that are concerned with auxiliaries are included in the pre-processing rule base. So in the final adaptation of the rule, the top label is left untranslated. This has the additional advantage that the same rule may be used for other labels than "E-GOV".

"do"-deletion pre-processing rule

```
[<Label>, do/[tns=<Tense>,frm=fin],     ⇒    [<Label>, <Verb>/[tns=<Tense>,frm=fin],
    [E-ADVA, not],                                [E-ADVA, not],
    [E-INFC, <Verb>/[frm=inf]                     {Subtrees1}+{Subtrees2}]
        {Subtrees2}],
    {Subtrees1}]
```

An interesting question, of course, is what type of rule should be formulated by the metataxis writer. In this case there is no **linguistic** justification to formulate the rule as a pre-processing rule and, intuitively, the metataxis writer will consider it to be a clear example of a metataxis rule. So, we would expect the rule to be written in a form in which the top label is translated (*do*-deletion rule 2). The formalizer will detect redundancy – there are other rules that translate the "E-GOV"-label – and reformulate the rule. Some caution is necessary, however. Although the indefinite article *a* has no direct translation equivalent in the IL, it is part of various constructions that do have a special translation, such as *not a single man* in our example. In this case deletion is not allowed in the pre-processing stage but has to be postponed until there is certainty that the word in question has no translation. In Section 3 we discuss how this and similar cases are treated. For the moment, we assume that *a* is either translated or deleted at some point in the process.

We will apply our pre-processing rule to the dependency tree for *We didn't see a single man yesterday*. The result is:

Pre-processed SL-tree

```
[E-GOV, see/[tns=past],
    [E-ADVA, not],
    [E-SUBJ, we],
    [E-OBJ, man,
        [E-DET, a],
        [E-ATR1, single]
    ],
    [E-CIRC, yesterday]
]
```

We now turn to the SL-TL transformation of this tree. Some of the rules and dictionary entries needed for the transformation are listed below. For the sake of simplicity, only a single translation of each word is given.

Metataxis rules:

1:	[E-GOV, <X>]	⇒	[GOV, <X>]
2:	[E-SUBJ, <X>]	⇒	[SUBJ, <X>]
3:	[E-OBJ, <X>]	⇒	[OBJ, <X>]
4:	[E-ATR1, <X>]	⇒	[ATR1, <X>]
5:	[E-ADVA, <X>]	⇒	[ADJU, <X>]
6:	[E-CIRC, <X>]	⇒	[ADJU, <X>]

Dictionary entries:

1:	[man]	⇒	[vir'o]
2:	[not]	⇒	[ne]
3:	[see]	⇒	[vid'i]
4:	[single]	⇒	[unu'op'a]
5:	[we]	⇒	[ni]
6:	[yesterday]	⇒	[hieraŭ]

The first rule that can be applied is Rule 1. The result is a hybrid dependency tree (the IL part is shown in italics):

Hybrid tree 1

```
[GOV, see/[tns=past],
    [E-ADVA, not],
    [E-SUBJ, we],
    [E-OBJ, man,
        [E-DET, a],
        [E-ATR1, single]
    ],
    [E-CIRC, yesterday]
]
```

The top of the single **untranslated** tree consists of the node *see*, so the next step involves calling the dictionary and applying Entry 2:

Hybrid tree 2

```
[GOV, vid'i/[tns=past],
    [E-ADVA, not],
    [E-SUBJ, we],
    [E-OBJ, man,
        [E-DET, a],
        [E-ATR1, single]
    ],
    [E-CIRC, yesterday]
]
```

The rules and dictionary entries given translate only one entity (a label or a node) at the time, so we have an alternation between the application of rules and dictionary entries. More complicated dictionary entries could perform the translation of one of the dependent labels and more complicated rules could involve translation of a label and a node. For example, we could have the following dictionary entry:

```
2a:  [man,                  ⇒   [vir'o,
         [E-ATR1, <X>]]              [ATR1, <X>]]
```

This entry translates the word *man* as well as the label "E-ATR1". The result of applying this entry is an untranslated part that starts with a word, so the next step would again be a call to the dictionary. In our example, the first item to be translated would be the word *single*:

Hybrid tree 3

```
[GOV, vid'i/[tns=past],
    [ADJU, ne],
    [SUBJ, ni],
    [OBJ, vir'o,
        [E-DET, a],
        [ATR1, single]
    ],
    [E-CIRC, yesterday]
]
```

In certain cases more than one rule or dictionary entry is applicable. In English *single man* also refers to an unmarried male person, for which there is a single word translation in the IL, *fraŭl'o* 'bachelor'. The dictionary entry for this alternative translation is:

```
2b:   [man,                  ⇒    [fraŭl'o]
          [E-ATR1, single]]
```

Adding this entry to the dictionary results in two alternative translations for *We didn't see a single man yesterday.*

Translation 1

```
[GOV, vid'i/[tns=past],
    [ADJU, ne],
    [SUBJ, ni],
    [OBJ, vir'o,
        [ATR1, unu'op'a]
    ],
    [ADJU, hieraŭ]
]
```

Translation 2

```
[GOV, vid'i/[tns=past],
    [ADJU, ne],
    [SUBJ, ni],
    [OBJ, fraŭl'o],
    [ADJU, hieraŭ]
]
```

Translation 1 is literal and interprets *single* as *distinct* or *separate*, whereas Translation 2 interprets *single man* as 'bachelor'.

There is a third possible IL-translation: *Ni vid'is eĉ ne unu viro'n hieraŭ*, which may be paraphrased as 'we saw not even one man yesterday'. The negation is moved away from the verb and modifies *unu* 'one' instead, with *eĉ* 'even' modifying the negator *ne*. The metataxis writer might formulate the following rule to describe this phenomenon:

```
[E-GOV, <Verb>,              ⇒   [GOV, <Verb>
    [E-ADVA, not],                   [OBJ, <Noun>,
    [E-OBJ, <Noun>,                      [ATR1, unu,
        [E-DET, a],                          [ADJU, ne,
        [E-ATR1, single]]]                       [ADJU, eĉ]]]]]
```

Although the tree contains SL "islands" in the TL-tree (<Verb> and <Noun>), it is evident that rules of this form are necessary. As we will see, there is an opportunity for the formalized rule to call the bilingual dictionary, thus ensuring that the output tree contains translated equivalents of <Verb> and <Noun>. Notice that this rule translates a large part of the tree. Its Application to the pre-processed SL-tree of our example sentence results in the following hybrid tree:

Hybrid tree 3

```
[GOV, vid'i/[tns=past],
    [E-SUBJ, we],
    [OBJ, vir'o,
        [ATR1, unu,
            [ADJU, ne,
                [ADJU, eĉ]]]
    ],
    [E-CIRC, yesterday]
]
```

Application of subsequent rules yields Translation 3:

Translation 3

```
[GOV, vid'i/[tns=past],
    [SUBJ, ni],
    [OBJ, vir'o,
        [ATR1, unu,
            [ADJU, ne,
                [ADJU, eĉ]]]
    ],
    [ADJU, hieraŭ]
]
```

The three alternative translations will be evaluated by the semantic system which orders them according to plausibility in the given context. The dictionary writer has the option of excluding the literal translation, if necessary, by marking the specific entry in the dictionary. Usually, though, there is no exclusion of literal translation alternatives. On the contrary, the function of the metataxis is to generate all translations of a particular SL-tree that are syntactically possible. Semantic evaluation of the alternatives is performed in a separate module.

In practice, the dictionary is the main source of alternative translations of structures. By default the dictionary will generate all translations possible from a particular pattern. In the metataxis, the rule that translates the largest part of the untranslated tree is usually applied, without considering the alternatives. Only occasionally a different set of rules is used to generate an alternative translation. This implies that the most appropriate rule has to be selected. Although it is possible to have a separate selection algorithm that compares the effect of various rules, a more practical solution is to **order** the rules in the rule base according to their effectiveness. A similar ordering has to be maintained in the dictionary, if it is necessary to exclude alternatives. So, in general, entries and rules that translate a larger part of the tree take precedence over those that translate a single word or label.

The TL-tree that is finally selected still contains the basic forms of the words. Therefore, post-processing is added to take care of form government and agreement. This is relatively simple in the IL, but in a language such as French many additional rules are necessary (see e.g. Tamis 1988). In the IL, for example, there will be a post-processing rule that expands the feature [tns=past] by replacing the infinitive ending *'i* of the verb by the ending *'is*. Another rule adds an *'n* to nouns preceded by an "OBJ"-label. Applying these rules to Translation 3 (assuming that this is the preferred translation) results in the following IL-tree:

Post-processed IL-tree

[*GOV*, *vid'is*,
    [*SUBJ*, *ni*],
    [*OBJ*, *vir'o'n*,
        [*ATR1*, *unu*,
            [*ADJU*, *ne*,
                [*ADJU*, *eĉ*]]]
    ],
    [*ADJU*, *hieraŭ*]
]

There is one final step in this first stage of the DLT translation process. Before it can be transferred to the second stage, the IL translation has to be linearized by the Tree-to-String Converter. This module contains rules that order the words in the tree according the IL dependency grammar. The result of application of these rules to the post-processed IL-tree is the IL sentence *Ni vid'is eĉ ne unu viro'n hieraŭ.*

3. Linguistic and formal expressiveness

In an ideal situation there would be a one-to-one correspondence between the metataxis rules "on paper" and their formalized counterparts. We have already pointed out that pre- and post-processing rules have to be added other than those formulated by the metataxis writer. But it is stated that it is up to the metataxis writer to document these situations. Also, the well-formedness condition that stipulates that the translated part in a hybrid tree should be one continuous structure places certain restrictions on the formalizer of the rules. An example from the previous section was the *do*-deletion rule which had to be reformulated as a pre-processing rule. However, there are cases that cannot be remedied by moving a rule to another rule base but require a different approach to the metataxis process.

As an example, we will have a look at two alternative rules from the IL-French metataxis (Tamis 1987: 11) that transform the same construction.

Two alternative rules for the same construction

```
1:  [<IL_Label>, <X>/VRB,      ⇒   [<French_Label>, <X>/VRB,
         [OBJ, <Y>],                     [F-OBJ, <Y>],
         [INFC, <Z>]]                    [F-INF, <Z>]]

2:  [<IL_Label>, <X>/VRB,      ⇒   [<French_Label>, <X>/VRB,
         [OBJ, <Y>],                     [F-OBJ, <Y>],
         [INFC, <Z>]]                    [F-APREP, <P>/PRP,
                                             F-PARG, <Z>]]]
```

The label variables in the rules are used to indicate that they hold irrespective of the value of the IL-label. The difference between the two rules is the translation of the infinitive complement ("INFC"). In Rule 1 it is translated into an infinitive complement ("F-INF"), but in Rule 2 it is translated into a prepositional complement ("F-APREP"). The reason for two rules is that the French verb that is the translation of the IL verb <X> has one of the two possible **complement sets** indicated by the rules, dependent on its **valency**.

An obvious solution seems to be to include the IL verbs with their complements and their translation in the bilingual dictionary. However, with many verbs the complements are not obligatory, so the verbs without their complements would have to be included as well, leading to an enormous and undesirable expansion of the dictionary. Moreover, the phenomenon holds for a class of verbs and, consequently, the metataxis writer has decided to formulate **general** rules in order to remove **redundancy** from the dictionary.

The preference for one rule or the other depends on the French translation of the IL verb. So, in order for the rules the work properly, it would be necessary to know the valency of the French verb before the translation of its complements. In the present DLT prototype, however, the metataxis control program or **metataxor**, always singles out a subtree with an untranslated label or node at the top. Therefore, it will not apply rules that refer to hybrid trees, such as the following, in which we specify the valencies (indicated as feature lists) of the French verb <X>:

Rules with valency control

```
1a:  [<FR_Label>, <X>/[obj=yes,inf=yes],      ⇒   [<FR_Label>, <X>,
          [OBJ, <Y>],                                   [F-OBJ, <Y>],
          [INFC, <Z>]]                                  [F-INF, <Z>]]

2a:  [<FR_Label>, <X>/[obj=yes,aprep=yes],    ⇒   [<FR_Label>, <X>,
          [OBJ, <Y>],                                   [F-OBJ, <Y>],
          [INFC, <Z>]]                                  [F-APREP, <P>/PRP,
                                                            F-PARG, <Z>]]]
```

This example shows the necessity of a more flexible metataxor. In the DLT prototype the initial solution has been to include rules like 1a and 2a in a separate valency rule base and to formulate a special metataxis rule that performs the following steps:

[1] translate the top IL-label;

[2] call the bilingual dictionary to translate the IL-verb;

[3] call the valency rule base with the resulting **hybrid** tree;

[4] translate the complements of the verb according to its valency;

[5] return the result.

So in order to obtain a similar expressiveness in the linguistic and the formal version of a metataxis it is necessary to introduce control elements in the formalized rules. This not a very desirable state of affairs and a future development will be a more versatile metataxor, such that the formalized rules are more in agreement with the rules specified by the metataxis developer. An intermediate solution, which we will discuss later, has been the implementation of an alternative control strategy by means of a number of dedicated rule bases.

To illustrate how the special rule operates, we will look at the translation of *Mi instigas vin bone fari vian laboron* 'I urge you to do your work well'. The IL-tree after pre-processing is:

Pre-processed IL-tree

```
[GOV, instig'i/[tns=pres],
    [SUBJ, mi],
    [OBJ, vi],
    [INFC, far'i,
        [ADJU, bon'e],
        [OBJ, labor'o,
            [ATR1, vi'a]]
    ]
]
```

Subsequent transformation of the tree starts with translation of the "GOV"-label and the word *instig'i* (steps [1] and [2] of the special rule). The result is:

Hybrid tree 1

```
[F-GOV, pousser/[tns=pres,obj=sub,aprep=à],
    [SUBJ, mi],
    [OBJ, vi],
    [INFC, far'i,
        [ADJU, bon'e],
        [OBJ, labor'o,
            [ATR1, vi'a]]
    ]
]
```

The feature list of the verb *pousser* contains the tense feature from *instig'i* and valency features (printed in boldface) from the French syntactic dictionary, which is consulted simultaneously with the bilingual dictionary. The valency features not only indicate that a valency is present but also specify the categories or the words that are acceptable as dependents. In this case the object should be a noun ("sub") and the prepositional complement should be governed by the preposition *à*.

The next step ([3]) is the translation of the complements of the verb for which the valency rule base is called. The verb *pousser* has valencies for an object and for a prepositional complement, hence Rule 2a applies, resulting in:

Hybrid tree 2

[*F-GOV*, *pousser*/[tns=pres,obj=sub,aprep=à],
[SUBJ, mi],
[*F-OBJ*, vi],
[*F-APREP*, *à*,
[INFC, far'i,
[ADJU, bon'e],
[OBJ, labor'o,
[ATR1, vi'a]]
]
]
]

Notice that variable <Z> in Rule 2a matches with a complete subtree. This is true in general; a variable may be bound to a single word as well as to a subtree.

Further transformation of the tree is straightforward. Although *far'i* (French: *faire*) is another verb of which the complements are subject to valency-controlled translation, the rule concerned (Rule 1a) is not applicable because of the absence of an infinitive complement. The completely transformed tree, then, becomes:

Translation

[*F-GOV*, *pousser*/[tns=pres],
[*F-SUBJ*, *je*],
[*F-OBJ*, *tu*],
[*F-APREP*, *à*,
[*F-INF*, *faire*
[*F-ADVA*, *bien*],
[*F-OBJ*, *travail*,
[*F-ATR1*, *ton*]]
]
]
]

The valency features have been deleted because they are no longer necessary. The tense feature determines the form of the verb *pousser* and this is taken care of by a rule in the post-processing part of the metataxis, resulting in *pousse*. Also, the pronoun *tu* is replaced by its accusative form *te*. The post-processed tree is linearized, yielding the French sentence *Je te pousse à bien faire ton travail.*

We already mentioned some shortcomings of the metataxor. In the DLT prototype it only checks whether the (sub)tree that has to be translated starts with a label (a syntactic relation) or a node (containing a word). If the tree starts with a label, the metataxor calls the metataxis rules, if the tree starts with a node, it calls the bilingual dictionary. The rules and dictionary entries are ordered according to the form of their input, in that those that would translate the largest part of a particular tree are put first. For example, a dictionary entry for *single man* precedes one for *man*, and a rule that translates a subtree precedes one that translates only a label. Consequently, as much as possible is translated during a call to the metataxis rules or the bilingual dictionary. A minimal **translation step** consists of the translation of a label or a node. This control configuration is shown in Figure 2a.

We have seen some examples in which the dictionary is called from a metataxis rule in order to prevent the forming of SL islands or to enable valency-controlled translation, indicating, in fact, that the one-item translation step is sometimes too small. Since a minimal dependency tree in the DLT-system consists of a label and a node, it is sensible to consider the combination of a label and the node it precedes as the minimal translation step. This requires a different type of control strategy which, in the DLT prototype, has been realized without modification of the metataxor (figure 2b). The metataxor calls a **control rule base** which determines when the three other rule bases and the bilingual dictionary are applied. The rule bases are divided into a **top-level rule base**, a **test rule base** and a **sub-level rule base**. First, the top level rule base translates at least the top label of the structure to be transformed, and, if specified, the top node and any dependents. Next, the test rule base checks whether the top node has been translated, and, if not, calls the bilingual dictionary. So any tree structure that is returned by the test rule base has had at least its top label and node translated. The resulting tree is sent to the sub-level rule base, which takes care of all transformations that can only be performed on hybrid trees, for instance, valency-controlled translation. After application of this rule base control is returned to the metataxor.

In general, ordinary metataxis rules will find a place in the top-level rule base, whereas rules for valency-controlled transformation (cf. rules 1a and 2a) and other rules which work on hybrid trees will be included in the sub-level rule base.

Although it is very difficult to specify in advance what the characteristics of a control program such as the metataxor should be, it is evident that during the development of a prototype the formalizer should have facilities to experiment with different types of rules as well as different types of control strategies. In this case, we benefit from the fact that the formalized rules of the DLT prototype are written in Prolog, which allows a tailor-made control algorithm expressed in rules. From these we can extract the characteristics needed to improve the the metataxor. As a result, the rules will be simplified since all non-linguistic control statements may be removed.

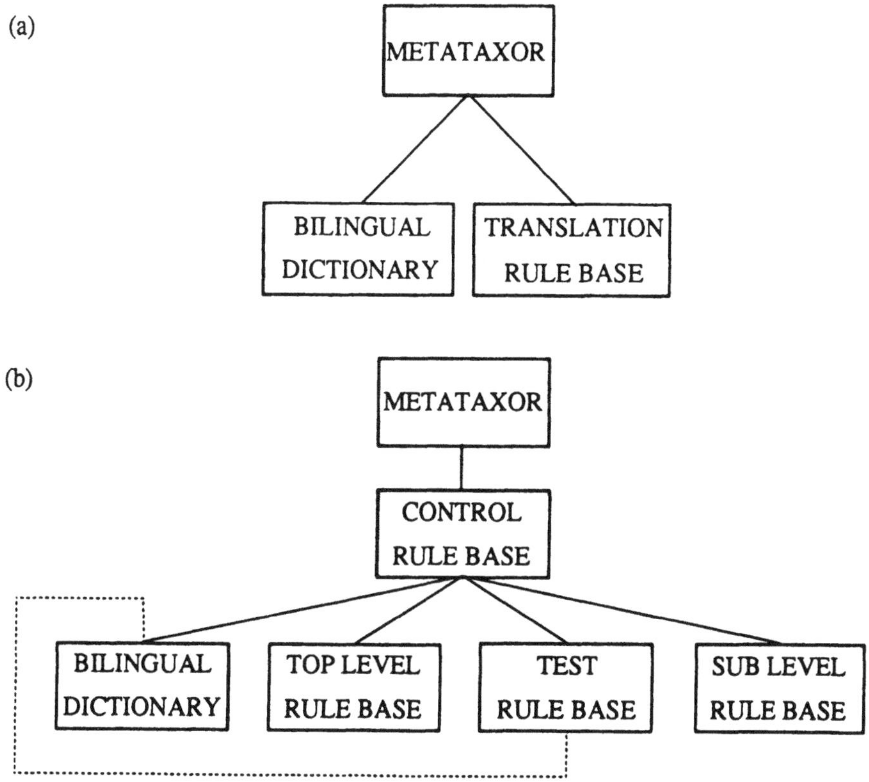

Figure 2. Control of rule bases and bilingual dictionary. In (a) the metataxor switches between translation rules and the bilingual dictionary. In (b) a control rule modifies the control algorithm such that valency-controlled translation of dependents is possible.

in addition to this adaptation of the metataxor, it seems to be necessary to introduce a rule type that handles **hybrid** subtrees. This would give the formalizer the expressiveness which the metataxis designer calls for. As we have seen with the introduction of a valency rule base for rules 1a and 2a, such rules have to be handled in a separate rule base that is called by an additional metataxis rule. This means that two rules are necessary to formalize a phenomenon that is formulated as a single rule by the metataxis writer. If rules such as 1a and 2a could count as properly formalized metataxis rules, specification and formalization of the metataxis would be more closely related.

The use of hybrid trees, however, is not restricted to valency control. In the previous section we have encountered a case for which postponement of deletion was necessary. The indefinite article *a* has no translation equivalent in the IL, but may nevertheless be part of an expression that requires a special translation. In the English-IL dictionary of the prototype we find for instance: *a certain amount of <X>*, *a cut above <X>*, *a number of <X>* and *a week* (as in *five times a week*). As a consequence, the possible deletion of *a* has to be postponed until its governor is translated. Again we would like to formulate a hybrid rule that checks whether *a* is governed by an IL word and, if so, deletes it:

"a"-deletion rule

```
[<IL_Label>, <X>,      ⇒    [<IL_Label>, <X>]
    [E-DET, a]]
```

Translation of verb-negation from the IL into French is another example of a phenomenon that is difficult to formalize and for which a hybrid rule would be desirable. In the IL, verb negation is expressed by a single adverb *ne*, but in French **two** adverbs are needed: *ne* and *pas*, both of which are dependents of the verb. As it is not possible in this case to translate *ne* by means of the dictionary (a translation is always a **single** word or subtree), a metataxis rule is needed which translates the verb and the negation in one step:

Verb-negation rule

```
[<IL_Label>, <X>/VRB,     ⇒    [<French_Label>, <X>/VRB,
    [ADJU, ne]]                      [F-ADVA, ne],
                                     [F-ADVA, pas]]
```

In the rule the top label is a variable indicating that various values and their translations are possible, similar to Rule 1 and Rule 2, which we discussed previously. Since there are also rules that specify the label translations for verbs that are not negated, the result is a **duplication** of information in the rules. Moreover, the translation of the governor is independent of the translation of the negating adverb, so we would prefer two different translation rules. By interpreting the rule specification slightly differently, we end up with the following hybrid rule:

Hybrid verb-negation rule

```
[<French_Label>, <X>/VRB,     ⇒    [<French_Label>, <X>/VRB,
    [ADJU, ne]]                          [F-ADVA, ne],
                                         [F-ADVA, pas]]
```

Notice, that, although this rule is to be preferred over the previous version, we still include the translation of words into a metataxis rule without any linguistic justification. So, it might be that we have to adapt the formalism of the bilingual dictionary such that **hybrid** entries are possible, comparable to hybrid metataxis rules, for example:

Hybrid dictionary entry

```
[<French_Verb>/VRB,     ⇒     [<French_Verb>/VRB,
    [ADJU, ne]]                   [F-ADVA, ne],
                                  [F-ADVA, pas]]
```

The verb is already translated, because IL *ne* may be part of a special translation; a possible translation of *ne sci'i* 'know not', for instance, is *ignorer*.

4. Tripartition in the metataxis

The SL-TL transformation rules in the formalized metataxis are preceded by pre-processing rules and followed by post-processing rules. The role of pre- and post-processing is characterized by Schubert (1987: 168) as follows:

Pre-processing: Syntactic variations irrelevant to translation can be detected and reduced to a standard structure.

Post-processing: Word-specific restrictions can be used to modify target language trees later.

This looks like a straightforward working definition. So in the English-IL metataxis we may find rules of the following type:

```
[<English_Label>, can't]    ⇒    [<English_Label>, can,
                                     [E-ADVA, not]]
```

The idea is that there is no difference in the translation of *can't* or *can not* and that, in order to prevent several entries in the bilingual dictionary or several translation rules that cope with the various variations of *can not*, we **normalize** all forms to *can not*. There might be stylistic significance but that is the concern of text grammar and falls outside the scope of sentence-based metataxis. If necessary, a feature could be used to indicate what the current representation is derived from, e.g.:

```
[<English_Label>, can/[orig="can't"]
    [E-ADVA, not]]
```

One might ask: (i) How is this different from morphological analysis; and (ii) shouldn't this analysis be done by the parser? This is a relevant question, and it is indeed difficult to decide where the parser should stop and pre-processing rules should begin. Since the source language of the English-IL DLT-module is Technical English, in which forms such as *can't* are excluded, no practical experience is available in this field. However, one of the general principles in DLT with respect to parser design is that the dependency trees delivered by the parser should contain **basic forms** of the words with additional syntactic information included in features. This suffices to exclude forms like *can't*, *don't* and the like. There is also a certain vagueness in the criterion. Stylistic variation could be expressed by a difference in word choice, for example, by the use of *must*, *should* or *have to* in a certain context. Although style is involved here, we would not want to normalize these words to any one of them.

Nevertheless, we may envisage a task for pre-processing rules. Their main function in the DLT prototype is to prepare the SL-structure for translation into the TL in those cases that a mere translation rule is not powerful enough. Again, this is a control function that should be removed from those rules in future. Another more interesting and, at the same time, linguistically motivated purpose is the conversion of SL-structures to a normalized form.

To illustrate the usefulness of normalized tree structures, we will look at a particular translation problem. The bilingual dictionary contains entries such as:

```
[evaluate/VRB,          ⇒   [taks'i,
    [E-OBJ, <X>]]               [OBJ,valor'o,
                                    [DET, la],
                                    [ADJU, de, [
                                        [PARG, <X>]]]]
```

If the verb *evaluate* is passivized, as in *The project is evaluated*, the pattern that matches with the dictionary entry is no longer available:

```
[E-GOV, be/[tns=pres],
    [E-SUBJ, project,
        [E-DET, the]],
    [E-PAP, evaluate/VRB/[ptc=pap]]
]
```

The direct object of *evaluate* in an active sentence is now the syntactic subject of the auxiliary in the passive sentence. To restore the pattern expected by the dictionary the following rule is applied, which transforms the sentence temporarily into an active form and adds a feature to the main verb to indicate its passive origin:

```
[<English_Label>, be/[tns=<T>],    ⇒   <English_Label>, <Y>/[tns=<T>,pas=yes],
    [E-SUBJ, <X>],                          [E-SUBJ, Ø],
    [E-PAP, <Y>]]                           [E-OBJ, <X>]]
```

Notice the introduction of a **zero element** ("Ø") as a placeholder for the subject. A by-phrase cannot be transformed into a subject at this stage because it is not possible to make a distinction on syntactic grounds between proper by-phrases or expressions such as *by hand* or *by accident* (which ask for a particular translation) as in, for instance, *The feet were removed by accident.*

Application of the rule to the passive example yields the following tree:

```
[E-GOV, evaluate/[tns=pres,pas=yes],
    [E-SUBJ, Ø],
    [E-OBJ, project,
        [E-DET, the]]
]
```

The dictionary entry for *evaluate* will match, so the translated tree will contain the correct IL expression:

```
[GOV, taks‘i/[tns=pres,pas=yes],
    [SUBJ, Ø],
    [OBJ, valor‘o,
        [DET, la],
        [ADJU, de,
            [PARG, projekt‘o,
                [DET, la]]
        ]
    ]
]
```

The following post-processing rule restores the passive form:

```
[<IL_Label>, <Y>‘i/[tns=<T>,pas=yes],    ⇒    [<IL_Label>, <Y>‘at‘i/[tns=<T>],
    [SUBJ, Ø],                                     [SUBJ, <X>]]
    [OBJ, <X>]]
```

Notice that the passive is formed by inserting the passive morpheme *‘at* (others are *‘it* and *‘ot*); resulting in a construction quite different from the English passive:

```
[GOV, taks‘at‘i/[tns=pres],
    [SUBJ, valor‘o,
        [DET, la],
        [ADJU, de,
            [PARG, projekt‘o,
                [DET, la]]
        ]
    ]
]
```

Another normalizing operation is concerned with the transformation of auxiliary+verb constructions into a basic form of the verb and features indicating the function of the auxiliary. This facility is used in all cases where the auxiliary is not translated as a word but as form modification of the verb. For example, *will see* expressing "future" is translated as *vid‘os*. A pre-translation rule adds a feature:

```
[<English_Label>, will,    ⇒    [<English_Label>, <X>/[tns=fut],
    [E-INFC, <X>]]
```

A post-translation rule adds the appropriate suffix to the basic form of the verb:

```
[<IL_Label>, <Y>/[tns=fut]]    ⇒    [<IL_Label>, <Y>‘os]
```

Both examples of normalization may be considered as transformation of the parser output into forms that are more abstract and approach the idea of **kernel constructions**, which – in the context of machine translation – has also been put forward by Teller, Kosaka and Grishman (1988). Apart from certain experiments in the

English-IL metataxis, no systematic investigation into the benefits of kernel constructions has been carried out in DLT.

In the DLT-system, the application of normalized constructions is dictated and restricted by the expectations of the bilingual dictionary. The translation of SL-words into TL-words is straightforward, but whenever larger constructions are involved, the lexicographer has to deal with the dependency grammars of the source and/or target language. So, although the constructions contain basic forms and feature sets, their geometry should be according to dependency grammar specifications. This points to a restriction on pre-processing: transforming an SL-tree into another SL-tree is not allowed if the result is not possible according to the dependency grammar of the SL. Since any grammatical construction may appear in the dictionary, the use of pre-translation rules to facilitate the work to be done by the translation rules is limited. As an example of the reasons for this restriction, consider the English *to*-infinitive, for which the IL has no equivalent. It is usually translated into a bare infinitive in the IL. So, it seems feasible to have the following pre-processing rule:

"to"-deletion rule

```
[E-TO, to,               ⇒    [E-INFC, <X>]
    [E-INFC, <X>]]
```

This rule deletes *to* and, as a result, a single translation rule for infinitives suffices. However, constructions such as *fail to see*, which include a *to*-infinitive and have a special translation, require a rule that matches with a *to*-infinitive:

```
[<English_Label>, fail/[tns=<T>],    ⇒    [<IL_Label>, <X>/[tns=<T>],
    [E-TO, to,                                 [ADJU, ne]]
        [E-INFC, <X>]]]
```

The *to*-deletion rule would disturb the pattern that matches with this rule, so we are forced to formulate separate translation rules for the *to*-infinitive and bare infinitive constructions. This clearly shows that the bilingual dictionary determines what normalizations are allowed in pre-processing stage.

In a previous example we discussed the temporary transformation of a passive into an active construction. A feature (**pas=yes**) indicates that the active construction we are dealing with originates from a passive and, as we have seen, enables us to restore the passive construction in a post- processing rule. However, it may not always be desirable to restore the passive; sometimes an active or some other construction is more appropriate. It is accordingly advantageous to look in a different way at this feature and consider it as an **operator** that gives a passive as the result when applied to an active construction. Usually the operator is not translated, but by translating the operator as well as the construction and then applying the translated operator in the post-processing stage, it is possible to opt for an active or some other construction in the TL instead of restoration of the passive.

The introduction of operator translation would simplify the tree transformation rules and at the same time enhance the expressiveness of the metataxis. Figure 3 illustrates the various tasks of the rule bases and the dictionary in this new approach to the

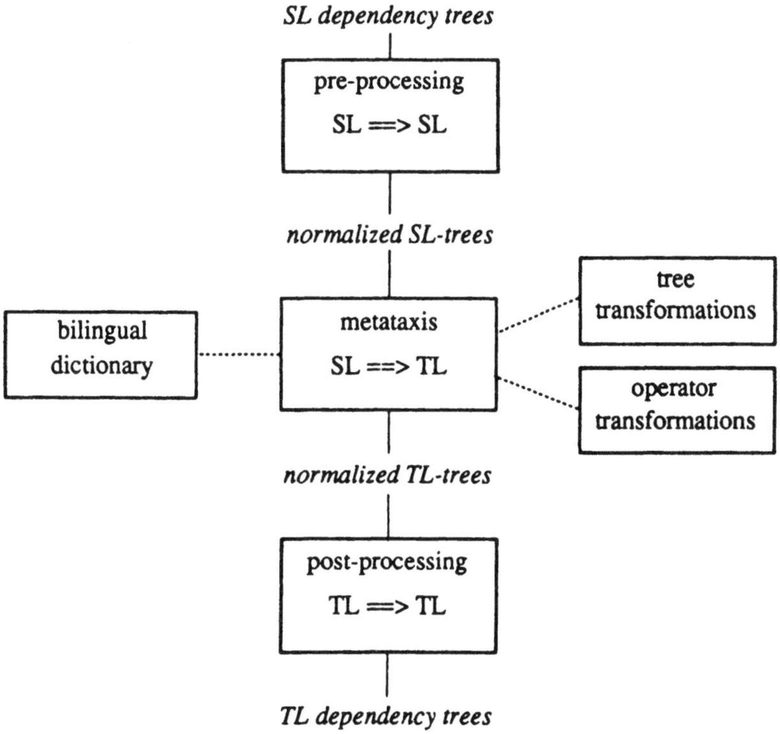

Figure 3. Various stages in the SL to TL transformation of dependency trees. Translation, or metataxis proper, involves only normalized tree structures.

metataxis. We see that pre-processing converts the dependency trees from the parser to normalized trees. A normalized tree consists of a structure and an operator. Both are translated separately and then post-processing generates a TL dependency tree by applying the operator to the structure.

We expect that the division of labor suggested will facilitate the linguistic specification of the metataxis, including all three parts, and of the bilingual dictionary.

5. Conclusions

In this article we have dealt with various aspects of the formalization of contrastive grammars for the translation system DLT. We have seen that, on the one hand, the linguist requires more expressiveness than can be presently formalized, in particular with regard to the transformation of hybrid trees. On the other hand, Prolog as a formalization language is too powerful, as it allows all kinds of control information in the rules. We argued that this control information has to be included because the current metataxor employs an inflexible control strategy, but it is important for the formalizer to have facilities for experimenting with various control strategies during prototype development.

We have suggested an alternative organization of the metataxis process to overcome the restrictions encountered in the present prototype. The SL-tree is first converted into a normalized SL-tree and an operator stating what kind of construction we are dealing with, e.g. active, passive or nominalization. The transformation part of the metataxis has separate rules for trees and operators. In this way, it is easier to translate a particular SL-construction into a different type of construction in the TL. After transformation, the post-processing part applies the operator to the normalized TL-tree to generate the proper TL-construction.

An important conclusion that may be drawn from the experience gained from metataxis formalization is that the knowledge used in the various processes of the DLT-system should be as modular as the processes themselves. That is, formalized linguistic knowledge should be **declarative**, so that it is close to the information provided by the linguist. The necessary control strategies should be formulated as separate knowledge sources, so that it is easy to change them in case it becomes necessary to modify the behavior of a process. The result of these modifications will be much more flexibility during the development phase of the DLT prototype.

References

Schubert, Klaus (1986): *Syntactic tree structures in DLT.*
Utrecht: BSO/Research

Schubert, Klaus (1987): *Metataxis. Contrastive dependency syntax for machine translation.*
Dordrecht/Providence: Foris

Tamis, Dorine (1987): La métataxe IL-français.
Unpublished report. Utrecht: BSO/Research

Tamis, Dorine (1988): The treatment of form determination for French in DLT.
In: *Interface, Tijdschrift voor Toegepaste Linguïstiek // Journal of Applied Linguistics* 3, pp. 45-56

Teller, Virginia / Michiko Kosaka / Ralph Grishman (1988): A comparative study of Japanese and English sublanguage patterns.
In: *Proceedings of the Second International Conference on Theoretical and Methodological Issues in Machine Translation of Natural Languages* (Pittsburgh 1988). Pittsburgh: Carnegie Mellon University, Center for Machine Translation [no pagination]

Index

Bei Fragen zur Produktsicherheit wenden Sie sich bitte an:
If you have any questions regarding product safety,
please contact:

Walter de Gruyter GmbH
Genthiner Straße 13
10785 Berlin
productsafety@degruyterbrill.com